1

ISBN: 978-1-7329900-6-7

Cover designed by Jeffery D. Chapman Sr.

Some names have been changed to protect the innocent.

Published by A&C Marketplace Publishing LLP as transcribed
directly from author.

Library of Congress Cataloging-in-Publication Data
Jeffery D. Chapman Sr.,
Printed in the United States of America

FAMILY BUSINESS
LIVING JUST ENOUGH FOR THE CITY

Jeffery D. Chapman Sr.

TABLE OF CONTENTS

DEDICATION

This book is dedicated first to God and
His Son Jesus Christ.

Thank you for giving me this task, this story,
and for healing me.
It is a privilege and honor to be used by God!

This book is also dedicated to my entire family,
especially my children.

In Loving Memory of My Parents

INTERLUDE

It was not long before I kissed my kids and wife good-bye to pursue $30,000 for a package of cocaine. The results, a drug deal gone bad! In 13 years, my life travels backwards, like that day, that hour, that minute, and those very bullets flying. I caught the slug, and I almost died ya'll! Satan does not play fair, neither do the streets.

FLASHBACK!

I'm lying in a pool of blood, my life was slowly but surely diminishing. The assassins have fled the scene. My family is in a state of hysteria. I'm technically in a state of crossing over to the other side. In one-second, my life has been altered. In one split second my destiny has taken a detour. The Emergency Medical Technicians (EMT) and a helicopter ride can't determine if I'll survive the "impossible." September 20, 1990, the day my life changed!

"12-years-ago I was paralyzed, and I was walking several months after that injury, so why can't I survive this injury?" Those were my subconscious thoughts at that time because my conscious was dead on arrival. For the first time in my life, it was just God and I.

While we take life for granted, God has already planned our lives, and we take different routes. Decisions are so important. If I had known what I know now, I would have re-routed the decisions that I made.

12 years later, my life story has no coincidences. I'm a quadriplegic, which means that I'm paralyzed from the neck down, living on a life support machine. The reason I write these words is to bring some awareness to how blessed we all are, and it's by the Grace of God. I've learned several lessons about being thankful for everything that the Lord has provided for my family and I, throughout my life.

You might think that scratching an itch isn't a big deal, neither did I until my injury. I have an extremely sensitive face due to the level of injury to my spinal cord. A lot of times I might have an eyelash, small piece of hair or even a piece of lint on my face, and it feels like a large piece of cotton. I can't scratch it, so I have to wait until someone comes into my room and ask them to wipe my face. I ask for medication sometimes, which takes several minutes before it takes effect. (Some say that an itch is mainly psychological, but I believe it is physical. Try to ignore whenever you have an itch---you wouldn't last three minutes). This is my everyday reality! After having said all of this, something as small and effortless as scratching an itch is nothing to the average person. Most of us even take that capability for granted. Just as we take for granted the gifts and opportunities that God gives us every day. You can't put a price on the ability to have your physical independence and good health. We take so many other things and people for granted; our spouse, children, health, religion, time and physical/mental independence. We are so busy doing everything that we want to do, we forget to give God His proper respect, praise, and time. We must "hearken to the voice of the Lord."

I am eternally thankful for my Lord and Savior Jesus Christ for giving His life for my sins so that I may eternally live through Him. I'm thankful to my family for being there for me throughout these years. I was divorced a few years back, but I still have to honor my wedding vows, until I die. A lot of you may think I am crazy for trying to still honor my ex-wife, but I first made those wedding vows to God, and then to my wife. I won't be free from my vows until I die. My wedding vows mean to me, *"Until death do us part!"*

What people need to realize is that things do happen. You might not always have that high paying job, or your health might start getting worse. A marriage is an institution, a commitment, it is special, but you must know how to appreciate each other. A man is supposed to love his wife and treat her like a queen through love and affection. A husband is to make his wife feel special everyday by complimenting her, embracing her, reassuring her, and communicating with her. Wives should always make her husband feel like a real man, lifting him up by making him feel like a king, being the wind beneath his wings, making him feel superior, and being submissive unto him. (Please read the 5th Chapter of Ephesians)

Fathers talk to your sons and daughters and be their role models. Don't be so caught up in yourself or your job, that you can't take time to talk with your children. Believe me they are listening. Don't let people in the streets and negative things on television program your children. Instead, communicate and build a relationship with your children. It is important that both mother and father partake in building a foundation with their children. Oftentimes, we complain about the things that we don't have, but we never thank God for the things that He has already given us. Just remember to always be thankful for what you have because in a blink of an eye, it can be taken away.

I'm not looking for sympathy or credit because all credit belongs to God. I just want people to appreciate and thank God for all things He has done. I hope you get something positive from my story. You may be asking "What have I gotten from all of this?" Well, I believe that it's not just about "Just Living Enough for The City." *"Anything worth having is truly worth waiting for and patience is truly a virtue!"*

God Bless all of you, In Jesus Holy Name!

JEFFERY D. CHAPMAN, SR. **FATHER OF TWO**

CHAPTER 1

IN THE BEGINNING

I was born, Jeffery Denorse Chapman on May 21, 1965, a native of Washington, DC. I was reared in one of the toughest, most dangerous areas of the nation's capital called "Barry Farms." Growing up in Barry Farms I learned how to survive and how to deal with life in the face of adversity, and most of all, the importance of family.

Before I can continue, I have to share the history about the community in which I was born and raised in for many years. Please let me share this with you because it's so important to know where you come from and it helps to identify where you made your life. But knowing the truth will also guide you and set you free. The Barry Farms community we know today was originally land owned by white farmers, David and Julia Barry, and it extended from the Anacostia River to what is now known as Garfield Heights. In 1867, after the Civil War, the Freedmen's Bureau purchased 375 acres of farmland from the Barry's. The land was then sold for $125 to $300 per acre to newly freed slaves and quickly became D.C.'s first African American home-ownership community. A portion of the profits from this were used to build Howard University, which started out as an educational institution for the residents of Barry Farm, who built their homes and the surrounding neighborhood from scratch. In 1954, the Redevelopment Land Agency acquired much of the land in the area and built public housing for displaced residents coming from the urban renewal in Southwest and other parts of the city. These "projects" which remain today, have been neglected for years and are facing demolition now. Barry Farm is a neighborhood in Southeast Washington, DC, located east of the Anacostia River and is bounded by the Southeast Freeway to the Northwest, Suitland Parkway to the Northeast and St. Elizabeth's Hospital to the South. In 1867, the Freedmen's Bureau (officially the US Bureau of Refugees, Freedmen, and Abandoned Lands) purchased a 375-acre farm from David and Julia Barry, white landowners, and transformed Barry Farm into a post-Civil War community of formerly enslaved and free-born African Americans. Earlier, the Commissioner of the Freedmen's Bureau, General Oliver O. Howard, had asked African Americans squatting on land in Washington, DC, what might help them to become self-supporting. They said, "Land! Give us land!" Howard promised to acquire land near the city. Howard transferred $52,000 from the refugees and freedmen's fund to be held in trust by himself, Senator Pomeroy, and Mr. Elvans for the use of three institutions: Howard University, Richmond Normal School, and St. Augustine Normal School in Raleigh. They used some of these funds to purchase Barry Farm. The Bureau sub-divided the farm into one-acre plots, which the Freedmens could purchase over a period of seven years. For an additional $76 they could buy lumber to begin constructing a house. By 1869, money from the sale of the land, reportedly $31,178.12, had been returned to the fund and distributed to the three institutions listed above. Everyone talks about the negative part of the history of Barry Farm, but there is African American history concerning the better days. Now it's being taken away from us, and yes, we had a factor, but so does the government, for allowing things to run down, crime rates to skyrocket and allowing the fluctuation of drugs and guns in the communities. Our government, so you can blame the people would have been suppressed, despised and not recognized as humans. Whatever happens in these neighborhoods will continue until we can take control over it, and beautify, but not while they are still there. The government can't allow us to continue to kill each other so that it would be easier to just walk in and take over the entire 300+ acres from them and call our plan again. Now I can continue telling you my story because this was a very valuable part.

My parents (Joe was what everybody called my father) were both born in South Carolina. They both grew up about 10 miles apart from each other. My grandparents also lived in South Carolina. I believe in the beginning, there were talks about where I was born. At the time my parents were waiting for me to come aboard. We were living in the Barry Farms neighborhood, our address was: 2700 Wade Road. The apartments are still there now. I guess after living there for several years, my arrival came. My parents chose to move down the street to another apartment complex that was a lot smaller and it seemed like a close-knit family with the neighbors. I was too young to remember this incident, but down the street, one of the neighbors had a problem with my mother. My mother kept to herself, minding

10

her own business. Occasionally when she would go shopping with two of her nieces, they would bring several bags back, to avoid the nosiness and unfortunate jealousy of several neighbors, there was a way to come to the back entrance of these apartments and that's what my mother did.   They just came to the back door to eliminate any unnecessary drama. So one day the lady and her husband started disrespecting my mother, and my cousin was with my mom outside on the porch. I guess it was during a summer day and this lady decided that she would challenge my mother, for whatever reason she brought this on herself. As my siblings tell me the story, the lady started disrespecting my mother along with her husband and my cousin already warned him not to put his hands on my mother. The lady and my mom got into it, and I'm not bragging, but that lady got a real good South Carolina, fed up with her husband hanging out and with a lot of buildup anger, became the recipient of a real good beat down. As her husband went to reach to touch my mother my cousin warned him to keep his hands to himself. My cousin hit the guy in the head with either one beer or a six pack of beer. We're talking about the late sixties, early seventies, there were no aluminum cans in those days so I know he did some damage to the guys' head. I don't know where my father was because there's a possibility that it would have gotten worse with the lady's husband, but my cousin took over and took care of business. My mom and my cousin were just sitting on the porch like everybody else and not bothering anyone. This must have been a weekend because my brother tells me that my mom and siblings got on the bus that following day. My brother described the ladies face after my mother finished beating her up. He said that she really looked like a RACCOON, not bragging, but both of her eyes were black after getting a real good beat down, that she brought on herself. But we didn't have to deal with that kind of drama anymore, we moved to the other apartment complex, nothing like that ever happened because everybody kept to themselves. Also, we did communicate with one another. Not to sound negative about the other residents on the other side of the apartment complex, but I know that the people in the new complex that we moved into were hard-working families. By this time, I was old enough to understand that our new neighbors were a working-class group of wonderful adults with a sense of community. We had to build this together, especially since we faced one another and were in close proximity, a lot closer than the other apartments. So we really knew our neighbors well, and they knew who we were, along with our parents and siblings, and everybody looked out for each other. I miss those days. These days people don't have time to get to know others. It's a very selfish generation these days, and with a robotic mentality, with all the electronics.

The address of the other building that we moved to after my mom shortly gave birth to me was "2636 Wade Road," only about a half a block down the street, but what a big difference. My mother kept to herself, didn't drink, didn't smoke. She was all about taking care of her husband and kids, that doesn't happen like that anymore, may she rest in peace! On the other hand, my father was out there, doing whatever, and all my mother would do was stay home with the family. This allowed my mother to stay home with all of us, what a blessing! I believe it was in 1971 when we moved up the street to another complex called Park Chester apartments and I think the owner of those buildings lived down in Barry Farms. My oldest brother provided me with this information because again I'm the youngest of the family and I had no knowledge of these incidents. These apartments were made for larger families. They converted two apartments into one, so they were very spacious with the exception of the kitchen. But we had a four-bedroom apartment with two bathrooms and that's a lot of space, even back in those days, and even today. Those apartments were made to accommodate larger families.

When we were younger, we were able to get away to where it all started in South Carolina. As a child, I only remember my father's parents. Occasionally we would visit them during the holiday seasons and sometimes in the summer. I remember spending the night with my grandparents most of the time by myself. I just enjoyed being able to be around my grandparents and with them as a kid, because they were getting older and you know, if we don't take advantage of time and opportunity, we might miss out on spending quality time with family. I really enjoyed being there with them. I used to remember eating breakfast and dinner in the kitchen with my grandfather before he died in the early eighties. He would joke around with me, just like my father used to do. They both reminded me of each other in so many ways, and I see where my father got the joking part of his life from, his father. My grandfather used to have a green reclining chair that all the grandkids would try to sit in. Whenever he got up for anything, if only for a few minutes, we would run to sit in granddad's favorite chair.

Growing up with my cousins, most of them were my uncle and aunt's kids, my father's nephews and nieces, but they did not live in the same community as my grandparents, so I only got a chance to play with them when they would come to visit our grandparents, knowing that we were in town. I would play all day at my grandparents' house or go up the road to my grandmother's youngest brother's house. Again, it was only me. There weren't a lot of kids around. This was a special time to be with my family on the Chapman side. This quality time was very rare, so I tried my best to take full advantage of every opportunity, every moment that I could spend with them.

In both areas, where my mother's family grew up at in South Carolina and also in the community where my father's parents lived, my grandparents' house, it was so much sand everywhere that it would get into your shoes. I'm a city slicker, born in Washington, DC where we didn't have the abundance of sand to walk on, and I did not worry about having sand in my shoes, or in my socks. Every time, without exaggerating, whenever I would go to bed, I couldn't help but to bring sand in the bed with me from my shoes and socks. It wasn't a way to avoid it. It was a way of living and in those days things were so much different from living in the city that I had to adjust to. Even though it was very annoying to sleep with sand in the bottom of the bed, an area in which both of your feet would lay. Normally, when I would visit my grandparents, I would always be by myself because I wanted to enjoy that special time with both of them. However, one particular visit, I brought my mother's brother's son with me to stay the night. It wasn't a problem bringing my cousin because we were like brothers and we did a lot of things together, good and bad. But this one particular time that he went with me to spend the night at my grandparents' house,

I woke up the following morning and my pajamas were soaking wet. In my mind I knew that I did not wet the bed. I knew it! You know when you urinate on yourself, so I knew something was strange about this situation. I asked myself the question; *"how in the world did I get wet?"* I knew that I didn't urinate in my sleep that night, and that the only thing that was different that I did was to wear socks in the bed. Because this night, I had decided that I was going to wear my socks to bed because I just could not deal with that very irritating feeling of those sand pebbles and trying to sleep. I told my grandmother that I didn't pee in the bed, but she didn't believe me because my excuse was ridiculous. I said; *"grandma, all I can remember was just wearing my socks to bed that night and maybe I sweated."* Again, a very lame and ridiculous excuse, but I was not lying to my grandmother, that was the first time ever, in my life that I wore socks to bed. I'm pretty sure that she may have told some of my other family members that I wet the bed and the lame excuse that I gave her. I didn't think for a moment that my cousin actually wet the bed. He was a couple years older than I was, so the thought of him doing that never entered my mind at all over the years, it was just a mystery until years later. I guess the both of us were in our twenties or close to it when I found out the truth. He finally confessed. If I could have told my grandmother right then when he confessed, I would have. I could not wait until we went back to South Carolina to tell her the truth about what happened that night, since in her mind she believed it was me that wet the bed. He started explaining exactly how everything took place, he said that he woke up early that morning and changed his pajamas and put on his clothes, before I woke up that morning. Now, that explains why I was the only one that had wet pajamas on that morning. He told me that he was embarrassed. In my mind I'm saying; "really, you were embarrassed," but I didn't say this out of my mouth. I didn't say anything because he was a lot older than me. It would appear that the younger of the two would have wet the bed, but that wasn't the case. He admitted that he waited until my father came to pick us up when he decided to put his wet pajamas in a bag and put them inside of the trunk of the car without anyone noticing him. He planned this out very well. I'm glad that he told me the truth because I never would have suspected that it was my big cousin. Unfortunately, he always had a problem wetting the bed so my uncle had to make sure he didn't drink anything before he would go to sleep. It was one of those things that he had to grow out of, which he did eventually.

On the other hand, when I was able to go down to South Carolina to visit my grandparents, finally I was able to tell my grandmother exactly what happened, *readers would you believe that my own grandmother did not believe a word I said!* I guess because when I told her that my socks were sweating, that was enough and she was already convinced that I did it. That sweaty sock business didn't help my case at all! Grandma said; "why should I believe you?" I responded; *"maybe grandma, because I'm telling you the truth."* I was telling her the truth for the second time concerning wetting the bed. Even over the years, and overtime, I still don't think THAT SHE EVER REALLY BELIEVED ME! MAY SHE REST IN PEACE!

I remembered the day that my grandfather died. The night before he passed away, I had a dream about him and the Shah of Iran, of all the people to dream about. What connection did the Shah of Iran have with my grandfather at that time? If I'm not mistaken, the Shah of Iran was killed. My grandfather died from a heart attack. Maybe the connection was DEATH. But wow, dreaming about both of them. They were both sitting on the front porch (not from my grandparent's porch, but it was this particular porch or side porch that was in one of the communities that I normally passed by, either driving or walking and it was a nice size house). My grandfather was telling the Shah that I was his grandson. I felt very proud and happy that my grandfather called me over to talk to the Shah of Iran, even in my dream.

The following day, my friend and I were on our bicycles about to enter the McDonald's restaurant located on Martin Luther King, Jr. Avenue, in Southeast Washington, DC. While we both were struggling to bring our bicycles inside a McDonald's, my parents spotted me before I fully entered the restaurant while they were driving down the Avenue towards our old community. I don't know exactly where they were headed but my father was driving pretty fast and he told me to go back to our family establishment which was a block or two from McDonald's. I didn't know what was wrong, but I could see the expression on my father's face, and I just felt that something was really serious or bad. I knew something bad had happened, so I immediately went to my family's mom-and-pop/beer and wine store. That was when I was that my grandfather had died. I started thinking about that dream that I had that night before, about my grandfather talking with the Shah of Iran, and I asked myself, "Was that dream symbolic or was it telling me that something was going to happen to my grandfather?" Again, I'm just a kid, but I remember it very clearly. After hearing this news of my grandfather passing away it caused me to think about the wonderful memories that I had with him. I can remember going into the "walk in box," the place where we kept all the cold beer, sodas and wine. I would sit down for a few minutes and drink a beer. I was probably about 15 years of age. I had never met my mother's parents, they passed away when she was just a little girl. My grandfather passed away, the late Mr. Alexander Wilkins. To this day, I still believe that they intentionally killed my grandfather, but they said it was an accidental death. When my grandmother passed away, I think my mother was a teenager at the time, so I wasn't blessed to meet them at all. But my father's parents, I was truly blessed to have met both of them. That's why I say that you have to cherish each and every moment and every opportunity that God gives you, EVERY DAY! We were able to all go to my grandfather's homecoming service. I think for the first time we closed down the family business until we came back. This is during the time that my first nephew was born and my brother drove my future car down to South Carolina, a 1979 Chrysler LeBaron. I didn't get my driver's license until the following year. But I have photographs of our family, while we were down there during my grandfather's homecoming service. They had the repass at my grandparents' house and I was able to see a lot of family members, uncles and aunts that used to live in the northern part of the United States, New York, New Jersey and Philadelphia. It was very sad that family had to get together when something like this happens, someone dies in the family, and everybody come together. I was always a family man and I truly believe that families should stick together. We also need to communicate with other relatives before another loss of a family member.

At the homecoming service, I was able to meet my oldest sister for the very first time. During my father's younger years, he met a woman much older than he and a relationship ensued and as they say; "the rest is history." After my parents got married, I believe this old relationship caused problems and left a scar on my mother's heart and maybe some un-forgiveness. Every now and then I would try to talk to my mother and tell her that she shouldn't let these things bother her. I would tell her *"this happened many years ago, so please let it go,"*

I would insist! Over the years, I tried to communicate with and find my oldest sister and my niece all the while keeping this from my mother because I did not want to stir up any bad memories. I let my father know that I was in search of my sister and he was okay with it. He told me that if I was successful in my search to let him know. *"No problem Pops"* was my response to him. I didn't like keeping any secrets from my mother. Unfortunately, I was unsuccessful in my search for my sister. It was many years that I found out she had passed away. I'm still in search of my niece and other family members out there. I'd love to know how they're doing! I'M STILL HER UNCLE!

Now, back to my grandmother, she was sweet, but you didn't want to make her mad because she really had a quick temper. She wasn't as friendly as my grandfather. After my grandfather died, I never stayed at my grandparent's house again. It just didn't feel the same without having my grandfather with us. My grandmother later married her daughter's husband's father - DON'T ASK ME WHY! After my grandfather's death, we would still visit South Carolina but I never again felt the same love. One year, we were having a family reunion for my mother's side of the family; the Lee-Wilkins. Lee was my grandmother's maiden name. I am still trying to find out more information about my grandmother Annie. I do know that her father was a Native American from the Cherokee tribe and her mother was an African American woman. My brother and I drove down together to the family reunion. It was a blessing to spend some time with my big brother, because while living in the city, everything was so busy. We enjoyed the quality time to get away together so that we could talk about whatever came up in our minds. It was very rare for the two of us to be hanging out. We started out driving on the Woodrow Wilson Bridge, headed south. My brother thought that he was just going to sit back and enjoy the ride while I do all the driving. We were driving in my brother's very nice car; a Turbocharged Chrysler LeBaron. It was canary yellow. It was beautiful and very fast. He said out of his mouth "do you have a joint or something so I get my head bad." I said to my big brother; *"We are not even fully out of DC yet, and you want to get high?"* I couldn't believe it, that he would say this so fast! I knew that the subject about getting high would eventually come up and it was just a matter of time. Despite the question about getting high so quickly, I continued driving and

THANK GOD, we made it down safely. I know this because I was carrying some illegal products that belonged to my cousin. It was best if we stayed in town. Everybody knew that if my cousin had some products they would come to her house, especially with two city slickers.

After we got settled in with our bags, we took a trip to go visit our grandmother. We went to show respect even though I felt as if she was always trying to get rid of us. She had a very bad attitude towards us. I believe that he was considered an outcast from his family because he decided to marry a black woman, my great-grandmother. Our intent was to visit our grandmother and say; hello, God bless and we love you. However, we never got a chance to say those words. My brother and I looked at each other and realized it was time to go back to where we came from. Again, out of respect, all we wanted to do was say hello to our grandmother. While we were visiting her one of our female cousins was there for the summer. We noticed how very cold our welcome was. That's if you call it a welcome! It was more like a very cold goodbye, see you later, you can go now, adios!

I don't think that my brother and I stayed 15 minutes. Although I did not hold it against her, I never felt welcomed. I was the fifth youngest grandchild! Maybe she was just having a bad day. Whatever the case, I still have a lot of love for our grandmother. Years after I got injured I would occasionally write letters and send her a few dollars in the mail. I tried to remember to get gifts for her birthday and Christmas. I think her birthday was July 24. My grandparents had about 13 children, and a few of them died stillborn or shortly after a couple of months or weeks. She lost several kids, but God blessed my grandparents to have at least nine children, including my father.

As I mentioned earlier, I never held that painful day of the cold shoulder, the neglect, but I must admit that it hurt! I mean it really hurt! However, all is forgiven! I made sure I stayed in my lane as a child. I always acknowledged my grandmother throughout the years even when we would talk over the phone. I had to pretend nothing happened. Sometimes I wanted to bring it up. I sometimes wondered if it would have made a difference if I said something about it. I had to be a big boy and realize that we all have our days; some good, some bad, and we just had to make the best of it. It is now a thing of the past. PAINFUL PAST! After receiving such treatment, I know some people would have said to themselves; "I'M NEVER GOING TO VISIT HER AGAIN." I thank God that I am not like that. I've learned over the years, a lot of years, that sometimes we must let things go. One day I decided to ask my cousin if she remembered that dreadful day and she said, "Yes." That was the end of that conversation.

My mother's father, my grandfather Alexander Wilkins, was a very powerful man during his days. He was in charge of all of the family business and land. He was a well-known sharecropper and handled all business matters along with one of his favorite brothers; Great Uncle Lewis. We still have the land that my grandfather owned, with the exception of about 100 plus acres of land, that UNFORTUNATELY his brothers took shortly after my grandfather died. Our grandfather was much older than my grandmother when they got married. I believe my grandmother was about 15 years older and they had 9 children, and just like my father's mother, she lost several kids when they were very young, or either stillborn.

Whenever anyone would describe my grandfather, they would always say that he was a very handsome man. He was chocolate covered with black wavy hair. He may have been a lady's man, but I'm not to sure about that because he was either a Minister or Deacon in the church. I never saw a picture of my grandparents. God willing, maybe one day someone will share a picture of them with me. One of my aunts accused my mother of taking a photograph of my grandfather that she never returned to them. During this time, I was very active in photography and if my mother had a photograph of my grandparents, I'm pretty sure she would have given it to me to make copies of that pressure photograph of my grandfather, so this remains a mystery.

I know for sure that my grandmother was a beautiful woman. They told me to just picture our mother's oldest sister who was also a very beautiful woman herself. She had high cheekbones, just like the Cherokee Indians had. If you ever saw photographs of the Cherokee woman with those high cheekbones, that was how my Aunt looked.

She looked just like a Cherokee Indian woman. The rest of my aunts had the same features including my mother, then the baby girl of the family. I have a special position as far as grandchildren on my mother's side of the family because I am the youngest male grandchild, then my cousin. Sometimes it is good to know your place in the family. I am honored to know that I am the youngest, male grandchild.

Unfortunately, my grandfather died a very tragic death. He was sitting on the back of a dump truck when someone accidentally, or intentionally raised up the back of the dump truck and he fell headfirst onto the paved road. I always believed that he fell into a hole and was covered with dirt and was buried alive, causing him to die of suffocation, but that wasn't true. He actually lived for three days in the hospital. The cause of his death was trauma to the brain. I believe that someone really, intentionally and deliberately killed my grandfather out of jealousy, envy. However, it happened, I believe it was not an accident. I just don't believe it was, even to this day. I really wonder who was there when this happened to MY GRANDFATHER. Was there any of his family members around that time OR WERE THEY ALL Caucasian coworkers? This was a time of the "ALLEGEDLY ACCIDENT." During those days, in the forties, fifties and sixties, RACISM WAS SPEAKING, and I can't falsely accuse anyone, but I was just wondering about these few questions that I have concerning who was present when the accident occurred. I think they are legitimate questions that anyone would ask during a tragedy like this and to some, he was just another man of color. That was my grandfather! All this time I thought that he had died on the spot, only to find out the truth.

My grandmother was now responsible for taking care of the family's sharecropping business by herself. When my great uncle died it really affected my grandfather because they were a lot closer to each other than his other siblings. If my great uncle was still alive, he could help my grandmother with the things that she needed because he was very knowledgeable about the family business. Unfortunately, her brother-in-law weren't very helpful to her or to her children. I know this because my mother had a lot of bad memories. When it came to her uncles, they had some sort of learning disability, so did my aunt. People would drive by the community and tease them.

People can be so mean at times. It's one thing when a stranger makes fun of one of your family members, but it is even worse when your own family would tease you or your brother. My uncle had a nick-name, they called him JIG-JAG. They would tell my grandmother to come and get "JIG-JAG" from up here, while laughing the whole time. They never would have treated him this way if my grandfather was still living. When she would tell me the stories she would start crying because the pain was still there. Being 14 or 15 years old, this was hurtful because it was their own uncles laughing and making fun of them. Although this may have been over 40 years ago, whenever my mother talked about it she would still feel the pain and get very emotional.

Yes, my family took total advantage of my grandmother because she was also disabled. They never got her a wheelchair, so she would have to use a regular chair and maneuver through the house that was getting older and needed a lot of repairs. My grandfather and my uncle was not there anymore and the other ones showed up like they didn't care. All they wanted to do was get a piece of the hundreds of acres of land that was left from my great-grandfather's inheritance. Greed is something else and it is one of the seven deadly sins in the Bible. There was a good reason why my great-grandparents and my grandfather's parents put my grandfather in charge of the family business. I don't like to use these words loosely but "jealousy and envy are amongst family!"

As I say this, it brings back memories of the night when I was shot several times, I heard one of them say; "I didn't like him anyway and make sure he's dead." I heard the same words that were spoken when they hung Jesus on the cross. He hung on the cross for our sins. Jesus Christ is the Son of God and the true Messiah! One of the soldiers gave the order and said to the other soldier; "pierce him in his side to MAKE SURE HE IS DEAD." Those same words that I heard the night that I got shot multiple times. They wanted to make sure I was dead. That means that they had it in their minds to continue shooting. BUT, GOD SAID THAT JEFFERY D. CHAPMAN, SENIOR, "THE WEB IS FORMED AGAINST YOU, MY CHILD WILL PROSPER!" Throughout the years, I have been trying my best to give God all the honor and praise that He truly deserves. Despite being temporarily and physically paralyzed from the neck down and placed on life support, no matter what I deal with every day, I will always give God the glory through His Son Jesus Christ! Always!

I believe that my great uncles only gave my grandmother 50 or 70 acres of land when my grandfather died and the rest they divided amongst themselves. Only God knows and prayerfully it is documented and recorded somewhere in my grandfather's name. They divided the rest of the land amongst all the siblings that were living at the time. I'm not certain of all the siblings that my grandfather had. At this time, it was very hard for my grandmother to raise her children because her health started to fail. One day she was walking on the side of the highway, just like everyone else did back in the day. She was all alone on that busy highway when she was hit by a car. We believed it was the same location that separates our family land. Because of the physical damage caused by the moving vehicle she lost the ability to walk again. She was crippled and physically disabled until the day she died. While writing my story, it brings back memories and reminds me of my paralyzed state. I'm physically not able to walk, YET! If you don't mind me sharing my hypothesis concerning my grandmother getting hit by the automobile at a very high-speed; I believe in my heart that my grandmother's death was deliberate. Racism in the South has always been evident, and I believe that was a factor in her death. As far as I can recall, no one was ever charged, nor did they turn themselves in for hitting my grandmother on that beautiful day that she decided to take a walk. During those times the KKK were very evident and had no regard for people of color and treating them like animals. Unfortunately, this is our reality. It's not rocket science, it's just basic observation. I'm not claiming to be a forensic scientist, but a lot of these things do not add up. If it doesn't add up and it quacks like a duck, it's possibly a duck! God knows the truth! It seems ironic that both of my grandparents were killed as a result of vehicle incidents; my grandfather at the hands of a dump truck and my grandmother, a hit and run. Today, this would be called vehicular homicide or possibly attempted murder.

My mother was a young teenager at this time. She not only had to take care of her mother, but she took take care of her two siblings. Although they both had disabilities, they were very strong. My mother struggled with helping out. That was a huge responsibility for a teenager to have to take on. But all those things made us STRONGER in many different ways. My mother and I both were forced to grow up fast. My mom had to help around the house with everything. Sometimes she and I would talk about the 'oldin days.' I heard the hurt in her voice and I could actually feel her pain. As they got older her siblings all had their own families, so the tasks of having one parent and having to take care of them was hard. During that time in South Carolina it was difficult for African American families to survive. There were the Jim Crow laws, discrimination, and economical pitfalls to face, but Thank God, we made it through some really tough times over the years!

I believe! I believe it is time to take my spiritual life to another level! There is still so much work that need to be done from me through the eyes of our Father, through His Son Jesus Christ, without complaint or excuses. I say these things as I am claiming all these things in Jesus Christ Precious Name. Thank you for not only hearing my prayers but also answering them so that I can continue in faith. IT IS IMPOSSIBLE TO PLEASE GOD WITHOUT FAITH! I shall be restored and take back everything that the locusts, the opposer stole from me and my family. I'm claiming these things with full expectation. I have to believe in order to receive His blessings with faith as my foundation!

✳ ✳ ✳

BOTH OF MY PARENTS WERE TRUE SURVIVORS

My father is a survivor. Together my parents and older brother came from South Carolina to Washington, DC, I think it was in 1956, when my brother was just a little baby. Times were very hard. While trying to find jobs and provide a roof over their head, my parents would sometimes rent a room for a few months or sometimes they were able to stay with my uncle (my mothers' youngest brother). He was several years older than my mother, again my mother is a baby girl, and the baby of the family. They were able to stay with my uncle and his family for a few months until something mysterious happened. The caseworker came to the apartment and saw that there were more people living in the apartment and not on their lease agreement. So, this meant that my parents had to find a place to stay as soon as possible. If I'm not mistaking, GOD arranged for this lady to let them stay with her until they were able to find their own place to live. God knows it was a blessing and they had a baby during that time. I must admit, it must have been very challenging for them and even frightening that sometimes they wondered whether they would find a place to live. Again, the caseworker just mysteriously showed up in their apartment. But thank God for faith! Thank God for favor! Thank God for the lady that they met that was probably an angel. I do believe in angels!

In the Bible, the book of Hebrews, Chapter 13 verse 2 says: *"Do not neglect to show hospitality, to strangers, for by this, some have entertained angels without knowing it."* As I mentioned, they must have said to themselves, "We don't know that many people here in Washington, DC, because we just recently came from South Carolina a few months ago." My father started working with a construction company called "Perry & Wallace." I believe my uncle was working with them first. He was able to help my father get a job. We always thanked him for helping my father and later my family found an apartment in Southeast, DC. I believe that they lived in the apartment for one year until my oldest sister was born. The apartment was located on Bangart Street, in Southeast Washington, DC. They must have felt really good and thankful to God that they were able to have their own apartment after being treated pretty rough and badly by others. All they were trying to do was find a safe place for their children, and you know, some people, can be so mean and so harsh to others. Where's the love?

Prior to my parents getting their own place, I believe they actually stayed with some good friends. These friends were also from South Carolina. They moved to Washington, DC a long time before my parents did. They stayed with them until their transition to their own. They always stayed in touch with my parents, especially my father to make sure that he was okay. I always considered the both of them family. I also considered him like family to us over the years and even now, to this day, I stay in contact with them. I remember when my parents needed help, they were there for them, and even after they moved they stayed in touch with the them. My father felt like he was the little brother because Mr. Burness was much older than both of my parents and knowing that they were from the same small town in South Carolina. This was during the time families looked out for one another. This world we live in today is very sad. It is very selfish and many feel as though someone owes them something, especially this generation of kids. I don't know what's up with that kind of logic or that kind of thinking.

Our family started growing and my parents had three children, my brothers and sisters were now born. At this time my parents were both working. Their income increased, and they were able to afford a much larger apartment. This is when they found out about the Barry Farms area. Shortly afterwards, they moved to the final community in the apartment complex. It was when my parents moved further down the street, four years later my mother was pregnant with me, yours truly and that I was! They both decided to move down the street to another smaller apartment complex, but the apartments had an extra bedroom. During that time my father was working in construction, and my mother was working at Washington, National Airport. Years later they changed the name, in the nineties the airport was renamed after the former president, Ronald Reagan, now they call the Airport, Reagan National Airport. Our mother worked very hard with the food service department. She was responsible for preparing all of the food that went on the airplanes. This was extremely hard work for a female or even a male to do, but back then everyone had to get used to doing manual labor. This is how this country was built on the backs of hard-working manual laborers and their job was to fill up those food carts and then push them onto the airplanes. My mother was a very beautiful young woman and I'm not just saying that because she is my mom, but it was the truth. She was sexually harassed by her manager on her job on a daily basis even though she told him that she was a married woman and she insisted that he leave her alone. But because she would not succumb to the stupidity, he would try to give her extra hard work to do until she couldn't take it anymore. All the heavy lifting eventually caused her to have a hernia and poor circulation in both of her legs. She had to stop working in her early sixties because of the broken veins. All of this started with a knucklehead supervisor who was trying to flirt with her. Just because she wasn't that kind of lady and he couldn't receive rejection, he caused her ailments. She was unable to endure standing for long periods of time on the concrete floors at the airport. After losing a paycheck, an income my mother was accustomed to, everything fell on my father's shoulder. He was a true soldier, not in the military, but a soldier of survival, and he knew how to make sure that his family was fed and had a roof over our heads.

My father became a bootlegger, one who sells liquor illegally. That was one way he used to diversify the loss of income that my mother no longer was able to provide. She had another full-time job and that was taking care of the four of us, being the best mother and wife possible!

I remember going to the liquor store with my parents when my father needed to buy more liquor. He liked different brands because he had established himself very well. Everyone knew that since all of the liquor stores were closed on Sundays they could get a bottle from Mr. Joe. He had two sizes available. My father really knew how to make a dollar and I inherited it from him. As I was growing up, I became an entrepreneur, but with different products. All of my siblings had this business minded mentality. My kids and nephews and nieces also inherited the entrepreneurship gift. I still can remember seeing my father coming out of the very small liquor store (for some reason seemed very small to me) with several large bags filled with alcohol. I'm pretty sure that the owner of the liquor store eventually offered my father some kind of discount because he was buying so much liquor from the owner's establishment at one time. This meant that my father was spending hundreds of dollars every time he would go to this particular liquor store. This was his business. After my father started spending so much money with this guy, the only thing to do was to give him a discount on each bottle of liquor that he purchased. This would've been the right thing to do as the owner of the liquor store and appreciating the large sales and practices that my father was giving him because not everybody that patronized that liquor store was making large purchases at one time.

He was well established as a bootlegger and he had quite a reputation. He had a huge clientele of adult customers. Both of my parents knew how to survive during tough times in the South. It didn't bother him that much because he had established an image and a little reputation for himself, despite the risk and the dangerous stick-up boys. One time someone put a gun to my brother's head and robbed him for the liquor that he was carrying for my father. He initially pretended to be a customer. My brother was only 10 years old at the time. I'm certain that my older brother and my father handled that situation. Because of our family's successful business, we had to endure these kinds of things.

In my neighborhood you really had to defend yourself, if not, folks in the hood would take total advantage of you. My father was our protector and provider! He really enjoyed driving fast cars and every now and then when he would get drunk and have a little alcohol in his system, he would hang out in the streets, doing whatever he wanted to do. This bothered my mother a lot, which was understandable. It was difficult for my mom because she knew that he had an undisclosed amount of money in his pockets while he was in the streets and she knew that the haters were waiting for the opportunity. If you found yourself sleeping, the stick-up boys would come around creeping. The only time he would hang out in the streets and race his fast cars was when he drank.

We finally moved our family from Barry Farms in 1970, to a neighborhood directly up the street from our old apartment. This area was called Park Chester Apartments. God had blessed my family to be able to afford a larger apartment, located in the Park Chester community. Since I was the other addition to the Chapman family, we needed more bedrooms. These apartments were remodeled to make them larger to accommodate bigger families. The apartment came with four bedrooms, two bathrooms, living room, dining room and a very small kitchen, but it was more than enough space to accommodate all of us.

My parents were not afraid of anyone because you had to have some tough skin back then. It was an absolute must because people would challenge you or try to take advantage of you all the time if you were not able to stand your ground and protect yourself from them. They knew exactly who to challenge or take advantage of, that's just what they did. If they could get away with it, the thieves would steal your personal belongings. I was the only one that called my father "pops" because it sounded cool to me, without being disrespectful. Pops made sure we had food, clothes on our back and a roof over our head. I loved my parents very much and we had a great relationship. A lot of kids nowadays cannot talk to their parents about certain things that bother them or threatens them. It is very sad, but I thank God that I didn't have that problem. I don't think any of my siblings had a problem communicating with our parents, and what a blessing that has been over the years to be able to go to either one of your parents and tell them what was going on with you in your life or what was troubling you.

My mother was a very quiet lady, she never drank, smoked or went to parties or hung out in the streets. She believed in staying home with her children and taking care of her husband. I'm blessed to have a mother like her because a lot of my friends' mothers were just the opposite. Mom kept the family together in many ways. She was the NUCLEUS and the DISCIPLINARIAN in our family. My mother was a very strong woman, and truly a God-sent lady. All she wanted was to make sure that she took care of her husband and her children and to make sure everyone was happy. But a lot of times, especially in times my father was hanging out in the streets, it weighed heavily on my mother's heart and mind, but she still stayed. On occasion he would hit the lottery for a large amount of money. We never knew the amount, but he made sure the bills were paid and all of the stock merchandise was purchased with his winnings. I guess having the responsibility of taking care of four children and a wife, running the streets wasn't personal, he just needed to get loose every now and then.

You know drugs have been a real downfall in some ways, directly and indirectly that affected my family and so many others.

I'm not trying to justify anything but in a lot of ways drugs destroyed the black communities, musicians, actors and a lot of other professionals. Many lost their lives due to the use of drugs. The devil and all of his demons knew that this would affect people of color and they found a way to spread it all over this country. The bible clearly tells us that the devil comes to steal, kill and destroy. He comes after as many souls as he can, and it is still happening today.

Getting back to how it affected my family; both of my older siblings sold drugs. My brother sold marijuana and he would leave me to do the cleanup job. He would use the top of the shoe box to separate the marijuana and seeds to make the $5 nickel bags of marijuana. My job at the age of eight years old was to clean up the marijuana from out of the top of the shoe box. It was a way for me to get a couple of joints out of doing it. That's why he left it for me. It wasn't a coincidence. In his mind it was the right thing to do, being as though I was helping. He told me after I cleaned up the shoe box I could scrape out any leftovers for myself.

Everybody knows that during the sixties and seventies marijuana wasn't hidden from anyone, it was out in the open. Even when you go to the movies we'd watch one of the big-screen movie stars smoking marijuana. Up in smokes was a movie. All about marijuana and even the movie Coolie High when the principal and the police officer smoked marijuana in his office and I think even Clint Eastwood was on a big screen smoking marijuana. I'm not saying that because they did it, that we should do it, but what I'm saying is that it was available. I'm not trying to justify my siblings selling marijuana and angel dust. It had formaldehyde or embalming fluid which was used to preserve dead bodies. A famous artist made a record about angel dust. The downfall of all of this was that the drugs were sold and used. This drug caused people to hallucinate. I didn't handle this heavy drug, only the marijuana, which was bad too. I'm not glorifying this act, I'm just letting everyone know what the sixties and seventies looked like for me and my family. Everybody in the neighborhood knew that my siblings were selling drugs. During the time of the drug enterprise, my family also worked on the ice cream truck. What a blessing to have three ice cream trucks. Sadly, after some of the people would smoke angel dust or wacky weed, both treated with chemicals, it would affect their minds and in a lot of cases, some people believed that they could fly. They would actually find a high point somewhere and jump off and unfortunately the result ended in death. A lot of people succumbed to the daily drug addiction at a very young age, even the older ones that you would think knew better got hooked. As a kid, I too was exposed to all of this and had the knowledge of these things that maybe I shouldn't have, or maybe in some ways having the knowledge protected me from a lot of the things at a very young age. There was an old saying; *"what you don't know, won't hurt you."* That is one of the biggest lies ever told. Knowledge is power and if you don't know some things you may get killed.

Our parents knew everything that we were doing because my oldest sister was the snitch of the family. When I was nine, she told my mother that I was smoking marijuana. She also knew that my brother was selling it at the time. My childhood went very fast! I started smoking marijuana when I was only eight years old. My mother found out what I was doing. There wasn't much she could do because it was what it was. It wasn't that my parents did not love or care for me, this simply was the life of the seventies. We had our own mom and pop store, wine store and ice cream business and now I'm exposed to almost EVERYTHING! As the seventies passed, someone changed the name from "wacky weed" to the "love boat" (It was the same drug, treated with the same chemicals, and had the same reaction as angel dust). Later as the years rolled on, and I got a lot older, the more street knowledge I obtained, not by choice but by force, as I was out of my parents' house in our family establishment. This was in 1974 when we purchased the mom-and-pop business. The store was located on Nichols Avenue, but they later changed the name to Dr. Martin Luther King, Jr. Avenue located in Southeast, Washington, DC.

Years later, my younger sister and I started our turn indulging with selling drugs. We were selling love-boat during that time. This may sound crazy but I did have a conscience, in that I refused to sell drugs to kids. It went to school with me. I felt so much older, running my family's business, starting at the age of 13 throughout Junior High School and eventually High School. Most of my customers were some of the dancers next door and strip club frequent goers. I never got hooked, it was all business for me. I couldn't say the same for my sister. Of course, this didn't last long. I eventually started experimenting with different drugs or let me say that I was exposed to many different illegal drugs as a teenager, for example; powder cocaine. I even tried crack once and I think I didn't get hooked, but that was a set up. By this time, I'm in my twenties and the apartment where my fiancé and I were living, there were two crackhead tenants that lived downstairs on the 2nd floor of the apartment building. They worked a job every day, but they loved smoking crack cocaine. I called it my crack house, that's what it seemed like. Some days I would go downstairs to check in on them to see if they needed anything or knew anyone that needed my goods. They would somehow claim that they had no money and being the kind of person I was I would hook them up and leave. No less than 30 minutes later, they would come upstairs to my apartment, knocking on my door with money to purchase more. Yes, I know it wasn't right, but at that time it was just business, a legal business in my mind. It helped me to pay my bills. Even though I had a full-time job and before my daughter was born I had to get ready to make sure the finances were available in order to take care of a child. My fiancé at the time was not working so I had to diversify my income, so in my mind this was justifiable; "supply and demand" that's what they called it.

Whenever you let people know that you are making money or you already have money they have a tendency to have things to sell. One example, before my daughter was even born, I already had a wardrobe for a couple years because my neighbor downstairs was a kleptomaniac who provided us with clothing that fit my wife, my daughter and sometimes, myself. Some kind of way, I got hooked up with this guy that was working for a company that sold Similac milk and other kinds of milk for babies. I would give him a little something and I always received at least 10 cases of milk before my daughter was born. I also made sure that I got a case of milk for my nephew as well because he was around the same age as my daughter, just one or two months apart. This lasted long enough, until the next time I had another order.

I can remember I ran into this particular guy, but it was actually a blessing. Not only did I get milk for my baby, he also had juice too. It was Gerber's apple juice and other different types for the babies. I also had a connection to provide me with pampers. I had access to get large bags of pampers from the hospital. Having access to the product of crack cocaine drew a lot of people around me. But there was somewhat of an even exchange in my mind; again, "supply and demand." At this time, I decided not to be as much involved with selling drugs of any kind. My son was born. I tried my best to trust in God and use my photography skills as my backup source of income which was very low during the winter months, but very lucrative at times, mainly during the summer months.

***

BREAKING IN ICE CREAM TRUCKS BY
GIVING ENABLED KIDS A TREAT

My father used to take so many kids and adults to McDonald's whenever he would get a new ice cream truck, maybe to him it was some kind of initiation of showing that he appreciated the support from the kids in the community of Park Chester. The first time he took a countless number of children and adults from the community out to McDonald's, was in the back of his pickup truck. Everybody got a hamburger, French fries and drinks. All expenses paid by my father. He drove all of us down to Anacostia Park until my mother drove up and saw him and they had a few words and then we went back to our community. I'm pretty sure that all the kids enjoyed themselves, including myself, and maybe a couple of my siblings. The second time was when we purchased our third ice cream truck, just like before, but this truck was a lot bigger, which meant that you could hold and carry more people and also, we had a cover over our head, that protected everyone, unlike the pickup truck. Everything worked out with that one, just like before we all went to McDonald's and got hamburgers and French fries and soda for everyone that was in the truck. I mean everyone! Nobody was excluded. I always liked a fillet of fish sandwich from McDonald's. That's what I ordered all the time and this time wasn't any different plus it was my father who was treating everyone. I thank God that we did not have any problems. We made it back, happy and safe. This was the kind of things that happened in our community in the neighborhood of Park Chester. This was also a way of my family giving back to the neighbors that patronized the ice cream truck business over the years.

As a kid, I observed and learned a lot about the other people at Park Chester, which was a black community. It was also a safe haven for kids and adults that did not have to walk to the Berry Farm's corner store and the chances of them getting beat up or robbed by the kids in the neighborhood. I mean you had adults that would take other adults' money and items that they purchased from the store and teenagers that would do the same thing to other teenagers. It didn't matter the age, even younger kids would steal candy or ice cream. By our family having the ice cream truck sometimes parked right in front of our building or in the parking lot was convenient and safe for kids and adults. But, no one really saw that positive side of my family as being a safe haven for the community, the people. Some of the haters in the community would call the police occasionally on my family because there was some kind of policy that if no one was at your ice cream truck at a certain amount of time we would have to move to relocate to a different area, but by the time the police would arrive, there would be customers buying stuff. It didn't matter though because the police didn't particularly like that our family was trying to establish a business in the community. Which brings me to this question; Why do we hate on each other so much as black people? When my family was just trying to provide and make a better living for the children. What was wrong with that? There were people jealous and envious of my family members. Sadly today, some of the same people have that same mentality and hatred towards my family and I.

My father had his haters, my mother didn't bother anyone but she had her haters. She wasn't one of those ladies that would go out and start gossiping, nor was she trying to steal someone else's husband, she was about family and the family business. Then my oldest brother had his haters, both my sisters had their haters and believe it or not, while growing up, I had my haters and still do to this day, WHY? Maybe because our parents were able to provide certain things that maybe some of the other parents were unable to give, for an example, a new car. My brother was able to get an automobile when he turned 16 years old due to all the hard work my parents did. Although he was a lady's man, he was my role model and my idle. I wanted the same things for myself when I grew up, although the young ladies liked me too. Nevertheless, my sister was a trendsetter, she also had a set of haters. She was into fashion and could dance which drew a lot of attention, positive and negative. My other sister, along with our adopted sister had their haters. Believe it or not, even I had my haters; me as a kid. What did I do to anybody to make them want to hate me?

We were all business minded children which we learned from our parents and we had leadership qualities. We learned how to count and organize money. Some of us, before we were even teenagers learned how to organize. My father taught us many skills. Later on in life when I had my kids I was able to teach them also about counting money. These are business skills, not bragging skills that you learn normally in school of business, but we learned as we went along, and no one in the community really understood that we had a systematic way of doing things. All they ever saw was people come into the ice cream truck and later the store and that we were making money and progressing. As I lay here year after year, I began thinking about things, how we indirectly put pressure on people because they wanted some of the same things that we had. There were positions that they were able to acquire, as a result they were blessed to have the same things we had and more. So, in a lot of ways, we helped the community do better in their desires to have more, but if you asked the average person in the surrounding areas, they wouldn't think that way. God willing, maybe they'll get it one day!

As we got older, my brother started a family and became an electrician. My oldest sister started attending cooking classes and was supposed to become a chef or even a writer. However, she chose a different direction as far as business. My other sister went to school and became a cosmetologist and that was her business. Our adopted sister decided to leave the family. I believe she was brainwashed by several people that lived in the Park Chester community. It was her fault and her choice that she decided to sneak out the house one night after my parents told her not to, but she did it anyway, and to teach her a lesson they locked the door and would not let her come back that night. It wasn't like she didn't have anywhere else to go for that night because her biological mother Mrs. Virginia, May She Rest in Peace, lived in the adjacent building to our building. This lesson was only supposed to last one night, but again, the people that were influencing her did a very good job and she decided to just move away on her own. After several years of being apart from our family, after making the decision to befriend my sister so that she could be a part of the family and enjoy some of the nice things that my sisters had, she made the choice to move out of her mother's house. Nobody forced her, but everybody would think that we did, but the truth is the truth. She was considered my sister no matter what happened or what transpired over the years. Unfortunately, she was brainwashed by the outsiders although she once called our parents mom and dad. Because of her complexion, a lot of people thought that she was our biological sister, being light-skin like myself and my mom, my father, brother and sisters were brown-skin, so she fit right in.

CHAPTER 2

GROWING UP

I'm the youngest of four, but at times I felt like the oldest, maybe it was because I grew up so fast. I had one older brother, two sisters and our adopted sister and my first dog named Lady. My brother was nine years older than me, and I learned a lot from him. Maybe more than I should have being as young as I was. He was my role model, and I wanted to be just like him. He was an excellent basketball player, and I figured if he made it to the pros playing basketball, I would have to be as good as him or better. The girls were crazy about him, and during the seventies we all wore afros, and I was no exception. I wanted to be so much like him. Whenever he wore plats for cornrows, I would have my hair done the same way. They called my oldest brother "Chap," and when they would see me somewhere they would say; "Hey! Aren't you Chaps little brother?" I kept a cool smile, and I would reply, "Yeah!"

My father's nickname was Joe, he was my first role model, but to be blessed to have two role models in your family, meaning my brother was the second one, is truly a blessing. I would dress just like my brother and that wasn't really normal for a nine-year-old kid to dress like an 18-year-old teenager, but that's what I did. Whenever he went shopping for clothes, my mom made sure he took me with him so I could get the same or similar things. I was a mini Joe and a mini "Chap". As I mentioned earlier, my brother had another reputation that wasn't so positive, he sold a lot of marijuana, and many people were aware of it. You couldn't tell me anything, I was the little man, and my brother was my big brother, who I truly admired. I believed that he was going to make it to play professional basketball. He was also very talented when it came to playing softball for the local adult team for the Barry Farm community. The softball team uniforms were yellowish gold, with black and white pants.

I used to get some of my friends in the hood to smoke, roll up after the cleanup, and some of the guys that I hung out with. Some were close to my age, and a lot of them would be older than me, but I would be bringing something to the table. Here I come at the age of eight or nine years old with a couple of joints of weed in my pocket. My parents never knew that I was smoking marijuana, they might have known but just didn't say anything to me about it, until one year, my oldest sister told my mother that I was getting high. Although my brother sold weed, he was intelligent. He attended two different colleges, Bowie State University, and the other college was South Eastern University. I'm pretty sure that my brother played one year of basketball, with Bowie State University, and he also played for South Eastern University in Washington, DC for another season. For some reason they displayed their basketball games at a local high school in Southeast, the Anacostia high school, because I've been to at least one of his basketball games. I tried to be around as much as possible to learn a lot of things, and again, some good, some bad. He is my big brother and I was very proud of my brother. Unfortunately, he dropped out of school. At the time I was uncertain of why my brother dropped out of college.

I will say one thing, my father wasn't into sports, he was strictly into taking care of his family, and finding ways to pay the bills. Many of my brother's friends and their fathers were very heavy into sports, but since my father wasn't I believe that my brother held that against my father. Unfortunately, a lot of people have a tendency to blame others because they may not have received the encouragement that they felt they needed. A lot of times, we have to be accountable for our own actions. As I lay here in this nursing home, or even when I had to go to the hospital, had surgery for whatever reason, I have to find ways to encourage myself, each and every day. Although I do have a lot of church members that stop by to pray for me and check on me, and also try to encourage me. I have heard this countless times from my visitors or church members, they would say to me; "I CAME HERE TO ENCOURAGE YOU, BUT YOU END UP ENCOURAGING ME MORE." I TRULY THANK GOD THAT HE HAS ALLOWED ME TO BE A BLESSING TO OTHERS AND TO BE ABLE TO BE AN ENCOURAGEMENT TO THEM. I truly believe that one of the main reasons that my brother didn't complete his college education was because he enjoyed getting high, hanging out with his buddies and also chasing those ladies out there. TEMPTATION IS VERY STRONG! I believe that my brother's social life was a big factor that interfered with his determination to finish pursuing his college career. His lifestyle, using and selling drugs not only hindered him. God only knows what my brother could have made of himself if he would've stayed in college, but his choice and his life, like all of us make certain choices in life that can help or hurt us and we have no one else to blame but ourselves. Unfortunately, I am reminded of this. Every time I think about why I can no longer walk yet or breathe on my own yet, is because of the one bad decision I made. I cannot blame ANYONE ELSE! I can't! It is totally my fault and I can't even blame the devil because I knew right from wrong. I have to live with this true reality that when I made the decision to sell a kilo of cocaine and everything went wrong. I can share this reality and the consequences of my mistakes, but all I had to do was use a very powerful, two letter word, NO!

"NO" is a very powerful word when you use it correctly. I KNOW NOW! As I struggle with the very thought of; *"should I do it, or should I not do it?"* constantly exposes the battle that we deal with every day between spirit and the flesh whether we know it or not. The enemy is the "INNER ME!" Making the right decisions determines the outcome or consequences. We have to face and deal with our sinful bodies and thoughts each and every day. I've been committed to make the effort to be more SPIRITUAL as I go to my pilgrimage and walk with the Lord. We serve God, not a man or woman. We should try our best to live a more spiritual life. A gospel singer made a song called "Spiritual," which explains almost everything that I just tried to say within this paragraph. Lord, help me to be more Spiritual!

Drugs have destroyed millions of lives, not just for my brother, but millions of young children, teenagers, young men and woman, entertainers, actors, those in Hollywood and those from all walks of life. This also affects the rich because they have access to any kinds of drugs that are out there, all they have to do is make a phone call and the supplier delivers. With all of the new drugs that are available today; methamphetamines, prescription drugs, synthetic drugs, man-made drugs, they are slowly killing us. It is critical that we continue on this topic of drug usage because the younger children are becoming more and more addicted. It first starts with prescription medication, namely opioids that they get from their parents' medicine cabinets. Then there is the heroin dealer. Many years ago, a lot of veteran soldiers who served in the military, giving their lives for our country, the United States of America, came home with a HEROIN ADDICTION! They made it home safely from Vietnam but experienced psychological death. It was more of a warfare in the mind. It was hard for them to cope with everyday life. The only way they could get rid of those bad thoughts, visions and memories, they felt was to medicate themselves with drugs. They thought that the drugs would help them block out those horrifying memories and casualties of war. Even seeing some of their friends get blown away because of Viacom planning, booby-trapped bombs, underbodies.

We need God to help us all to spiritually overpower the negative addiction of drugs that causes us many temptations in life. A drug dealer is anyone that is selling drugs, they don't care who they are selling the drugs to, all they are looking for is the money. No one knows anything about the consequences of selling drugs or the effect that it has on different families and each other as a race. During the eighties the drug epidemic was terrible. They inundated and flooded the African-American community with crack cocaine, one purpose was to kill black Americans. This is the true fact! I wonder why our people of color have been hated and targeted all over this country for centuries by the powers to be. They try to find ways to kill us all, that's not Godly to say, but it's a fact!

For me, it really was a struggle choosing to sell drugs. Even if I sold a bag of marijuana, I was considered a DRUG DEALER! I really never cared to continue to sell drugs, and I could stop at any time, but it always seemed like I could use this method to fall back on whenever I needed some fast money. NOW, I'm about to say something, that may sound like an oxymoron. Have you ever heard of a drug dealer with a conscience? Well, that was me. I struggled and fought against myself to continue doing this. I knew that it was affecting my people and other's family members. At one point, I knew I had to stop! I was just fed up! I didn't want to make this lifestyle an everyday thing.

I was faced with public embarrassment after receiving an eviction notice. My wife and daughter had to move back with my parents. I had just lost my job at St. Elizabeth's hospital as a psychiatric assistant. To avoid embarrassment just out of the blue, I saw a guy that had a U-Haul truck, and I asked him how much he would charge me to use his rental truck for a couple hours. I gave him the money that he requested, and I had to tell my fiancé, my sweetheart at the time that we had to make a quick move. I did not want to become a full-time drug dealer, and believe it or not, when I was working at the hospital most of my customers were there, my coworkers. I'm truly thankful that she was willing to move quickly without questioning me about my decision, and truly thankful for being understanding.

After several months of living with my parents, I had more products to sell, but first of all I did not want to bring this to my parents' house. I didn't want to put them in jeopardy nor did I want to get caught. I certainly didn't want them to lose the house because of me. I was truly thankful that my parents didn't question me when I moved back in with my fiancée and daughter, they were very understanding. Early one morning I went back to the neighborhood that we had moved from and went to this wooded area, it was like a dead-end street. But you can either go left or right, it could've been a metaphor that I really didn't pay attention to until now as I'm talking. I was at a crossroad and I had to make a quick decision. I remember going to a wooded area where I dug a hole and destroyed about $400 or maybe even $500 worth of drugs. That was a lot of money during the eighties. In all reality that still is a lot of money in today's standard. A few weeks later, I thought to myself that maybe I should've waited until after the holidays were over. Since my wife wasn't working at the time, I had to take care of everything financially. My wife was seven months pregnant with our daughter. I had to step up and take care of my family, working at the hospital, and diversify my income was selling drugs. I had to make a split decision on whether I was going to continue selling drugs or to get a real job. I had the strength and my mind was made up at that particular time. Using my photography training and skills allowed me to make extra money and it kept me away from hustling for several years. Now that the three of us are living with my parents, I have to try to generate some income without selling drugs and get a real job.

I'm not trying to justify or rationalize all the things that I did, right or wrong. However, I had to deal with the consequences

Of the decisions that I made on that cold, fall night, Thursday, September 20, 1990. I'm just praying to GOD, that I am able to help someone. I'm praying that thousands of my readers get a chance to read this story of mine, GOD WILLING and receive something positive from my message, my life story and not make the same mistakes that I made. I'm still living with the decisions I've made, thus my story "LIVING JUST ENOUGH FOR THIS CITY."

God knows everything that we were dealing with. The scriptures remind me that anything worth having is worth waiting for, but also not to be anxious about anything, but in everything with prayer and supplication making my requests known. I was impatient with the Lord. I KNOW NOW! Unfortunately, for so many other people, dealing with financial problems, especially in the African-American Communities and Neighborhoods, drugs are so easy to get and very accessible for anyone that wants them, as long as you have the money. You can also get any kind of guns and weapons that you want as well.

There is a conspiracy theory! A true conspiracy exists, as it was given by the orders of the people that are positioned in high places. These people that run this world have the power to make orders to have African Americans killed by any means necessary. First it started with the availability of drugs; prescription also, and the availability of weapons, which are so convenient to get their hands on. It's nothing for a teenager these days to buy guns or to become drug dealers. It seems as if they don't want us to have any positive occupations. Instead, they see our occupations as: drug dealer, killer and criminal. These were caused by broken families, babies having babies and the blind leading the blind. They made it so convenient, so that we could get addicted to drugs or the younger generation become killers without a conscience. We're taking each other's lives, pulling the trigger as if they're playing a video game, but this is real! This isn't a game! When the young kids start using drugs, they become a slave to the product and they would do whatever it takes to get it. It doesn't matter the cost, they are even willing to "take someone out" if they get in the way.

During the late 1980s or early 1990s, around the time I was shot, Washington, DC, was labeled the "Murder Capital of this

Country." This was a part of the plan, for black people to kill and exterminate each other. This is not an exaggeration. Remember the border babies? People were hired just to hold the babies because they were born addicted to crack cocaine. This was to kill the seed of the next black generation.

Then there's my oldest sister but we called her "Babby." I don't know where she got that name from, but it wasn't in my power to question her name. She was just my big sister. Growing up, Babby was a wild young lady. She liked to go out to parties and clubs every weekend. She used to sneak out of the house late at night, just to hang out. She was an extravagant dresser and most of her friends envied her because of that. During the seventies there was a popular Go-Go band called Chunk Brown & The Soul Searchers, and wherever they played, you could find her. She had a good reputation for being well-dressed and a good dancer. Yet she carried a bad reputation for selling Angel Dust. Angel Dust was wrapped with individual pieces of aluminum foil and it needed to be kept refrigerated because the chemicals would get weak. You could only get about five or six joints out of a $10 bag. Babby made a lot of money and several enemies came with selling drugs. Angel Dust is a chemically imbalanced drug whose side affects made one hallucinate. One day she was at a pool party with her friends and they smoked some Angel Dust. As a result, one of her friends stripped down, butt naked, and jumped into the pool. It was a normal reaction, hallucination. It made you feel as if you were on fire. Everybody there tripped out on what he did, and that has been the talk for many years. Angel Dust was made of Parsley Flakes, the regular old flakes that you would cook with, but it was treated with formaldehyde or embalming fluid. Everybody knew there were two things to be prepared to do when someone began hallucinating, we would give them milk or stick them into a cold shower which would shock them back to reality. YES, the drug people used to preserve dead bodies and had to be refrigerated, just like a cadaver or dead body so chemicals would not get weak. This chemical not only causes one to feel as if they're on fire, but it affected people differently. It caused some people to think that they were flying like a bird and they would jump off of a high area or platform. I never tried this particular drug because I was too afraid of what would happen to me mentally.

My sister and I had a good relationship and before she would leave out for the night, for some reason she thought that I was her personal photographer. She wanted me to take a photo of her in whatever outfit she was wearing that night. She also had a problem with taking whatever she wanted out of stores. Although she didn't have to steal, but I believe it was part of her rebelliousness. She had a little crew that would hang out with her when she would take clothes from clothing stores. My parents would have bought her any clothes that she wanted, but she had to do it her way. One day she looked up the definition of her name and it read, "Determined Purpose." That truly was an accurate description.

My younger sister and I were only four years apart. She has always looked after me throughout my life and I am so grateful to her. Like most lil' brothers, she is one who I looked up to. My family kept this picture of her holding me on her lap while I was trying to pick up the telephone. She was probably about three and a half years old. She had a lot of "tom-boyish" ways about her, but she will always be my little, big sister. I can't discuss her without mentioning our adopted sister. She started living with us during the early seventies.

She was a young girl who lived adjacent to our apartment building. She and my sister became really good friends. The two of them were like twins. Every time my mother bought clothes for one, the other would get the same outfit in a different color. Both of them were very good friends and they did everything together. Even their boyfriends were friends of each other. My adopted sister was light skinned like myself, and everybody thought that she was my biological sister, we wouldn't tell them any different. She enjoyed scaring people, especially me. I remember one night I was leaving out of the kitchen, in the apartment in Park Chester. It was really dark between the kitchen and the living room area, so she laid down beside the stereo system. As I walked by, she grabbed my leg and she scared me real good. I was so mad at her. I kicked her and she retaliated by punching me in my eye. I saw stars for a few minutes. She just kept laughing at me and that made me extremely upset. I was about 9 or 10 years old at that time. She would scare everybody and get a big laugh out of it. Both of my sisters were very good in karate classes and they moved up very fast in the rankings. They used to have some other females taking karate, but after my sisters started being so aggressive the other girls dropped out. They were so good, they'd spar against the black belt instructor because there were no other females in the class to practice with. They took karate for about three years and nobody bothered either one of them at school, in our neighborhood or at our store.

Although my adopted sister's mother lived in the apartment building connected to our building where we lived, she wasn't always around. Instead once she started living with us, she called our parents mom and dad. She got along well with my mom because she liked cooking and cleaning up around the house, whereas my other sisters couldn't take cleaning. I believe in some ways "Babby" felt some kind of way about the relationship that my mother and sister had. After she moved in with the family, I would say that my mother did not neglect my oldest sister, but she was so quick to do anything that my mother would ask her and maybe, my own sister might have felt she was trying to take her place in our family. Just maybe my mom started to favor my adopted sister because she was quick to do whatever my mother asked, whereas my other two sisters may have hesitated or stepped back and watched how our adopted sister would react so quickly. She had other siblings, but she did not live with them. She had four brothers (*the oldest boy, who was killed the year of 1982 by one of his friends that lived with their uncle*). He was stabbed several times with a knife. After he was stabbed, he made his way to his mother's door and collapsed and died. Her other brothers worked in our store. After being locked out of the house after sneaking out of my mother's house, she moved to Maryland with her step-father's sister for a while, never calling home to say anything to our family. If I'm not mistaking, she tried to stay with us the next year, but we had another fight and it was pretty ugly, so that put an end to her second chance of living with us. Until this day, I feel really bad that she had to leave.

After I was shot, five years later we were able to get her address and telephone number. We found out that she had moved to New York, got married and had six children. I used to call her while my mother's sisters were here visiting with me. When my mother finally had a chance to talk to her after all those years, I could tell that my mother really enjoyed talking to her. She would start talking about the good old days and my mother and sister would be

43

laughing while they were talking to her. I enjoyed hearing them talk and laugh with each other while I was on the telephone, a three-way call. I would always ask her to send me some pictures of her and her children, but she never would send any pictures and I don't know why. Occasionally, I would purchase a case of corn chips that she used to like when she was living in our area. They didn't sell that particular brand in New York. I would mail several cases to her and her children, but she would never write me a letter or call me on the telephone to say thanks or to show her appreciation. After doing all that to try and keep the lines of communication open, I got tired of always being the initiator. I have not talked to her in over three years or more. I pray that they are doing well!

CHAPTER 3

HOOP DREAMS

I was placed in advanced sixth grade and after I was tested I decided I wanted to be transferred to another class. I really should have stayed in the sixth-grade class that I was in before going downstairs to be tested because a lot of the students that were in that class were older, by approximately two years and I was on the lower grade average. I learned that later, but they had so much freedom to do a lot of things, which I enjoyed, like watching television and the singular radio. These things would not have taken place in the class I was in before transferring downstairs and now I understand why. There was so much freedom to do whatever they wanted to do. Lessons are learned, even at a young age, if you take heed to the lessons that are presented to you and believe me I know better. I just want to work hard, like I should have. I have big regrets even to this day.

I was one of the smartest students in the class. I guess I would've been considered the "teacher's pet." I would finish my class work so fast that my teacher would ask me to help her around the classroom. Sometimes, in the classroom I didn't feel as if I was being challenged at all. During those days they didn't have the Xerox copying machines. They had a different kind. We had to manually turn with our hands to make duplicate copies of our daily assignments and that was my regular job that I did for my teacher and also for my classmates. As I mentioned some of the students were much older than I was. I should not have been in that 6th grade advance class, but they became my friends. It didn't matter to me if they were older, and even sometimes if I was to give them my finished assignment for the day. They wanted to look at my papers. Sometimes, I wanted to look at other students' papers and assignments that they had finished before me. This was all very new to me and flattering in some ways. In no way was I looking down on anyone, but for some odd reason, the tables were turned.

Around 2:00 p.m., on any given day, I would ask my teacher to go to the bathroom, and she would give me permission. I never went to the bathroom, and she knew this. She also knew that I had finished my assignments earlier that morning while all the students were just waiting until 3:00 p.m. to come. So, I would leave school early every day, and go home. My teacher would watch me walk up the street out of her window and she would never say anything to me the following day. Even after lunch I would go to my brother's girlfriend's house and stay until 3:00 p.m. Then I would catch the bus or walk to my parents store which was a nice walk, probably close to one mile, but that was good exercise. My parents opened our mom and pop store during my last year of elementary school.

I was only in the 6th grade and I was moving too fast. I shouldn't have stayed in that advanced 6th grade class because when I got to the 7th grade my skills were very weak. I really learned the hard way. After only being in the new school for a couple of months I got injured at my parents' store. This is where I had suffered my first experience with paralysis and one of the reasons why I had to repeat 7th grade. The other reason was because I missed a lot of days out of school and I didn't take advantage of the tutor that the District of Columbia school system was going to provide for me while I was out of school and while taking outpatient physical and occupational therapy, and again another one of my mistakes. I'm not taking advantage of opportunities that was presented to me because I thought I knew better, shame on me. It didn't bother me that much that I had to repeat the 7th grade over again, because I felt that if I were to move to the next grade without repeating that previous year of education, I would be missing something really important before going on to the next grade level of education along with some other important lessons.

In 1976, I graduated from Berney Elementary School and I started attending Friendship Educational Center in the fall of the same year. Prior to me starting junior high school, In the same year of 1976, I started playing basketball with #11 Boys Club. That was my first year playing organized basketball. We had some great players on our team, and our tallest player Moony, was about 6-feet-tall. At the age of 12, I wasn't that aggressive around the referees, but when playing ball amongst my peers and some guys that were older than me, much older, I became aggressive. I didn't have any problems shooting the ball and even scoring points against the older guys and even guys my age when we were just playing pickup ball. I enjoyed calling the next

46

shot, especially when the older guys would try to take over the basketball court from the younger kids. Whoever made the first two free throw shots would choose the teams. A lot of times I made the first cut and we would challenge the other teams. Unfortunately, I didn't feel aggressive or even play with any kind of aggressiveness when we would play against the other 12 and under teams from the other Boys Clubs. Whenever we played our regulation games against other teams on our 12 and under squad in our division I will get nervous. When we played other teams, I would just freeze up, and I would be afraid to shoot the basketball in front of the crowd. Our team drew a lot of spectators. I would get a rebound or even block a shot every now and then, but when it came to scoring or shooting the ball, I felt pressured that if I attempted to make the shot and miss, it would bring embarrassment. No excuses, but I really was new when it came to playing organized basketball. The other guys were exposed to playing well. Midway through the season, the coach had another tryout. I felt that I was going to be replaced. There were two spots left, one guy in particular was much taller than I was, but I was determined not to let them take my place on the team. So, I practiced when I had to play against them, total defense, defense, defense, block shots, rebounding against them! I wonder sometimes what my coach thought about me. Even when the second half of the season came by and I didn't let that guy take my position, I just wondered what he thought about me. I guess I'll never know. I was determined to be better and get better and play basketball in all aspects of the game.

The next year I would become a starting playing with the 12 and under team for the Boys Club. We finished the regular season without losing a game. The only game we lost was in the Christmas tournament. But as far as a regular season record, we were undefeated, and the only team at number 11 Boys Club with that winning undefeated record. After the season was over, there was a major tournament for all the teams in the United States or maybe the Eastern region of the United States. It was held in the state of Buffalo, New York, right across from Niagara Falls. The name of the tournament that our teams played in was called P.A.L., which stood for the Police Athletic League. Since I was not productive during the season, they selected two additional players to take the place of another player and my position *(which we learned later on that they falsified the papers with their age and birth certificates),* so they can play on the 12 and under team, go figure! I wasn't allowed to play because they lied, and of course because again I wasn't as good as I thought I was. Although we were unable to play, we were still allowed to travel to Buffalo, New York. This is where the tournaments were played. I felt like I was still a part of the team. But in reality, I think I had some resentment with what the coach did to me and I never attended any of the tournament games, I just stayed in a hotel. It was still an honor to know that the #11 Boys Club, brought four different teams represented from our club, and all played in the big tournament. That said a lot about our basketball programs in our local Boys Club. All of our coaches were police officers who we gave much respect to at all times growing up.

My parents were not familiar with the weather in Buffalo and neither was I. It didn't matter, I was a little kid that was able to travel away from home with a lot of friends and teammates. Sometimes we were a little underdressed for the weather, but it didn't bother me at all. It was a 12-hour trip up to Buffalo, New York. When we arrived, the snow was covering the ground at an alarming rate. There was about 12 inches of snow on the streets and I later learned that was one of the largest snow storms in Buffalo's history. We settled in our rooms after arriving that night and would you imagine that I had to share rooms with someone other than my teammates, it was no problem. I ended up hanging out with one of the guys from the 18 and under team that was from my neighborhood. The next day was strictly business, all the teams had their assignments. GAME ON! The other teams did well in the tournament but the 12 and under team (my team), was magnificent! We played so well that we beat the favorite team from the Big Apple, New York. The score was 111 to 26, that's right, our team crushed the favorite team. We were victorious in more than one way, and we made the Buffalo newspaper because of our great performance or my teammates' great performance. It was a great experience for me because it exposed me to a side of life that I wasn't used to seeing, coming all the way from Washington, DC, local Boys Club. This was the first time I was able to visit Canada and we were right on the Canadian border. The only thing that was separating us was the Niagara Falls Bridge.

In between days of playing in the tournament, one day a group of us decided to go to Canada. So we did, we had to pay 10 cents to walk across the Niagara Falls bridge. Then we came to this place right across the bridge that had video games where we had to convert our American coins to Canadian coins in order to play the games, but it was all fun and games to all of us, especially me. Again, I really felt some resentment from not being able to play with my teammates in the tournament. With the team that we had we didn't need the other two guys. We had great shooters, rebounders and a big six-footer. We had the whole package! Well, I was praying that I would be ready for next year and I worked very hard over the summer to get ready to be a starter on the 12 and under team for the year 1977. I had even started trying out for my Junior high school basketball team. I was trying to do the same thing as some of my former teammates that used to play for their junior high school when they were the same age. I made about three practices but that too came to an end, not by choice. It was totally out of my hands. I was so excited about playing with both my Junior high school and getting ready for the tryouts for the Boys Club 12 and under team, which it would've been my second year playing 12 and under basketball, BUT IT DIDN'T HAPPEN!

∗ ∗ ∗

MY FIRST YEAR IN JUNIOR HIGH SCHOOL

The first couple of my months, while attending Junior high school my mother took my cousin Kay and I to school every morning. Every morning when we would get in the car, my mother would have the group called the Emotions playing their songs. I'm always thinking about the music that we listen to today in comparison to the music back in the day, real music. After we got comfortable with going to Friendship Junior high school, we started catching the Metro public transportation bus to and from school. Friendship Elementary and Junior High School was one of those schools that you could smell the fresh paint off of the walls and new materials in the facility.

The school was only going on the second year of being open when we started attending. September of 1977, if I'm not mistaken, the school had thick glass windows that you could not look out of. I guess it was the way it was built, so that the students would not be distracted from the outside activities or negativities. One part of the school was for the elementary students and the other part was for the junior high students. The only thing that separated the two parts were the doors and the walls, but you can walk through a door and have access to either side of the school.

My second year in junior high was much better. I was used to catching the bus with some of the new friends that I met. I was no longer a new kid on the block. This was my 2nd year in the 7th grade when I met my friends. I had made a few other friends the last year there and every now and then we would get together. During lunch time we would put our money together to buy a "nickel bag" of marijuana and a couple of bumpers of beer. I just don't know how I was able to focus during those years. This was my second year there (remember I had to repeat seventh grade because of my injury and dealing with paralysis and also because I didn't take up the opportunity to get it during those months that I was home), that was my fault. During the 70s, everybody smoked marijuana, it was the cool thing to do. By the time I got to the eighth grade, I started hanging with other people who smoked weed, just like the second year in seventh grade. I really know how to pick up friends. Everybody really didn't get time with us, some tried to hang out, but they were smart enough to know that they needed to not get high, that's a lesson I had later on in life. As I mentioned, I started out being exposed to so many things, more than I think any of my friends even in high school ever had to deal with. My last remaining years at Friendship wasn't about getting high as much. It was me getting ready to graduate and go to high school. The getting high part of my life during the last years in junior high school eventually subsided and I thank God that I was able to make that decision to graduate like I was supposed to. I had another type of education which was street knowledge and everything else negative that went with the surrounding area. So, now I'm ready to attend high school. I was told that I had several options to attend a vocational school half day and school for academics which was Frank W. Ballou Senior High School.

PHOTOGRAPHY INFLUENCE

My last year at Friendship, I learned a little bit about photography. After I was injured I was influenced by some older friends of mine to get into photography. One friend was about five or seven years older than I was when we started taking pictures at the police Boys Club after being shown how to develop film and how to print black and white photographs. That started me on the road to becoming a photographer. One of the officers showed us how to use the dark room. Since I wasn't able to play basketball the way that I used to, photography was the other option for me.

What really inspired me to continue in the photography field was a few years prior to my accident. I attended a funeral in New Jersey, my fathers' brother past away and I was supposed to take pictures. I had other uncles and aunts that were there and some of my cousins that I hardly knew. There were other relatives there that I did not know as well. It is really sad that you have to meet your relatives and other family members on occasions like A FUNERAL. It is really sad! Families should try to get together at reunions and any other kind of family related occasions, but as usual we meet each other at funerals. After leaving the repass and being around so many family members, I felt empty. There was some history that I missed. Although I had my camera, I didn't have film or the batteries that I needed so I wasn't able to take pictures of this occasion. However, I thank God for other means, I had another chance to get it right. The following week was my grandparents (My Father's Parents) 50th wedding anniversary. This would be held in South Carolina and I told myself that I was determined to get things right and photograph this event. I told myself that I wouldn't never miss another opportunity for documenting any other family events or gatherings. True to my word, every time we traveled to South Carolina I documented my pictures which was considered my history books that I will later show my kids, one day. So, in all reality, I got into photography for the memories.

Both of my sisters may have indirectly had a part with helping me start photography. My youngest sister used to take a lot of pictures and my oldest sister would wake me up to take pictures of her either before she went to the club or when she got back. I became her personal photographer. But in all reality, that really wasn't the motivating factor for me becoming a photographer, but indirectly they had something to do with it, maybe!

When I graduated from junior high school to high school in the year 1980 to 1981, that's when I made the decision to go to the Lemual Penn Center, to learn more about photography. I attended two different schools; Ballou Senior High School for academic classes and the other school was named after Lemual Penn Career and Development Center, where I learned commercial photography for my trade. All the years that I attended the Lemual Penn Career Development Center, I never knew who Mr. Lemuel Penn was until I decided to look him up and I discovered that he was a military soldier. He was an African-American military soldier and that Lt. Col. Lemuel Augustus Penn (September 19, 1915 – July 11, 1964) was the Assistant Superintendent of Washington, DC public schools, a decorated veteran of World War II and a Lieutenant Colonel in the United States Army Reserve who was murdered by members of the Klu Klux Klan at the age of 48, nine days after passage of the Civil Rights Act. He joined in the Army Reserve after graduating from Howard University and served in World War II in New Guinea and the Philippines, earning a Bronze Star. He was the father of two daughters and one son. It was sad that all four years that I attended the Lemual Penn career center, I had no idea that Mr. Penn was a Lt. Col. in the United States military and that he was killed by the KKK. This information is very important, and I thank God that I was able to attend the school in his honor.

But I believe that if I was older and out of school, I could have given more of myself to my parents' business and try to better it. I already had a very rigorous schedule at such a very young age, but the old saying is, *"If I knew then what I know now, things really would be a lot different."*

* * *

COUSIN KAY

She is my mother's great niece by way of my mother's oldest sister. Kay used to live in South Carolina with her father (who has been deceased several years after some kind of incident with a tree crushing him, MAY HE REST IN PEACE) along with her three sisters. They moved to Washington, DC in the '70s to live with their mother, but this was before their father died. After my sister moved out of our parents' house, shortly afterwards Kay started living with us.

Kay and I went to Friendship Junior High School for a couple years together. She is a few years older than I am. Her mother and three sisters lived up the street from Friendship, she attended Friendship one year before I got there. Now, we were attending it together and she knew a lot of the students. Kay lived with us for several years and helped us a lot around the house and at our family store. She really was a big help working with the family business. She was also an attractive young lady just like my mom and sisters, that attracted certain customers. She worked in the store with us for a long time. I don't remember why she moved out of our house and stopped working at the store, but we were good friends. While she was working at the store she met her daughter's father and he was crazy about her. I mean really crazy about her and they end up dating. After she moved out, I would make it my business to still see her and my other cousins, her sisters occasionally. I tried to always keep the lines of communication open with all of my family and friends after they went their separate ways. I've learned over the years that people in your life are sometimes there for a short season and sometimes for a lifetime, but they are for a reason, so we should value all of them as we go through life. A couple years later she had a little girl. They were dating while we still had the family business on the Avenue. They later moved into their own apartment and I would stop by if I was in their neighborhood. Billy was a hard-working guy, and I can remember him taking me to one of his jobs. Because for years he worked two jobs, a real good guy, and when he and my cousin started dating, he became a lot like family. You could ask for anything, he really had a big heart. I can remember during the lowest points of my life, especially when we lost the family business and I didn't have many friends and not much money in my pocket, he came and took me to a club. That's not what I really did, but I had to get away for a while and I really enjoyed myself. I thanked him because I really needed to get away. As the years went by I met my wife. Shortly afterwards we moved together and got an apartment. Unfortunately, I learned that he started smoking crack cocaine and developed a very bad habit. Once he came to my apartment with a dress that he was trying to sell so that he could get high. I really felt bad for him, knowing that he was such a good guy, and doing well for so many years and now to fall victim to crack cocaine. *"The CIA really did a good job when they conspired to kill us, millions of us directly and indirectly and broke up so many homes, even killing all seeds when they were born addicted to crack cocaine, thanks for nothing!"* One day I learned that he was strung out on that crack cocaine, more than before. When I saw him this particular day, he had another young lady with him standing outside watching. He grabbed a ladder and climbed into a big-time Jamaican drug dealer's apartment. Sadly, he was never seen after that. I believe they killed him and dismembered his body. There were speculations that the Jamaicans chopped up his body and put it into the trash can. They were known for doing things like this. During the 80's the city was flooded with Jamaican drug dealers. They came down from New York and started living in the low-income areas, especially where they were housing single women with kids to live in apartments. Those were the target areas. Some of the mothers eventually got addicted to crack cocaine. This was a very bad thing that the kids had to suffer because of this. A lot of guys hooked up with them to buy drugs. They were famous for the "working fifty" which was a $50 crack cocaine rock that they would break down and make even more money with. These guys were treacherous people to deal with and very coldhearted, but it was all business and it came with the territory. GOD only knows what really happened to him. WHEREVER YOU ARE YOU, BE AT PEACE!

* * *

MY YOUNGER DAYS

As a child growing up, life was pretty good for my family and I. I was the youngest child and things were a lot easier for me because of the support from my older siblings. Every now and then I would have to defend myself at school or sometimes in the neighborhood. Often, I would just get tested. When we lived in Barry Farms, my babysitter was also our next door neighbor. She had three sons and later, a daughter. I also had a friend upstairs. He had an older sister and a younger brother and their parents. We were the same age and we attended Birney Elementary School together. Those two guys were my best friends.

I remember when I was in the 6th grade, he was visiting my classroom and one of my classmates was kicking him, I immediately jumped up into his chest—let's just say, we never had any problems with him anymore and believe it or not, after that incident the guy and I became friends. Well, that was back in the day, not these days. I felt like I was his protector because he was a little guy. When we were in the fifth grade, a lot of times he would come to school with a $20-dollar bill almost every day. He told me that his grandmother gave him the money but I believed that he was stealing from his mother. He would ask me to go to the local store. Mr. B owned the corner store in Barry Farms, right across from the elementary school that we attended. One of my friends would always tell me to buy myself whatever I wanted. He never wanted any change because he was scared that if any of the other guys knew that he had some money they would take it from him. Now! I'm not claiming to be a tough guy, I just didn't have to worry about everybody messing with me. I was a good kid, but negative influences growing up caused me to partake in the mischievous deeds that the rest of the kids in my neighborhood were involved in. I was the teenager who smoked marijuana and drank beer with my friends. I had family members that sold drugs, and if I asked them, they would provide me with drugs. I thought getting high at a young age made me more mature for my age, but it actually made me paranoid.

* * *

OFF THE HOOK

When I was younger my friends and I would set the trash cans on fire, just to get a quick ride on the back of the fire trucks. At that time we were living in Park Chester Apartments. These were large trash dumpsters that we were setting on fire. These were the kind where large rats would be all around them, and in some ways, we thought that we were helping with the trash overflow. After we would set the trash dumpsters on fire, I or someone else would pull the fire alarm. The last time I did it I jumped on the back of the fire truck for another ride. The fire truck seemed like it wasn't going to stop, so I panicked and jumped off of the truck while it was moving and scarred up my arms and legs. That truly was my last time setting the trash cans on fire.

I always used to hang with guys older than me. These guys were about three or four years older. We would go up to the local Safeway, they would steal hamburger patties and other stuff so we could cook out in the woods behind our apartment. After stealing a bag of M&M's from Safeway, I was too scared to steal again.

Back in the seventies we had iron milk crates that we would drape aluminum foil over, turn the milk crate over, stuffing the inside with paper, and then set it on fire. The aluminum foil would protect any germs from underneath the foil. We cooked some of the best hamburgers ever! The last time I hung out with those guys I really got in trouble. We walked to a shopping center called Eastover, located in Maryland, and it was quite an adventure. On our way down there, we saw this girl and a guy riding a mini-bike. One of my friends, our adopted sister and oldest brother threw a can at them, don't ask me why. We kept on towards Eastover, and it was just our luck, we ran into the girl's brother. We walked right in the direction of where they lived. He punched our friend in the face for throwing the can or bottle at his sister and we all ran. Just above the hill we were stopped by some other guys on bicycles. They demanded money, but my pockets were dry, and I had no money at all. They let me go and some of us got away before they could catch us. After getting away from that ordeal, we met up with some guys that knew our parents. They gave all of us a ride home, and that was when I received my punishment. I tried to pretend like I was on the playground all of the time, but my parents knew better. They sent my sister to find me and bring me home. My father gave me a really good beating. I started hollering and crying as if he was killing me so that he would stop. It worked and when I went into my room, I started laughing to myself, but not out loud. Really, it didn't hurt me at all! I was just glad that it was over.

When we were living in Park Chester apartments, I would always hang in the woods behind our apartments. My friends and I would just go exploring throughout the woods, making club houses, climbing trees, looking for all kinds of animals, and other different wild life. What amazed me about the woods was the freedom to play and explore, and then the mystery. One day my sisters and their friends were walking in the woods behind some old houses in the Barry Farms area, when one of the guys kicked in one of the back doors of an old house. When he kicked open the door, I saw a scary old lady sitting in this dark room, combing the hair of a baby doll. This lady was very old, with long white straight hair, and she looked like a witch! We all ran after we saw her, because it really was a frightening scene. I was so scared. I started running away and I tripped over an old tree branch that was lying on the ground. The lady resembled an old female prisoner in a dark basement. I can remember that day like it was yesterday, it's still very vivid in my mind.

We used to have a German Shepherd dog, named Lady. We bought her when she was just a puppy, and she was absolutely beautiful. The rental office personnel always complained about everything we had, so after Lady was a little bigger, they said that we couldn't have an animal in our apartment. Lady would sometimes break her chain and chase some of the kids on the basketball court. That meant that one of us would have to go and restrain her. She never attacked anyone, she would just chase them a little. Anyway, my father rented out another apartment across the street from Park Chester apartments. It was across the busy Avenue called Nickels Avenue, but later renamed Martin Luther King, Jr. Avenue still located in SE. It was in a very small and quiet neighborhood. My mother, father, Lady and I, would stay there most of the time. My father also kept his liquor supplies there. On one side of the street were small apartment buildings, that held four to six apartments in each. On the other side of the street were all town homes. If you were to walk straight down the street, you would end up in a wooded area, but beyond that was a nice grassy area that you could have had a cookout or picnic in. Further down was a busy parkway, called Suitland Parkway, located near their Junior High School, named Frederick Douglas. They would walk across that busy parkway, to go to school. We used to take Lady, our dog into that grassy area and have a ball and play with her all day. Finally, we gave Lady away to the owners of the ice cream company where we used to get our supplies from.

A couple years later we gave Lady to the owner of the ice cream company. They used her as a guard dog, but she still remembered us. Whoever we visited the ice cream company, we always stopped to say hello to Lady and she always remembered us, all of us! One year, Lady had some puppies and we wanted one of her puppies, but the owner did not want to give us the puppies, so my sister jumped out of the car and took two of the puppies for our family. Lady was our family and her puppies were our family too. We named the puppies Kim and Duchess, we later gave Duchess to one of the friends of our family. We kept Kim because during that time we had moved into our family store and we had control over what went on in our store. Our family business was like a mom and pop store. Kim had a couple more sets of puppies and we kept some over the years. We later gave Kim to a man that lived on top of our store, Billy with his elderly mother Ms. Helen. He was a little weird and it was a lot of speculation about him having a sexual relationship with the dog. Nevertheless, I feel like those were some of the 'wonder years" of my life. I'm an old soul, and it seems like I've been here before.

CHAPTER 4

OUR SECOND FAMILY BUSINESS
CONGRESS BEER AND WINE

We purchased the store while we still lived in the apartment complex called Part Chester. Yes, there was still a lot of jealousy and envy, because of the progress that my family was making. I don't mean to sound pessimistic, but that is the way it was at that time. We eventually sold our ice cream truck to some friends in the neighborhood, but that didn't last long, because they didn't know how much was involved in running that ice cream truck business. That also was the end of our illegal bootlegging business, we were now totally legitimate business owners.

We purchased the business from an elderly couple Mr. Mike and Mrs. Anne. I believe they were Jewish. They really were a nice couple. They had very little supplies in the store. My father really built that business up fast, adding most of the candy and potato chips and other stuff to the business. It went well for several years with the exception of our second year at the family business.

* * *

STICK UP BOYS (ACTUALLY, THEY WERE MEN)

Our second year running our family business, some guys set my family up to be robbed. My mother, sister and I were walking to our car when two gunmen approached us and demanded my mother's pocketbook, which she had laid in the back seat of the car where I was. I thought about grabbing it "meaning the pocketbook" but I kept thinking that they would shoot me in the back of my head. My sister ran around to the driver side of the car where the gunman was holding the gun up against my mother's head. She came from the other side of the passenger side of the car and came to the driver side and knocked the gunman's hand up in the air and he shot off a round in the air. Then he knocked my sister to the ground and shot down at her and I had to run out of the passenger side back to the store for help. All I could think of was that my sister was dead. I decided that

I had to run back to the store where my father and some of my other family members were inside closing up the store.

By the time I arrived in front of the store, and started banging on the store door, my mother was also behind me with her head bleeding. The stick-up boy hit her in the head with his gun while he demanded her purse. When they opened the door to the store to let us in, I ran directly to where we kept our hand gun. I grabbed it and I was going to run outside of the store to see if I could find them. I realized that I didn't know what direction the two of them went so I gave the gun to my father instead. I was only about 10 years old at that time that the robbery occurred. Shortly afterwards I saw my sister walk into the store. I was so thankful to God that she was alive. Then all of a sudden my mother disappeared and we looked for her in the car. Someone noticed that she had driven the car in the direction in which the gunman ran. She had attempted to drive the car and try to find the people that robbed us but because of the injury to her head, she passed out behind the stirring wheel of her car. She was only about 100 feet away from where it all happened. When I saw my mother with her head laying on the stirring wheel, I thought that she was dead because of the blood that was on her face.

That night was very traumatic for me and I blamed myself for not running for help sooner and I promised myself that it would never happen again while I was in the store. I always knew where the guns were in the store and sometimes I would have it on me waiting for someone to try and rob us again. I would hide behind boxes or set somewhere in a high area of the store watching everybody. From the age of 10, up to the age of 18, I carried this burden with me all of those years without anyone knowing about it. But to be honest, if I could have remembered who those guys were, I would've killed them! I don't care how young I was, and you know, I probably saw these guys numerous times as the years went on. But I could never remember what they looked like. Thank God that I didn't remember. Never stop me from wanting to protect my family by any means necessary. People of color, we are always complaining about getting along and not being treated right, when we ourselves don't treat each other right. Where is the brotherly love in that? We are too busy trying to take advantage of each other. We had to go through hell trying to just make an honest living and the struggle STILL continues!

MY FATHER WOULD HAVE TO OCCASIONALLY WHIP OR BEAT SOMEONE UP IF THEY CAME INTO OUR FAMILY ESTABLISHMENT INCORRECT

I'm not bragging on my father, but he had to defend his business. People would constantly try to catch you sleeping and attempt to take advantage of you, so he had to do what he had to do. I respect my dad for that and I thank God, I reminded him several times about these things, as the years went on. I pray that as I get older, I can be half the man THAT YOU ARE POP and I know I will be okay! I was trying my best to give my father his flowers while he was living. I would do the same for my mother as well. Everyone knew how much I loved and appreciated her. My heart is filled with joy as I reminisce on the years that they were with us.

There were times when troublemakers would come into our establishment and try to steal or even try to take over. My father would grab anything, it could have been an extension cord, a broom, a blackjack or a machete. He would get his hands on anything to let them know that it was no joke in there. He would run those knuckleheads out of the store. He made sure he kept the troublemakers out of his store. Back in those days, you had to protect your stuff or others would take advantage of you. My father came to this area with my mother with only a few dollars in his pocket, but God blessed them. The Lord really blessed both of my parents to find one another, and they later got married and raised a family together.

Growing up in Barry farms and Park Chester, back in those days, some people had very large families. Now I'm talking about my parents age. Some guys had five or six brothers and sisters. Some had more. My parents had to protect the family and home businesses throughout the years.

There was a man named Mr. T, he had a wife that was like my mom, she kept to herself, and she worked very hard for her family. She had two boys and a girl. On the other hand, her husband was just like my father, a bootlegger. He also was banging his lady upstairs from the apartment they all lived in, the same building, and he had his loving wife, just like my mom. But I can't say that he was always right or wrong, you know. Sometimes when the woman see that the men had a little money, they would present themselves. It sometimes didn't matter that they were married. I don't know if it was a money factor or whether they were set out to take someone's husband, or both.

Anyway, I remember my mother telling me the story about what Mrs. T's son told her. It was something that eluded her mind for years, something he told her one day while they were in church. He said; *"Mrs. Chapman, thank you very much for what you did for my mother years ago."* My mom was kinda caught off guard. As he explained to her and said; "Do you remember when my mom came running to the ice cream truck for help and you came out of the ice cream truck with a baseball bat and they tried to rip her clothes off while she was running away from them?" My mother stood in between the two ladies and told them that if they wanted to get to her, they would have to go through her first. I guess both of them thought about it for a while and decided, maybe this is not a good idea after all and we should leave her alone or we will have to deal with Ms. Chapman. Again, I'm not bragging, these are all true stories and I felt good and so very proud of my mother because she stood up to help Mrs. T. Most of all her baby boy was telling my mother many years later, while they were in church, how much he was appreciative of what my mother did, a standup lady. My mother worked very hard for our family and so did Mrs. T. Again, very quiet ladies, and they both just wanted the same thing for their families.

My mom just wanted her husband to be home with her and the kids instead of running the streets. However, I think because of the love that he had for my mom and the rest of us and our family businesses, he couldn't get loose like he really wanted to, like some of the other guys that he was friends with, THANK GOD! I'm not trying to justify my father hanging out in the streets, maybe he felt that he had to get away from everything, married, with four children and responsible for EVERYTHING that went on in the house and the family businesses that we were blessed to have throughout the years.

As I'm reflecting back on the day that my brother and one of his friends had an encounter with a guy who deliberately pushed our youngest sister into a fence, I can't do anything but laugh. This guy (who had a little sugar in his tank) decided to push my sister into a fence because she beat him in a race and during that time my sister with a tomboy. This was during the time we still lived in Barry Farms. He pushed her into the brand new fence that they put around the outer walls of the community and also for the safety of the kids so they wouldn't get hurt. This all happened because she beat him in a race contest. She beat him badly and he must've been embarrassed. He got mad because he was a sore loser and pushed my sister. This caused her to be hospitalized with a fractured jaw. Now, it was time for my big brother and one of his friends to straighten this out! His friend was also dating my oldest sister so that made him family. My brother and my sisters' boyfriend finally caught up with that guy and physically beat the mess out of him for what he did to our sister. It was the right thing to do. You can't let anybody hurt your family and not protect them no matter what and that guy was wrong and he was "cruising for bruising." You don't get mad because you're a sore loser. He learned a lesson that day and after that butt whipping he was never seen again in the neighborhood even though he was really visiting family members that lived there. He disappeared, I wish you well, but I also pray that he truly learned a lesson about getting mad and being a poor loser, but also causing harm to someone.

When my parents moved to Washington, DC back in 1956, my father did not have his brothers up here from South Carolina to watch his back. He had to stand alone and set an example to all these big families in our neighborhoods. A lot of guys knew that he had a big family and they would back down or take a beat down from one of the members of the family, knowing that they had so many other brothers. They took advantage of guys that would normally take advantage of other guys, in different ways. Thank God they knew where my father stood, Joe (my father's nickname). They would make such statements as: "That guy will shoot you, or kill you, or that guy is crazy." It really worked and they knew it was for real. I wasn't as aggressive as my father was nor was my brother, who is the oldest child. He would get into some fights as he grew up in Barry Farms because people would TRY you and we had to stand up for ourselves. (I can't tell you how many times I've made the statement of people trying to test or TRY you growing up in these different neighborhoods) My big brother was just a little guy, but he was the oldest child in the family and that meant protection over your siblings and parents if necessary. But one year, Thank God, my brother started a growth spurt, the more he played sports the taller and stronger he became. He is always my big brother (and you have to realize that this is my big brother and this is the way I see him, regardless of what everybody else thought, you can't change my mind. This is my big brother, my role model, and so is my dad). I was truly blessed to have both my father and my brother that I could look up to.

A lot of people knew my family members, either from the ice cream truck business, the bootlegging business, the family business, or in the streets, and my brother from sports and selling drugs. My sister was known for fighting and taking care of herself. My entire family was known for fighting and protecting ourselves but my sisters took fighting to another level. Most people didn't realize how much my family had to go through. All they saw was the fruit of our labor and the material possessions that we worked hard for. No one gave us anything. We had to endure the controversy, fighting, envy and jealousy. We had to literally fight for everything that we had. No matter what we did positive in the community, we came up against opposition.

It also helped that my sisters were one step away from obtaining their black belts. I regret not staying in karate classes, instead I started playing basketball. We all have regrets in life, and I truly believe that if I was able to remain in karate classes it would have helped me with my basketball skills. But my sisters would take care of any females they came in our family establishment acting like knuckleheads. Sometimes fights would break out right in front of our establishment. Most of the fights initially started at a strip club or with the "Go-Go" girls, that is what we used to call strippers during the seventies. Instead of them settling their differences where it happened, they'd find their way in front of our store for some reason. These fights would result in broken windows or broken showcase glass pieces. My sisters weren't having it, they would go out there and straighten them out. It was a survival game called life. It was always something going on, dealing and stressing with all walks of life. Everybody was doing something and the Avenue had a tendency of drawing them to that particular spot. We had a lot of clientele that used to buy beer and wine from our store, that also was a contributing factor of what happened or what was happening on the Avenue.

I know that God was protecting my family and myself from the beginning until we got rid of the store and even now. We knew a lot of people and their lifestyles; somewhere killers, stick up-boys, heroin dealers, cocaine dealers, marijuana dealers, and so many others did heinous crimes. But those were the people that we dealt with on a regular basis and a lot of times we would help them out, especially at closing time, which was 12:00 midnight. We closed our business but the club was still open until 2:00 a.m. These guys had reputations that other people knew about. Again, we dealt with these guys all the time but at midnight they didn't want to drive all the way to Maryland to get some beer and sometimes they would knock on the door, and depending on who they were, we would let them purchase whatever they wanted. There was one stipulation; they had to wait until we all walked out together because it was illegal to sell anything after 12:00 midnight. They had to walk out as if they were family, even though they had a brown bag in their hands. Some of them were appreciative of the things we did. There was one instance where a guy came in and wanted to count his money that he just made from selling marijuana. I took him in the back of the store so that he could take care of his business. Things like that, the guys appreciated. There was a sign of protection because of the respect. I believe the word got out; "hands-off" this family. They say, "Honor among thieves." Not to mention the respect they had for my father and brother and overall family. The females had to deal with my sisters and of course, my mother was no joke. I would lay back until something kicked off, and even though my parents and my brother were there I had to take the initiative first to make sure the problems were resolved. I can remember as a teenager I was standing by the front door inside our family business, this guy was trying to steal a bottle of wine. I was about 15 years old at the time. I snatched the bottle of wine out of his hands and pushed him out of the store. I told him not to ever come back. You had to keep your head on a swivel for various reasons and at all times.

I speak frequently about the hatred amongst our own people, but it was something that we had to deal with almost on a daily basis and unfortunately, this issue is still in existence today. Our own people have a tendency of hating on each other. I remember when a Korean family moved into the neighborhood and they started selling beer and wine. We did not contest like we should have. We did not have a business organization on the Avenue like they did in the Anacostia area, but they should have been contested. Because we did not contest it, they eventually owned the whole community. Some of the people that used to patronize our store started supporting the Korean stores just so they wouldn't have to buy anything from us. I'm thankful for all of the loyal customers that we had over the years and my family is grateful for the support. They lowered their prices just to bring in the customers. They brought competition and a lot of them are crooks and the Government is certainly aware. The Asian Business Association here in the DC area were illegally connected to their counterparts in Asia. I believe that every governmental agency was aware of what was going on, even today. They are occupying and buying property in the black communities, so they don't care. They are allowed to get away with all kinds of crimes and the government looks the other way because they refuse to go against the Asian business leaders. THANK YOU TO ALL THE FAITHFUL CUSTOMER'S THAT SUPPORTED OUR BUSINESSES OVER THE YEARS!

* * *

THE BULLIES ON THE AVENUE
(WINE HEADS, ALCOHOLICS, DRUNKS, BUMS)

These are the names that stick out when I think about the guys on the Avenue. This group of guys were younger than the older drunks on the Avenue. They would try to beat them up and take their drinks from them. I was much younger and they seemed so much older than I was. But in all reality, they were probably in their twenties. They just looked much older.

I can remember one particular guy in the neighborhood, I remember him very well because of some of the things he did to the older guys and to the mentally ill patients from St. Elizabeth's hospital. He was slightly older than me, but probably around my brother's age. I can remember clearly the time that they took a mentally challenged patient from St. Elizabeth. He was feebleminded and had the mind of a child. They took him behind the car wash that was located on Dr. Martin Luther King Junior Avenue, S.E. There was a shed on the side of the car wash. I noticed the guys taking this patient into the shed, so I creeped up and looked through the broken glass and saw them doing horrible things to him, sexual, explicit things. After a few minutes of witnessing this, I couldn't take it anymore and I just walked away, shaking my head and in disbelief. He was also famous for intimidating the old alcoholics on the Avenue and anybody else that he could intimidate. He didn't come up against my father or brother because he knew better. As I got older he tried bullying me as well. That didn't last too long. After many years of being the way he was, I believe he finally got himself together because the younger generation was not having it. He had a choice to either stop bullying and threatening to beat up other people or getting killed. This new generation wasn't fighting, they were shooting. In order to live longer, he had to change his way of living.

The other guy's name was Bones, again he was around my brother's age and they did the same thing, intimidate the winos and made them give them something to drink, meaning alcohol or wine and sometimes money. He eventually changed his ways a little bit and became a Rastafarian and started growing dreadlocks, but his girlfriend would also be on the Avenue with him all day long. What kind of crap is that? He had his tender being a bully, but eventually he got away from the Avenue and woke up. Then this guy named Randolph comes along, I think he was a boxer back in the day and he did the same thing that the other guys did to the older winos. He also would try to take their drinks and their money and intimidate them. He thought about challenging my father, and I'm not bragging but I think they all knew that their chances of winning were slim to none. My father would kill anyone that would try to threaten his family or home business. They knew that he was a little crazy and that he would do exactly what he told them he would do if they were to get out of place. By my father warning the guys about what he would do to them if they even thought about doing something stupid, it gave them all something to think about.

As I got older, I knew that they probably wanted to challenge me knowing that I was younger. But then they would have to deal with my father and brother. I did nothing to make them look at me that way, it was just their mindset. I never portrayed any hatred or jealousy towards them. However, I didn't back down from any of them that I named and if they did try me they would have to deal with the consequences. I mentioned early in the story that we were robbed by a couple of guys that watched us in the store. They strong-armed and robbed us and I've always felt like I didn't do my part to protect my family. Although I was only 10 years old at the time, I became a victim of anger and frustration. I carried this anger over a decade, until we got rid of the store. I was determined that no one would rob us again. I was willing to take action by any means necessary to make sure I step up first to take care of the situation. It would have been redemption for me. I carried this for a long time, not knowing it, but always waiting for an opportunity to relieve the anger that was lying dormant. Now mind you, I'm the youngest of the family. At the age of 13 my parents entrusted me to run the family business, something that I did not ask for. They gave me my own set of keys to the family store and gave me the opportunity to go inside of my family business anytime I wanted growing up, but I did not abuse the opportunity. I was there to take care of my family business. I did not abuse or disrespect my parents who put me in charge of making sure everything was right. I came close to killing someone though. One night after we closed down the store my siblings and other employees, I heard a loud crash. I thought someone was shooting at us, but these guys outside were actually trying to break into the store and climb through the window that was iced over, but I reacted quickly and I ran to get our registered shotgun. When I went outside my sister's boyfriend John was fighting one of them until we came out. One of the other guys ran away and that's when I pulled the shotgun on the guy. My brother was standing right beside him with a hand pistol, but the guy was still talking smack and disrespecting us. I asked my brother to please just move away from him. It was the first time that I had loaded the shotgun in my life. If my brother wouldn't have moved away, I would've killed him. Honestly, I would've pulled the trigger, but I THANK GOD that I didn't pull the trigger for various reasons.

We put that knucklehead into our establishment and now I can really do anything I wanted to him. I kept the shotgun pointed on him long enough to call my father and the police. I had a clear shot and could have pulled the trigger without anyone else getting sprayed by the pellets. He started getting nervous and asked me to put the gun down. Frustration and anger continued to build up in me. The police and my father finally arrived and I unloaded the shotgun and put it back in the place where it was safely kept. The police made this knucklehead empty his pockets, he had about $40. He put the money on one of our beer iceboxes that was about waste high. The police officer searched the room well and then handcuffed him and took him away. My father asked the officer, as he was walking the would-be burglar out of the store, *"What about the $40?"* The officer responded; "What $40?" In other words, Mr. Chapman, you use the money to fix your window. I can't remember if I took everybody home and my father stayed in the store that night or not because the window was broken or if I came back to the store the next day. Normally, whenever the alarm system was set off I would go outside ready to fight. I was a police and security at night with a shotgun in one hand and a pistol in the other. This happened numerous times. It wasn't going to happen on my watch. I'm telling you, I had this dormant anger of revenge because it would happen when I was only ten years old and I had been holding this anger and frustration. My blood was boiling inside of me for years. A lot of times, I wasn't aware of it until a situation came about and trickled these emotions.

There were so many different people that fell on hard times for various reasons that just hung out on the Avenue all day and every day and night and drinking until we closed our store at midnight. They all found somewhere to go until the next morning, but they would not be out there after 12:00 midnight because that drew another crowd of people. These next group of people eventually fell on hard times. It could have been any of you or your family members. THIS IS LIFE!

Mr. J.J., a former boxer, I don't know how far he got in his boxing career or even what weight class he fought in but you could tell that he used to box by the way he would hold his hands sometimes while punching and playing with others on the Avenue. He would throw a punch followed by the words; "Bam, Bam, Bam Bam." He always tried to prove that he still had skills. I really don't know the truth about what might have turned him into an alcoholic. I don't know what triggered that off, but it looks like he had arthritis in his hands. Some of the guys knew that he used to be a boxer because they would still challenge him even though they knew he was an alcoholic. They were disrespectful to him and one time bust his lip. My father would intervene and stop them from harassing him. He had a wife and three children. I know they were embarrassed when they would see their father on the Avenue and must've heard them a lot. Sometimes I would see them coming from the grocery store and walking past our family establishment and most of the time their father would be outside drunk. I pray that everything worked out for them over the years.

Then there was CJ. He was a real Cherokee Indian from North Carolina. He was one of the closest that we would allow to hang around and in the store. He was like family. We enjoyed the laughter and jokes. I can remember him singing a few songs and I never knew the artist until many years later, it was Ray Charles songs. His favorite song was POISON IVORY. He sang that song all the time. His favorite drink was WILD IRISH ROSE, the other guys liked THUNDERBIRD too. There used to be a saying concerning this wine and it went something like this, "What's the word, THUNDERBIRD, what's the price, 30 TWICE, who like it the most, COLOR FOLKS." Those were the two most popular wines that the guys on the Avenue liked to purchase out of our store. Since the Wild Irish Rose came in two different sizes, they really enjoyed that one. Sometimes he would sit in the store and report everything that went on, which was cool. One night he got into a fight and they messed up his arm. I think they had to put a screw in his arm, he wore it in a sling for a while until it got better, but it never fully healed. He was still able to use it and that's all that matters. He had two children. Sometimes we would sit around and talk about his family and he would mention how much he missed them. He would just sit around and talk about his family and you could see how much he missed them. Sometimes he would get teary-eyed and I would quickly end the conversation because I could see that he was hurting. Whenever his family needed to contact him they would call our store because we were the only communication that he had. One day he got a telephone call that his daughter was expecting a baby. He was so excited. My father would extend credit for him until he received his check, although he kinda built up a large bill that was never paid but. It was all good. My parents arranged transportation for him to go to North Carolina, so he could see his grandchild and children. That was the last time we heard from him and I pray that everything worked out for him and his family and that he was able to stop drinking. God only knows how things worked out for CJ. As far as the bill is concerned, my father just let it go.

A Young Lady named Donna. Donna was a very beautiful young lady in high school, everybody talked about how beautiful she was. Unfortunately, somebody turned her out to be a junkie and she got hooked on heroin. I could always tell when a customer got hooked when I looked at their hands. Their hands would be bloated like a balloon as a result of the injection needle missing the vein.

Then there was brother T. Who was a very humorous guy, but also a very sneaky, stick-up boy, unfortunately he was a baby boy in the family. He only had sisters but he also got hooked on heroin. All these people that I mentioned I never saw them for what they used or what they did. They were people that I saw almost every day and dealt with, they were associates/customers that patronized my family's business. I can say that I developed a friendship, but in my mind and heart, they were never considered my enemies. They were people that got caught up in the difficulties of life and ultimately became a product of our environment.

* * *

THE FRIENDS THAT I MET WHEN I ARRIVED ON THE AVENUE IN 1974

I mentioned earlier that I did not like to do a lot of work in the store. As soon as I would get there, I would disappear from the store. I would either be around the corner with the guys. Others would join in later. We would either ride our bicycle, play basketball or football. But one of my favorite past time was trying to invest or make something; plant watermelon seeds, make boomerangs (out of clothes hangers) by wrapping masking tape around the bottom of the hanger, after shaping the hanger and removing the top portion. I used to try and create all kinds of stuff, maybe my friends were bored with my creativity.

Joe was my first friend that I met on the avenue. He used to stay at his grandparents' house to be eligible to go to a local Catholic elementary school there called Assumption. Then I met Tom, he also lived across the street from Joe, we always called him Mann. Tom lived with his grandmother as well and went to the same Catholic school that Mann went too. Mann was one year younger than me. Tom was the same age as I was. Then I met Bob, he lived down the street from both of them with his parents and brothers and sisters. They had a big yellow house towards the end of the street. Bob was a few years older than we were, maybe two years older. But we would sometimes play football, basketball or ride our bicycles around the neighborhoods together. I later introduced Rodney to them and we all just started hanging out. Sometimes I would notice that they would be hard to find, then one day I noticed them running and hiding from me. I believe that Rodney had a lot to do with it, but I know that I was a spoiled kid, although I would like to use the word loved, but the truth is the truth. I was always a leader but didn't mind doing other things as well.

One day we all caught the bus to the movies to see a movie called "When a Stranger Calls." We didn't realize that the buses stopped running into Washington, after 8:00 p.m. so in some ways we were stranded, until I noticed this young lady from our neighborhood. I asked her could she give us a ride back home because we missed our bus, she said okay. We walked outside to wait for her to finish with her nephew and niece. While we were standing outside talking two guys approached me and asked me where I purchased my glasses. I told him, but then I started thinking to myself that he does not know where I'm talking about. Then he asked me if he could try them on. I said no because they were my prescription glasses. His friend said well, suppose we take them? My friends were just standing there scared. I took them off and put them in my coat pocket and said to them; you have to take them. I walked back into the movie theater and asked my friend how much longer it would take her. I let her know I was having some problems with some guys outside. She said, what about your buddies? I told her that they were scared. She rushed her nephew and nieces off of the pinball machines. As we approached the exit of the movie, one of the guys stepped in front of me to block me inside. I reacted by pushing him away from me into the wall or the vending machine that was opposite my direction. I just wasn't going to allow them to pin me in so I had to make it outside. As I walked out of the movie theater, it seemed like a hundred guys were waiting for me outside, me alone!

As I walked towards my friend's car, another car pulled up in front of the guys that I pushed, and someone handed him a green gym bag. It had a gun inside of it and as I opened the car door, it separated him from me, and the young lady hollered and said to them to get away from her car with this craziness. After I got into the car one of my friends was the last one to get in. One of the guys pushed him into the car. Now he decided he wanted to get brave. I said; *"Man sit your ass down!"* Now you want to do something because they touch you.

I apologized to the young lady for what had happened and thanked her for the ride home. I was mad at both of them for not saying anything to the guys in the beginning. While we were in the car on our way home Joe said; what were we supposed to say? I said; at least let them know that I wasn't by myself. I never forgot about how they "punked out" on me that day. After we got home, we had someone to get a bumper of Malt Duck, it was an alcoholic drink. We used to have a little club house downstairs in the boiler room located near one of my friend's grandparent's apartment. I was really, really mad at those guys, but I never brought it up as we got older to embarrass them. At one point they started avoiding me. I didn't have time for games like that, if they didn't want to be bothered with me, oh well! I knew one day it would be time for me to move on.

＊ ＊ ＊

HANGING IN THE NEIGHBORHOODS
NEAR THE STORE

The surrounding area of our store was where I did a lot of exploring. This was a very exciting area. On the left side of the street was where my friend's grandparents lived and on the right side of Labum was where Tom's grandmother and Bob's parents lived. From the left side of this one-way street began with the parking lot of the Atlantic Auto Car parts store. At the end of the parking lot was a drive through alleyway that connected Labum Street which was the one-way street. Mellon street was the next street over, which was a part of my hang out. Labum street was divided in half by apartments and single-family homes on the lower half of the street. It had some four-unit apartment buildings on both sides of the street, where Mann's grandparents lived, next to them was another four-unit apartment building, and adjacent to them was a double five story apartment building. After the large apartment buildings were the beginning of the single-family houses. On the other side of Labum Street were four more unit apartment buildings. Between the second and third building was a nice area of grass. That was where we played football a lot, if the landlord, Mr. J didn't catch us. After the fourth building, the other single-family houses started from there. We were going to purchase one of those houses but thank God that we did not buy that house. Bob's parents lived in one of those houses and occasionally we would hang out there. They had one of the largest houses on that street and it was a bright yellow color. We knew just about everybody in the other houses and in most of the four-unit apartments, that was our turf. At the end of Labum Street on the left side was another alleyway that also connected to the next street which was Mellon Street and another apartment building. We used to go exploring in those woods finding all kinds of junk. It was a very steep slope from the top of the woods to the very bottom. We were all over that area and we knew a lot of people. We would frequently ride our bikes or just found ourselves walking around the neighborhood. We also spent a lot of our time at the Boys Club playing basketball. One day the fellows and I were playing in the alley behind the store. It was this old abandoned car behind this clothing store. We would take turns pretending that we were actually driving this car. While we were there, this old guy came by and started talking with us. I believe that he was an old pervert, maybe even a child molester. He was sitting in the back seat of this old car and he was trying to expose himself to us. We grabbed a handful of gravel and through it at him. He still was hanging around us. I probably was just turning 11 years old. I hit him in his face with my fists, but it didn't faze him. We told another adult what this older man was trying to do. The adult took matters into his own hands and called the police. We believed he was a mentally disturbed man. When the police arrived, we took them to where he lived. It was beside this convenient store in a green house. After a few minutes, the police brought him out in handcuffs. I truly don't know the outcome of the mentally disturbed man, because when it was time to appear in court, Mann's mother didn't pick me up, instead she and Mann went to the police hearing without me. When my brother finally brought me to the police headquarters, all they wanted was my statement and that was the end of that. I don't know if Mann and his cousin went to court concerning this situation or not. I just know that they never called me anymore concerning that whole ordeal.

This situation could have gotten very serious because this old mentally disturbed man was not leaving us alone until the older gentleman came by. But not only that, I pray that because of our encounter with this elderly man, God allowed us to save some of the kids from being snatched up in a house. His house was positioned and located in a very busy area where kids would come all day long. McDonalds was right across the street from his house. Right next door to his house used to be a Highs small convenience store and down the street from his house was the Boys Club. So, there was a steady flow of young children passing his house each and every day. Again, I pray that no one was victimized. There were many opportunities for that man to snatch a kid at any time located where his house was. God does things in ways we don't understand, sometimes we will never understand, but I believe it was a part of GOD'S PLAN!

* * *

THE SURROUNDING AREAS BY OUR STORE

On the Avenue where my parents store was located, I saw any and everything. Like most kids from the hood, I became a product of our environment at a young age. I was exposed to drugs, alcoholism, prostitution, and the irony was that St. Elizabeth Mental Hospital was one block away from our family business. Even when we moved to our house located on Alabama Ave., Southeast, Saint Elizabeth's Hospital was right across the street. Being surrounded by this hospital that was placed right in the middle of Southeast Washington, DC, we moved everywhere around it. We must remember that Mr. and Mrs. Barry purchased a lot of property in that general area of Saint Elizabeth's Hospital.

In this area, the air was filled with spiritually lost souls and a polluted sense of despair. There was a stench of envy, helplessness, and often hopelessness. Our family was one of the few families that wanted to better ourselves and because of that we had to go through so much that no one ever knew about. We just received the envy and jealousy and hatred because we wanted better, not because we were looking down on anybody. There was just a desire to have a better life for the family. I just don't get it and maybe I never will understand why black people are so envious of each other. They would rather see you do bad things than good and would do whatever it takes so that you will not be successful. What's wrong with our people? In my community we had a beauty salon around the corner from the store, our mom and pop store was on the front side of the Avenue, a cleaners beside the hair salon, and years later it was turned into a pest control store, and a strip club was located to the left of my family business, called The Beehive. This strip club was where grown, old men would get their cheap thrills. Everything was X-rated, X-rated, X-rated!

∗ ∗ ∗

THE OWNERS OF THE BEEHIVE
(WHICH WAS THE STRIP CLUB NEXT DOOR
TO OUR STORE)

When I was 10 or 11 years of age my friends and I would help clean up by washing dishes, setting up tables, taking out trash, sweeping and mopping the floor in order to get paid a few dollars on Saturdays. I was a very young kid and my hormones and my curiosity were working overtime. Sometimes my friends and I would sneak a quick peak at the naked ladies while they were dancing on the stage during the afternoon hours. You had to go through the front door first and then there was a secondary door that you could enter into the club. We really had to take a quick peak and then run out before we got caught, which never happened. During the 10 years that we had our family business, the night club changed owners and names several times. It was called the Beehive first and then the Rio and finally the last owner called his club the "Manhole."

When I was 14 or 15 years of age I started coming inside of strip clubs whenever I wanted without a problem because at that time I was running the family store. I appeared older than what I really was because I had a full beard at a very young age. I conducted myself like an adult. Two doors down from the store was an upholstery shop.

Next to the shop were some apartments where I recall strange things would take place inside. There was a man who was an old pervert. He would offer guys money to give them oral sex, if not intercourse with him. Although he was a nice guy, I found that aspect of him disgusting. One day he offered my sister's boyfriend sexual advances. Her boyfriend was a boxer, so you can imagine what he did to him. Then there was our neighbor who lived upstairs, he was okay with me, but one day they found him dead in his apartment. Someone had shot him up several times. I don't think the police ever found out who him and after a few years the guy we thought was strange died as well. Right across the alley from the upholstery shop was a motorcycle shop and then it turned into what is now a liquor store. Several years later the upholstery shop was turned into another strip club that stayed open for about three years until they closed it up because of all the violence. So, at one period of time we had a strip club on both sides of our family business. It brought a lot of drugs and violence, but it did not affect our business at all. As a matter of fact, it improved our business because they would purchase beer from our establishment and sneak it into the clubs, so they did not have to pay for the more expensive beer inside of those strip clubs.

* * *

POLICE RAID

I forget to mention about the police raid on our house and our store. I think it was a couple of weeks after I came home from the hospital. My mother and cousin Katie, who was staying with us, left our house and was on our way to the family business. An unmarked police car put on his serene and told us to pull over. We knew that we didn't do anything, so we did as he demanded. He approached our car and showed us his badge. He told us that we should turn our car around and follow them back to the house. They came in and searched our entire house for stolen goods. The only thing that they found was a refrigerator that we had purchased from a liquor store owner named who was former "dirty" police. He had sold my father this refrigerator about one month prior. After the police couldn't find anything else they told us that we could lock up our house and go wherever we were headed. We had no idea that they had closed our store up for hours looking for evidence. The police officers helped themselves to whatever they wanted to eat. They said that my father was running an illegal numbers racket from our store which was a lie. My father just played a lot of Maryland lottery. They found tickets everywhere and they tried to use them as evidence. They took over $2,000 of our money and we never saw a red cent of it. I remembered one of the officers was very eager to check out the money in the cash register. They found no lottery tickets, but they took the money anyway. Those police officers were some of the most dirty and very dishonest group of people that we had in our community. They arrested my father and we covered his head with his leather jacket because of all of the news reporters and cameras were taking pictures outside. All of the police officers, those involved in the illegal raid of my parents' home and establishment should have been arrested and brought up for charges. **No real JUSTICE** was done that day, it was called, **JUST US,** with the badges and the power. They never found my father guilty of anything, but they took the refrigerator and all of the money we had in the store that they helped themselves too. Talk about dirty police. We believe the "dirty" copy sent the police to us so that he wouldn't take the rap. We finally opened up the store about 6:00 p.m. and continued throughout the day. My mother asked a friend to take her to the police precinct to get my father out of jail. That whole day was quite an experience. We later saw this incident on the news as they were taking my father out of the store while he was being arrested. It was just like a gang, where they would do what they wanted to you because they thought they were above the law.

I'm still talking about these dirty police officers and they are still doing these things to the day and worse. I have several family members that are police officers and as I mentioned growing up with the Boys Club, I have much respect for the police officers, but these crooks I have no respect for them. Even up to today for what they did to my family and they did it to me. Remember the lady that stands the blindfold over eyes with the unbalanced scale is called the lady of justice. Two of those symbols, if you pay attention to them will tell you there's no real JUSTICE, the scale is unbalanced, and she had the blindfold on. *"I say justice is blind for those who can't see or refuse to see the truth."*

* * *

THE 70s

The 70s brought nothing but drama for my family, especially my father and I. My father liked to drive fast and race cars. The first fast car that he purchased was an orange and black 442 (Oz's) Oldsmobile. It was street and track ready for racing. People would wait until we closed our store and then they would drive up to my father's car to race. Martin Luther King, Jr., Avenue SE, had about a half of a mile between two traffic lights. That's when they would get their engines ready and as soon as the traffic light would turn green, they were off to racing. I hated riding in the car with my father once he decided to race. One night after we had closed our store, my father was drinking some alcohol that night. One of his buddies asked him to race with him later that night. He worked around the corner in the alley where they had a mechanic shop. They had a race-car in the parking lot of the Safeway that they would test out every now and then. My father's friend thought he had a faster car, but he couldn't beat my father's car and sometimes it depended on the driver. My father took all of us home that night and they left later that night to find a place to race each other. My mother later that night received a telephone call from the hospital stating that my father was in a car accident, but he was okay. When my father came home from the hospital he had some bandages on his face and he had a small cast on his leg. Driving under the influence of alcohol is one thing, but to race under the influence of alcohol would lead in most cases to an accident and possibly death. I thank God that my father survived!

After the accident with the orange colored 442 Oldsmobile car that was street legal but could be put on a racetrack at any time, my father bought another car that was pretty fast, but he didn't race it like he did the other one. However, I do remember one afternoon, we were headed up to our family establishment on Martin Luther King Avenue, there was a drag strip near the store. At the first traffic light there was an entrance to the hospital, Gate No. 1. While we were sitting at the traffic light, a motorcycle pulled up, revved up his engine, and of course my father did the same with his car. The light turned green and they both were off to the races. My father pulled away from him, meaning that my father won the race. As for me, my butt never touched the car seat. I was standing straight up in the car, of course when the race was over my father started laughing at me because he saw me standing straight up, my feet to the floor and my head and back against the seat. Periodically he would tell the story to his friends while laughing at me. But that really was the end of his racing career, again, thank God! Believe it or not, my father really was an excellent driver.

I guess by now you can tell how much I really loved my father and my mother and how much I honored, respected and obeyed them, it was the thing to do. They both deserved it, for all that they did for my siblings and I and for everything that they went through, especially raising children in the Washington, DC area, coming from the South. I did whatever they told me to do, without questioning, well without questioning them out loud, either way I still did what they told me. IT'S CALLED RESPECT!

AFTER SEVERAL YEARS OF BEING VERY SUCCESSFUL WITH OUR FAMILY BUSINESS, THE LATTER 3 to 4 YEARS WERE TERRIBLE

✳ ✳ ✳

MISHANDLING OF THE FINANCES

After years of working on the ice cream truck business I can remember we were finally able to get a legal wine, mom and pop business started. I remember my mom standing behind the counter near the register. I was so excited because it was a new chapter in our lives. NOW, there would be no more illegal selling of alcohol and beer. The store was initially empty but that didn't last long before my father put his touch on it along with my mother's management and direction.

Approximately two weeks after opening, the whole layout of the store had changed dramatically. The shelves that were very empty had been filled with candy and potato chips, and then the many different bottles of wine and beer that my father started purchasing. It quickly turned from just a beer and wine store to an official community store that was now children friendly. It was not only just for adults to buy beer and wine but the kids could now purchase different kinds of candy, lollipops, sodas, potato chips, etc. The previous owners did not have a lot of varieties of goodies that a child could come in to buy. It was more adult friendly. My father pulled up the ice-cream truck and unloaded everything into our new establishment. Funny thing, after selling ice cream on our ice cream trucks over the years, for some reason we didn't sell ice cream, and that was pretty strange, knowing that the ice cream was our primary source of income. I didn't think about it, nor did I ask my parents about it, "MAY THEY REST IN PEACE WITH THE LORD." I will never know why they never sold ice cream or even snowballs over the years because they were our biggest sellers. We stood out over all the other ice cream trucks. We sold the old-fashioned snowballs that a lot of the other ice cream truck owners did not sell. It was kind of iconic, very well known to everyone about the snowballs. My father had that snowball system down to a science. Twenty plus years later, it was time for my nephews and nieces and my kids' turn to learn about the ice cream truck business.

During the times they worked on the green line subway for the Congress Heights or Alabama Avenue subway station, my father started selling snowballs right outside in the front yard of our house. I don't want to get off the subject of the topic of discussion, but I'm just thinking back on when we started the family truck business. I can remember taking my father with me to Baltimore, Maryland when I had to meet up with one of the artists that used to make my backgrounds for me. While talking to the artist, my father had noticed across the street that a guy had a snowball stand. Curious, he walked across the street and inquired for himself, he forgot about me, but that was motivation for him. When we got back to the house that's when he decided to start selling snowballs again, old-fashioned snowballs. Even the fireman would drive pass the house, pull over to the side and purchase the nice refreshing snowballs that a lot of them said brought back childhood memories. I didn't mean to drift off from the topic of discussion concerning the first years in the family business, but this is how the second-generation of my nephews and nieces started with the ice cream truck business.

Finally having a stationary, established business in the community was a huge accomplishment. It was a very lucrative business. I remember driving around to different communities throughout the neighborhoods. It was totally like day and night, and different in every way. No one really outside of the family knew how hard, and how many sacrifices that we all had to make in order for everything to be successful. We were committed! Once we got established and started meeting new people, my father started providing a credit service to our new customers, establishing credit to a lot of them, as we got to know them better. Even after we lost the store a lot of people that established a line of credit with us, most of them never paid the bills off. Again, this was a way to help some of the people purchase different items until they got paid. We had almost everything in it from bread, soap powder, can goods, and some things that some of the local grocery stores would carry. We had it in the ice cream truck and the store. In a lot of ways throughout the years, we would get a lot of haters. I never understood why people would get mad at my family when they were simply trying to better themselves. In a lot of ways, having the family business was an indirect motivation, although a lot of people did not like us. I hoped they would one day see the vision and want to own their own business one day. I always liked to see other people succeed despite all the challenges that they had to deal with, they were achievers. I'm pretty sure that those same people that showed hatred towards my family 20 or 30 years ago, have the same mentality and hatred. Some people just won't let go. I'm reminded of the scriptures that tell us not to think of ourselves more highly than we ought. Romans 12:3 says; *"Do not think of yourself more highly than you ought, but rather think of yourself with sober judgment, in accordance with the faith God has distributed to each of you."*

Ultimately, we lost our businesses for various reasons; particularly mismanagement of finances. We started out doing all the right things, but for some reason we made a wrong turn. A lot of it came from some of the people that we had working for us. Some of the workers were stealing products and money from the cash register. My father trusted too many people. There were guys that considered themselves my friends, which really wasn't true, but my father trusted them and allowed them to work in the store. I believe that accounted for a lot of money being stolen. My father also had several older guys working in the store and they would also help themselves to the cash register. Even my brother's friends had their hands in the register. They would brag to other people about how easy it was to take the money. It was up to me to try to catch these guys in the act of stealing.

There were just too many hands in the cash register that my father trusted. Unfortunately, we had to learn about this situation, the hard way. A message to those with a business, take it from me, make sure that you are the only one, or just one person that handles the money, not everybody. Lesson learned! If you look at the history of Asians and their management of money can be a good business lesson. They are accountable for the money that comes in and stays in their establishments. I'm sharing this information for business owners so that you won't have to experience the same things that eventually caused our business to fail. Those last three or four years were very difficult to handle. Everything started dwindling down on a downward spiral. It was very embarrassing. One specific time towards the end we hardly had any merchandise, even though we were about to embark on another business in the Anacostia area. Some people remained supportive, but others were glad to see that we were losing the battle of having a successful business. I believe they were happy to see this. It is very sad when you can celebrate when someone else is down. Whatever happened to being your brothers or sister's keeper?

I remember the song; "Nobody wants you when you are down and out, and nobody wants you, nobody wants you!" During those difficult years, I learned exactly who our friends really were. I really didn't have any because I wasn't able to do the things that I used to do. I remember the times when I would treat my friends to McDonald's, I would purchase whatever they wanted, but I never received the same reciprocation. These were very harsh, but Bible lessons learned. I've learned in life that IT'S IN THE VALLEY, WHERE YOU GROW AND LEARN, IT'S DEFINITELY, NOT ON THE MOUNTAINTOP.

* * *

.22 CALIBER PISTOL

I thank God, my father's life was not taken when he had his accident. A few years later, my father was hanging out with a guy named Randolph. His family was known for starting problems, but again my father was under the influence of alcohol. Randolph was driving another one of my father's fast cars at the time. It was a brown 455 Oz. Anyway, Randolph was driving the car that night and they parked outside an apartment complex. Apparently, my father was sitting in the passenger seat with a handgun under his seat. He was prepared just in case anybody else tried to do something to him (under the influence mixed with a little paranoia). My father went to sleep in the car waiting his friend to come back from whatever they had stopped to do. While my father was asleep, he had dreamed that Randolph or someone was trying to rob him, by going through his pockets (Now this is what he told us). Still dreaming, my father reached underneath his car seat and pulled out the handgun. The gun accidentally discharged and he shot himself in the leg. I would imagine that he woke up very fast after that. Randolph came back and saw what happened to my father. He drove him to the closest hospital. Mr. Randolph was always cool with me. After my father made it to the hospital and the doctors examined him, he was blessed that the bullet didn't do any serious damage because it went straight through his lower part of his leg (I believe near his calf muscle). The only real part that was damaged was my father's pride. During those days, and even now, people will shoot you, but to shoot yourself, now that's another story!

After all of what happened to my father, getting shot with his own .22 caliber handgun, thank God that it was not one of his larger caliber guns that he had. He was afraid of getting needles from the doctor. My mother said that he had gotten all the way outside of the hospital when the nurse had to bring him back into the hospital to get a needle. I mean my mother said that he was hopping out of that hospital when he heard about a needle. Now that was funny, here's a man that just got shot with a real gun, and he was scared of a little needle. Oddly enough, I don't care that much for needles myself. It didn't take long for him to recover from that injury. We just thanked God and He provided the rest, thank you Jesus! As you can see, a lot of things that was done within my family was our fault. In fact, my father hanging out and drinking, shooting himself, we thank God for all fools and babies. Babies don't know any better, but a grown man, yeah he should've known better, but again we thank the Lord Jesus Christ, that he lived. I prayed that God would continue to watch over my family. My mother was a praying woman. I know that prayer changes things. I'm a living witness, never give up on God and never stop praying for your loved ones. Continue to pray for yourself. A

84

lot of times you don't have to ask somebody to pray for you, PRAY FOR YOURSELF!

* * *

BLINDSIDED

My father had a couple of other car accidents prior to that one. One time he was taking these two guys to the drug store for something for one of the guy's wife. My sister was sitting in the front seat with my father, and I was sitting in the back seat between the two guys. I was just looking everywhere and I enjoyed hanging out with my dad. We came to a four-way intersection that didn't have a stop sign anywhere. It was around some old apartments and I guess the District government overlooked that area. Nevertheless, we were driving along and a car came speeding from the left side of us and hit our car. If it wasn't for God and the quick thinking of my father, I probably would not be writing this letter now. My father stretched out his right arm and prevented me from flying through the front windshield. My sister hurt her nose because she hit the dashboard. The other two gentleman were okay physically, but a little shaken up. One guy asked for his hat, which disappeared during the impact. The other accident that my father was in took place in our neighborhood. He was leaving out of the bottom half of our apartment complex, which ran into the main avenue, Martin Luther King, Jr., Avenue SE. A car ran directly into him. I'm not sure about the extent of the damage that was caused by this particular accident. My father didn't get injured that time, but some damage was done to his car. Another close accident that could cause my father's life. It seemed as if a lot of things happened to my father over the years.

* * *

1978 MY MOTHER WAS SICK
AND I STARTED WORKING MORE IN OUR STORE

This begins my taking charge and starting to get more serious in running the family business. I was in junior high with keys to my family's store. This was only the beginning. The next year after my accident, my mother got sick, and had to be taken to the hospital for surgery. It was during the Thanksgiving holiday. I remember writing a letter about not having my mother home for Thanksgiving. It was the first Thanksgiving holiday that my mother wasn't able to cook her traditional Thanksgiving dinner. When I was a little boy, she used to sing to me this old Thanksgiving-day song about this turkey that didn't like Thanksgiving Day, and how he would wish that it would go away. I really missed her during that week. We still opened the store and my family and I worked that busy holiday. A friend of the family was one of the first employees that we hired outside of the family. When we purchased the store, he was just a young guy. But he ended up being a part of the family for several years, until he started attending high school and playing football. He was a pretty good high school football player too. I used to go with him to a couple of his practices and I think it got to be too much for him to work in the store and go to school and play football. After his second year in high school was when he decided to quit and pursue his football career. During that Thanksgiving holiday when my mother wasn't there, because she was hospitalized, I made a vow to God and to myself, that when my mother came home from the hospital, she wouldn't have to work hard anymore in the store, as long as I lived. My father would sometimes go on a drinking spell, for a few days and then he would get his act together and get back to work as if nothing ever happened. My mother would then have to open the store and wait on the customers along with trying to take care of the other business matters throughout the day while my father would either be asleep or outside running the streets.

I was only 13 years old when I made this decision about helping my mother. True to my words, I started taking more responsibility in our store. I used to make sure that the money wasn't overflowing the cash register. I would leave only enough money to make change (15-$1 bills, 5-$5 bills and 2-$10 bills). As for the loose change the quarters, dimes, nickels and pennies, I would make sure that they were filled to a certain level. I made sure that all of the beer, wine and sodas were all cold and fully stocked. I was responsible for making sure that the cardboard boxes were torn up and taken out back to the large trash can. I started learning how to stock up the walk-in box. After our close friend stopped working for us that responsibility became my responsibility. I enjoyed stocking the large refrigerated storage boxes. I considered it as a physical workout. While I was inside working, stacking all of the different kinds of beer, I would be listening to the radio. I had to fully stock the refrigerated box once a week. I would put several cases of beer inside of the walk-in box throughout the week as needed. This was just another added responsibility that I had to do throughout the years, without complaint. It is amazing the things that we can do when we are young. I also told myself that once I got older, I would make a schedule for my parents. Yes, I was about maybe 14 or 15 at the time and came up with a schedule, keeping in mind that we were robbed many years prior. I wanted to make sure that my mother got home early before she had to deal with the winter months when it would be less daylight. So, this was a schedule that I came up with; my mom would be home by 5:00 p.m., my father would open the store at 8:00 a.m. and stay until I came to relieve him at 8:00 p.m., because he was only supervising for the most part, no disrespect to him. I wanted to make sure that my mother got home safely and that she didn't have to stay any longer than she had to in the store. I think when I turned 16 years old, we implemented this schedule, and there was no problem with it from either one of my parents. Can you believe being this young and coming up with a schedule that was acceptable by both parents? Thank you, Lord!

* * *

MENTAL

We used to have a lot of patients from the local hospital as regular store customers. Sometimes the local winos would get the female patients so drunk that they would take them to the balcony of the upholstery shop and take turns having sex with them. This didn't happen every day, but it happened enough. My sisters and I would observe their obscene behavior from behind our store. We would see the winos receiving oral sex from the male patients. On that avenue was considered, "No Holds Bar." As a result of seeing so many sexual acts at an early age, I became numb to this kind of behavior. Although living in the city life, surrounded by the hood, it could have been a distraction for me, but I took full advantage of education and experiences that I had while growing up. As the years came and went the survival skills that I learned while being on the Avenue helped me a lot especially dealing with different people.

Working in my family's business, all kinds and types of people came into our establishment and we had to learn how to treat them. Behavior is usually unpredictable on both parts. We had to be spiritually strong and mentally strong as well. It takes a lot of different strengths to deal with so many different walks of life and the attitude of the public. But I truly believe that we did the best we could and I know that no man could effectively grade us. He may give us a low-grade but thank God He is a judge and jury and whatever grade the Lord gives us, will be honest and truth. We didn't have a lot of problems with any of the outpatients from the nearby hospital. It was the surrounding knuckleheads. They gave us problems all of the time. As I got older and started thinking about what those guys did to mental patients, I felt guilty. Now that I know better, why didn't I say something to them all or why didn't I call the police? I can blame everything on being 10 or 11 years old, but not knowing right from wrong, because I knew what they were doing was wrong. I can only speak for myself, I can't speak for my sisters. The ladies that were being abused were somebody's sisters or someone's daughters and mothers. They meant something to somebody and they were somebody. I dropped the ball! Once again, they say that self is your worst enemy, THAT'S TRUE!

* * *

WITNESSING SOMEONE GET SHOT AND LATER DYING

I saw a lot of things growing up on the Avenue. One day a friend of mine almost got shot by the police. If we would have delayed walking down the alley towards the Boys Club. We had just walked through the open gate of the Boys Club, and I heard some gun shots. I didn't know exactly where they were coming from, but I thought that I heard them coming from this grassy area. It was a football game being played at the Boys Club, and all of the officers responded to this call. On one particular occasion, I went to court for a particular guy and testified against the police officer for using excessive force. Well, he was the guy laying on the ground. He was an older gentleman, he was a nice guy. I cannot remember ever seeing him causing any problems. An off-duty police officer that I knew from the Avenue shot him several times.

The police from the Boys Club heard gunshots, stopped the football game and came to the area in the alleyway where he was laying and slowly dying. He couldn't go anywhere, he was surrounded plus as I mentioned, he was slowly dying and after 30 minutes I saw him breathe real hard. That was it! He died shortly after he had already collapsed from running and from the bullet wounds. They had pronounced that he was dead, right there in the alley. I saw him lying there dead. I went to the Safeway and the man that he had cut up was setting near this glass window, and you could see them trying to put bandages on all of his cuts. His skin had opened up like a hot-dog and started to swell up and then it would split apart. That was the way the man's skin had opened up from the knife cuts. That was a very confusing night for me to have to see all of this happening right in front of my eyes. Again, another situation where a kid my age should not have to witness. But, I had to grow up fast and grow some tough skin because I had already been through a lot, starting with the robbery, and so many other things that took place during the decade of having our family business on the busy and dangerous Avenue. That Avenue was no joke!

* * *

RESPONSIBILITY

When I turned 13, it was the beginning of me taking more responsibilities to help my family out. 14 still the same, 15 I got my learners permit and a little more responsibility started. I can remember one night I went to a supply store in Maryland to get some cigarettes and candy and it was raining very hard on the highway, a friend of mine that had a driver's license road with me, but I was very nervous because this was new to me. I remained calm and only went in to get the supplies. Thank God we made it safely and when we came out the rain had stopped which was another blessing.

I remember when I was only 16 years old and my father had purchased a very nice car from a family member that could no longer pay the car note and he didn't want to mess up his credit, so he asked my father could he take over the payments and transferred the car into his name. My father helped the guy out and purchased the 79 black Chrysler LeBaron. I really wasn't thinking that my father was getting this car for me. But when I started learning how to drive my sister would ride with me while I was driving this car. I thought that I was ready to take my road tests. I took the car on my road test which I failed the first time. The second time I took the road test, I used their vehicle and changed the testing site to the Brentwood area. Well, I finally passed the test. I have been driving a whole lot more and getting very comfortable driving everybody home at night while my sister was my passenger and co-pilot. When I officially received my driver's license shortly after my birthday, the responsibilities of running the family business quadrupled, it was like overnight. I started getting more responsibility and yes, I enjoyed driving nice cars, but it came with a price. Now, remember, I'm only 16 years old now. I had to get the supplies for the store from two different warehouses for the cigarettes and candy. We would get them from the wholesale place, and I would have to get several cases of wine from another warehouse business. They never questioned me about my age because I conducted myself like an adult and I also had a full beard. I would arrive back to our store around 5:30 p.m. I had no time to study because I had to be back at the store at 8:00 p.m. to relieve my father. I made this schedule for my parents, so that my mother would not be getting home late at night. It also helped my father get home so he could get enough rest to open up the store for the next morning (in other words I created this problem myself). I was in charge of making sure that the money and store responsibilities were executed before closing each night, which was at midnight. I started to carry out these duties when I was 16 years old. One of our employees, who was considered family later robbed us without a gun by stealing money from us seven days a week. Sometimes my father would leave out of the store for whatever reason, and he would have the freedom to do whatever he wanted. Sometimes he would give the customers store credit, and he would collect money on the low, outside of the business. My brothers and sisters worked the same shift, but they too had other things to do around the store, so none of us could keep our eye on him, with the exception of my mother. She knew exactly some of things that he wanted and he could not get away with anything when she was working and watching him.

I would go to two different schools for my Academic classes and the Penn Center for my Commercial Photography classes every day, and I would go to the supplies store every day. On Saturdays, I would do household responsibilities of cleaning from the 3rd floor all the way down to the basement, for several years without any excuses or complaints, starting with vacuuming the top level and 1st level of the house that had carpet on both floors, and cleaning throughout the whole house. We had shag carpet so I would use a carpet rake first to loosen up the flattened carpet and then vacuum it starting with my parent's room, the hallway, bathroom, and the other two bedrooms upstairs. Then I would sweep the stairs from the top level to the living and dining room. From there I would go to the basement where we had wood floors. On alternate weekends I would wax all of the furniture in the house. I had a lot of responsibility from 15 to 19. Some of my siblings had moved out of my parents' house, and I was like a robot, in addition to working for my parents. The only time I really had free was Saturdays during the daytime until 8:00 p.m. and Sundays were very busy so I would come in early to make sure that the money was counted and tried not to allow the employees to rip us off, so I would get to the store early on Sundays. This is my family and I had to protect our interests, business and finances.

I started taking more pictures at my high school during lunchtime before I would drive across town to go to photography school and some days I would make $40 or $50 and sometimes more. Again, it was all business and I continued my business throughout my years of high school, which was a blessing. It made me even more self-sufficient and independent. As a business owner, I was able to get the teacher at Ballou high school to make me some business cards. My first cards didn't come out that well. If I was thinking, I could have had them made professionally at the Lemual Penn center where we had classes with printing presses and all the necessary tools. Although I was cool with the instructor, I never thought to ask for help. If I had asked him, I know he would've made them for me, mainly out of respect. I believe it was a missed opportunity to help take my photography business to the next level. I just had so much on my plate. The thought never entered or crossed my mind, but I was thankful for what I did get from the teacher at Ballou.

* * *

I WAS THE NIGHT SECURITY OFFICER IN OUR STORE

When our store alarm wasn't working I would return to the store at night after taking everybody home. I would go home real quick, take a shower, then I would go back to the store and wait until my father would get there in the morning. I would lay in this small closet area in our store where we would take our naps during the day. It had a small mattress in it and not much more room for anything else. In one hand I would have a .32-caliber pistol and near my other hand I would have the shotgun ready. Sometimes I would sleep out in the open, just so I could be ready. My last night sleeping there, and believe me I slept there enough, someone broke into the store. Early that day we had the alarm fixed. God only knows what would have happened if the alarm had not gone off. It is a known fact that most criminals are not that bright, I know that first hand. The alarm scared him off. He ran down the street into the housing area and into the outside basement staircase. A friend of our family was a Metropolitan DC Police officer who arrested him and called his fellow officers to come and take him away. We later learned that we knew the guy's father. He used to work in the old upholstery shop next to our store.

We believed that the old owner of the manhole and the owner of the building that our store was located in wanted the guy to break into our store and find our lease agreement for the store. I believe this because he had lost his night club and wanted us to lose our store. Again, this is all just speculation. One other break-in happened while we were still inside the store. We had just closed, about 30 minutes later there was a loud smash. One of the guys threw a hubcap through the window. My sisters' boyfriend was outside at the time and he was fighting one of the criminals. I ran to the closet place where we kept the shotgun and I grabbed it and ran outside to try and catch whoever it was. My father was also an enforcer and I guess you could call him a bouncer. Some days these criminals would try to start trouble. As fast as they came in my Pops would send them right back out by any means necessary, most of time by force. He would hit them with whatever he could get his hands on. A lot of times he didn't have time to think about what to grab, he would just react and reach for whatever was close by. They would have insisted on breaking in our store if we didn't stand up and protect our livelihood. As time went on a lot of people got the message, don't mess with that crazy man called Joe.

I had to carry a gun under my apron every day and night. A lot of it was because of being traumatized when I was only 10 years old and I never let it go. I was determined to get them before they got us again. I am not exaggerating or trying to make myself and my family seem larger, but these are the things that we dealt with every day with the public, they had warped minds and hidden motives. Although I had my siblings around, it was a huge responsibility on my lap that I never asked for. I had to grow up and do the things that needed to be done. Typically, it should have been the oldest that these responsibilities were passed down to. It didn't work out in that order, things do happen.

Even in the Bible, there were two twin brothers Esau and Jacob, even while their mother was carrying the twins in her belly, God told her that the older was to serve the younger, which ended up being true. It was said that Jacob stole his brother's birthrights, but that really wasn't true, his mother heard the voice of God before they were born and just arranged things so that they would be fulfilled. But he really didn't steal his brother's birthright, as a matter of fact Esau sold his inheritance to his brother Jacob for a bowl of soup, which meant that he didn't care anyway. God knew this before they were born. I'm not saying that my siblings were serving me, I'm just trying to give an example of how sometimes things are not like they are supposed to be. This analogy was used only as an example of an illustration of how things change, even in biblical days.

CHAPTER 5

DRUGS

The years were in 1982-1985, and the center of attention was crack cocaine. I was a product of "Reagonomics," an economical system that divided rich and poor, and gave Black folks an opportunity to be buyers and sellers of crack cocaine. If you lived in any urban ghetto at that time, your role model was the neighborhood super hero; the drug dealer, and its cohort: the drug addict. My brother at that time was smoking crack cocaine, and I was concerned about my sister falling into the drug lifestyle. One of my sisters had a bad drug habit! She would knock on my door at all times of the night, and she did not care if I was sleep or not. Many crack users lived in the vicinity, and I sold crack, so there were financial benefits to that. People back in the day used to call powder cocaine; "The white lady." I referred to cocaine as "Satan's New Eve," because of its deception. Cocaine is doing the same thing to our people today that it was doing yesterday, and that is deceiving them.

Yes, crack cocaine did a lot of damage within the black communities all across the country. What a lot of people did not know that the secret government agency was spearheading the annihilation in the killing of black people in the United States. The conspiracy to kill black people in the experiment started in Southern California; Compton and Watts. In those areas at the time was a lot of gang violence so what better place to start the experiment of killing black people, than where they were killing each other all the time. This was around the time when a rap group in California started their music career.

They had a guy who helped the government turn crack cocaine from the pure cocaine that they got from the drug cartel, in exchange for United States military weapons. The plan really worked, because the cocaine that they were getting from the drug cartel was pure and very potent. A lot of times when the people would try smoking the crack cocaine, it was instantaneous addiction, one-hit and they were hooked and it started spreading all over the United States. This guy, an African American, was a sell out to his own people and he didn't care. He was making money, but a government in itself made millions of dollars each day. In my opinion, this operation should have been annihilated because this caused so much death to the black people across United States.

A military man that was responsible for distributing the weapons to the cartel, in exchange for the drugs and he never did a day in jail. All he said was that he was following orders which was true, nobody ever did any real jail time, even he might have done two years in jail but he was protected by the government all the time he spent in prison.

Many years later they made a movie about this information that I'm telling and I know a lot about what was going on. But the movie helped you put everything into perspective. The movie was titled "Kill the Messenger." It wasn't a very catchy title. To the average person, if we heard a title such as this, it would make them think about someone working in the post office or something. So, a lot of black people did not watch this movie or had any real knowledge of it, because if so, it might have opened their minds and their eyes and might have stopped a lot of them from using crack cocaine. Millions and millions of black people were killed, incarcerated, addicted to this drug that was put out there by our government to kill our people. INNOCENT, INNOCENT, NEWBORN BABIES were born addicted to crack cocaine and they were only minutes and seconds old. They called them border babies, some called them crack babies because while their mothers were pregnant with them they were addicted to crack cocaine and it affected the babies, even before they were born, killing our seeds. They never had an opportunity to live. This was some cold-blooded stuff, that thing that Satan is best at; to kill, steal and destroy people of color, mainly black people.

Thank God that one day, everybody that was involved in trying to kill us and prevented us the opportunity to live, will be held accountable, one day! Again, it reminds me of the biblical times when the Hebrew Jews were enslaved because they were getting stronger in numbers. These are the original Hebrew Jews. Jesus Christ was a Hebrew Jew. Pharaoh at that time started to enslave the Hebrew Jews and try to make it difficult for them, because they outnumbered Pharaoh's people. This is biblical truth! The Israelites were brought to a strange land by Joseph, who was in second command to Pharaoh, and he brought his father and brothers and other family members to a strange land, and they grew and grew for over a century and that was not the original plan. They were born on a strange land to them, just like here in America, the Africans were not born here, they were brought here to a strange land, and was in slavery just like the Israelites were during the biblical years. Just a little food for thought.

I took part in this evil of selling drugs and unfortunately my sister was my right-hand sales lady because she and my other sister were able to get one of those section 8 apartments and they knew a lot of people. The government once again put all the black people, single mothers in the box/neighborhood which wasn't only the breeding ground for newborn babies, but a perfect opportunity for the drug dealers from New York to move in the apartment and get the mothers hooked on crack. The government renovated the entire neighborhood that had abandoned apartments for these single mothers with kids. Although this kept the single mothers from living on the street and being homeless, they would not allow the babies' fathers to live with the mothers, even though there were a lot of guys that were good fathers, they didn't want to see black families together. They were determined to keep the fathers separated from their kids and they wanted to make sure that the fathers were either incarcerated or had a record to make sure that they weren't able to be there with their family, and if they could get a job, daycare cost a lot of money, even back then, they could at least help out with the kids. The drug dealers became their providers and not the biological fathers. This was also one of the communities that I previously spoke about earlier and how these drug dealers came down from New York and took over the single mothers' apartments. These drug dealers moved in and invited their friends from back home to come down and do the same thing. I really don't know why strong brothers that lived in Washington D.C., could have allowed these things happen. Were they afraid of them? They sure didn't fight for their neighborhood or the black system and the kids, instead they started buying drugs from them. Once they moved in, they were able to get the single mothers hooked on crack cocaine. This was taking place every month. I met a lot of them when I had the photography studio. I witnessed these events with my own eyes. I'm not exaggerating or tying to make things sound dramatic in any way, but unfortunately, this was a very bad time for those single moms and their family members that were using and became hooked on crack cocaine. No one was exempt from being a crackhead, everybody suffered. It was a mess and very sad for the kids to have to grow up watching their mothers using crack and also now the drug dealers being their boyfriends. Even if the biological fathers wanted to visit, there was tension between them. The fathers became nonexistent. Now, the mothers are drug addicts and given the label as being crackheads. All over the United States, especially in the black community or neighborhood, illegal drugs have found a way to destroy the lives of black people in one way or another. That community of Congress Park Southeast was devastated with drug trafficking, shooting and killing and one of the most sad and embarrassing things about all of this was that the police department was located just a block down the street. Street drugs and nowadays prescription drugs are still killing people of all colors and races, drugs do not discriminate or make a difference in whether you are male or female. They are just still killing us! They are killing us by the millions and that's NO EXAGGERATION! I became one of my number one clients and that's one of the first rules, believe it or not that a drug dealer should never do, is to be your biggest customer, getting hooked on your own product/supply. I snorted my own cocaine product often with my cousin, and my friends and other family members. It was a socialization thing that I did, not with strangers but with friends and family.

* * *

I THANK GOD THAT I NEVER TURNED
INTO AN ALCOHOLIC!

I'm so thankful to God that none of my siblings turned into alcoholics, having so much access to beer and wine, not necessarily liquor, but alcoholic beverages on an everyday basis. Especially having the keys to our family establishment at such an early age, anytime of the day or night that I wanted to, especially in the closing time. I NEVER ABUSED or misused my privileges and opportunities in a negative way. It was always business. Even though every now and then, if I wanted to drink a cold beer, I had no problem grabbing one and drinking it real fast. A lot of people took us for bad, especially those that were employed by my father. They sometimes would steal beer and wine. Some were customers and we allowed them to pay us later. There was no one else to blame. It was our own fault for trusting the employees. I knew that one of the employees had to be stealing a lot of money every day because he lived in a very expensive apartment complex and the money that my parents were paying him, it definitely wasn't enough to afford those apartments. So, he had a lot of ways to take the money and at different times. My father gave him too much freedom to do whatever he wanted. When my mother was working in the store, she really had to keep her eyes on this guy. Again, my father gave too much freedom and leisure time. He gave a lot away. He also had a strategy of how he collected money sometimes. He had this elaborate system where he would collect money outside the store. Unfortunately, this guy also became an alcoholic. Although, I don't believe it was totally his fault, as it was somewhat genetically in his DNA.

I believe that if I was older and out of school, I could have given more of myself, to my parents' business and try to better it. I already had a very rigorous schedule at such a very young age, but the old saying is, "If I knew then what I know now things really would a lot different."

And again, I had so much freedom to do whatever I wanted to through the years. My schedule started on Monday. From Monday to Fridays, I was required to get supplies for the family business. I was only 16 years old and even before I was 16 years old I was driving to the warehouses to purchase wine, cigarettes and all kinds of items that we needed every day and not once did anyone, especially when I was buying the wine, question me for identification. I started growing a beard when I was about 15 years old. That may have something to do with them not asking about identification, but also the way I conducted myself, like a mature businessman.

I told myself many years ago that I would make a different schedule for my parents to work. As soon as I got my driver's license at the age of 16, I did just that. My mother came in to work about 11:00a.m. I made sure that she would be on her way back home around 5:00p.m. So, remember we got robbed many years ago and I did not want her to have to be out too late, especially during the daylight-saving time when it got dark outside, very early. My father would open up the store at 8:00 a.m., but all he did really was supervise everybody. The schedule was from 8:00 a.m. to 8:00 p.m. Then I would relieve him along with the rest of my family members. My siblings and some other workers would be there from 8:00 p.m. until 12:00 midnight, this is seven days a week.

This was a very hard thing to do, especially for a young man like myself. It was extremely hard to try to even study. Whenever it was time to put my head in the books I had to worry about the money from the cash register that was disappearing. It became very hard for me to study, which affected my grades throughout the years, but I didn't have any problems with my grade in commercial photography classes. I had a 4.0 grade average in photography school and I was one of the top students, not bragging, but as I mentioned before I got exposed to photography at a very young age. I guess I was about 11 years old when my friend Officer Bailey taught us how to develop black and white portraits. I was very advanced in my conversions even before I started taking the commercial photography classes. I kind of submerged myself into learning about photography because when I started learning about it, I was only 11 years old and then when I turned 12 years old, that's when I was faced with being injured and learning how to walk all over again because of the paralysis that I talked about earlier in the story. I can no longer play basketball with a little aggressive attitude that I had, so photography was the next option for me.

I started early with a lot of things that the average 12-year-old, let me take that back, the average 8-year-old would've been exposed to, when it came to getting high, and sometimes drinking something called Malt Duck, which really was an early version of a wine cooler. I used to drink this with some other guys my age, but also the older guys, again not abusing the premises I had. Every now and then I would get a bottle and go over my friend's house and we would drink and smoke. But never abusing either one of the alcoholic beverages and the marijuana joints.

I know that I danced around many different summaries within this part of my manuscript, but that's how it was, it would really be hard to try to put all these things in chronological order because so many things were happening in my very young life, it was like I was playing tennis or ping-pong here and there and all over the place, while still maintaining my sanity, thank God. I remember one of the guys that was like a brother, who also worked in the store, would give some of the guys that I hung out with some free items from our store. I caught him a couple of times because of the expression on my old friends faces when it came to buying some MALT DUCK. They were surprised a lot of times, but that was his way of trying to fit in with everyone.

My oldest sister told me one day that she would occasionally see the guys that I normally would hang out with running and hiding from me when I would arrive with my mother, but I never saw it, but she did, and she told me about it. I said to myself, I don't have time to be playing games and these guys running away from me as if I was a player or something. They had me looking all over the place. When I was 11 years old I played basketball with the older guys. They had to be at least 16 years old because he was driving his father's car. Again, they were straight up with me and I appreciated those guys. One friend considered me to be like a cousin and I fit right in. But the things that they exposed me to were like an entirely different world. This guy was old enough to drive. These are not the same guys that would hide from me when they would see me getting out of the car with my mother. My friend who considered me to be his cousin, his father used to be in the Marines which gave us guys access to go ON THE BOWLING AIR FORCE BASE. I had never been on any kind of military base in my life until I started hanging out with the guys. It was the city within a city! They had everything that the outside stores had and more. Everything that you wanted was right there on the base, EVERYTHING! This was very exciting to me, we went bowling, something I had never done before. Or we would go to the gym and play basketball. They also had a movie theater on the base. I was very excited about this and enjoyed every day that we went onto the base. We had to be mindful of the time because whenever we walked outside after a certain time, the bugle would go off and you would have to wait until it was finished before proceeding. I think it was the Star-Spangled Banner THAT WAS PLAYED EVERY DAY. So we always had to be mindful of the time. As long as you were inside the building, you did not have to worry or stop doing whatever you were doing. But you couldn't get caught outside during this time. I think it was around noon every day.

Even though these guys were much older than I was, I did not let them use me any kind of way and they never tried to talk me into getting bottles of MALT DUCK, which was all of our favorite drink. But every now and then everybody had to contribute something. I would sometimes contribute a 32-ounce bottle of Malt Duck or a nickel bag of marijuana. It was like a mutual understanding that everybody had to bring something to the table. I was the exception, even though I was the youngest of all of them. We used to have a good time, back in the day!

One close friend was like my little brother until he started selling drugs on a large level. I can remember when I first found out that he was selling marijuana, he was in the alley behind our family business, across the street from his grandparents' apartment building. I can remember jacking him up one night against the wall, asking him, "Man, What Are You Doing selling marijuana?" We're just young teenagers at that time, and he said to me, "Well, you sell weed!" I told him, "Please don't do everything I do." I was a bad influence on not only him, but to a lot of people that we grew up around because of my early exposure to drugs. Although I never forced anyone to use them, they wanted to try and do the same things that I did. Well, after talking to my little brother about the marijuana thing several years later, he was surprised that I had been selling illegal drugs. There was a reason I was getting powder cocaine to sell, one example was if I brought $500 worth of powder cocaine, he wanted me to give him half back which would've been $250, but I would give him only $200 back. I wasn't just anybody, like the rest of his runners. I was supposed to be considered a big brother. He never had a biological older brother. Then he started acting petty towards me. After everything that we had been through growing up together. That all changed when he started having new friends and making them more money. A lot of times he would show that he didn't want to be bothered with me, it was cool with me though. If someone we knew got injured, and mainly if they were killed, he had no problems calling me, no matter what time it was. Most of the times it would be during the late nights. He had no problems calling me and asking me to come over and hang out and talk for a while (Only when he was stressed or

101

maybe even a little scared). I would tell my fiancé that I was going over to his apartment to talk to him. I would try to explain to her what was really going on and why he was really calling me during those moments. During out conversations, the majority of the time there would be a large bag of powder cocaine on the table for us to snort as much as I wanted to snort, as long as I stayed there with him that night. I would socially get high with him and maybe drink a couple of beers while we snorted the night away. I'm not saying that I was anybody special, but he wanted my company anytime we would receive news that someone we both knew was killed. Sometimes there would be a couple of his other friends hanging out with us, getting high.

But you could only get but so high off of snorting cocaine. I knew my limit. I wasn't being greedy, trying to snort my brains out because it was so much there. I just needed enough to get mellow, but he would try to get me to take another hit and another hit! I would always tell them that I was good. I had enough! But if I wanted to take some with me he didn't go for that. As long as I was with him I could have as much as I wanted. He thought if I took it with me, I would sell it. But it was all good. I was glad that I could be there whenever he wanted to talk. I always tried to be a big brother and a friend to him over the years. But, he had new friends and this caused him to believe somehow that he was better than me because he had more money, nice cars and clothes. He always tried to out do me!

Again, growing up and watching the success of my family over the years, there was always some kind of competition going on. When I got injured when I was 12 years old, they never came to the hospital like I thought my friends would. I was a very good basketball player, much better than he was and a couple of my other so-called friends. But when I got injured and was paralyzed I had to learn how to play the game all over again and a lot of people, including him was very happy. Now that I could no longer play basketball the same way, his basketball skills improved and he developed to be a pretty good basketball player. I had to learn the game all over again using my left hand because of paralysis that I suffered on the right side of my body. When I was right handed my basketball game was pretty good, compared to a lot of people and I had to learn how to play the game now as a left-handed basketball player. I tried my best to still play the game with the guys at the Boys Club. Most of my friends became better ball players than I was and I couldn't hang out with them anymore. My basketball skills in the game itself never got better, and I'm serious when I say that some people, including a few family members were glad that I could no longer beat them like I used to. I never tried to embarrass them, but when I played basketball against them before I got hurt, I was just better than they were.

I had to live with knowing that I was not a basketball player anymore and they were very happy to know that they could finally take over the game. I really loved playing! I started out learning how to play the game at the age of nine, teaching myself, and I always wanted my big brother to help me get back playing the game that I love so much. But my own brother never helped me get back in shape or help me with my skills. I needed the help to regain my skills and I was waiting for him to teach me. That help never came from even my former coach at the Boys Club. He never pulled me to the side to try to work with me. Maybe he was mad at me because of the way I did not participate during the basketball tournament that our team won in Buffalo, New York.

Only one person, a female named Kathy tried to help me. She was like a tomboy. She wasn't a bad looking lady. After the injury, my mother did not want to let me out of her sight, especially knowing that I would go to the Boys Club to play basketball, so I had to sneak out of the store. One day Kathy saw me struggling, trying to shoot the basketball with my very weak right arm and hand. She said to me, "Jeff, why don't you try to shoot the basketball with your left arm and hand." That's how I started playing basketball again, shooting and dribbling and bouncing the basketball with my left hand. You would be surprised how a little advice can help someone out. Just imagine if I had a little more help. With recovery and help I may have been able to learn the game all over again. The downside of all of this, I was surprised to see just how many people were glad that I could not play basketball the way I was before I got injured. People were happy to see me as a failure. Okay, enough about this subject of my not being able to play basketball anymore.

My wife, my daughter and I had moved into the apartments on Oakwood Street, another neighborhood that was close to our family business. It was a three-story building, we lived on the third floor. I met some guys that lived downstairs on the second floor on the same side of the building, it actually was like three sections to the apartment building. I found out that these guys loved smoking crack. We became associates. I couldn't really say that they were my friends, they were cool to hang with because they liked to smoke that crack. I was able to make a lot of money from those guys. Every once in a while, I would walk downstairs, mainly during the weekends because both of the guys were able to maintain jobs even though they got high. On one particular Saturday morning, I went downstairs and knocked on the door to see if they needed anything. They indicated that they didn't need anything at that time, so I asked if I could borrow their pipe. I put the crack in it and took a hit only to leave the rest with them.

Honestly, I knew I was wrong, but it was business. It would take them maybe 10 minutes before they would call me and tell me that they wanted more, every time. I knew that they had money and I didn't mind giving them a freebie every now and then. I would just light up the crack pipe for them and go back upstairs and just wait for a few minutes and just like clockwork, I would get a call, or they would beep me on my pager and ask me whether I was still home. I would just walk downstairs to make $25 or $50, within a few minutes. It did not take them long to respond and in turn they would get a lot of customers for me and sometimes I would give them a rock of cocaine for their help. I had this little business of selling crack to downstairs neighbors for several months. This was quite a system that I had and I considered this "my crack house." I thank God, and truly I THANK GOD, that I never got hooked on smoking crack cocaine!

I also sold Marijuana to some of the female tenants in the building and I made sure that they were taking care of by making sure that no one was trying to beat them out their money. I only sold marijuana to some of the people in my building, and some of the older guys around the way would also buy from me. A couple of the guys lived across the street in other apartments. I sold a lot of love boat to two special ladies. I think they were sisters or related to each other. They also lived on the second floor, but towards the middle of the building away from the guys that had the crack house.

I had a system going on throughout the building. No matter what I had they always wanted to make sure they got a nice quantity, whether it was marijuana, love boat, or crack cocaine, or a fat nickel bag of weed. I would make a special bag just for them. They didn't have to be outside on the street trying to get it. I would make sure that it was right for them. One of my clients was a beautiful, pretty young lady, and I knew her baby's father, but this was just business, nothing more. She was very tempting, but I had to control my hormones, which I did. Since she had the clothing for sale I would allow her to come upstairs so she could talk to my wife. I would just pay my bill. We purchased so much clothing for my daughter, we didn't need to buy anything for a whole year, until she turned two years old. I had to take full advantage of this connection while I had a chance. She enjoyed smoking love boat along with her sister. On occasion I would give them a free bag and enjoy a smoke with them. We would talk about whatever subject they wanted to talk about while we were neighbors. During my last days living in the apartment, I started feeling uncomfortable with the people in the crack house because they were always involved in unnecessary drama that caused a lot of unwanted attention.

I remember the night that I was moving out of the apartment, they were so bad and got in a very big argument. The police had been called to the crack infested apartment. These guys started really slacking and smoking a lot of drugs. I had to stop coming downstairs. We decided to move because I lost my job and I did not want to depend on selling drugs for a living. While I was packing up the U-Haul truck to move out of the apartment the guys started fighting each other inside of the apartment. I believe that if I would have stayed there any longer, they would have snitched on me to the police. The police were called and had to break them up. I knew it was time to leave. I was ahead of the game. The main reason for living in this apartment was to stack enough money to buy an ice cream truck. I tried to do what my parents did when we lived in the Park Chester apartment complex. I wasn't there long enough to achieve that goal. I met quite a few people in the area and we all seemed to get along with one other. When the ice cream trucks would come into the neighborhood, I would buy most of the kids that lived in my apartment building ice cream. It was summertime and sometimes their parents didn't have money to buy ice cream, as long as I had their permission I would get all the kids ice cream. I made it my business to treat the kids because I always believed that we should help our children in the community, and by helping them, we helped the mothers. There were a lot of single mothers living in my building and I did not do this to show off, I did it from my heart. Again, I wanted to help the parents out a little bit with the expense of purchasing the ice cream for the kids.

I was really well-connected with a lot of resources while living in the apartment buildings, especially the young lady that provided the clothes. Everyone benefited from that, especially my daughter, wife and sometimes my brother-in-law. She carried all sizes and she knew that if she brought them to my apartment chances were, I was going to purchase them. I also purchased some items for her little daughter and her sister who had a kid and a few guys that lived across the street. One of them worked in the hospital and I would get an army bag full of pampers. All I had to do was give them a little something which saved us a lot of money.

Someone introduced me to a guy that worked at a warehouse that sold Similac and a soybean brand of formula that I would get my nephew, trying to help out my oldest sister. I would get at least 10 cases of Similac. The guy even had Gerber juice that I got for my daughter and my nephew, again saving us a lot of money and all I had to do was give them maybe a $50 bag of powder cocaine, which was really nothing to me but that's all he wanted. I think he came by at least once a month. I would stock up again, a real blessing because baby formula was very expensive. I wished I had those connections when my son was born, but I had to stop selling that poison for a while. This is when being a drug dealer's mind-conscience stepped in, which is an oxymoron because most drug dealers would sell drugs to their own mother and brothers and sisters without even thinking twice. The saying was, "If you don't get drugs from me, you're going to get it from somewhere, so why not let me make the money."

* * *

MY SISTER MARCIA AND HER BOYFRIEND KEVIN

Kevin was my sister Marcia's boyfriend who my parents really liked. He had some positive things going for him versus some of my sister's other boyfriends. They did not have the same business qualities. It was unusual for a father to admire his daughter's boyfriend, but that just meant he was doing something positive. Every real father wants to make sure their daughters are safe and are taken good care of by their boyfriends and eventually become their husbands.

His father also had his own barbershop down the street which gave him the experience at cutting hair at a very young age and when he was old enough his father purchased him a barbershop across the street from our family store. It was a nice, small size shop that had about four barber chairs in it. When Marcia and Kevin started dating, he became family, instantly after dad's approval. I used to help him out around the shop by duplicating keys for customers. As a way of helping him out, I asked if he could show me how to operate the machines. It was also a way to show my appreciation for them giving me free haircuts. So, I learned how to master using the key machine. Since the barbershop was so close to our family business we became pretty close and began hanging out together. He was like another brother to me and like a son to my parents. My mother would always send him a plate of home cooked meals. When he and my sister really started dating, real serious dating, he actually lived with us in our basement for about one year until they got their own apartment. They really were a nice couple. They both came from families that were business owners, and I believe this was sure motivation for my sister to pursue her own entrepreneurial dreams.

Kevin had a nice looking, fast navy-blue Camaro, that he loved driving fast in. He and I smoked a lot of weed together, and I would hang with him when he went on some of his errands. The local girls were jealous of Marcia because she was dating Kevin and they wanted him. They wanted to break their relationship up. The two of them dated for about five years until Kevin moved his barbershop about one block from where his first barbershop was located and their relationship started getting weaker. He started selling a lot of drugs and making a lot of money in his barbershop and it brought even more women in his face, which eventually started making him feel like he was all that. I never understand why woman sought after men that were married or in serious relationships, especially those that made a lot of money. They didn't care about their husband. They just wanted to get some fast money anyway they could. They wanted to be that one that was going to break up my sister's relationship. They wanted to be the one to brag about. This was familiar in that my father was also tempted by foolish pride that eventually was the failure of their relationships because of the "tricks" that were chasing after their success. That's all they were "tricks" trying to get that treat money or bragging rights to say that they were the one that took someone else's husband or boyfriend away from them.

Kevin was moving up in the drug game and his brother came to join him in the new shop. I think his brother just got out of the military. The barbershop name was eventually changed to their names. The more drugs that Kevin acquired, the more material things he bought. But he also bought on a lot of negative attention from some of the jealous guys and also this caused the stick-up boys to watch him closely. When he was dating my sister, because of our family reputation, he was protected because he was dating "Joe's" daughter. His first large purchase was a home, somewhere in Maryland. After he moved into his new house a few months later, approximately three to four "stick-up guys" came into his house to rob him. At this time, he was not dating my sister. I always believed that I knew one of the guys. He was able to get his gun and he shot one of the guys that tried to rob him and the other guys drove away. One of their friends on the street wanted revenge but he later died. I learned later on who all of the robbers were and I know they would not have tried to rob him if my sister was in the house, or even if they were still together at that particular time. Being a show off, brought much negative attention his way. No one liked a showoff or someone who bragged about what they had. However, he was still considered my brother and we would smoke a joint of weed together every now and then, mostly in the back of the barbershop. He still gave me the family discount and getting that much needed haircut.

EGO TRIPPIN'

I tried to rent an emptied space next to Kevin's shop but some of his friends requested to rent the space out to build an auto shop that specializes in auto accessories like nice car rims. Prior to me asking to rent out the space, we had a misunderstanding that led to a fight between us that really never should have happened. That caused a huge problem because Kevin made the mistake of going to my oldest sister's house and then my brother's house because of a misunderstanding concerning his youngest sister. He thought that he could just do what he did and maybe even try to intimidate my oldest sister and my brother by bringing some of his punk buddies with him that one day. Neither of them were intimidated. He attempted to show off because he always had a lot of guys following him. He came to my sister's house with some of those guys as if he wanted to fight, which wasn't going to happen. Why would you try to intimidate my family after my parents embraced you and protected you? If he really wanted to fight he should have found the guys that gave his sister the "love boat" drugs that eventually turned her out and caused her to walk into moving traffic and could have been killed. Once I learned that he had been to my oldest sister's house while my oldest niece and my nephew were home, I started looking for them. They could have been scared or shaken up by these guys coming into the house like that. It takes a punk and punk friends to do something like this. The fight was provoked by him disrespecting my brother and my sister. We were trying to keep his sister from getting hurt. I don't know what made him start looking for my brother which I thought was drug related. I thought maybe my brother owed him some money. Even if he did, why would you go to such extreme? This caused Kevin and his boys to get hurt really bad, especially since a lot of people didn't like him anyway. We found out later that it was all about his sister being high and delusional. He could have resolved the situation in a more sensible manner by finding out what really happened, especially since he once lived with our family and dated my sister.

I had been looking for him for at least three days coming to the barbershop to talk to him and to confront him about how wrong he was. In the day that I would find him was on July 7 which was my friends' Randolph's birthday. Randolph and I had been smoking weed most of the day and we drank some beer. After running out of beer, I asked him to go to the store and purchase more beer. One hour later, I decided to go and see what was taking him so long. He was behind the counter working. What! I was already tipsy from drinking earlier. While I was there, I decided to purchase a few wine coolers for myself. I placed them on the front seat of my car. My venture was back on towards finding Kevin. He had just recovered from another incident where he was shot for messing with someone's wife or girlfriend. In my mind, he is still my brother. I didn't want to cause harm to him, I just wanted an explanation. I approached the barbershop and they were actually closed, but there were people still inside. I began talking to him through the locked gate, but I could still see inside. I'm dressed, sly in my shorts and my nightshirt and some nice summer loafers. I was ready to fight. He began antagonizing me by asking; "What's up? What's up?" Are you looking for me? I told him that he was wrong for going to my brothers' and sisters' house. I took it upon myself to step to him and tell him he was wrong. He approached me and was bold enough to take my glasses off my face and laid them on the car. I hit him low and then went across his jaw and he dropped to the ground. By now, I proved my point! He tried to get into my car and he grabbed my legs and tackled me to the ground. We tossed and turned each other. I tried to get away because I remembered his recent injury not too long ago. Nevertheless, he decided to show off in front of the people in the barbershop. He knew that I had been drinking because he could smell the aroma by now. Although I was prepared mentally and physically for the fight, I was heavily intoxicated.

One of Kevin's friends saw his sister tripping out while my sister was trying to help her and they called him and told him some kind of story that my sister was responsible. This caused him to come over my sister's house with a few of his buddies and he started kicking my sister's front door numerous times. My sister and my niece were inside of her apartment during the time Kevin and his boys were trying to kick her door in. When I heard about what he had done to my sister, it made me mad and I had to straighten that situation out because I know that both my sister and my niece were scared. I don't know why Kevin felt that he could do what he did to my sister and brother without anybody stepping up to him. He really was a punk that hid behind his buddies. But together they felt strong, A group of punks! That was the other reason why I had to step to him because of the way he went about the entire situation was wrong. Again, this is the same guy that used to date my sister Marcia and lived in my parent's basement for almost a year, he was truly tripping.

This was a time when I had to step up to the plate and defend my family. The next day after the fight came and I saw a couple of guys that were outside that night and they asked me why didn't I stomp him when I had him on the ground. These were some of the same guys that were probably telling him something different. My father found out about what had happened the next day. I don't know who told him what happened, because after I had finished making my point with Kevin that night, I went home with my lady and my beautiful baby girl. I told her what had transpired on the Avenue with Kevin and I. My shirt had a little cut on it, he ripped the pocket of one of my favorite shirts, but I was able to get over the shirt. The two guys who were supposedly with him the night went to my sibling's house because they were cousins of my lady. I had squashed it! Everything in the past was over as far as I was concerned because he was still my brother. I just didn't like that he disrespected my family. I don't know what he was tripping off of or thinking. It was resolved. For some reason he thought that I was gonna call my father to come up to the barbershop. I did what I needed to do so there was no need for me to call my father. The word got out that my father was coming to the barbershop, so they closed it down early. They were in a hurry to close up shop, thinking that my father was going to come up there and tear up some stuff. For what? I already took care of what was needed to be taken care of and the scuffle was over. Randolph was the one that told us that they were in a hurry to close the barbershop, thinking that my father was going to come up there, and do some damage. Even though in some ways Kevin disrespected my father, it caused them to no longer be friends. He began to say negative things behind my father's back. This hurt my father because he took him in as if he was his very own son. It was time to let this go!

Several months later after Kevin and I had our altercation, he had an argument with his brother on the side of the barbershop near the customer parking lot, after they had closed up for that night. I took the opportunity to explain to Kevin. I told him that he should have handled the situation with his brother inside and not in front of all the people surrounding the shop. But remember, he loved to show off and he loved the negative attention. It made him look like he was hard-core. He actually threatened his own brother with a gun. He told him if he got into his car he was going to shoot out his tires. I did not want to see their relationship deteriorate so I explained to him that he was going against his brother. I also told him that all of the people outside wanted to see the both of them go at it. They wanted the satisfaction! They eventually went inside the shop and was able to resolve whatever the situation was between them. I also followed them in so that I could resolve the situation that he and I had previously several months ago. I told him that some of the same guys that wanted to witness our disagreement were there to instigate the argument between him and his brother. I let him know that they were actually haters and hypocrites. We resolved a lot of things because I reminded him that he was also my brother and my father took him in. We thank God that we were able to make amends!

✳ ✳ ✳

LOOKING FOR A PLACE TO OPEN UP MY OWN STUDIO

I found an empty place around the corner from my parent's old store. Kevin was supportive during that time because I was trying to rent out an empty store that was next door to his barbershop, but one of his friends had already requested the property. If I was able to rent the property from him, it really would have been very lucrative, because of all of the guys that were trafficking in and out of the barbershop with money. It was also located on the front of Martin Luther King, Jr. Avenue which would have attracted even more business, but it wasn't meant to be.

Although I never got my hair cut at his barbershop anymore, we were on the same page again. After five months of renting the studio, Kevin died somehow. According to witnesses he had fallen off the roof of one of his friends' houses. I also heard that he was at a married woman's house and her husband came home while he was there and he tried to leave out of their house by exiting out of one of the windows upstairs and subsequently lost his footage and fell off of the roof. They told me that immediately after the fall the people nearby came and took all of his personal items that he had on him. I really don't know what happened to my brother. We don't know if someone intentionally pushed him or whether it was an accident. BUT GOD KNOWS! So, I don't need to speculate! After the accident, I learned that he was in the hospital after my wife talked with her cousin on the telephone. Her cousin's brother was one of Kevin's best friends. After she told me what hospital he was in, I immediately got dressed and went to Howard University Hospital. They told me that only his immediate family members could visit, but for some reason, the nurse felt compassionate towards me and she gave me a few minutes to visit with hm. That was called the favor of God! He was not conscience, but I looked at his eyes and they appeared to be open, just a little. He had several tubes and medical equipment connected to him, and I really felt sorry for him, and to see him lying there like that, my brother, I couldn't help but get emotional. I said a few words to him, and said a little prayer, and a few days later he died. Despite our past misunderstanding, I always considered him as a brother and I used to think about him a lot, even years after he died. I remember that his birthday was either March 20th or the 21st.

* * *

JUST SAY NO!

Reflecting back, I realized that I made stupid decisions, that I hope young people will learn from. I see now that the drugs for the 21st Century is Heroine, Cocaine, Marijuana, methamphetamine, opioids, Marley and Ecstasy. What people must realize is that there are consequences that come with selling and using illegal drugs. God only knows what else is awaiting to kill our children. It is not worth playing Russian roulette with your life. Once you loose your brain cells, you'll never regrow them back again. This was only the beginning of a terrible ending for me. It started with my first puff of marijuana, along with the exposure that I received from my family. But all I had to do was say; "No!" That two-letter word has a lot of power. You have to know when to use that word, NO! It can be the difference in life or death. Please listen and take heed to what I'm saying to you, BEFORE IT'S TOO LATE!

CHAPTER 6

DEEP ROOTED TRAGEDIES

On the weekends the Boys Club was closed, my friends and I would play basketball outside with the older men. They would have their coolers full of beer and they would try to bully us to the point of frustration. That was the only edge that they had over us, because we were a lot younger, and faster than they were. Every chance they got, they would give us a hard block. It was a psychological game and that was their way of balancing the playing field. During that summer of 1977, the Boys Club had to close down their gym because of renovation. I couldn't wait for the new season to start, and I was so excited because this would be my second year playing 12 and under basketball. I would be one of the starting players, so I worked very hard all summer trying to improve my basketball game. I would not only be playing basketball for the Boys Club, I was also trying out for my junior high school basketball team, (Friendship Educational Center located in another area in southeast Washington, DC). It was a new junior high school and elementary school all in one. It was a very large building and I wanted a new start and I didn't want to go to my neighborhood school. I was excited about everything until that night of November 26, 1977.

Earlier that evening one of the officers at the Boys Club let me shoot the basketball around in the gym for a few hours. I don't know why he allowed that, not knowing it would be my last time hanging around in the newly renovated basketball gym. I was visualizing myself playing against another team in the upcoming basketball season. Because they had renovated the Boys Club basketball gym, everything was like brand-new. The floor was painted a gloss, the backboards were all bright white with the square right behind the rim to help you when you wanted to shoot shots off the backboard. Number 11 Boys Club was entitled to have this for renovation because the four basketball teams made it all the way to the championship and to the PAL time. That was in Buffalo, New York. So, I guess that's where he got the funding from because he did so well representing number 11 Boys Club. The only age group that did not make it to the championship and to the economy was the 14 and under basketball squad.

During that time it was all about Dr. Julius Erving, playing for the 76ers. He was a very exciting basketball player and I wanted to model my basketball game after him. I further developed skills and fundamentals in this game of basketball. There was no Michael Jordan to be thought of during that time, instead it was all about Dr. J and a few other NBA stars.

After shooting around in the renovated gym, I was so excited, on cloud nine. I was anticipating the time when I left the Boys Club, that night I was elated and anxious about the tryouts, which would have been the next two weeks. I just knew that I would have a starting position. It was mine to keep and no one would be able to take it away, because I worked too hard all summer. Maybe a few hours later that day or that night, after I left the Boys Club and went to our family store that was just a couple of blocks away, two knuckleheads were trying to steal stuff from our store and disrespecting my sister. It really was a quiet night until these two rascals came into our family establishment. My sister Marcia was working in the store at the time. Remember my sister had some tomboyish ways as she was an expert in Karate for several years. Well, my sister wasn't going to let these guys steal from our store, so she kicked them out. After she pushed them out of the store they called her a Bitch! One of them had already stolen a coke, and he placed it inside his coat pocket that was draped over his arm without our knowledge. I followed Marcia outside in front of the store to help protect her, but also to bring her back into the store without having to fight either one of them. I turned my back to one of them (I do remember his name), swung his coat with that thick Coca-Cola bottle inside. It hit me on the left side of my head. *Everybody should remember those thick Coca-Cola bottles.* A lot of us used to tease people who wore thick glasses, we would call them Coca-Cola bottle lenses.

That very hard, deadly blow to my head, caused me to be paralyzed on the right side of my body. If anybody know a thing about the human anatomy, they know that the left side of your brain controls the right functions of your body and vice versa. I learned the hard way about human anatomy, because that's how it affected me. I remember seeing people that had a stroke in their brains that caused them to walk slightly bent and they would drag their feet. I didn't realize until years later that in fact that blow to my head caused the stroke in my 12-year-old body. I often wonder to this day, what kind of physical threat could I have been to those almost grown men that would cause them to viciously attack me. What was that knucklehead thinking when he struck me in the head with that bottle? I was only about 12 and he was around 16 or 17 years of age. There are real, evil people in this world and he was definitely one of them, and so was his friend. Shortly after I got injured, it came a time for them to answer and be accountable for the things they did to people. That injury ended my basketball career, hopes and dreams, and almost ended my life.

∗ ∗ ∗

STEPPING STONES

I had to learn how to walk all over again at the age of 12. The doctors told my mother that night that I wasn't going to make it alive due to my injuries. I remembered the doctors wheeling me pass my mother on a stretcher, and she was weeping hard. I said to her, "*Mom don't worry about me because I will be Okay!*" I don't know if she even recalled those words, but I thank God that He gave me those words to say to my mother to try to comfort her because I never wanted to see her cry like that again. The irony was that I was supposed to be getting baptized that following week. **The devil was and still is a liar! God had something in store for me!** After I was struck in my head with the bottle, my parents brought me into the store. They did not wait for the ambulance, instead they put me into the back seat of the car and drove me to Hadley Memorial Hospital, about 20 minutes away from our business. It was located in Southwest, Washington, DC. When I arrived at the hospital, they wanted to transfer me to Children's Hospital, but they did not have a helicopter at Hadley's, so they transferred me by way of ambulance.

I finally arrived at Children's Hospital, located in North East Washington, DC. I remember the doctors taking a lot of x-rays, but nothing much more than that. I later learned that I was paralyzed on the right side of my body. All I was worried about was getting well so that I could go to basketball practice. I didn't know how serious my condition was. I couldn't see out of both of my eyes at the same time because of the swelling that built up in my brain. I stayed in the intensive care unit for three days. I can remember those three days very vividly. Again, two things were on my mind; basketball and being able to get a girlfriend. I'm just being honest, at the early age of 12 years old that's what I was thinking about. I also wanted to relieve all the pressure from my mother's heart caused by seeing her baby boy in the condition I was in.

* * *

FLASHBACK - THE INJURY!

While I was in Children's Hospital, I tried to watch the Washington, Redskins game one day but the medication made me so sleepy. After I left ICU they gave me a private room on the fourth floor, Four-Green. This was a brain injury unit and I was slowly getting stabilized each and every day. My room was located right across from the nurses station. My mother, God Bless her, stayed with me every single day and night. They had a couch that turned into a bed that she slept on. They fed us breakfast, my favorite was pancakes and sausage. Almost every morning I requested that same breakfast. They would make this especially for me almost every day. The doctor would come every day during the early mornings to see if I had any sensation in my right foot. Mrs. Catherine Hammond was a neurologist. For the first couple of days she would ask me if I felt anything. I did not have any feeling. They would use the clipboard to touch the bottom of my foot to see if I could feel anything, but I felt nothing. But, one day I started getting an unusual sensation in my body. I would look at television with one eye at a time. I had to switch from the left to the right. One day, I forced myself to look at the television with both eyes at the same time. Thank God! Thank God! I slowly was able to get my vision back, everything started coming back into focus. That was the very first sign of progress as the swelling started to subside in my brain. I thank God that He gave me the courage to force myself to watch television. I truly believe that it triggered the nerves that operated in my brain.

I then started getting a sensation feeling in my right foot and leg. I couldn't wait until the next morning when they would come around to make their rounds and test the bottom of my foot. I was able to say; YES, Dr. Hammond I can feel the clipboard. Thank you, Jesus! Thank you, Lord! They were happier than I was. I thank God for everything! I had physical and occupational therapy every morning. My physical therapist and occupational therapist were wonderful. I had many visitors. Members from the church came to my room and they all gathered around my bed and prayed for me. This was not my neighborhood church, this was a church that the police officer attended and a lot of the kids in the neighborhood would come to the boys club, this was the church that he would take all of us to sometimes I was thankful for the visits and their prayers for me as they gathered around my bed. I truly believe that their prayers helped my recovery. Even my adopted sister came to visit me and it was the first time that I'd seen her in months because she had moved out on her own and none of us had seen her since she left our house. She came to visit me and I was so happy to see my sister and she brought her new boyfriend that she met in West Virginia job corp. He was from DC, small world. But I was glad that she took time to come out to see me.

Officer Bailey came by but my so-called friends and my so-called little brother never came by to visit me in the hospital. I thought he was like my little brother and even at that young age I learned a lot about life and people and how quickly things change from good to bad and vice versa. It also taught me a lesson about my friends. My mother needed a break that night so she had my sister Valencia stay in the hospital with me that night. Valencia wanted to go outside to smoke a cigarette, and possibly a joint. While she was out of the room, I was left alone. I needed to use the bathroom, so I decided to try to go by myself. Well, I only made it three steps away from my bed, and then I fell to the ground. I jumped up so fast, and got into the bed before the nurses came in. One of them asked me what happened and I told her that I fell trying to go to the bathroom. I really didn't want to get my sister in trouble with my mother, but I had to be honest. I could not lie to them. The breakthrough came when one day I was sitting in my wheel chair, and I was looking down at my right thumb. I noticed that I was able to move it a little bit. I was very excited about being able to move my finger again! I called my mother over to witness what was going on with my finger. Several days passed by and I didn't have very good coordination, but the more I tried to feed myself a popsicle and while trying to eat the popsicle, my right hand was all over the place and on my face, because I had no control of my right hand yet, but I kept on trying and the more I tried, I began making progress.

The next morning, they took me down to the eye doctor, and they used an instrument to push my left eye back into its correct position. After my head injury, the swelling went directly into my brain and the swelling was the reason why my left eye was pushed out of position. My vision was even better after they repositioned my eye. Often the nurse would walk me up and down the hallway. I used to hold my right arm in a bent position, and when I walked, I would drag my foot. That was how I was able to identify anyone that had a stroke. Although I was never informed that I had a stroke. It was never mentioned to me about my condition. I learned this many, many years later after getting a CAT scan, which revealed a stroke. When it was time to be discharged from the hospital for about three weeks later, I learned about the nervous system and how it worked in relationship to my body. Taking a hit on the left side of my head affected the right side of the body and vice versa. Because of the way that the nervous system is made up in the human body, the nerve in your brain is reversed. The left side of your brain controls the right side of your body. I made the basketball team, while I was in the hospital, but I wasn't in any shape to play. When I finally got home, the family had moved back into our house that caught on fire. We had a stationary exercise bike that I would use for hours every day, and that helped me to walk faster. But I really needed to work on the upper part of my body, which I did, but not as aggressively as I worked my legs.

My mother was very protective of me and she did not want me to play basketball again. I had to sneak out of our store to go to the Boys Club and try to play basketball again. I was right handed before the injury. It was a very long road learning how to shoot and dribble the basketball with my left hand, because my right hand was still very weak. I practiced by myself and learned how to play the game of basketball all over again. I wished that I would have had a coach or someone older helping me to get my basketball game back together, so I could get back to my aggressive attitude, and playing better than I did before I was injured. I was out of school for maybe three months, they wanted me to have a tutor during my days out of school. This would've been provided by the district government, but no I didn't take advantage of it. When I went back to school I was so behind that it was impossible for me to pass that 7th grade year. If only I would have taken advantage of the tutor that they offered me. (We live, we learn and most of the time we learn life lessons the hard way. I know I have sometimes throughout the course of my life). I still played basketball with my friends sometimes, but it was not the same. I could no longer play one hundred percent like before. They knew it and was happy.

While I was in the hospital one of my friends who was light a brother started a fight with the guy that hit me while at Ballou Senior High school. My sister Marcia witnessed the fight and she said that he was winning the fight, until he slipped and that's when the other guy was able to get some better punches in. But "my friend, my big brother" had a very big heart. Let me tell you a little bit about him. He was only about 5'5", if that tall, but he was everybody's big brother. He would be the first one there to help all of us out. You never had to ask for help, he was always there, like a protector over all of us and he was the shortest of all of us whether we were younger or older. It didn't matter how big that person was, he would find a way to bring that person down to the ground.

I did not know that that my good friend Bo got into a fight with that coward that struck me in the head with the bottle while they were in the high school cafeteria, but because he was my friend, he felt that he had to straighten everything out and he did that for all of us. He took it upon himself to look out for all of us that lived in the neighborhood. Bo would do anything to help anybody, he had a gigantic heart. He was the oldest of three children, he had a sister, and a younger brother. He used to work at the corner drugstore, on Mellon Street. We also had another good friend like a big brother that worked at the drugstore and I'm pretty sure that he was the one that got him the job working in the drugstore just like he did a couple of guys in high school. Gary was a huge father figure. He was a very cool guy. He would give me a film discount sometimes. In the eighties, cocaine came to the neighborhoods like a wild fire. Everybody was selling it, including myself. My brother/friend Bo, would help Marcia's boyfriend Kevin out sometimes with things around the barbershop and illegal favors. One day Kevin took him and me to see his mother who was in the hospital at Capitol Hill

Hospital. She was a very large lady and very sick. About one week after we visited, his mother died in the hospital. Of course, he was devastated! I offered him my condolences because I knew that to lose a mother meant to lose a part of yourself. Now! He was the head of the household, then he started selling and using drugs about two years later. I really felt sorry for him, but he seemed to be handling the situation okay.

It wasn't that long ago after he lost his mother, that he also lost his job working at the drugstore. He therefore began hanging in the streets and getting high. A person that helped so many people and in his times of need, nobody really was there for him like they should have been. I was limited to what I could do for him. But if he ever asked for something if I had it, he had it too. I have a lot of respect for my brother and even my sisters will let him stay over sometimes at night when he was out there in the street. His caring for other people was never reciprocated. Most people used him for what they wanted. The last time I saw him alive was when my friends and I were sitting in my car on Mellon Street. His clothes were very dirty, and he had a bad smell from his shirt. That day we drank beer together and I gave him $5 or $10 dollars. We parted, and I told him to be strong! I guarantee you that everybody that he helped when he was doing good and he had a lot of money a lot of times, didn't try to help him when he needed help. Anytime I saw him I would talk with him to see what was happening in his life. I would buy him some food or give him a few dollars if I had it to spare. Three days later I got a call and I was told that someone shot and killed my friend. He was found right behind the drugstore where he worked for many years. This was in 1988. He would always call me when someone else was killed. I kept saying to myself that I just saw him the other day. I was truly saddened and hurt emotionally to hear about his death. Before he died, he would sometimes go over both of my sisters' houses, and they would feed him food, and let him clean himself up. They both liked him like a brother. MAY HE REST IN PEACE ETERNALLY, NO MORE WORDS, AND NO MORE DISAPPOINTMENTS, JOB WELL DONE, MY BROTHER, JOB WELL DONE!

I pray to God that whoever killed him pays for the crime.
It had to be someone he knew because of where his body was found.

FIRE DESTROYED ALMOST EVERYTHING WE HAD
WE MOVED INTO A HOUSE

Earlier that same year tragedy would happen, we had purchased a new house. We moved from Park Chester apartments and moved into our first house located on Alabama Ave. SE Washington, DC. This was only five minutes away from the family business and only 10 minutes from where we used to live. My father and one of his friends helped us to put panel on the walls and we worked really hard to make the new place look even better with the new paneling on the walls. We put carpet all throughout the living room and the dining room, on the stairs, and all of the bedrooms. In the basement, we had an artificial fireplace that we plugged into the wall. In the basement we had a full bathroom with a shower, but after the fire, for some odd reason they didn't replace it. We had a built-in radio in the wall of the basement wash room, carpet on the floor, a brand new washer and dryer and a brand new stereo. All of these items were destroyed in the fire. The company that was supposed to fix the house did a very shady job and did not put the correct wiring throughout the house. They put a lower gauge wire which became very weak and hazardous.

We moved into our new house before I was paralyzed. After moving most of our stuff from the old apartment, one night the gas furnace exploded, and that is what caused the fire throughout the house. Our house was burned really bad. The basement completely burned down and everything that we purchased new for the basement was destroyed. The kitchen area was burned and the living room and dining room areas. Every plastic item melted from the intense heat. I was asleep when the fire started. I remember going to sleep on the top bunk beds. When I woke up I still did not know what was going on. I turned on my bedroom light switch, and I started walking out of my room into the hallway rubbing my eyes, because the smoke was burning them. I started to turn around to walk back into my bedroom. I don't know why I wanted to go back into the bedroom, but while I was walking in that direction, thank God I ran into my father. He grabbed me and both of us slid down the stairway. I was still dazed and while he was opening up the front door, I was still laying on the stairs trying to figure out what was really going on. I woke up and still couldn't figure out that our house was actually on fire. He picked me up and brought me outside. My adopted sister and Marcia came out later. My mother was still on the telephone with the fire department trying to give them the direction to our location. She finally came out of the house safely, Praise the Lord Jesus Christ and our Heavenly Father that all of us got out of the house safety!

We watched our house from the side of the street burn up, the flames from the basement was ready bad, it was like watching an inferno. We were only living in the house for maybe two weeks, when disaster came. We had to move back into our old apartment in Park Chester, while the insurance company renovated the house. It was a good thing that we moved out of our old apartment during the middle of the month. Because, we had not notified the rental office about our moving. I was injured several months after the fire took place in our brand-new house. It really didn't take the repair men a long time to renovate the house, maybe about six months. I believe that was one of the reasons why it did not take so long to renovate the house from the fire damage was because they cheated us and did some shady renovation work. They didn't do a lot of things they were supposed to have done during the renovation. If my memory serves me right, my family was moving back into our new house while I was in the hospital after I got hit in the head with a bottle that caused partial paralysis. GOD worked everything out in my family's FAVOR! THANK YOU JESUS! THANK YOU FATHER GOD! THANK YOU HOLY SPIRIT!

"I spoke earlier about how my father and I went through a lot of things physically and also life-threatening, more than our other family members had to go through. Now this was my season of dealing with life-threatening, and physical challenges as I explained further on about my battles. Well, the battle is not mine in all reality, the Lord was fighting them, for my father, my mother and myself and these are just a few of the things that God brought us all through. God protected me through the paralysis, family house fire and close calls."

ANOTHER CLOSE CALL

I had another close call during the July 4 holiday season. To the right of our store was the front door of the upstairs apartments. A guy named Bryson decided to stick an M-80 inside the mail slot of the door. I shouldn't have let him do that because it was a few elderly ladies living upstairs, but I didn't stop him. We waited for a few minutes for the explosive to go off, but it took a long time to explode. Well, me being the smart guy, I looked under the crack of the bottom of the door, and as soon as I put my face down there, the dynamite exploded in my eyes, "BAM!" My left eye had a lot of fragments inside of it and a piece of something hard hit me right in the left corner of the outside, inner corner of my eye. My ears were ringing, blood was shooting out of the corner of my eye, and all I could say was; "M-80-M-80-M-80!" My parents rushed me again to Hadley's Memorial Hospital instead of waiting for the ambulance to come and take me to the hospital. Because of the explosion and all of the debris the doctors had to flush my eyes and stop the bleeding. The bleeding was caused by some kind of sharp debris from the concrete on the ground. It cut me right in the corner of my eye and the blood was pouring out like a squirt gun. It could have been worse! It could have caused blindness.

An M-80 is a small piece of dynamite that is illegal, but a lot of people get their hands on them and they can be very deadly. This is normally around the 4th of July holiday when these types of explosives are available for sale. Again, it is illegal! They pack a very powerful punch when they explode. There is about an inch and a half small fuse that you light shaped like a metal pipe. But instead of metal it is made of cardboard material with plastic that holds explosives inside. These things are dangerous and can kill you or bring bodily harm when used improperly. As I mentioned, I never should have allowed him to light that device and stick it inside of the mail slot. It could have seriously brought harm to other people that were upstairs in the building. I got exactly what I deserved for allowing this to happen. God spared me of my vision. I can't blame anyone but myself for my involvement. Again, I can't even blame the devil for something that I did. After I was released from the hospital I was instructed to keep a patch over my eye for two weeks. I was definitely accident prone, but in all actuality, this was simply a bad decision on both parts.

CHAPTER 7

MY HIGH SCHOOL YEARS & MY PHOTOGRAPHY BUSINESS

My first three years at Ballou was pretty exciting. I had my own car. I met a lot of girls and I had a couple of girlfriends. I was known as the camera man and I had one special spot where I used to take the majority of my pictures at. It was right near the cafeteria door and by the side door where most of the students came out for lunch near a tree. They had to see me before they left the cafeteria. I would have the people lined up waiting to have their pictures taken. I charged $2 for one picture, and $1 for a duplicate, and $2 for the frame. I was guaranteed to make $5 to $7 off of each person. I would tell my customers to give me a $1 deposit before I took their pictures. I would normally have their pictures ready within two days. I sold most of my pictures in the boy's bathroom, or as I walked to class, but mostly at lunch time. I've taken thousands of pictures over the years as a student at Ballou. I would average about $30 to $50 daily, sometimes more, and I would only be at the tree taking pictures for about 20 minutes. After I was finished taking pictures during the lunch break at Ballou, I would drive across town to go to the Penn Center, where I took my photography classes. I was one of the top students in my photography class and anytime that my instructor needed a student to go somewhere outside of the school to take pictures she would call on me.

I started this business at a young age, during my last year in Junior High School. I was self-sufficient in a lot of ways. I didn't have to worry my parents about a lot of things. I was able to purchase things for myself. I can't help that I came from a business background and environment. My last name is Chapman and we definitely were known as entrepreneurs. So, being a businessman at a young age was part of my DNA and history of the Chapman family. One day my photographer instructor saw one of my friends looking at some of the pictures that I sold at Ballou. She was mad at me for selling pictures. Sometimes she would occasionally get one of the other students to go with her to certain events that she sponsored. She would take photos or flicks of people and sell them their pictures. I can understand why she was mad at me because I was taking pictures and getting paid. Unfortunately, I couldn't afford a Polaroid camera at the time, but I still made it work with my 35mm camera. One of the biggest differences is that I had a middleman which was a processing company that developed my photos and film. It was the same thing that she was doing, but she had a Polaroid camera connection and a background, and all I had was my 35mm camera and a natural background outside the school cafeteria. Why would you get mad at me for learning how to do something? It seemed as if she wasn't impressed that I was able to work the same job, almost the same skills as she had. But, I didn't have a Polaroid professional camera like she had, but I still got the job done. She didn't have to question me about what I was doing, I was just trying to make some money for myself. I was able to do it on a professional level, just as she was doing. I didn't have the background. My background was a natural, outside background. I didn't have the instant photo on the spot that she had. I learned my commercial photography skills from the best instructor in town. She was one of the best photographers out there and I can't help that a lot of her professionalism naturally rubbed off on me. I respected and admired my instructor. I did all of my class work, but also was successful in this side business. It never affected my classwork. It was just a matter of time that I would get a Polaroid camera just like she had. She was also mad at me because I did not take either one of the two job offers that she had prepared for me. I was truly appreciative of her finding these jobs for me, but I was also running my family's business, even before I started attending the commercial photography classes at the Penn center. I tried to explain that I had to help my parents with their business. She said to me; *"What if one day, suppose your parents don't have that business anymore, what are you going to do then?"*

That statement later came true, but it was too late for me. It seemed like any pictures that I took during my last year at the Penn Center, wasn't good enough. She called me one night at my parents' business and told me that I was going to be getting a photography award from Miss America. I thought that she was playing, but she was telling the truth. The next day, one of my classmates went with me to the hotel (in DC) where they were holding the awards banquet. I wish that I had a nice dress suit to wear, but I just went casually dressed. Three other students were awarded certificates for their outstanding performance in their class. One was for drama, graphics design, art, and mine was for (Commercial) photography. I did not have a family member there to represent me at all, so I represented myself. NASA, Smithsonian Institute Museum, and other organizations were sponsoring these awards to open up Black History Month. Vanessa Williams, the first African American woman to become Miss America was present at the ceremony. She was very beautiful and reminded me of my father's youngest sister, Aunt Dorothy. They really looked a like. I asked my friend to take some pictures of both of us with my camera, so I could have some pictures to show my family members. When we developed the roll of film, he had taken about 95 percent of the pictures of her. I don't know if he did this intentionally, out of jealousy, or maybe he just was caught up in the moment. One of my female classmates took some color pictures of Vanessa giving me my certificate. I did not know until later that Vanessa and I had made the front page of the school's newspaper (One of the students from our photo journalist class took the picture of Vanessa and I). Within the same year a porno magazine exposed pornographic pictures of Vanessa Williams and as a result her crown was taken away from her. I refused to support the magazine that humiliated Vanessa. Despite the exposure, she still came out a winner in my eyes. Vanessa Williams has aged over the years, yet she is even more beautiful. Anytime one of my family members would see something pertaining to Vanessa Williams, they would tell me about it, as if I really knew her like that. I wish I did really get to know her as a friend, but that was wishful thinking.

After receiving that VERY prestigious award from Ms. Vanessa, I felt that I had made history and I began to really think way ahead of time. I thought that one day I would have a daughter and she would recognize her father's achievements. I would also show her the picture of Miss American, Vanessa Williams presenting me with the award, and I hoped that I would motivate her. Maybe even my daughter would also be interested in some kind of beauty pageant, especially the Miss America pageant. I was thankful and honored that my instructor put me in that position to receive a Commercial Photography Award, representing my class, and the Lemual Penn Career Development Center. This was a very big honor and I THANK GOD for being in a position to receive this award, along with the three other DC public school recipients. I never knew that she thought that much of me that she would allow me to represent the entire class. That in itself was an honor and a privilege. I apologized if I disappointed her in any way over the years and I pray that she knew that I really appreciated her and the principal of the Lemual Penn Career Development Center. He also gave me high honors and in return, I gave as much respect as possible and appreciation that he himself thought very highly of me.

* * *

MY MODELS

My nieces and nephews were my models. I took a lot of pictures of both of them when they were younger. I didn't see my oldest nephew that much, as much as I would like to have seen my oldest nephew, but there was not a lot of communication between the mother and my brother. My niece was something else, she was a little grown woman when she was two years old. She would be all over the store and sometimes outside of the store. She loved eating bubble gum, and I remember how she used to try and take a package of gum when we had our store. She would face me but she would slip her hands behind her back and grab a pack of bubble gum and run away while putting the bubble gum in her mouth, because she knew that I was going to take it from her. She would put the paper and the bubble gum in her mouth at the same time. She was a very sneaky little girl, but she was my baby and she still is my baby. She thought the penny bubble gum machine in the store belonged to her. Anytime other kids would try to get something from the machine, she would be right there looking at them. One time she bit a little kid after she bought some bubble gum from the machine. I don't know why she did that, it totally caught all of us off guard.

After my sisters moved to a neighborhood called Congress Park, I would ride my bicycle around the area, checking up on my nieces and nephews and my sisters. When the ice cream truck would be in the neighborhood I would get them whatever they wanted. They always had their little friends around them and I would have to get them something also. I didn't mind and was thankful that I had some money to even be able to purchase whatever they wanted from the ice cream truck. My nephew in particular would always run around the neighborhood with his friends. I used to take a lot of pictures of them when they were younger. I spent a lot of time with the two of them, more than I did with any of my other nephews and nieces. I was their uncle, but I also tried to play the role as a father to all of my nephews and nieces.

When I had my photography studio in 1988, I enrolled the two of them into karate class. The classes were held at the Boys Club. They went for a few months, but I couldn't get any help from my sisters to take them and pick them up after karate classes were over. I would have to get someone that was in my studio to go and get them from the Boys Club. After they would get to the studio, I would let someone take them to McDonald's. I did this as long as I could, but it was hard to try to run the studio and make sure that they were able to get back home safely, again I had no support from their mothers. Eventually they had to quit taking karate because I did not have anybody to take them to class. But I thank God that I tried. I tried my best to expose them to karate classes just like my sisters and I were until I quit taking karate and started playing basketball. I always really wondered what would have happened if I had stayed in karate. Both of my sisters were one step away from being black belts.

* * *

HARD KNOCK LIFE

I remember a few months before school was letting out for the summer time, a friend of mine named Ticker whom I've known since we were 12 and played basketball together at the Boys Club, became one who I would occasionally hang out with. Ticker went to McKinley Tech, near the Penn Center. I unfortunately had to repeat my 12th grade year at Ballou because I had so much freedom and I abused it. I was taking as many lunch breaks as I wanted. I would just jump into my car and leave. I had unnecessary attention and trouble coming for me. That summer I went to Anacostia High School to attend summer school so that I could graduate during that summer. I started getting lazy and decided to wait until the fall school season to complete those courses because I only had three classes.

One night we were having a rough time in our store and I met our church's Reverend and I asked him to pray for my family. Later he told me that he was having his church renovated and I really needed some money, so I started working in the church as an assistant to two guys that were doing the renovation. I enjoyed working there because that meant that I wouldn't have to be in our family store with the embarrassment. I worked with them until they finished the renovation of the church. That was my summer job and it was truly a good learning experience. I learned a lot about different projects like how we build the pulpit, how we built two bathrooms starting with the framework, they had already done the plumbing work, which meant that they had to break up the hard-concrete floor and then put the drainage and plumbing in the ground. We put the sink in first and hooked the drainage. We fixed up the kitchen in the back area and touchup painting that needed to be done. These guys were very good and if I knew what I know now, I would've continued working with them when they finished renovating the church.

I also learned that these same guys were in the Anacostia area that protested against us getting our beer and wine license. Guess who the biggest person that was against my family? The Reverend, the same person that I was working for in his church doing renovations. If he wasn't so much against us getting our license, we might have received our letter and license to sell beer and wine sooner. We eventually received our license and kept it for a few weeks, but all of a sudden it was taken away from us just as quick as we got it. It was taken away which was a real disappointment, after all the expectations and excitement to be relocated in a really nice area right by the bus stop. I think we could have developed a very nice business in that location. Initially I was very angry at those people. The other proprietors, most of them were black business owners in the Anacostia area, and they had a business organization for business owners in the area that would get together at least on a monthly basis and talk about things. This was lacking while we were in Congress Heights as black proprietors and family business owners, which allowed the Koreans and Asians to get their beer and wine license and gradually they started buying everything up in the community. Now they own everything, but if we had some kind of business organization, we possibly could have denied them receiving their beer and wine license. Many of the black business owners in our area did not want anybody else selling the same things that they were selling. I learned to respect that in their business minded approach.

My mother tried another adventure, she loved cooking, so we decided to start a carryout business. My mom's cooking was homemade style, it wasn't regular fast food and everyone enjoyed it. That wasn't my forte, but it was my mother's desire. Although my family was very successful with businesses, this one just wasn't working out and I had to make the decision to break the news to my father. I told my dad that I really could no longer work at the store because I had to focus on trying to pass two classes; one at Ballou so that I could get my high school diploma. I truly apologized to him, but I had to focus on passing these class. I know that my father was disappointed. I was disappointed and occasionally I was still trying to come down to the store to be supportive, but it just wasn't happening. This was the first time out of all the years that I was in school that I was able to truly focus and do my homework. I was running my photography business a lot more than ever because we needed the money. I was able to make some money to help my parents with purchasing food, other much-needed items and necessities. We really hit rock-bottom and I was so thankful that we were able to sell the business after several months of trying.

* * *

THE CONSPIRACY

I was out of school for a few weeks until I decided that if I didn't finish school this year, I would probably not finish at all. How could I tell my future children to finish High School if I didn't finish myself? I stopped seeing the young lady that I was staying with and I started trying to help my parents. One day while my mother and I were in the basement, I heard on the radio that some students at Ballou Senior High School were arrested for selling drugs at the school and more arrests were expected. After hearing that, I told my mother; *"mom I guarantee you that they will try to include my name in that mess."*

At this time, I was still attending Ballou, and I had just started going back on a regular basis three weeks prior to these illegal allegations came about. So, I was avoiding the principal at that time because of my attendance. As I was walking to my third period class, she called my name. I said to myself, now I'm in trouble, and she is going to kick me out of school. She said; "Jeffery, I have been looking for you." I replied, "I've been here." Then she said, "You know that your name has come up involving you selling drugs at the school?" I immediately told her that it was a lie. "What are you going to do about this?" The principal inquired. I told her that I wasn't going to do anything, because they were lying. Her response was for me to have a nice day, but she left the door open so that I could come to her regarding this issue. I was relieved that she wasn't kicking me out of school.   Since I was not at school all day, I did not know that they were asking students about me until one of my best customer and friend told me that the news reporters asked him was I selling drugs at school. My friend told them emphatically "No, Jeff only sells pictures" and he showed the reporter several pictures that I had taken of him and sold to him. Everybody at the school knew about them accusing me, but no one would say anything about it to me, I was totally naive about this whole issue.

After talking to my principal and my friend, I seriously started thinking about how I could clear my name. If I was guilty, all I would simply have to do was stop selling drugs, but I was innocent, and I wasn't going to let anyone lie on me. Later on, that same night, after I talked with the principal, I was telling a friend of mine Jack that I wasn't going to talk to Channel 7 reporter, Mr. Berry. He was an investigative reporter and a voice for the people. Jack replied, "Man you are not going to talk to Mr. Berry! He won't have time to talk to you." That angered me to hear that my friend would not support me. I told him that I would catch up with him the following day. When I was in my homeroom class the following morning, everybody was talking about me being accused of selling drugs. I had heard enough, and I asked my teacher could I have a pass to speak with the principal. He granted it, and I went directly to the principal's office. I asked her if she could call Mr. Berry at Channel 7, so that I could clear my name from the drug dealing allegations that were made about me. She called Mr. Johnson from Channel 9 because he was investigating this case.

She spoke with him, and he said that he would be at Ballou around 1:00 p.m. The principal told Mr. Johnson about how long she had been knowing me and what kind of person I was. She also mentioned that she knew at least three guys that didn't like me and would say or do anything to hurt me. I thought of several people that could fit that category. I was truly surprised to hear her say this, even though she didn't give out any names. The interview took about one hour, and he asked me several different questions. I told Mr. Johnson about how I helped the DC School Superintendent at time who was running for a city council member seat. Over the summer, I volunteered to help him with his city council campaign. I explained to Mr. Johnson about how the previous principal accused me of selling drugs last year. They made it clear that I wasn't going to be coming back to Ballou. My brother and three of my sisters attended Ballou, so I wanted to keep the family tradition alive, I explained. The principal also explained to Mr. Johnson that the DC School Superintendent signed me into Ballou personally that year. My principal couldn't understand why he would get me back into the school, knowing that I was accused last year of being a drug dealer. Mr. Johnson said that he was going to interview him after he finished interviewing me. I had no idea that the person who falsely accused me of selling drugs with the same person I helped with their campaign over the summer. I said to myself; What would he gain for lying and making false allegations concerning me selling drugs? What was this all about? Mr. Johnson informed me that the accusation was that I was selling marijuana. I'm thinking to myself; "this is ridiculous." How could someone just make up something like that? When in all reality, his nephew was the one that the police needed to be investigating. But for some reason the blame was put on me. I know that he had a hidden agenda and maybe, because I did not roll away with him like the other guys did, he thought he could retaliate against me because I didn't do some things that he wanted me to do. I did not have a secret lifestyle like some of the other guys did. Not Me!

* * *

MONTHS BEFORE GRADUATION

We lost our second store around Christmas 1984, and I was finally able to concentrate on school by studying and reading. My attendance was great, I didn't miss five days from Christmas until graduation. I would do most of my studying in my bedroom until I finally got a larger one. I really wished I could have had this opportunity earlier to get more involved in school. I only had three classes during the morning time, but sometimes I would go to yearbook class after lunch, because I still received credit for it. I would take pictures of all of the events that took place during the school hours. I used my own money to have film processed. I would take the pictures at lunch time like usual, and sometimes I would go to the Penn Center. My instructor was still disappointed with me and I could understand her position. She went out of her way to get me these good jobs and I let her down, but not intentionally. After leaving the Penn Center, I would catch the bus from there, and transfer at the Navy Yard to catch another bus to the hospital where I still had to catch another bus out to Iverson Mall. This was where I would get my film developed. I would drop one roll off and put another roll in the shop. By that time the bus would be coming back towards the other direction home. I had it timed perfectly. When I returned to the bus stop, I could transfer to another bus, or just walk about five long blocks home. After I would get home, it was time to separate the new pictures and the frames, so that I would be prepared for school. I also had a finance sheet where I would count the pictures that I would take out to school that day and make a prediction on how much I would make that day. I also would count the money that I made the previous day. I had quite a system going on.

I had a studio in my parents' basement and I decided to take some pictures of the most attractive girls in the school. Then I would show them to hopefully gain some future customers. I never took advantage of these girls sexually, but the thought did enter my mind. One of the girls later ended up hating me because I didn't try to have sex with her, but if I knew that she wanted that, I wouldn't have disappointed her. I didn't want to have a reputation that all I wanted to do was manipulate the girls into coming over my house to have sex with them. I was being pressured from three different directions in my final year of High School. My father was pressuring me about getting a job, my principal was mad at me because I didn't take the jobs she offered, and at Ballou, I was constantly accused of doing something illegal. I used to ride my bicycle after I would do my homework and after separating pictures. I would ride to several different neighborhoods to sell and take more pictures of people. I had a backpack on me with all of my equipment, camera, flash and pictures, just waiting for business. I made a fair amount of money considering that my pictures weren't Polaroid. They were taken with a 35mm camera, and the photo was a 4X5 print. I initially had a problem with the way my frames looked, they were wooden frames. I had to do something different and I couldn't settle for average. I was very successful in some ways, thanks to God for guidance and strength to persevere. Even as I was under attack by so many different directions. The easiest thing in the world to do is to give up and I had to remind myself a lot of times; "WINNERS NEVER QUIT AND A QUITTER NEVER WINS!"

I've had a lot of practice on forgiving people that have tried to wrong me even cause me bodily harm. I learned at the young age of 12 to be able to have a forgiving spirit, that doesn't happen overnight. Believe me, I've had a lot of practice on learning how to forgive others. As my Lord and Savior Jesus Christ said while He was being crucified and dying on the cross; "FATHER, FORGIVE THEM FOR THEY KNOW NOT WHAT THEY DO."

* * *

GRADUATION DAY

The day of graduation arrived and I was so excited. My friend had one of his family members give me a ride to Constitutions Hall where the graduation was held. We had a very large class (399) students graduating that evening. I felt so relieved after my graduation ceremony was over. I told my parents that I would find a ride home! All of a sudden everybody was gone and fortunately I saw one of my schoolmates outside of his car. I asked for a ride home and he said no problem. I felt so good that night that I probably would have walked home. We went to a party that night, but we never went inside, don't ask me why. I was finally free of all of the pressure from those three areas. I then capitalized on photography.

My intention was to use my parent's basement as a full-time photography studio, if possible. Most of my clients would have been all females because I didn't want to deal with the jealous hearted and envious guys. I was willing to take a chance with all female clients and maybe if they had kids. I just didn't want to have to deal with the guys or even allow them to come into my parents' house. As my business progressed, I was going to pay my parents mortgage every month as rent, but also to give them a break for allowing me to use the basement as my full-time photography studio.

Maybe a few weeks after I graduated, I met my future wife and the future mother of our kids. I was at the Amoco gas station putting gas in my parents' car and I noticed a young lady that got out of a little red Toyota Corolla Tercel. She was wearing all white with a red belt around her waist and red shoes to match along with a red purse. When I went to pay for the gas, I said, "Hello, how you doing tonight?" She said, "Fine." I asked her what her name was, she said, "My Name Is Paula," and I asked her if she ever needed any photographs taken. I gave her my business card and she gladly accepted. (Which was my pickup line and my way of meeting beautiful young ladies) I smiled and as she got into the car, if I'm not mistaking I closed her car door and that was all the discussion that we had at that particular time. She drove away and I said to myself, she's not bad, she's not bad at all! And I left everything like that. She would be my future wife, but I had no idea at that particular time. Would I ever see her or hear from her again? If I'm not mistaking a couple of weeks later she called me, but I wasn't there to answer the telephone. She wasn't able to leave a message because my noisy brother answered the telephone that day when she called me. In all reality, she initiated the continuation of our conversation. Later on that day my brother told me that someone named Paula called me. I kept thinking to myself, "Who Is Paula?" I couldn't remember who was this young lady named Paula. I know that we had a cousin in South Carolina by that name, but that wasn't her. My brother would've known that was his cousin that he was talking to. He told me that he talked on the telephone with her for a little while. I asked him why he would talk to someone that called for me. He said that they just started talking about whatever. I said oh, okay! I'm still puzzled and trying to figure out again to myself, who was this young lady named that was calling me? Throughout the day, I passed out several business cards, so I honestly couldn't remember everyone's name. The curiosity got the best of me. My brother wrote down her telephone number, so I had to call to find out exactly who she was, and that's exactly what I did! I called her and we started talking and she reminded me that she was the young lady that I gave one of my photography business cards at the Amoco gas station. Everything came back to my memory, even the outfit that she wore on that particular day. She was very easy to talk to. We talked on the phone for a little while, until we set up a date to go to the movies and that was the beginning of everything. On our first date, we went to the movies although I can't even remember the name of movie that we went to see that night. I remembered a lot about her. Whenever we were together I made sure to make a good impression by purchasing an expensive wine called Asti Spumante. I made sure that she knew that I wasn't cheap.

CHAPTER 8

PHOTO MEMORIES

The thing that really inspired me to study photography took place a few years before my accident. I attended a funeral in New Jersey because uncle Victor passed away and I was supposed to take pictures. I had other uncles and aunts that were there, and some of my cousins that I hardly ever saw were present (They lived in New York and Philadelphia). After leaving the city of New Jersey I felt very empty and there was some history that I missed. The following week was my grandparents' 50th wedding anniversary, and it was held in South Carolina. I told myself that I would not ever miss another opportunity for documenting any other family event or gathering. So in reality I got into photography for the memories (I always made sure that when I photographed my parents, they were always together, because that's how I always wanted to remember them, together). After my grandparents' 50th Anniversary, all of my family members in South Carolina would see me coming with the camera and they would scatter. They would pretend like they didn't want their picture taken, but I would take it anyway. When they made the statement that a picture is worth a million dollars, it really is a true statement. Over the years I have lost a lot of my family members, but I will always have the memories of them in my heart, mind and in a picture.

When I graduated from junior high school and matriculated to high school in 1981, I attended different academic and vocational schools so that I could finally take commercial photography for my trade. I did not have to always catch the bus because I had my car. It wasn't until after we went bankrupt in my final year in High School, that I started catching the bus. I was in a car accident during my senior year on my way to the photography school, a taxi cab ran into the left side of my car, causing major damage. After my car was fixed, it was parked in our backyard of our house for a couple of months. I did not have the money to pay for the insurance on the car at that time. But because my family was doing pretty bad at that particular time and they really needed some finances, they had to file for bankruptcy, money was tight. I could remember one particular day, my father asked me if I could sell my beautiful, black 1979 Chrysler LeBaron with red interior. My very first car and without hesitation I said to my father; "No problem Pops, you can sell the car if you really need the money that bad". In all reality, I probably could have made the insurance payments, but ever since my parents gave me the car, I had so many problems by having the car, not a problem with the maintenance of the car. Some problems came just because of all of the envious and the jealous people that didn't want me to have such a nice car, including the police harassing me all the time. I just got tired of all of it and I did not want to have to deal with all the negativity and all of the problems that came with me having such a nice car, especially since I was so young. I didn't want to deal with it anymore. I believe that both my parents were surprised that I didn't give any negative feedback. I did miss driving my car, but sometimes you get tired of being sick and tired. So again, it was no problem for me to sell my car to help out my parents because this car was giving me so many problems. Although I enjoyed the attention that I got from all of the beautiful ladies when I had my car, but some things must come to an end.

I had a studio in my parents' basement and I started my first photography business. Having a studio was somewhat lucrative in some ways. I also had an apartment in the back part of the basement. I was thankful that my parents gave me free range to do almost anything that I wanted to do. The studio was okay but I really wanted to have a studio lighting system that my instructor had at the school, but I made do with what I had. In school they call it continuous lighting but what I wanted was studio lights that would not be on continuously, but it was a flash lighting system, which was the type of studio lighting that I was trained to use while taking the commercial photography classes.

I would take pictures of some of the most attractive and beautiful young ladies while I was still attending high school when I had my photography studio and I was praying that I could build up my clientele, so I could help my parents more financially.

My intention was to build a portfolio for future customers. I never took advantage of these beautiful young ladies sexually or in any other kind of way. One of the girls had a problem with me

139

because I didn't attempt to have sex with her. With all the beautiful ladies, the thought definitely crossed my mind, but I had to withhold my hormones and sexual thoughts of being sexually involved with any of these beautiful young ladies. The temptation was very strong and overwhelming at times.

I did not want to have a negative reputation or a negative name for being a photographer that was known for having sex with the ladies and using photography as an excuse. I couldn't take that chance of developing a bad name for myself. I didn't want the negative marketing while showing my brag book/small portfolio to potential clients. I developed a small portfolio book that I was aiming for in the beginning and most of the photos were the young ladies that I had taken pictures of in my studio. I tried my best to deal with females. Dealing with the guys was a whole different ballgame and most women liked having their photo taken and some of them would still try to flirt with me. In the back area of my parents' basement where a small bathroom was located, was where the young ladies would change into other outfits. One of the young ladies intentionally pushed open the door so that I could actually see her partially naked. I was coming to see how long she would be so that we could get done faster with her photo session and when I came into the room, I was a little taken back because I thought she was fully dressed. She intentionally wanted me to see her that way, and again the temptation, the temptation to restrain myself was very hard. I'm a young man, a teenager and sex is on my mind. I can't tell you how many times I had to deal with those sexual thoughts, each and every day. Sometimes it was overwhelming, but I maintained my professionalism throughout the photo sessions. I wasn't sexually involved with any of them. Some of the guys thought that these were my "girlfriends."

As a matter of fact, one of the young ladies that I photographed in my little portfolio was really mad at me because I did not try to make sexual moves towards her. This young lady insisted on changing into different outfits, a short red miniskirt and very tight jeans. I loved to see beautiful women with nice fitting jeans on. I can't think of the name right now of the jeans that was very famous at that time but a lot of women wore them during the eighties. It wasn't the one by Gloria Vanderbilt, now I can remember, they were called CHICK JEANS, they were nice and tight fitting and that was one of my weaknesses, a beautiful woman with tight fitting jeans. I'm a man and I thank God that I'm a man and I love beautiful women and being a photographer allowed me to be in the presence of so many BEAUTIFUL WOMEN.

While I would be showing other young ladies the pictures, sometimes the guys would want to look at them and I had no problem with that, but the first thing that the guys would ask me was "Jeff did you hit that?" Meaning, did I have sex with them? I would respond quickly, "Man this is business," but I had a lot of "wannabe" Jeffery D. Chapman's photographers out there that wanted to take pictures and be like me. Thank God that I was a cut above the rest and knowing that I went to school for this made a lot of difference because this was my professional career.

Unfortunately, they all had a hidden agenda. The majority of the male photographers at that time wanted to have sex with women and I know that a lot of photographers today are still doing that. But, I was a cut above the rest. However, I have to be honest with you all and myself, when I had my business cards I would always pass them out to beautiful women, while in high school and after I graduated from school and yes, I would have loved to have a sexual relationship with some of the ladies. That was what I did when I met my future wife was give her one of my business cards and the rest as they say, is history.

* * *

PREPARATION

My father began pressuring me about bringing some money into the house, so I could help pay some bills. At that time, because I didn't take the job offers that my instructor offered me, when I decided to take her up on them, they were no longer available. I could still hear her voice saying; "What are you going to do when your parents no longer have their business?" NOW, I could really use one of those jobs that she had before, but they were not on the table anymore doing that extra year that I had to attend high school.

I never bothered to ask her about the availability of those jobs afterwards. I needed one very bad. There are several things that once presented or spoken, YOU can never get them back.

141

WORDS-once a word is spoken, go out of your mouth, it is impossible to retrieve the word or words because the damage has already been done!

OPPORTUNITIES-the opportunities that she had for me with those jobs two years prior to my family losing our family business, those opportunities were no longer available, doors were closed.

TIME-we have to seize every moment and utilize all the time that God gives us each and every day. I mean every second, every minute, every hour, and finally every day we have to seize the moment and squeeze every bit of life from the time that God gives us. You can never get time back once it is gone. An example is that even a clock that is hung on the wall is correct twice a day, even though it does not have batteries in it or is not plugged into any electric outlet. That time will catch up with the time on the clock and eventually go pass the time that is showing on the clock. The time would come back around every 12 hours later, and that same time will come back around again.

I was constantly being accused of doing something illegal in high school almost every year when they saw clearly that I was getting money from my customers that were paying for photographs. All of the years that I attended Frank W. Ballou Senior High School, with the exception of my first year there, I was accused of selling drugs. I was harassed by the principal and by the Metropolitan Police Department. I really believed that it all started when I started driving my car. There were plenty of students that were selling drugs, and they stood out from the crowd by the way that they dressed and all of the expensive gold jewelry. My car wasn't a sports car, it was a four-door family car. I dressed very nicely because I liked to represent myself well. I didn't have the very expensive clothing or jewelry which was a sign of a drug dealer. The police would follow me. I caught them one day taking pictures of my car and I know that I was under investigation for about three years without any arrests. I thank God for helping me make it through that year and gradually all of that pressure that I had on my shoulders was diminished, so I thought.

As the days went by my father and brother decided that I needed a real job immediately. We were eating dinner one night and they both were talking about something and eventually about me. I was explaining to my father about everything that I did during the last five years of my young life, while trying to be respectful, and obedient to my parents. That's when I asked my father, "What about the time that I put in over the years?" His response was, "That was in the past, I need some help now!" They had some nerve, especially all that I did for my father. I even stopped several of my family members and employees from stealing the money from the cash register. After hearing my father say these words out of his mouth, that's the kind of appreciation I got from him and my parents didn't owe me anything. I did all of these things because they needed to be done. Again, I did these things because I love my family. I have the upmost respect for both my parents. I made a lot of sacrifices over the years for the family, even turning down three jobs that probably would have afforded me the opportunity to help our family more during the years that we didn't have the family business. But, because we did have the business I was designated and appointed to be the overseer and responsible for everyone doing their part. For my father to say these things, knowing that I was trying to get my high school diploma, despite everything else that I was trying to do to help my family, was very painful to hear. He was so focused on making money! I was trying my best to make some money taking photographs so that I could contribute something and most of the time I would give the money to my mother and she knew that I was giving her $30 or $40 almost every day. But we never gave my dad any of the money because he would have played the lottery with it. Sadly, he had an addiction with gambling and he used the money from the family business any way that he wanted to use it. That showed me my father and brother's true colors. I was really disappointed and hurt deep down inside of my heart, knowing that I had sacrificed my photography career, and a job that was offered to me while I was in the 11th grade to learn how to use computers. I never held it against either one of them over the years, but it really opened up my eyes a lot, and my thinking changed tremendously. I truly thank God for a forgiving heart, and even after I had been emotionally slapped in my face. Perhaps this type of emotional disrespect was preparing me for the future emotional pain that I would experience.

* * *

DEVELOPING

I couldn't wait to get out of that house. I planned on using my parent's basement as a studio and I would pay them rent for the use of the space. I had it all figured out. I was going to use the back door of the basement for the entrance of my photography studio. There was a walkway from the front of the house and down the side of the house that led to the basement stairs. My second option was to join the Metropolitan Police Department as a Criminologist or as a Forensic and I could have put on hold being a photographer and then finally to become a Radiologist.

I had a lot of plans for my future. I even thought about going into Job Corps, but I met Paula and she was the last person that I photographed in the studio. I was going to try to find out what kind of courses they offered which was located in Junior Village. I believe it was near the police Academy. But I never got a chance to explore that option. NO REGRETS! NO REGRETS! Meeting Paula was a true blessing to me and we were blessed to have two children from the marriage.

"No one plans to be a failure, they just failed to make plans"

CHAPTER 9

LOVE OF MY LIFE

Genesis 1:23 And Adam said; "This is now bone of my bones, and flesh of my flesh; She shall be called Woman, because she was taken out of Man."

I met Paula in 1985, at a gasoline station on the avenue, south side of DC She was purchasing a pack of cigarettes, and I was paying for some gas. I still can remember that day like it was yesterday. She had an aroma that was brand new. She wore a white blouse, matched with white pants, accented with a red belt, red shoes and a red purse. I gave her one of my business cards that indicated that I was a photographer, and I asked if she ever considered modeling, that was always my pickup line and it worked most of the time.

We started dating and I would tell some of my family members that she was going to be my future wife. I felt so comfortable with being with her. It just felt good! I know she must have been thinking that this guy is tripping, because I just met him, and he is telling everybody that I am going to be his wife. When I met Paula, I had just sold my car, a Chrysler Labaron 1989 and my family had just filed for bankruptcy and they needed the money that I received from selling my car. I had no problems with them doing what had to be done, and I thank God for me not being selfish. In August of 1985, my family had a reunion in South Carolina, but again we did not have the financing prior to filing for bankruptcy. I prayed to God that we would be able to attend this reunion because it would be my first time bringing a girlfriend to South Carolina. Prior to all of the following visits and reunions, my siblings were always able to bring their friends with them, now it was my turn. I borrowed some money from a friend of mine. We rented a 15-passenger van, and everybody was able to attend the reunion, thanks to God. Three months after Paula and I were together she got pregnant with our first child. When she told me about the pregnancy, I was very happy, because I always wanted my own children, even though I had some nephews and nieces that were like my own children. She probably was surprised that I handled the news the way that I did, knowing that we were only together for three months. When we met I did not have a regular job because I was a freelance photographer. That wasn't making a lot of money, but she still excepted me and that was a blessing. I believe that both of us were a blessing to each other in many ways.

* * *

PICTURES OF MY FIRST BORN

I must have taken several hundred pictures of my baby girl throughout her childhood. I was always taking pictures of her doing whatever she was doing. Rolls and rolls of film only of her. Every time we had a family gathering on either side, I made sure that my baby had her picture taken with her grandparents, uncles, aunts any other family members that were there. It's always true that you take a lot of pictures of your first-born child, more than you do any other children that you have later in life, it's just a known fact. My daughter as a baby saw more flashes in her little years as a toddler, than most of my nephews and nieces. Before she was born, I had to put together a couple of special events for her mother pertaining to her birth. Taking pictures was natural for me. I also had a lot of pictures taken of her mother. The excitement of being a father and also very thankful and blessed for my baby's mother. Again, between the both of them, I took a lot of photographs. Not to mention my other family members that I had taken a lot of photographs of them as well. Taking pictures of my parents was also a must! I had to always try to get pictures of my parents together. I took a lot of candid shots because I wanted the memories. I loved the photo memories of my loved ones.

* * *

BABY SHOWER

I sponsored Paula's baby shower because it didn't seem like none of her friends or family members were going to give her one. So, I took it upon myself to handle the business of making sure that she had a very nice shower. I was reminded of many years ago when my sisters had their baby showers in my parents' basement and they all were very nice. A lot of people attended their baby showers. I wanted to make sure that Paula had a very nice baby shower, with our first child, again I was not getting any kind of feedback from either one of her sisters or friends concerning them putting together a baby shower for her. I couldn't allow this to happen, so I had to make sure that she would have a nice shower. I know that it seemed very odd for the father of the baby to plan the shower, but I was that kind of guy. I was different from everyone else in many ways. I continued to have a flashback of the successful showers my sisters had. I asked her sister Adrien to contact her friends and other family members and let them know that we were having her baby shower at my parents' house. I believe that she had the baby two weeks later.

I tried to remember how my sister Marcia had her baby shower setup for my nephew. We used the large sinks in the basement and filled them with ice and beer and soda. Quite a few people came to the shower and I felt good about the outcome. It was very unusual for the expected father to sponsor the baby shower, but I'm just an unusual kind of guy. I wanted nothing but the best for Paula and my family.

I was growing and learning a lot about life and being a father. I had some previous experience of being an uncle/father figure to my nephew who was the oldest grandson and my niece who is the oldest granddaughter. My other nephews were born three months before my daughter was born. But it was nothing like having your own child. Now I was somebody's father. Paula received quite a few gifts from her friends and family at her shower. I genuinely think that everybody felt good about the both of us. I made sure that I did the belly rubbing thing with her and I tried to make her feel beautiful. I was always told that when women are pregnant they feel less attractive, but Paula didn't have to worry about that, I made sure she felt beautiful, at least I tried my best!

* * *

FINALLY, I WENT BACK TO WORK!

I finally went back to work after being off for several days. I almost forgot that I had a job because of the celebration of my beautiful baby girl. When I returned to work, I told everybody about my beautiful daughter. Some of them may have been sick of me talking about her, but that didn't stop me. I had to get adjusted to working on the night shift, because as I mentioned before, Paula was in labor with our daughter on my first night working the night shift.

I went back to ward 2-C where I established myself with the residents. For the most part, they were sleep during my shift, and I really had it made working nights. My first encounter working with a person with AIDS was on that unit. He was in isolation, because it was an "all-male" facility, and if he was to have any sexual relationships with the other residents, it would cause a serious epidemic there in that small unit.

My assignment seemed to always be in the isolated area with that resident. I would speak to him if I noticed that he was awake when I came to his area. Sometimes we would hold a general conversation, most of my conversation was about my daughter. He seemed to enjoy talking with me and I tried to respect him as much as possible, even though I wasn't quite educated about the AIDS disease during that time. One gentleman died three years prior to me working there and the whole world was very ignorant to this disease. Every morning I had to take his vital signs. I would use my protective gloves, but I tried not to make him feel like he was contagious, and I think that he appreciated the way that I treated him.

After I would get off from work, my first priority was to take a shower and put my dirty clothes somewhere away from my daughter. She was about one month old and when I would come in from work during the morning time she would lift up her little head, and look in my direction, as if she was saying; "Okay dad, you're home, I'm going back to sleep." And that's what she would do every morning. That made my day! They always say that a baby recognizes their parents' scent and smell and that was confirmation enough for me. She would never cry or stay awake, just give me a little smile and go right back to sleep. I used to tell everybody including Paula about this phenomenon concerning our daughter every morning. One morning I took a picture of her with her head up in the air looking at me with a smile on her face. I don't understand why some men don't appreciate their kids or take care of their responsibility. Just to get that little smile and to see her looking at me was worth me working 100 jobs seven days a week, priceless! How could that not make any man or woman feel special to get a response like that every morning? The older she got, I think the more she resembled me. Paula would get offended when people would ask if our daughter was her baby.

148

She would quickly answer; "Yes, she is my daughter." There was no resemblance at all, at least in my eye sight. My daughter would attract attention anywhere we would take her because she was so attractive. She had the prettiest curly hair. It looked like she had a jerry curl.

CHAPTER 10

STRUGGLES OF LIFE WHEN OPPORTUNITY KNOCKS

One day Paula and I went away for the weekend. When we returned to our apartment, she had to go to the bathroom, remember she was only a few months pregnant. The bathroom ceiling had fallen completely down to the floor. We reported that on a Monday and they sent a maintenance crew to clean it up. We refused to live in those kinds of conditions, especially since she was pregnant. We refused to pay our rent until they gave us another apartment which eventually they did, after a week. I explained that it was unsanitary to use the bathroom in a bucket while she was pregnant. As a result, they gave us another apartment on the third floor, but I made sure that both of our names were on the lease. I learned that part of the game from my brother Chap and his girlfriend Mary.

Everything was working out just fine. I would drop Paula off in the morning to work and I had enough time to pick her up and make it to work. I was making money from three sources by now; my job, taking pictures and selling drugs. I stopped buying drugs from one of my other dealers and I began doing business with my supervisor because he was a large drug dealer. He knew all about my family, and the store that we used to own because he hung out at the night club next door. He was giving me a better deal than the rest. I was purchasing it raw, the cocaine was not cut, yet I could cut it with a Vitamin B, a white powder supplement, and it tripled my money. I think the Vitamin B supplement was used a lot to cut the powder cocaine and when you went to the GMC store they wanted you to sign a receipt, but I had a different name. Every time I would purchase something from them, I guess in some ways they knew that people were using this Vitamin B supplement just to cut the powder cocaine back in the day.

Everything was working pretty fast. After all these years and not really having a serious relationship that I really wanted, but I thought all the time that most of the females were dating me because of the status of my family, not to look down on myself but most of the time it was some kind of hidden agenda on their behalf, so I had to be cautious. Again, I'm not trying to sound like I'm conceded or anything like that, I just didn't think I was a bad looking guy at all. After watching my siblings' relationships over the years, I had to use caution when I dealt with the girls, and for the most part most of my relationships were very short. They knew the type of business schedule I had and that made it hard to get involved with the long-term relationships. I wasn't able to be committed or even spend the time that I wanted to with the young lady. I had never went this far in a relationship before and knowing for the first time ever in my life that I was a father, that changed everything.

When I started hustling and dealing with this guy who also knew all about me and my family, this guy was from a different country, so how could he know about my family and I? He mentioned everything about where we lived and the family business. The Avenue was where he knew about my family. My supervisor and I became really good friends over the course of that one year working at St. Elizabeth's hospital as a psychiatric assistant. He had a much higher position and was a very cool guy. The more I got to know him, the better friends we became. He also was a very good cook, very good! This is where I learned about Caribbean foods, because he used to cook the black rice or curry chicken. I think every now and then oxtails, but whatever he would cook, everything tasted very good. I also learned about plantains and a few other Caribbean dishes. If he didn't call me, I would call him. He would let me know what kind of food he had. Before he could hang up the telephone, I was already knocking on the door. I know that I'm exaggerating, but the brother could cook very good!

I used to get the products from my connection, an old friend of mine and then he started acting shady. But before that I used to be able to borrow his scale, and I would be right there in his apartment, so it wasn't like I was asking to take his scale out of the apartment. A lot of times I would call him and tell him that I needed to borrow his scale, just for about 30 minutes or an hour. If he was not there, because I knew him very well and we worked together, he would say yes sometimes. Everything was all good, again, until he noticed that I was doing my own thing. We were not in competition or at least I wasn't in any kind of competition with him, after all, we grew up like brothers. I was the oldest and he was about one year younger than

151

me. I always considered him as my little brother until he started climbing the ladder and started selling heroin, and that's a whole different level. Now you had to put your name on a product and then put it out there. The people liked what you had, they would ask for it by name. For example, if it was called, "Red Jacket" and the people/junkies liked your product, they would ask for it by name. Everybody that knew my family knew that he was a friend of mine and a part of our family. Just like when my other friend was out there, they knew that he was associated or related to our family. There were a lot of other people that didn't hate our family, and they were cool with us and so were the rest of the people that ran with us in our circle. It was all organized, BELIEVE IT OR NOT, BUT WAS STILL WITH THE GAME, the game of life! It really is a small world, a very small world. So you have to be very careful who you talk to and how you talk to them. Because you never know who you're talking to or talking about to someone they can be related. So, the best thing to do was to mind your own business and pray always. I was able to continue to use the scale to weigh out my products until my friend realized that I was no longer selling his products, I was now doing my own thing. He started acting flaky and didn't want me to use his scale so I went down to the local liquor store near my Junior high school which was close to the Eastover shopping center. It was right before you cross the DC, Maryland state-line. They sold all kinds of paraphernalia, from the small Ziplock bags that you could put the crack cocaine rocks in, the plastic tubes that had the multicolored tops that you could put the crack inside of, and even the old brown nickel bags. I needed to get the triple beam scale so that I would no longer have to ask my, supposedly "little brother and friend" to borrow his scale. That digital scale was more expensive, so now I had to learn everything on my own. I needed to do my own thing. The product that I had was much stronger than his watered-down powder cocaine and a lot of people started waiting for me to come by to get my products. Several people compared what he had to what I had. Even the color was a lot darker which indicated to me the potency of the cocaine.

Since I began doing my own thing, I tried to keep everything ON THE LOW, LOW! I was looking to get paid twice, which was very good for me, because I didn't have to be out on the streets trying to get my hustle on. Every morning after work my friend would call me and let me know that a lady wanted to see me. I knew that meant she wanted $100 of crack cocaine. This was five days a week and very consistent. I don't know if she worked on the night shift as well, but she was a nurse. Yes, she was a nurse! This product affected everybody, from all walks of life. I don't know how people were able to function and maintain a job while they still got high off of this crap. So, every morning I would have to drive a few miles from my apartment just like the guys that lived downstairs in the other apartment. By the time I got to my friend's house that young lady was there waiting for me. I gave her the same deal I gave my friends. By the time I left, they were lighting up their $25 hit. I would roll out and go back home and try to get some sleep. I knew that Paula would have plans for us later. I'd at least try to sneak in a couple of hours of sleep. We were all involved in a lot of activities. Plus, I was always busy trying to capitalize on any business opportunity that presented itself to me.

* * *

PROPOSAL AND A NEW BEGINNING FOR US

Paula found a job with this accounting office and that must have been some new-found freedom for her to get away from that house. I finally was hired running a photography portrait studio called Olan Mills. It was located in Temple Hills, Maryland. So now we both had a job and now all we needed was to move out of my parents' house. I was thankful that they let us move in, but I was very uncomfortable for a lot of different reasons. One night Paula, our daughter and I went for a ride to this area that overlooked a certain part of Washington, DC. It was very romantic during the night time looking out at the city lights. I had saved up enough money to get an engagement ring. I bought that famous bottle of wine/champaign, Asti Spumante. This was a cross between a good champagne and a good wine back in the day. I didn't get down on my knees or the old traditional way to propose for a wedding. But I was creative in my own way. I asked Paula would she married me and she said yes. That meant a lot to me knowing that what we were going through during that time.

For a while I felt like a loser, failing, disappointing to her because of my moving out of our apartment and losing my job. God stepped in again and blessed me with the financing from my car accident settlement. I didn't get as much as I thought I would get but I was truly thankful for what God had provided us with. I received some of my money shortly after my birthday. I gave my parents several hundred dollars without telling them my total amount I received. We found an apartment in the next building where Paula's sister lived. It wouldn't be ready until June and that was good enough for me. Everybody knew that when you are living under your parents' house, you have to play by their rules. After being out on my own with my little family in our apartment, we had to move back with my parents for several months. In the times I would feel comfortable walking around our apartment in my underwear or Paula walking around freely, this was not an option in my parents' house.

During the time that we were living with my parents, my sister Marcia felt some kind of way. My sister and her boyfriend were also back with my parents. Since my mother and Paula began to hang out and go shopping together, it caused my sister to feel some kind of way. Now, there is an intense complex going on. We set up the basement to look like an apartment but when my sister moved in, they also tried to take over the basement which made us feel like prisoners, stuck in one bedroom. We no longer had the freedom that we had before. Now, we really had to move out of my parents' house as soon as possible. We felt like we were held up in one room while they were able to enjoy our furniture in the basement. It was certainly time to go. This made things a little crowded and tough. At times my sister would complain that there was not enough food for everyone. Now! It was time to buy some new furniture starting with a bedroom set. We were blessed enough to get a two-bedroom apartment. When we went to look at the apartment it was a homeless guy living in there. Shortly afterwards I was able to see who he was. I found out how he was able to get in and out of the apartment. He would use a utility door that was connected to our balcony. After we cleaned up the apartment, I made sure that the door was sealed and the inner part was boarded up before we moved in to prevent any unwanted visitors. We finally moved in and it was such a blessing to finally have our own place and privacy. A place to now called our own home. My daughter had her own room and so did we. I used a lot of the money from the settlement to buy furniture for our new place. We moved in on June 1, 1987, and we planned our wedding for October 3, 1987. Life again was looking good while we were living in our new apartment.

My old friend that I sold cocaïne to stopped by to visit me but also to try and talk me into joining back up with him again. I considered him a friend because we worked together on the job for a while. We also went to a couple of clubs located on Georgia Avenue in Washington, DC. together. He was the friend that cooked that good food from his homeland of Panama. Whenever he would be cooking some food from his homeland Panama, I was there. I enjoyed that cuisine. I wished that I could have learned how to make a few of those recipes so that I could have made some for my family to enjoy. After we talked outside for a few minutes we went into my apartment building, but I didn't take him in my apartment for various reasons. Instead we went downstairs into the laundry room. He showed me a shoe box full of blocks of crack cocaine. He asked me was I interested in getting a larger quantity of products from him. I quickly said no. I have a lovely wife and a beautiful baby girl, who I never introduced him too, because I did not want him to know them. But what he really wanted from me was to be a lieutenant with his drug ring. He was aware that I knew a lot of people in the area, from our store, and the neighborhoods in which I grew up in.

This position of lieutenant had a lot of responsibilities, they made a lot of money, but they were really flunkies. They do all of the dirty work for the head guy. Once they accept that job they no longer have a life. When the big guy calls any time of the day or night you better be there. Sure, you get some perks like money and material items, and everything your boss does not want. I couldn't live that type of lifestyle, that's probably another reason why I did not join the military, but the thought did cross my mind a few times. Another reason why I refused to get involved deeply into his organization was because I didn't want to know too much. I believe that was the main reason. A lot of our young black men are getting killed faster these days because they found out too much about the illegal drug operation which becomes a threat to the head drug dealer. Once this happens, the mentality is; now he must go! It's almost like selling your soul to the devil.

I'm guilty of selling and using poison and because of it I have been victimized, but again I can't blame anyone but myself. Even though I sold more drugs after I prayed to God to help me get away from this drug selling business. I learned a valuable lesson later on in this story concerning my prayer to God about this whole thing about selling and using drugs, they both are a dead-end street called "UNDERLINE LOSERS LANE." BECAUSE YOU CAN'T WIN THIS GAME! YOU CAN PLAY THE GAME, BUT YOU WILL NEVER WIN THIS GAME!

* * *

MARRIAGE OCTOBER 3, 1987

We finally set a date for the big day, October 3, 1987, one day after Paula's birthday. We paid for the entire wedding by ourselves. I was able to use some of the money from the car accident settlement. It took a lot of work on our behalf to make all of this work with no financial help from either of our parents. Paula and I was able to make it all work out. She had some help from her friends and family, as far as getting her wedding dress made by one of her aunts. We picked out our flowers and all of the other necessities that goes with it. I had to also get all of the alcoholic beverages including a case of champagne. We had a fairly large wedding party, which included six bridesmaids and six groomsmen. Out of the six groomsmen, I had to rent about four of them a tuxedo including mine. My brother's nephew was the ring carrier. Each tuxedo cost $75 to rent and you would get a $10 cash refund after returning them. I had to pay for them myself. If I'm not mistaking, Paula's friends paid for their own dresses, with the exception of two of them.

I didn't think that it would be so hard to get friends to participate in your wedding. I almost had to beg some of them to be in the wedding. I was so glad after it all was over. *If you are planning to get married, please make sure that your friends have some money!* I'm not trying to sound negative, it would just be a lot easier on you and make sure that they are sincere. Paula's sister and her boyfriend helped us with the food for our wedding reception. One of the groomsmen provided us with a limousine. We used the ballroom of Paula's grandmother's senior citizens home to have our reception.

156

They let us use it for a reasonable price. We were trying to save as much money as possible to stay at a reasonable budget. For our honeymoon, I really wanted to take a cruise, but that was just a little more money than we could afford considering everything else that had to be paid for. So we decided on flying to Puerto Rico for one week with a one day shopping trip to St. Thomas Virgin Islands. It cost us about $1300, if not more, but it really put a dent into our finance department.

Paula had her freedom party with her girls and I believe that they had a wild time. I wasn't that fortunate; my friends really didn't give me a real bachelor party. We went to this club for a few minutes and stopped by one of my friend's house to drink a few beers, but it really wasn't nothing to brag about. Not like the one that she had, but I was thankful for the effort that they gave. I was home early, about 11:00 p.m. or 12:00 midnight. I went to bed and Paula called me. We talked for just a few minutes. I don't even remember wishing her a happy birthday. The next morning, I was up and partially ready to begin the rest of my life with my wife and daughter. It was a rainy day and I believe that it is an omen for that, but I don't know what it was to represent.

I was informed that a driver was coming to pick me up from my apartment, I said okay. My brother-in-law also road in the back of the limousine with me holding the wedding cake in his lap. When I arrived at the church it was hardly anyone there including Paula. As I waited nervously for hours, Paula had not arrived yet. So, while I was waiting the guys and I were taking some pictures downstairs in the basement of the church. Being a photographer, it was hard for me not to have a camera and take a few pictures. Well, I had a pocket camera and I snapped a picture here and there. My brother Chap was my best man and the groomsmen were a few of my good friends. Finally, Paula arrived, I really felt embarrassed that my bride was hours late, it usually is the male that is late, but I tried to keep a cool head. They said that they were ready to start the wedding ceremony. I just wanted to get this all over with. We said our wedding vows and the ceremony was over really fast. They sang a song or two and we were finished at the church. When we walked out of the church it was still raining. We arrived at the reception hall and it seemed like it was more people there than at the church.

After we arrived, time seemed to move a little faster. We took pictures, danced, ate cake and I really felt relieved, but very happy. My parents took our daughter home, and we stayed to get all of our gifts to take upstairs to her grandmothers' apartment. We left all of our wedding gifts there until we came back from our honeymoon. We didn't realize that after everyone left including the limousine that we didn't have a ride back to our apartment.   Thank God that the photographer was still there. She gave us a ride back home and later we became really good friends. She wasn't a professional photographer because I wasn't going to pay anyone hundreds of dollars knowing the true expense of it all, call me cheap, but wise.

Our intentions were to go directly to the hotel in Baltimore next to the airport. But that meant spending some unnecessary money when we could use it more on our trip. So, we decided to stay at our apartment that night and get a friend to take us to Baltimore airport in the morning. A few of our friends came over to the apartment that night and we celebrated a little bit. My downstairs neighbor came to the wedding and later came upstairs. I gave him a little bit of cocaine to help me with my expenses during the planning of the wedding. So, I shared some of it with my company that night. I was even dumb enough to take $100 dollars' worth with me for personal use on our honeymoon.

* * *

HONEYMOON

That morning our ride arrived and we were on our way to Puerto Rico. It was the first time I'd ever flown in an airplane, I'm not sure about my wife. We had a quick breakfast and took a few pictures and then it was time to board the airplane. They didn't have our seats together. We were across the aisle from each other. We met a couple that was sitting beside me that had already been to Puerto Rico several times.   They told us what to look out for and what not to buy, especially any alcohol from the Rum factory, because it was cheaper at the local stores. As soon as I stepped off of the airplane, I started taking off my leather jacket, because it was really hot. We needed a cab to take us to our hotel. I noticed that when the guy called for the cab, it seemed strange. I noticed that the cabs' meter was not working properly, and every time we hit a hard bump in the road, the meter would skip a few numbers. It was defected and he was trying to take the long road to the hotel. I told him that the hotel was over there, and I asked him why he was going into a different direction. When we finally arrived, he tried to charge me almost $15 dollars and an additional 50 cent for each bag. I gave $10 dollars and said; "that's all I'm going to give you because your meter isn't working properly, and you are trying to cheat us" and we walked away.

It started raining really hard and within 10 minutes everything dried up. I never saw anything like that before in my life. The rooms were nice but smelled musty and damp. We got settled in our room and I believe we went to the bar. We stayed in the hotel for the remaining of the day. The next day we ventured out into the area. They had a really bad fire in the hotel one block away from our hotel several months before we arrived, and a lot of people died from that fire because they were jumping out of the windows. A McDonalds was a few walking blocks away so we went to get something to eat. That food was very expensive and tasted a lot different from our local McDonalds. We walked to the beach and the beach near our hotel wasn't that nice. The next day they took us to visit another hotel for a timesharing deal. This hotel was very beautiful and the swimming pool was also nice. We met an older couple and they took us to another hotel and we played the slot machines for a little while. They brought us back to our hotel after a few hours and their room was just down the hall from our room. The next night we went to an expensive restaurant to enjoy ourselves, later we learned that it was another restaurant next to the one which was less expensive, and they had some good food.

Now! It was time for our trip to the Virgin Islands. We chartered a small plane that landed and took off from the water. It only held about six passengers. It wasn't that bad on the way there and it probably took about 30 minutes. We landed on water safely and I thank God for that because the plane was small, and the motor/propeller was attached to the wings. We could hear the motor making a lot of noise. It was definitely no comparison to the larger airplane at all. I forget how many hours they gave us to shop but we didn't have any problems. Our credit cards were maxed out, but they still would accept them and we took advantage of that. We bought some gold jewelry for ourselves, alcohol - many different kinds, and souvenirs for everybody. We didn't tour the area that much because we were focusing more on buying stuff. KFC was another restaurant that we were familiar with, so that was what we had for lunch. Now, it was time to get back to the airplane site because we were running out of time. It truly was a beautiful island. The plane arrived and we boarded it with all of our goodies. When we were up in the airplane it started thundering and lightning. I was getting nervous because the airplane seemed like it was struggling a little bit. But, I thank God that we arrived safely.

I didn't want to get ripped off again by these gypsy cab drivers, so I told Paula that we would catch the bus back to the hotel. My baby really stuck in there. I told her that we would sit near the driver to get the correct bus stop near our hotel. When we finally arrived close to the hotel, the bus driver told us where to walk and we would be there in no time. I noticed as we drove through some local neighborhoods that it was pretty rough. I lived in Southeast Washington, DC., and it wasn't no utopian. We arrived safely to the hotel after walking a couple of blocks. After we were settled in our room we went to the downstairs bar. The bartender was friendly and she would give us some pointers about certain stuff concerning Puerto Rico. We told her that we caught the bus from the airport, she seemed surprised. She told us if some of the local people knew that we were tourists, they would have probably robbed us and even killed us. We did have over a thousand dollars' worth of stuff in our possession. Again, God protected us like He had been doing throughout our lives.

It was time to leave and I thought that I would use a little strategy this time with the cab driver. I told him that our airplane leaves in 45 minutes but truly we had about an hour more to wait before our airplane was ready. He was an older gentleman, but an honest one. We arrived at the airport in no time and the total cost was only $7 dollars. I gave him a $3 dollar tip. I knew that the first cab driver cheated me and I wasn't going to fall for that trick again. When we boarded the airplane we made sure that we would be sitting together. I noticed a man sitting in a wheelchair when we walked through the terminal. After we were seated, we were delayed for an hour. The seat beside me to the left was empty and I said to Paula; "hopefully this would a better flight home." Boy! I was so wrong. They brought the man that was sitting in the wheelchair to the emptied seat beside me. He really had a bad, bad smell coming from him. That three-hour flight couldn't have come fast enough. I was sick from the smell that was coming from him. When we arrived, our ride was already there waiting for us at the airport. I was so happy to be home with my daughter and my wife. I truly counted my blessings every day. After a couple of days, it was time to go back to work. Paula was still working at the accounting firm and I was working at Olan Mills portrait studio.

* * *

BACKTRACKING, MY FIRST REAL JOB

I finally realized that I couldn't make enough money to support Paula, the baby and I just taking pictures on the street. So my first real job was at St. Elizabeth Mental Hospital as a psychiatric assistant. You know how they say; "never say never!" Well, during the years that we had our beer and wine store, I watched some of the employees that worked at St. Elizabeth's Hospital coming in to our store acting crazier than some of the out-patients. My father would allow one of the employees to sit in the back of our store on his lunch break and drink a couple of beers. He would sit in a chair and start staring at me constantly. Then his eyes would start blinking, I did not know what his problem was. I said to myself, if working at that hospital makes you act crazy like him, I don't ever want to work at there. Guess what, it was my first real job. Remember "Never Say Never!" I started working there in 1986. The hospital was in the heart of the hood and the patients stood out like a chicken with its head cut off. One day I was transferred to another unit to cover for a party that we were having for the residents. But at any party there is always a bad apple in the bunch. He weighed about 300 pounds, he was a feeble-minded grown man with the mental capacity of a child. This same man was supposed to be on a diet. The delicacies didn't promote diet. The tech that was in charge told me to tell the residents that he could not have any more cake. I responded to the tech; "why don't you tell him in Spanish, too?" I walked down the hallway to observe the other residents. All of a sudden I heard a lot of a commotion

161

coming from the dining area. I ran to see what was going on. Apparently, the resident hit the Tech in his face and knocked him to the floor, he even hit the nurse. I grabbed this 300-pound resident by his arm and another psychiatric assistant grabbed his other arm. While we were de-escalating the resident, another resident aimed a piece of ice at the one we were restraining, but the ice hit me. My nose started bleeding. I didn't care that my nose was bleeding, I was worried about the other residents trying to start a big fight.

Apparently, he had been taking some of the other residents' food and snacks and they were mad at him. I believe this was why he hit the female nurse. I didn't find out about this until a few days later. We took the resident to the isolation room. The crisis team came running to our unit to prevent any violence. They asked me why "I didn't rough the guy up?" Right! This guy was so scared that he went voluntarily to the isolation room. I didn't want to provoke him anymore. After everything was over, they sent the technician and the nurse and I to another part of the hospital so that our injuries could be checked out. I just went because I wanted to go home early. My nose only had a little cut across it and after a couple of days it was healed. That night we didn't have our regular staff working, they would have prevented that situation from happening. Nevertheless, I enjoyed going to work and punching a time card but most of all I loved getting my paycheck every two weeks. Of course, with the bitter there is always the sweet. About the bitter there were many crazy incidents that happened and that was expected due to the environment.

* * *

OLAN MILLS PORTRAIT PHOTOGRAPHY STUDIO

After I stopped working at St. Elizabeth's Hospital, I started working at Olan Mills Portrait Studio as I mentioned. During the time that I was working there the studio had a very bad business reputation. The photographer had a very bad habit of taking too much time with each client, either talking too much or trying to position/pose each client in several different poses. In that profession they will show you several different poses and you have to do them in a reasonable amount time. I learned that they would sometimes have to wait for hours before taking pictures. This was told to me by several of the customers that I took pictures of during my one year working at Olan Mills. They had a weekly progress booklet that would show the sales and pictures that were taken at each studio. I'm not bragging but after about two months working there, our studio ratings started appearing in the weekly booklets.

When the customers would come and get their portraits taken in a reasonable time, they would always compliment me and tell me about the horrible experience that they had in the past. The other customers in the waiting room also noticed that people were coming in the studio and leaving out faster than in the past. Not only was I taking their pictures faster, but I also gave each customer quality portraits to choose from, which also made them buy more pictures. During the year of 1987 while working there, Paula and I were married, and we purchased our first brand new car. After several months of working there, they had their annual banquet. They would give each studio that performed well that year and the employees an award for their outstanding achievements throughout that fiscal year. I would look at the weekly booklet very closely to see how our studio matched up against the other studios in our region.

They gave our consultant and secretary an award, but they discriminated against me and gave the rookie photographer of the year award to another photographer. Remember I always looked at the weekly progress booklets and I know that my picture rating was higher than anyone else. This was an eye opener for me. After all of the hard work that I gave the company, this was my reward. The consultant would not have made the sales that she made if my pictures weren't good quality. It was time for me to leave Olan Mills for several reasons, including the one that I just mentioned. I sponsored a shopping trip to New Jersey and New York several months ahead of time and I notified my supervisor that I needed that weekend off. He approved it, three weeks before my trip he told me that I needed to put my request in writing, which I did, again ahead of time. The night before I was to go on the shopping trip that I sponsored, my supervisor called me and asked was I going to be at work the next day. I asked him what part of the request that I put in several months prior did he not understand? He said something disrespectful and I hung up the telephone. He called me right back and apologized.

Again, I told him that I would not be in because of the obligation that I already committed to.

After the following week, I felt very uncomfortable at the studio. Three months prior to taking that weekend off, my supervisor came to the studio to give me my performance evaluation (what a joke he was). When I looked at the pictures that he had taken during the weekend that I was away, they were horrible. He was supposed to get them ready for sale. Customers complained to me that he was very rude and he was rushing them. I had started taking more pictures at home of the guys in the hood with their fancy cars and putting their names on the large poster size photos. I made sure they were personalized. One day the consultant who worked there wanted to see my large poster photograph, but I would not let her see them, so she told the supervisor that I was using the pictures that I took at Olan Mills and getting them enlarged and selling them to the customers at the studio. This was not true at all. Olan Mills had a proof protection mark on the bottom of their photographs. The companies were not allowed to copy any of the photographs if they were taken the current year. All of the photos had the year that the pictures were taken on them. There was a clause that stated that photographs had to be more than five years or more before you could copy them. So, I could not copy any of their pictures even if I wanted to. Well, they believed her without any proof and they terminated me from Olan Mills wrongfully. I had a feeling that they were going to fire me before I went to work that day. When Paula took me to work I told her to wait for a few minutes, but she didn't, she pulled off, so I had to find a ride home. I felt like the guy that was working there before I started working at the studio, it was exactly the same way that they terminated him, it was on a Saturday.

After I lost my job with Olan Mills, I was okay, because I had learned a lot about taking portraits and it was during the summer months. That is the busiest time for my photography business and I had started taking several poster size pictures of a lot of drug dealers with their expensive cars. I was selling them for $50 each and I did very well. Several months later, I started looking for a place to open up my own photography studio. I was going to use the same concept as Olan Mills. I was blessed to learn a lot about the photography

164

business and how to run a brand-new professional studio. To be honest about the whole situation, I didn't have the proper studio lighting and some props to run the studio on a professional level. Some of the choices that I made along the way and some of the people that I dealt with, I should not have involved them. I totally went about it the wrong way. You live and learn as you go on in life!

The saying goes; "If I could've, would've, should've done things differently" after the fact, but you eventually recognize how you would've done things differently.

* * *

PHOTO MEMORIES PORTRAIT STUDIO

I opened up my own photography studio, but with a serious price. I found a vacant building, it was around the corner from my parents' old store. When we had our store, it used to be a Dry Cleaners, then it was a Pest Control/Extermination store. After we closed our store, a few years later it was the Headquarters for a campaign office. That was in 1984. Four years later I opened up my photography studio called "Photo Memories." I was hoping to redeem my parents' loss of our family business and turn my studio into a success, but that didn't happen like I thought it would. I found out that the owner of the property was owned by a Korean who purchased the entire building that my father could have purchased years ago, but that's another story.

The real-estate representative who was renting the property out for the Korean owner was my junior high school science teacher. They were renting the property out for $750 a month. I was so anxious about finding a place that I didn't consider negotiating a lower monthly price. I asked my friend to loan me some money as a down payment for my first month mortgage. That turned into a partnership and I did not stick with my original plan which was to start out with some sample office dividers and work my way up. Instead, I let him talk me into getting the place renovated which took several months and wasted a lot of money. I should have purchased a more tangible asset instead of a fixed asset which later was more beneficial to the owner of the building.

I hoped that this business partnership would work out because I wanted him to get out of the game and we both could become legitimate business owners. That was wishful thinking. I could not pay off the expensive studio with $750 a month rent, telephone, electric bills, and other bills that I had at home. I could no longer take the pressure of running the studio alone and not really making enough money to operate the studio without the proper equipment or financing. The Small Business Administration (S.B.A.) kept selling me pipe dreams. I would go and talk with them, so they could help me get a small business loan from one of the neighboring banks, but they just kept on making more excuses and stringing me along for months. All I needed was about $50,000 dollars and I could buy the equipment that I needed along with some working capital, but that never happened. I was going to try and pay my buddy off for helping me get started because I knew that as long as he was affiliated with me and doing what he was doing, the business would never be successful. The S.B.A. sold me promises for several months and I wish that they would have been more honest with me. I really didn't want to be a failure, despite the outcome. I began concentrating on family and letting the drugs go! It was a relief to get rid of the studio. I was under so much pressure trying to be a successful businessman and not become a failure.

I've learned over the years that when you try to do something, and it doesn't work or turn out the way you wanted it to turn out doesn't necessarily mean that you were a failure. It just means that it was a learning curve, something that you would have never learned if you didn't try. I put a lot of pressure on myself and received a lot of indirect and unnecessary pressure from others. At the end of the day, I can say that I tried. I tried to run a successful photography studio without the proper equipment and working capital. It is almost impossible for this project to work especially since Small Business Administration had been stringing me along for several months, knowing that they really didn't want to help me be successful. Somehow, I inherited a bad name along the way and I believe that is why they didn't want any involvement or dealings with me. It was my desire to borrow several thousand dollars for equipment and working capital. I know that I needed the money and I know what I needed the money for, but instead of them being upfront and honest with me, they continued to hang me out there. I can say that the only thing that was positive dealing with the SBA was that they helped me put my business plan together. But they did not go all the way with me to the bank, which I did really need their support when it came to presenting my business plans to lenders or the bank. I believe that if they would have stayed when it was time to borrow money from the lender or bank, it would have made things look a lot more professional. I never received the much-needed money. I also contribute this to the people I was friends with. This one person in particular was heavily into selling drugs and I truly believe this was a factor and they refused to go any further with me. It is what it is or in my case, it was, what it was!

∗ ∗ ∗

OUR SON WAS BORN, JANUARY 25, 1989

When I had the studio, Paula was pregnant with our second child. On the morning of January 25, 1989, I was about to go and get a haircut, but before I took off I put a quart of oil in the car before I left, and it was a good thing that I did. This guy called me and said that this lady was trying to get my attention. Paula was calling me to tell me that she was in labor. We quickly rushed to the hospital and this time I didn't get lost. We arrived about 2:00p.m. at Columbia Hospital for Women, where both my daughter and now my new baby boy was born. When we arrived, I was so nervous, I accidentally locked the keys in the car. The doctor-understudy was there, and he was trying to make us go to another hospital. I told him that if he wanted us to go to another hospital he was going to have to send us by ambulance. I wasn't going to take my wife to another hospital when we were promised that our child would be delivered there. Paula had a scheduled appointment to see her doctor on that same day and exactly at the time that our son was delivered. After I told him several times that we weren't going anywhere I demanded that he call our doctor and tell him that we were at the hospital. Shortly after that our doctor arrived and our son was born at about 3:00 p.m., weighing at eight pounds. They had to tell me to move to the side because I was waiting to check out his gender and apparently, I was in their way. God had finally given me the little boy that I wanted along with my beautiful daughter.

Afterwards, I stayed with Paula and the baby for a little while. I went downstairs to the souvenir shop and bought a box of bubble gum cigars with the words "It's a Boy" written on them. When I got into the neighborhood, I purchased some regular cigars and passed them out as well. It was time to get home and start painting the bedroom for the children. I had a friend of mind named who helped me paint the children's room, the hallway, and the living room. We worked very fast because the next day Paula and our son was coming home. We had aired out the apartment all that day so that the paint smell wouldn't be in the house so strong when they arrived. I always felt bad about not staying at the hospital with Paula after she gave birth to both of our children, but I had to do the same thing both times. That was to have an apartment painted and ready for them before they came home. I was just trying to do the best that I could to make her happy when she came home.

Again, I gave my wife another baby shower. It was a few days after they had come from the hospital. I wasn't thinking about bringing so many people around my newborn son. It was just because nobody offered to give her a baby shower, with the exemption of the people at her job. They had given her a baby shower a few weeks prior to her taking maternity leave. We had quite a few people come to our baby shower at our apartment from both sides of our family. Now! I'm the proud father of two beautiful children, and my head and chest had gotten even bigger. They are only two of the many blessings that God had given me.

I used to tease my friends sometimes by asking them, how are your wife and kids doing, even though they weren't married or had any children or even old enough to have kids. We are in Junior high school when I was saying these things to them, some of them, might've thought that I was crazy, asking them about their wife and kids. I was just joking around (this was a question that would be posed to an adult). We were just kids. In all actuality, some of them could have been parents at a young age, it happens, but now it was true for me as I got older and became a father twice, and I had no regrets!

∗ ∗ ∗

THE AVENUE

Summer was dozing into a deep sleep and autumn was surely rising. I lost the studio and I began taking pictures on the 'avenue.' I started setting up my backgrounds outside of this vacant store that used to be an auto store. I would pick up Paula and the kids and go directly to the avenue and set up shop. I would probably average about fifty dollars to one-hundred-fifty a day, and sometimes more. I knew if I didn't establish myself every day, someone else would. I would probably be out there three to four hours every day with an exception of weekends. I would be so happy when it rained outside because that meant that I could spend time with my family. Nobody wanted to be outside taking any flicks/photos on a rainy day and I definitely wasn't going to be outside in the rain, so I truly welcomed when it would rain. But on a clear day and night, I had to take advantage of the opportunities in order to make some money to pay my bills for my family. Thursday was the day that I left early from the avenue because my wife and I would watch a couple of our favorite TV shows. On Friday's we would always stop by the DC Wharf and get some seafood. My wife really learned how to cook and bake a lot of different dishes and it seemed like she got better each and every year. She really could fry some fresh fish and I loved coming home to the aroma of delicious fish frying, shrimp or whatever seafood she was making on Fridays. YES, all Fridays were considered a seafood day, and we always had to have fresh fried fish on the menu. It was a blessing that my wife and kids and I were able to eat dinner at the table and enjoy eating together as a family. (We were able to do this for years until I got hurt) I truly missed these priceless times, moments and memories together. Nowadays, it seems like no families have the time to really eat dinner together anymore, living in this MICROWAVE SOCIETY AND a CONCRETE JUNGLE!

On Thursdays and Fridays, as I mentioned, I would get in late those days between 8:00 p.m. and 9:00 p.m. on the days that I was out taking pictures on the Avenue. I just had to take advantage of the opportunities to make some money during the summer months. It was just business, THAT'S ALL! I wouldn't be taking pictures all day long, just long enough to make a few dollars so that I would be able to provide for my family. These days working one job isn't enough and taking pictures was another way to diversify my income. It was an honest, legal business. I wasn't out there just because I wanted to hang out there, I was out there to provide for my family. I religiously and faithfully made sure that I made two telephone calls before I came in after taking pictures for the day. I always called my wife, my second telephone call would be to my parents' house to see if they needed me to pick up anything from the store before I came home. I always said, once I came in the house for that night, I didn't want to come out anymore until the next morning. I stayed on the avenue until the weather started getting colder as the fall season was coming in for that year. As a man, I believe that I should always have money in my pocket to help my wife, children, and my parents and even other family members, when they needed something, ESPECIALLY my two sisters.

I am old school and I'm not trying to say anything disrespectful towards my nephew's and niece's fathers, but as their uncle, I truly believe that it was my position spiritually, and as I tried to be a positive, male figure in their lives, if my sisters needed anything to help them out, I believed it was my God-given responsibility to be there for her and them. But also, to show some kind of guidance for my nephews and nieces as a man, and a strong father figure, especially for the females, my nieces. The reason why I put emphasis on my nieces is because a lot of females, young little girls and teenage school girls need to see a strong male figure in their everyday LIVES! It is so important for them to grow up seeing this. Okay, I was uncle Jeff, but I also was a husband to their aunt Paula, again a husband and wife with kids. They could see how my wife and I interacted whenever they visited or whenever she and I visited them. My kids and my nephews and nieces were blessed to have my parents and my grandparents that they could watch us interact with each other on a regular basis, and that's very important. Also, the young men needed to see how a husband and wife interact with each other. We weren't perfect, but we still did our best and I pray to God that my kids, but also my nephews and nieces were able to grasp something positive from watching us interact with each other. I want to make this perfectly clear, I had nothing to do with what my sisters and their babies' fathers did or didn't do, I just know what I had to do as their uncle as well as my kids father. I did my best and God knows I pray that I could do more and can do more in the future, no matter how old they get. Being a strong positive male figure in the family, we all need to see this on an everyday basis, how to interact with one another.

I don't understand men who want a woman to take care of them. Where is the sense of REAL PRIDE, NOT FOOLISH PRID, when a man can just contribute anything towards bettering their family or themselves for that matter? How could they allow a woman to take care them? I wasn't brought up that way and God holds a man to a high standard of being a provider in many ways, as the old school. Where I come from there are certain circumstances where there are men that are home and taking care of their families and their wives are out there working, some situations are different, BUT JUST BEING LAZY, and not even trying to go out and be a provider, these are the guys that I'm talking about. How do they live with themselves, but most importantly, why would a woman accept a lazy man to let them? Is it out of desperation that they've allowed this to take place or have things gotten that bad now? In some cases the system has made it hard for some men to get a job when they are always trying to find reasons to keep them away from the family and keep them caught up in the system and in the revolving door of being incarcerated. That is also a major factor that a man can be at home because the system has blocked them out from being able to be a major contributor to the family. Some government systems have been in place to make sure that the black man is not able to live with his family and to keep them either incarcerated or in the streets.

September of 1990 was the last time that I took pictures on the avenue. There were many people out there, waiting for the opportunity to steal and possibly take me out (when I say take me out, I mean to rob me or even take my life, without exaggeration). Sadly, to say; there were many people waiting in line to do bodily harm or to shoot me. I recognized how much I was hated, not because I was a bad person, but this is the real truth! So many were waiting for the opportunity to take my camera, money or even my life. It didn't matter how much hatred was shown towards me. I could sometimes see it on their faces. I knew a lot of them hated me, but I didn't hate them. They made the choice to hate, but I certainly was not stupid or naive to the situation and always tried to be on guard. It didn't take

171

much for me to see their jealousy and envy. I didn't like to think that so many people hated me and I certainly didn't think more highly of myself as the Bible speaks of. I was humble then and remain humble now, even to this day. But, inheriting this type of hatred from others was my real reality. This was the night that I got shot and heard the guys say; "I didn't like him anyway, make sure he's dead."

* * *

NIGHT CLUB ACTION

My neighbor downstairs told me about a night club that where he frequently hung out. I decided to try it out. My first night I only took about 10 pictures, but the customers noticed that I was a lil' more professional than the other photographer, and they were satisfied with my pictures. I talked with the owner's son and I told him that I had a couple of backgrounds, and I asked for permission to bring them the next time I came. The next day I prepared to set-up the background in one of the corners of the club. Everybody noticed the background and it was mostly women who wanted pictures. The guys in the club did not like me at first and I could feel the hatred from them. I got a lot of dirty looks from the men but that also wasn't anything new, because I've always had problems with jealous men. The more pictures I took of women the more evil looks I received from the men. You could cut the tension with a knife. The name of the club was called John's Place. After everybody found out that there was a photographer in the club business started getting better. In that club there were pimps, drug dealers, killers, stick-up boys and hustlers that would come out every night. (None of these people were any different from the guys that I dealt with when my family had the beer and wine store on the Avenue). The only thing different were the days, the time and also the location of the club, but everything else I WAS USED TO!

My clientele grew and people were getting to know me. It was this one guy that I knew who was a stick-up boy, and I felt that he would try to stick me up later if he had the chance. After I started coming for a while, we became friends, or at least I thought because we conversed during the nights that I worked. When I would go to the club, I would bring a couple of my friends and my wife's uncle and my cousin with me. One of my friends was with me the night I got shot but didn't say anything while it was happening. Most of the time I took these guys with me to keep me company, but also hopefully to be my eyes and ears for me and to help me with the equipment, setting it up and breaking it down for the night. Most of the women that I took pictures of would try to hold conversations with me, flirt with me, and dance with me, but I would direct them to my friends. I wasn't trying to get to know any of them because I had respect for myself and my wife. My wife did not believe that I had respect for her, even when she wasn't present, but God as my witness, I had more respect for her than she gave me credit for. God knows exactly how I felt about my wife and her safety when it came to me being in certain places and taking pictures. I just cannot take her with me to certain places, again because of her safety. I always said to myself that I couldn't live with her getting injured while with me somewhere. Again, it wasn't because I didn't want her with me, I just didn't want her to be in the line of danger, and there are several places and events that I could take her because I knew it was safe.

As my business boomed, the owner's son became a little headstrong. I think it was because his girlfriend was a very friendly young lady. She also worked in the club and she and I would talk about whatever because she was a very friendly young lady, and I knew how to say things, not being disrespectful, but to maybe make her laugh or smile, that was it. This would be before the crowd would start coming through the doors, before it was time to get down to business. Again, his girlfriend and I would sometimes just talk or we would say hello to each other. This is all a part of the business. I wasn't out to get his girlfriend, that was the furthest thing from my mind. I had my wife and kids at home and that was the reason why I was even out working in a club in the beginning. A lot of nights, I would rather have stayed home with my wife and kids, but I was there on certain nights, because I was providing finances for my family. I wasn't there to pick up or flirt with any of the women, other than trying to make that dollar bill or put a smile on their faces by saying something funny or just giving them a compliment. It was always about the money, and I had the gift of gab, and I knew just what to say! *(During the Christmas month, after leaving the club about 2:00 a.m., I would go to United States Post Office, on Brentwood Road and work another four or five hours as a casual employee, to make some more extra money)*

I knew how some of the guys were when it came to talking to their woman, and I totally understood that. I'm a man and I wouldn't want my wife to get too friendly with other guys while we were out, I'm just being honest. I believe that he was trying to show his authority to his girlfriend over me. I think he bumped his head because I didn't work for him. I'm my own man with my own business. One day he wanted me to go in the back near the kitchen to take pictures, this sounded ridiculous. He did not realize that I had a brand-new background of a gold colored Mercedes-Benz which was a very nice background. On this particular day I was going to bring it out which I did and everything worked out in my favor, even though he was trying to degrade me or regulate me, GOD WORKED EVERYTHING OUT! I had no problem, so I moved my equipment into the kitchen area of the club. I didn't argue with him that night because I knew that my brand-new background would be a hit. Instead of him hurting me, he really helped me a lot because he wasn't able to clock my dollars and see just how much clientele I had on that particular night of all nights.

Later on, he realized that he had made a mistake by sending me all the way in the back of the club, in the kitchen, of all places. So at the end of the night, he asked if I could return to the front of the club the next time that I came. I wanted him to make up his mind because in all reality, I liked working in the kitchen, for various reasons. Again, he wasn't able to count my dollars or clock my money or the customers while I worked in the kitchen. Before I decided to quit there were a group of guys that were acting like fools. One of the guys started complaining about the way he was positioned, and he wanted me to take another picture. I refused to take the photo over again because I gave them enough time to get positioned right. I counted to three and snapped the picture.

The guy that paid me for the picture never said anything bad about it. So the other guy threw the picture into my camera bag and said he didn't want it. Ten minutes passed, and he came back to get the picture. From that moment, I started preparing myself for something to jump off. I told my friend who was with me that night to get ready for something to kick off. They did not know that he was with me and he heard what they were planning to do to me. Anyway, the club had a side door that I would use most of the time and it was where I parked my car so when I leave I didn't have to carry my equipment that far to my car. I told my friend that I would leave out of the side door because I felt that they would be waiting for me to exit from the front door. I wasn't about to walk into the lion's den. I wasn't trying to prove anything to anybody. I wanted to get home to my family as fast and as safe as possible! I knew they wanted to stick me up. My friend wanted to fight, but I wasn't going to give them the opportunity. After we started riding home he understood. He was an older guy and he was from a rough part of town. He was also a good friend of mine and I considered him like an older brother.

* * *

MO MONEY! MO PROBLEMS!

My friend lived on top of the studio that we were renting. He also had a problem using hard drugs, the drug of choice was HEROIN. I would take him with me to get him away from his drug addicted friends. I considered him as a true soldier and a real friend. Nevertheless, I was getting tired of the club. Sometimes before I would leave home, I would tell my wife that I really didn't want to go, but sometimes she would encourage me to go anyway. Two weeks later somebody threw a cocktail inside the club. Shortly thereafter, a gunman came inside and killed three people. Timing is everything and I was starting to get tired of working in the club. I had made my mind up that I wasn't going back and even before the incident of the cocktail bomb, and then later on the shooting inside the club. I thank God that HE HAD ALREADY TOLD ME THAT! It was time to stop working there. Thinking for a moment, if I was there that particular day, I may have been shot or even killed. It was the same location where my backdrop was located, once you came through the second door of the club. I was positioned right in the corner, so there was a strong possibility that if I stayed there, I wouldn't be writing this book. When we hear a word we must move right away, to flee right now without hesitation, we need to move WHEN GOD SAYS MOVE!

175

It seemed as though the more material things that my family and I acquired and were blessed with, the more problems we had. There were absolutely too many haters lurking around in the neighborhood, waiting to steal, kill, and destroy! That sounds like the devil, and his demons. One brisk morning I recall going outside to get the car warmed up for my wife and my daughter so that I could take them to work and school (this was before our son was born). That night I had the car cleaned up, I washed it and waxed it so it would be nice for my wife in the morning and clean, but to my surprise, the car wasn't there. I knew that I had a couple of beers the night before so I thought that I may have parked the car around the back of our apartment. I walked around the block and no car was to be found. I ran into the apartment and told my wife that the car had been stolen. I thought that maybe the car company repossessed it because I was a payment behind. So we called the car company and they said that we should call the police because they did not take it. The police said that it would take them several hours before they could come to talk to us about the situation, but I took it upon myself to look for the car.

I had one of my neighbors who was living downstairs to give me a ride around the neighborhood and about 30 minutes later I spotted my car near my old high school. We followed the car thieves, who were driving my car for about six or seven blocks. They had the music blasting with the sun roof opened. To see these guys enjoy my car, more than I could, being a married man, I had to be a little more conservative and not being able to blast my music with the sun roof opened, I got a little jealous. It was my practically brand-new Toyota Camry that they were enjoying more than I could. I was very angry, and even being married, I couldn't enjoy that car too much. I told my friend that I was going to jump out the car, so my friend went to the driver's side, and I went to the passenger side, and reached my arm inside of the car, and told the guy that if he moved his hands, I would break his damn neck!

I didn't know if they had guns but I didn't care. It was three guys in the car and between my friend and I, we kept kicking the back door closed, so they couldn't get out. An off-duty cop that my friend knew, noticed what was going on and he had his wife, to call the police for back-up. The police arrived thereafter, and they thought I

176

was an off duty police officer, because they asked the question; "what police precinct are you from?" I explained that I'm not from no precinct. This is my car, but I'm taking it back! After I pulled one of the thieves out of my stolen car, I reached back for the police to pass me the handcuffs, so I could cuff one of the guys, the one that I was choking. I guess I watched too much television and police shows and I wanted to put hand-cuffs on the car thief. The officer explained to me that he could not allow me to handcuff him. I think I was excited and lost myself for a one moment!

I gave them the okay to take my car to the precinct and I followed them. After getting all of the paper work done, they released my car to my custody and I had contacted my insurance company. The damages were estimated at $4,000 and they didn't get the car fixed immediately. I still drove the car for several weeks with the ignition and the door still broken. I had the car in my possession. While I was waiting for the insurance company to fix my car, I was still working part-time during the holiday season with the post office as a casual worker. I used my personal vehicle and I never got compensated for the gasoline that was burned while I delivered the mail in the different communities. At least my car was no longer sitting idle in the neighborhood, only at nighttime, which is when they stole it the first time. One month later the car was stolen again but they didn't get far because I didn't keep a lot of gas in the car for that reason. I received a telephone call from the police department telling me that my car was found and that I could pick it up. A couple of weeks later my car was repossessed and I just gave up on the car. There were too many problems that came with it. When I went to the "Impound" to get possession of my car, it was embarrassing to see my brother's car just a few cars away. His car was repossessed months prior (that was during the time that I had just started working on my photography studio and money was very tight). Things were "falling a part." My wife was soon to have a baby, we had no transportation, the bills were steadily coming in and the studio was not generating a lot of income. My cousins told me that I could rent cars even though my credit wasn't good, but all I needed was to present them with a credit card. I needed transportation very bad so I started renting cars. I paid cash since my credit card didn't have any money on it, just a limited amount, but it worked. Renting cars was costing me close to

$500 a month, which was $200 more than my regular car payments before my car was stolen and later repossessed.

* * *

POST OFFICE

I started working at National Airport Post office as a casual worker through the holiday season. I always wanted to get into the Metro Transportation service because they paid well and had great benefits that could help my family. I had to report to work early in the morning and it was hard for Paula because she had to get both of the kids up, take them to the babysitter, and then she would have to get on the subway and go to work because I needed the car to get to work early in the morning. The subway didn't open up until 6:00a.m. I worked both jobs driving the shuttle bus from 4:30 a.m. to 2:30p.m. Then I would go directly to the post office and work there from 3:00p.m.-11p.m. Some mornings my wife would drive me to work and pick me up. I was working at the post-office located at the Ronald Reagan National Airport. During the time I worked at the post-office it was a good experience. I wish that the Post Office would have hired me as a full-time employee. I even wish they would have hired me for a part-time position, which would have truly been a blessing and change a lot of things, but it didn't happen. I just wanted to get into the Postal Service system. (Between working with the Metro system and the post office, I would have received some great benefits that would've blessed my family members and I.

I ran into one of my childhood friend's father. He was the daytime supervisor at the post-office. When I first started working there, it was during the morning shift. I really worked hard so that I could impress my supervisor so that I could get a regular job there. I even talked to the head man in charge of the department about getting hired full-time. I had already taken the Civil Servant Test and passed it. My friend's father only stayed there for about a month after I started working there, and then he was transferred to somewhere else, and later retired. I learned a lot about the different stages of how the mail was distributed throughout the country. Sometimes I would take quick 20 minutes naps in the bathroom, but it was this one female supervisor that would come looking for me. Our locker room was a unisex locker room, but we had separate bathrooms for the female and males. She (my supervisor) would come into the locker room calling my name, and I would say; *"Look, I'm using the bathroom, why are you looking for me?"* I knew that she liked me and was just trying to catch me by myself to talk with me about my feelings towards me. I'm not saying this to make myself look bigger, but you know when someone likes you and they're trying to catch you by yourself, but I wasn't having it. When she would call me, I wasn't that friendly and I did this intentionally, hoping that she'd understand I wasn't interested in her. I had to be a little mean, not to hurt her feelings, but again, hoping that she understood that I wasn't one of those guys that was interested in other women at all. Again, I'm a married man. (I do know that if I fed into what she wanted me to, there was a possibility that she knew someone that could help me get into the post office as a regular employee, but it wasn't worth it) she would leave without saying anything, this happened more than one time. Now, I'm only making about $7 an hour, if that much. One day I explained to her during our lunch break that this was only a second job and I would get to the airport at 4:30 a.m., and stay until 11:00 p.m. I explained my situation to her and I talked to one of the supervisors about her behavior towards me. I had no problems from her after that and I believe she liked me a little bit. I wasn't making as much as a regular employee, but I was working harder than anybody there. This was during the evening time, I didn't have any problems during the morning shift. After they wouldn't hire me as a regular employee, I stopped working there and I worked for the shuttle bus company.

There were a lot of nice people that worked in the post office and I really wanted to be a part of that family. I worked very hard, more than a lot of the casual workers and the full-time employees. Well, they allowed me to do a lot of different things, I guess they felt that if he wanted to do it, let him do it, and we would get a break. I wanted them to recognize that I was a hard worker, but it didn't work in my favor no matter how hard I worked, I was just a casual. But I really enjoy working with that group of people and it was like a family. Even though it was a small post office, it was one of the busiest in the metropolitan area. The post office received mail from all around the United States and other countries. I remember them telling me and the rest of the people that was on orientation team that if anyone was to open up your mail without your permission that it was a 15-year federal crime. Also, in orientation, they said that you could really hurt your back even picking up a pencil off the ground. I'm thinking to myself, first of all, that was very light, but it wasn't about the weight, it is about the mechanics on how you bend over and pick up different objects. These were two very important things that I learned amongst the other things while working at the United States Postal Service. Even after I stopped working with the Postal Service, I was still able to come into the facility, say a quick hello to some the staff or even get something from the vending machine. Since the post office was located in the back of the airport, there were no vending machines anywhere closer. No one ever questioned me about what I was doing there. They understood my situation and I appreciated everything and all of the support while I was working there.

∗ ∗ ∗

WORKING TWO JOBS AT THE AIRPORT

I finally realized that I couldn't make this work with the photography studio. So I started working at the airport driving airport shuttle buses. I also knew that one day somebody would try to rob me of my money, and camera equipment, while I was outside in different neighborhoods taking pictures. This was motivation for me to choose the jobs that I did at the post office and with the shuttle bus company. If only they would've hired me full-time, I probably could have worked just one job, instead of trying to work two jobs.

Again, it was about benefits, not the hourly pay that made a lot of difference in the choices that I made and how much I desired to have either job with the post office or Metro. I thought that by me working with the shuttle bus company, it would give me some experience driving a larger bus with Metro, although I did gain a lot of experience while working there.

∗ ∗ ∗

WORKING WITH THE SHUTTLE BUS AFFECTED MY WIFE, MY KIDS AND I FROM ATTENDING CHURCH LIKE WE USED TO

I figured that if I worked there for about one year, I would have a better chance at getting a job with the Metro Transportation Company. I had some really cool employees that I worked with while driving the shuttle buses at Washington National Airport. My supervisor was a young lady, and she really looked out for me. I told her that I was a photographer, and that I did late night parties. When I would get to work that morning at 4:30a.m., I would tell her that I only had two hours of sleep because I just came from late parties taking pictures. She would allow me to take a quick break about 8:00 a.m., and I would drink a cup of coffee and maybe eat some breakfast. I would treat her to lunch or breakfast depending on what she wanted. She would also look out for me when I wanted to stay home and do a photography job, and during the morning graduations from all of the many different DC High Schools.

Graduations were held normally at Constitution Hall. The way she helped me was when I would call her early in the morning to ask her if they had enough buses for all of the drivers, if not, we would get paid for four hours that day without coming in. That really helped me a lot because the money that I would make taking pictures outside after the graduation ceremonies for one hour would almost amount to the 40 hours that I would work during the week driving buses. I really took full advantage of those days off. I really missed her when she left that job, all of my special privileges were gone with her. Several of the drivers had more seniority over me, and I had to wait until one of them wanted a schedule change in order to get certain days off. If I would have known then what I know now, I would have told my supervisor that I had spiritual obligations to worship my God on Sundays.

After work, my friends and I would drink a few beers, or sometimes go to the local basketball court to shoot some hoops. I had hours to hang out with the guys, and then I would go pick up Paula and the kids. Often, I would go to my parents' house for a while before going to work. One of the main reasons was so that I could bring some ice cream to my nephews and nieces. When I would pick up my daughter from school we always stopped at this store right beside her school to get some ice cream for everybody. Sometimes I would get all of them together, and just take a quick ride to pick up Paula. Finally, I would stop by to check up on my parents. Sometimes I would ask my wife to drive home and give me a break, since I had been driving in airport traffic for seven hours, but with a quick attitude, I had no luck. So, I just went with the flow.

My days off with the shuttle bus company were on Monday and Tuesday, and this interfered with us going to church. When I had the photography studio, Paula and I started going to Shiloh Baptist Church in Northwest. My wife was baptized at Shiloh, and when she was seven months pregnant with our son, we were in the Sacrifice Circle Group. The church was divided into circle groups. Before I started driving the buses, we tried to go to church every Sunday. My mother would go with us most of the time. I was trying to lead my family to the Lord. I was the head of my household and it was my spiritual responsibility to direct my family in the path of righteousness. The devil has always tried to interfere with me living a spiritual life. After I started working with the bus company, I missed taking my family to church on Sunday. Our family unity wasn't the same without the spiritual guidance and church atmosphere.

Sacrifice circle at Shiloh Baptist Church

After I Got Married, I had to take pictures of a wedding that was held at Shiloh Baptist Church. So I told my wife that maybe we should come by one Sunday and check out the service. That's what we did. We came by on a Sunday and we enjoyed the service. As I mentioned the first person that I met was a deacon who made us feel really welcome. His name was Deacon Hough. I sometimes would try to make it to my childhood church Matthews Memorial Baptist Church, even though I just wanted a little change and get away, knowing that I just got married several months prior, we started going to Shiloh Baptist Church every Sunday, and I would also make sure I picked up my mother.

During that time past, Rev. Gregory was the senior pastor at Shiloh. The circle that my wife and I joined was called the Sacrifice Circle. It truly was a blessing when we started meeting some members from this circle. I was trying to do my best to participate, while also struggling to do the right thing. Shortly after I got injured, some of the members from our circle were very supportive to Paula and the kids during a very difficult time for me, getting shot. The Hough's grew even closer to me and they also tried their best to help Paula out by being spiritual supporters to her while she was dealing with my situation.

After I came back from Delaware and started living in Reston Virginia, some of the members from our circle, the Sacrifice Circle, would come by every year, even though he was not a circle member, he was my friend. They came periodically, again, most of the time around my birthday, which is in the month of May and will be outside in the courtyard praying and talking. They did this for a while and then I think that some kind of way we lost communication with each other.

A lot of times when I was in rehab, I would find that the Houghs would be sitting in the chair beside my bed praying for me while I was asleep. They never seemed to be in a hurry to leave me and always made time to come visit me. The same thing was going on when I went to the nursing home in Reston Virginia. Over the years it would be different members from the church. Also, they had different presidents. But I was in charge of the sacrifice circle, they made time to come see me. I appreciate that. I can remember going to the church one year with the Wiggins. I was able to speak to the congregation about whatever God put on my mind and heart. I also started meeting some of the deacons and members from the church like. They would drive the bus to bring the members out.

Rev. Felton would also come to visit me. Sometimes separate from my circle, most of the time he would come with Deacon Kearney and maybe another Deacon from the church. When I was in Reston Virginia and at the facility, located in Hyattsville, Maryland. We lost a lot of members from Shiloh over the years and shortly after I got injured, Rev. Gregory passed away. Then some kind of way, Shiloh Baptist church caught on fire. A lot of damage took place in the old sanctuary and they had to do a total remodeling job on the church. I think they did a great job and then they had to find a new Shepherd to minister to the members at Shiloh and that's when Rev. Smith came in. But how many people can say that they have been a member of two different churches and was able to share my experiences? Even to this day they continue to show me love and I'm so thankful. I met many Reverends, Pastors, Ministers, and Deacons from several different churches over the years, especially during the time that I was in Reston Virginia. At the Cameron Glen facility, God is watching over me and blessed me with so many beautiful people over the years and I pray to God that in some way, that the Lord has allowed me to RECIPROCATE MY LOVE AND APPRECIATION!

* * *

STRUGGLING TO DO THE RIGHT THING, TRYING TO MAKE MONEY, AND TRYING TO STAY AWAY FROM ANY INVOLVEMENT WITH DRUGS

One of my sisters used to want me to get some "love boat" for her that was in the neighborhood where I lived. I would because I was a lil' depressed and disappointed that I wasn't successful in running the photography studio like I had always wanted to. Having a photography studio has always been a dream of mine that came to reality, but that dream did not turn out like I thought it would. I was trying to stop using and selling drugs. Getting rid of my studio wasn't a hard decision to make, if I wanted to support my family, I had to stop using drugs. Plus for the jobs that I applied to I faced random drug testing and if I wanted to support my family, it meant staying clean.

It really was a no-brainer for me, getting high, and possibly losing an opportunity to work with the post office even as a part-time casual holiday employee. I had to quit smoking "loveboat" or drugs in order to have the extra income to help my wife and kids. It was my responsibility to financially provide for my family. Again, it was a no-brainer, so I stopped smoking and using drugs. I am truly thankful to God for the willpower to be able to stop just like that.

* * *

GRADUATION SEASON

During the graduation season, sometimes we didn't have enough buses for the driver, and I would call to check before I left my house. If there wasn't a bus for the drivers, we had an option. Either we would go to work and give breaks to the other drivers or take pay for four hours and go home. I would take four hours of pay, and go to many different graduations and get paid. I did this for about three weeks. I would take Paula to work and go directly to Constitution Hall where all the DC. High Schools held graduations. They would have three graduations a day, and I would average about three to four hundred dollars a day, until this photographer created attention from the police. This brotha was working inside doing video tapes, until he noticed that I was making money outside taking pictures. It was too much for him to see. The next morning he had to set up his background right outside on the side of Constitution Hall on their lawn. After the graduation, he crossed the street and he realized how much attention my backdrop was getting. He was envious, so he started telling me that I was not licensed to take pictures, and then he walked away laughing at me.

Before we could take any pictures a Metropolitan police officer came and told me that I was not allowed to take pictures in front of Constitutional Hall with a background set-up, but I could walk around and take pictures of customers anywhere they stood. The cop gave me a verbal warning and I told him thanks for the advice. Before the police officer finished talking to me he asked me was the other guy with me, and I told him no, sir! He said to me; well I'm going to go there to arrest him, because he's definitely in violation because he is on our Constitution Hall property. I said to the officer; thank you very much and have a nice day. It doesn't pay to be negative to people and because this guy was so negative towards me and laughing at me, he was definitely arrested and just as he told me, he was going to lock him up. I was wondering to myself, was he really laughing now? Even after he laughed at me, I was in line all the time, I JUST PUT EVERYTHING IN GOD'S HANDS! The police officer locked the other photographer up because he was on the property of Constitution Hall, and he wasn't licensed. I know I had a license, but when he said that I didn't, all the time he was the one that didn't have a license. Sometimes it pays to be quiet! I could have been locked up for being on private property for taking pictures, even though I had my license on me. I also would set-up shop on the grounds of my daughter's elementary school.

The reason why I had to relocate my background was because the owners of the carry-out wanted to charge me for setting up in front of their building. The spot by my daughter's school was better anyway because I had a large fence that I could pin the background against. It was also a nice grassy area which helped me to enhance the photos/flicks. That area was also on the avenue and everybody that walked and drove by had to see my background. I could only take pictures at the school on Monday and Tuesday because those were my days off of work at the airport. I traveled many times with this local, popular "go-go" band, but I did not want to bring my wife with me because of the crowds that the go-go bands attracted. Most of the times "young-ins" ended up fighting and violence occurred, and of course I did not want to subject her to any of that. Although I received many offers from women when I was taking pictures, I was about making money, and returning safely to my family.

∗ ∗ ∗

LIGHTER DAYS

It was the summer of July, 1990, on a Saturday, we were having a birthday party for my siblings and one of their friends. This was the first time that I was able to enjoy one of their parties. The first time, I was working at St. Elizabeth's Hospital and on my break I drove to where my parents lived, I was looking at the party from behind the gates of the hospital. My parents' house was directly across from the hospital. It looked like they were having a real good time. The second time they had a party, I had too much to drink. I didn't realize I drank so much that fast, normally that's not me, to drink as much as I did. I had to deal with the consequences and I missed everything about the birthday party.

But the third party was a delight, indeed. I was more established with my polaroid business and I learned from the previous two parties that I needed to be more responsible. Just like in the previous birthday parties, my wife was there and one of her girlfriends that I truly never trusted was there with her at the party this time. I could not get caught up and wondering what my wife and her friend was doing, I just had to remain focus. I'm prepared this time, I had two different backgrounds set up with the lights shining on them. I invited a few buddies of mine from the airport, some of the guys that would normally get together every now and then, also, we would play basketball. This was a pretty good group of guys that I enjoyed being around and I pray they felt the same way. There were plenty of people, plenty of money, and that was sweet. (I know the real story. I talk about money a lot. I understand that God says that THE LOVE OF MONEY IS THE ROOT OF ALL EVIL! It wasn't about the love of money in my case, it was about having enough money to pay my bills and taking my family which was never enough, no matter how hard I worked. I was trying to make it to that next level of professionalism, to work smart not hard, but I never had a problem with working hard, but sometimes you can just use your brain and be smart about how you work).

I cooked on the barbecue grill, but I couldn't snap photos and cook, so one of my co-workers took over the cooking part. Again, I was truly appreciative for him helping me with the cooking. It felt like my birthday party. I was supposed to go to work on Sunday, most of my co-workers were there, so I made sure I called in early to let them know I couldn't make it. Paula was there with one of her sneaky girlfriends that I didn't care for because she would change when she was around her. My sister's boyfriend was around during that time and I had a fifth of cognac in my camera bag for special people. Before everybody got there I made my mom some barbecue wings and she loved them. After all, my mom spent so many years cooking for my father, my siblings and I over the years and decades, I was really glad that I was able to cook something for her that she liked and that was the barbecue chicken wings. I enjoyed it more than she did. Again, because I was able to RECIPROCATE and show her my appreciation for all the years that she cooked for me.

Though the party was jumping, you always have that one jealous neighbor. The police came and said that the neighbors were complaining, and my brother was about to say something wrong, but I told the officer that I would keep everybody within our yard. After talking to the officer, I made the announcement to everyone who

187

wanted to enjoy the rest of the party to stay within the yard, or we would have to terminate the party. Everybody agreed so the party went on. While my coworkers were outside, I went into my parents' house and called my job to tell them that I would not be able to make it in the morning. I was able to make some finances that night and everybody had a wonderful time. When I came back to work the following Wednesday, my coworkers said that they had a blast. I truly and really felt like it was my birthday. I had so much enjoyment being there with my family members, loved ones and associates. But also, it felt like redemption, for missing the previous two very large birthday parties. I was determined that I wasn't going to miss this one, not this time!

CHAPTER 11

GOD & I

On September 20, 1990, I took Paula to work, my daughter to school, and our baby son to the babysitter. After completing my daily routine with my family, I received a call from Paula's uncle. He called to see what was up with me. I replied that I was trying to make some quick money by helping a guy sell a kilo of cocaine. I believe that added up to about $30,000 for the package. He later caught the bus to my house and we snorted a couple of lines of cocaine together. I had to sample it to let people see that the quality of cocaine was like the color. If this deal worked out, I had plans to take my wife to the Poconos resort in Pennsylvania for our third-year wedding anniversary. Upon our return from our vacation, I would start my new job working for the Metro Transportation company and everything would be all right, SO I THOUGHT IT WOULD WORK OUT THIS WAY!

I put a lot of pressure on myself, because I sensed that Paula was involved with another man, and I was trying to keep our marriage together. My mind was running rapid, my marriage, having more money for our family, and the Metro job would have helped me to buy photo equipment for my portrait business in private homes. I estimated with the combined income of my wife and I, we would be bringing in a significant amount financially every year, and we would be able to move out of the neighborhood within a year's time, or maybe even earlier. I even had plans on going to college for radiology. I did have many big plans or was it just wishful thinking? I've learned that anything worth having is truly worth waiting for and that patience is truly a virtue. If I only could have waited for everything to fall in place, and not be so anxious.

The day was running slow, and I asked different people if they were interested in getting this package, but a lot of people became reluctant because it was powder. I proposed this deal to about 10 people within the day, but no one responded. So we decided to drink beer and just chill, until he asked me to take him downtown to this department store.

I spotted my cousin that was on the avenue and asked him if he wanted to ride with us downtown, just for a little while. Since we were waiting for my friend to return, I gave my cousin a couple of toots of cocaine, and before I knew it, time had caught up with me and I had to quickly pick up my family. I picked up our daughter from school first, then quickly went to get my son from the babysitter, and finally we picked up Paula from work. I can't remember if my friend was with me when I picked up my wife, but I do know that I had dropped off my cousin back on the Avenue. It just didn't seem appropriate sometimes to have people with you, especially when you're picking your wife up from work, especially guys. I told Paula that after I dropped them off at home, I had a couple of stops to make with her uncle. After I walked all three of them inside, little did I know that this would be the last time that I would be able to hug my wife and kids. Little did I know that it would be my last time with my family in our apartment together.

Paula made a statement awhile back that if I sold drugs, that we would not be together, she was right!

I wish I would have consulted Paula before I made the decision to do what I did. Maybe just hearing her reminding me of what she said again might've stimulated my brain cells. I remember hearing this song, and I said that I never wanted to have to sing this song in my life. It was called; "If I could have, would have, should have," but it was too late for me, I had already committed this stupid act.

* * *

WRONG WAY

As my wife's uncle, who had recently got out of jail several months prior, I considered him family and I drove off from my apartment, we started looking for a buyer for the kilo of cocaine. He knew some guys that lived in his neighborhood that would be interested in purchasing the kilo (this sentence really says a lot to me now). We went to the neighborhood where my "so-called," prospective customers would be----I was truly over my head trying to sell something of this magnitude. One of my ex-coworkers called me on my beeper and I called him back, he said that he was at a club not too far from our neighborhood. I told him that maybe I would stop by for a few minutes after I was successful in getting rid of the package.

My beeper went off again and it was the people who were interested in getting the kilo. I told them to meet me in front of my parents' house at a certain time. I then called my ex-coworker that had the drugs and I told him to meet me at my parents' house at a certain time. Now everything was set-up, and I had Paula's uncle sitting in my car facing my parent's front porch. He was supposed to be watching my back because I gave him a .22 caliber pistol (Believe It or Not, this is the same pistol that my father accidentally shot himself in the leg with many years prior). When they arrived I was standing on my parents porch and the guy who owned the cocaine was there also. I asked him if he could get someone to watch our backs but he said that he couldn't find anyone. So I assumed he had our backs, but I assumed wrong. (You know, they tell us to never, assume anything, and they were right) Two guys came to the front porch and we started talking. The next thing I remember saying was; "man why are you doing this to me?" They had pulled out their guns and I recall pushing my sister back into the house and I closed the door so that she wouldn't get hurt. I thought I remembered one of the guys saying, "Make sure that he is dead, I didn't like him anyway." Later those words were confirmed by my parents' next door neighbor. He was a neighbor that was aware of everything in the community, and it is nothing wrong with that, because it is said; "WATCH AS WELL AS PRAY." So I know if he heard when the gunman said that to his partner, and made the statement, it was confirmation. It wasn't me imagining that I heard something like that as I was slowly dying. IT WAS REAL!

Bullets went off! I was shot three times, once in the neck, that was the bullet that paralyzed me, one in the left arm, and another bullet grazed me across from my right cheek. The first bullet hit me, and I didn't feel it I guess because I was in and out of consciousness. I tried to act like I was dead, after hearing one of them say, "Make sure he is dead." They didn't shoot the guy who the drugs belonged to, he escaped with no injuries. Although my car was parked 100 feet away from my parents' house, my so-called lookout friend was looking at everything, but did not do anything to help me. Immediately my sister came running out of the house behind the guys and thank God that she was not injured. They got away with no one seeing them. There were bullet holes in the front door and in the wall of my parents' house. I was shot with a few different pistols including a .22 caliber pistol, which I think was the bullet that grazed my face, because if it would've gone inside me, it would've bounced all around in my brain.

The gun I gave my friend, the look-out guy was returned to the owner, which was my father. I came to talk with my father earlier, briefly about the situation and I think that all I told him was that I was trying to get some money to help him get the trailer that he converted into an ice cream truck. I told my father that I needed to get some tools and I needed to get a weapon, because I wanted to protect myself, and again without going into details about exactly what I was about to do, he handed me the .22 pistol without question and I said; "Pop, everything will be okay." My father trusted my judgment and he didn't question me too much about what I was about to do, but being a standup guy that he is, he gave me the .22 pistol. I was truly thankful that I could always talk to either one of my parents about anything, but this time I didn't say anything to my mother about what I was about to do or my wife. I was told that the gun had been fired several times, making the person I was with a suspect. What really hurt was that my parents had to come outside on their porch to see their son lying in a pool of blood, almost dead. They could not hardly get out of the front door because my body was blocking the doorway, according to my sister. He was standing beside me, trying to help me. My father said that when he saw me, I had taken a breath and closed my eyes. He thought I was dead, and he started taking off my ring, and other personal items.

∗ ∗ ∗

MY FATHER FINDING ME OUTSIDE OF THE FRONT PORCH DYING

That night I got shot my father came out of the house to see me lying on the front porch slowly dying. When I think about it, at times, I can't imagine how my father must've felt, seeing his son laying on the porch bleeding out from multiple gunshot wounds. I really feel bad that my parents had to see me dying on the porch. Even now as I'm writing this, I really feel bad. I really felt bad to have put my parents in this kind of traumatic situation and just a visualization of their youngest child dying in my father's arms.

Many years ago, when he told me about when he came out of the house and he saw me laying there again slowly fading away. He told me that I said a few words; "I'M JUST FAKING, I'M JUST FAKING!" And then he said that my head just fell back against his chest, and in his mind I just died in his arms. He told me, presuming that I was dead, he started taking my personal belongings off my body; my wallet, and other possessions that I had on my body and in my pockets and I think my wedding ring and a pinky ring that I used to wear. I still cannot imagine how he must've felt and God knows I had no idea what my status was when my mother came out of the house, and had to see me laying on the front porch. I'm so sorry that I took them through this as well as my wife and my kids. My niece was about nine years old and I think she called my wife and told her; "uncle Jeff is dead!" Now I can imagine how my wife felt to hear this kind of news.

I really don't think that the average person living really think about how much their lives mean to others. When they make bad decisions and mistakes it affects so many other people, BUT I KNOW! I was telling my father that I was just faking because one of the stick-up boys stated; "I DON'T LIKE HIM ANYWAY and MAKE SURE THAT HE'S DEAD" I CAN REMEMBER HEARING THESE WORDS VERY CLEARLY! So I guess self-consciously I was selling my father those words that I was just thinking, because I didn't want to get shot anymore and I was pretending to be dead, but in all actuality, I was dying. Probably for the short period of time, I did die for a moment, until the paramedics arrived. Everything happened very fast because when my father said he started taking my possessions off my body, I wasn't conscience and the paramedics must have arrived, minutes after I said those last few words. MY GOD WAS ALWAYS ON THE SCENE! I thank the paramedics and helicopter pilots for their very quick response.

Over the years I have met many people and sometimes I would have to go to a doctor's appointment by way of ambulance. This one ambulance driver transported me to a couple of appointments. One day I began talking about what happened to me and he said that he used to work in DC as a paramedic. He also said that he vaguely remembered this happening and he said. *"I believe that I was on a call that night, because you had to be transported by helicopter, and we had to take you to the empty parking lot where the helicopter landed. As they transported you from the ambulance to the helicopter he said I was in God's hands now!"* NOW, what are the chances that you will meet someone years later, in my case a paramedic that was on the scene that helped stabilize me. What are the chances and you get to meet him and become friends over the years. I REALLY NEVER BELIEVE IN COINCIDENCES, I BELIEVE IN GOD!

One of my family members told me later after I got injured that they received a telephone call from the hospital and was told that I would be paralyzed for the rest of my life. I could give credit to the devil for helping me loose the blessing that God had waiting for me, but I won't! It's too late to sing, "I could have, would have, and should have!" I can't blame the devil for everything because I knew right from wrong!

When the paramedics arrived, they called for the helicopter to transport me to the Washington Hospital Trauma Center. The helicopter landed across the street in the parking lot of St. Elizabeth's Hospital. They drove me from my parents' front porch to the helicopter across the street. On the way to the hospital God had given me another chance, and the paramedics were able to revive me. Once I arrived at the hospital my parents received a phone call from the doctors telling them my condition. I someone told Paula that I had been shot, and that I was paralyzed. The only thing that I could remember about being in the hospital that night was the rotating bed that I was laying on, because my body was being rotated in a circular motion, in and out of consciousness because of drug that they had me on in the hospital.

CHAPTER 12

NOW FAITH IS

Hebrews 11:1-2 "NOW faith is the substance of things hoped for,
the evidence of things not seen.
For by it the elders obtained a good testimony."

MY SISTER HAS TRULY BEEN A BLESSING
IN MORE THAN ONE WAY!

I truly love all my siblings and I know if they could have come to see me over the years like my sister Marcia did, they would have, but they've helped in different ways as well, mainly keeping me in prayer and that's big! However, my sister was the one that had been driving out to see me almost every week, when I was in Reston Virginia to bring me that home-cooked food. My sister Valencia and my Aunt would try to cook whatever I wanted whenever they came to visit, and again I praise God for that. My sister Marcia would faithfully come to visit me every week, to bring me home-cooked food, to cut my hair, they grow like wild weeds, at one time she was cutting my hair every week, then years later she would wait to cut my hair on the top but would always cut my beard. Within one week, my hair grew back so fast that I had to get it cut again. But I'm truly thankful for commitment from any of my other siblings. BUT every week she made it her business to come help me out. I also remember before my parents passed away when my sister Marcia used to have a very small car, just a little bigger than a Volkswagen, and both of my parents, both of my sisters, sometimes my kids in the summertime and several of my nephews and nieces, would all fit in that small car. It kind of reminded me of the circus and the clown car when all the people would seem to appear out of a very tiny automobile. These were the early stages of me living in Cameron Glen Nursing Facility, located in Reston, Virginia. Over the years through the cold weather, summertime heat, rainy days all the elements, with the help of God, HE MADE A WAY for my sister to be able to come and visit me with the additional help that I mentioned earlier.

All I know is that I was so blessed, and still blessed to be able to have family to visit me for so many years, over two decades since I've been in these nursing facilities. I've seen my roommates hardly get any visitors. It didn't take much for me to realize how much of a blessing to have family that would come to visit you at times when other visitors and these longtime siblings have been forgotten for whatever reason. THANK YOU JESUS! My sister Valencia has been living in South Carolina for more than 20 years as I mentioned, whenever she did get a chance to come up to visit with her daughter, granddaughter and son, she always asked me what I had a taste for dinner and if I wanted her to make me something special. I was truly appreciative of it, and most of the time, I couldn't think of anything.

My brother came to visit a few times when I was in Reston Virginia and I think it bothered him that he didn't know who did this to me. I don't know, and I'm not worried, and I am not going to lose any sleep over it. But sometimes you get these knuckleheads saying things like "you didn't straighten that business out or handle that business concerning your little brother!" That's a lot of UNNECESSARY PRESSURE! It was almost like the devil whispering in your ear and I understand that this bothered my brother at times, and I tried to remind them to just put it in God's hands. But HONESTLY, I am being a little HYPOCRITICAL, because I would've felt the same about trying to find out who were the people responsible for this. This is how a lot of bloodshed and innocent blood takes place, when someone is trying to get back at someone for something they may have on them, or one of their loved ones in their family. But over the years I have been praying and every time a conversation between my brother and I comes up concerning that night that I got injured, I always tried to remind him to just let it go, just like I did 13 years ago when I experienced partial paralysis. I had to tell my earthly father to just let it go AND LET GOD TAKE CARE OF IT!

My brother told me several times that it bothered him to see me like this, again I understand, some people may not. My big brother is nine years older and I am. He sometimes called me by my nickname "Bug" short for Jitterbug. I don't know where my father got that name from, but he cut it short. My brother reminds me that he used to put my diapers on and he reminds me that he is my big brother, like a father and he didn't like seeing me like this. He sometimes questioned himself about why I didn't tell him what was going on that night or what I was about to do. I tell them all the time, "Bro, it wasn't meant for me to tell you because things could have turned out even worse than what it did." There could have been an ongoing battle and more people could have been killed because of my stupid decision. I thank God that He knows what He is doing. I got shot multiple times, nobody is talking, and somewhat the bloodshed ended with me, the way that it was supposed to be. I didn't have to worry about any of my other family members getting injured, my wife and kids, my parents, my brother or sisters, and neither my nephews and nieces. In some ways it ended with me. Again, the way it was supposed to be, or supposed to have happened.

When I say, what I'm about to say, it may sound crazy to a lot of the readers, but if those guys weren't trying to take my life, didn't shoot me, then there were other guys OUT THERE WAITING FOR THE OPPORTUNITY, for various reasons. I will not elaborate, but it wasn't because I was a bad person at all, not perfect, but I wasn't trying to ever hurt anyone. Who knows, the person or persons that pulled the trigger may read his book. I want them to know that I have totally forgiven them all and I pray and put all of you in the hands of God. A lot of times I say this to people, sometimes before I get a chance to explain myself, they may respond and say "those people that did this to you might be in jail or dead," and my reply is always; "I pray that they are not in jail or dead, I pray that they may have turned their lives around and maybe in somebody's pulpit preaching the gospel and asking God for forgiveness!" What kind of a real child of God would I be if I did wrong for wrong, or evil for evil? Then I'm reminded of my Lord and Savior Jesus Christ, while on the cross, dying for my sins AND SAYING TO THE FATHER IN HEAVEN; "Father, forgive them for they know not what they do!"

SOMETIMES IT IS EASIER TO SAY SOME THINGS WHEN YOU'RE NOT GOING THROUGH SOMETHING, BUT WHEN YOU'RE BEING TESTED, YOUR TRUE COLORS SHOW. YOUR FAITH IN GOD SHOWS! THE REAL YOU SHOWS! IT IS TRULY IN THE VALLEY WHERE ALL OF US GROW WHILE DEALING WITH TRIALS AND TRIBULATIONS,

RELATIONSHIPS, UPS AND DOWNS, SAD AND DIFFICULT TIMES, WHEN WE ARE TRULY GOING THROUGH THE STORMS OF LIFE, AND BEING TESTED, THEN WE WILL SEE HOW YOU RESPOND OR ACT TOWARDS A PERSON OR SITUATION!

But as I mentioned I don't lose any sleep, or try to worry about who did this, as long as God knows, and I'm able to forgive them. Knowing that, I had to take FULL RESPONSIBILITY for my own actions and the choices that I made on that night, that led up to me being shot multiple times and diagnosed as a dependent quadriplegic and placed on a ventilator at the age of 25. I'm not even blaming the devil or anyone else, because there's something called ACCOUNTABILITY that we all must deal with concerning the things that we do or even say out of our mouths, especially the words that are spoken out of your mouth from anger.

Think about the Bible story concerning King David, a man after GOD's own heart. 2 Samuel 11 and 2 Samuel 23:39, when he took a man's wife, Uriah and got her pregnant, Bathsheba a Hittite women, and then to try to cover it up. He had one of his loyal soldiers killed after Uriah the Hittite did not fall for King David's trap. He was to try to get Uriah pulled from the battlefield as he fought for the Israelite Army, against their enemies, for the King. King David invited him to the castle and tried to get him drunk so that when he left the palace, like most military men do when they come home from service, had been deployed for so many months or years. The first thing they do when you get time is make sure that they make love to the wife (and this had been going on for centuries). But brother Uriah didn't fall for that trick, being a just man. He said to himself, my soldiers are out there fighting and I should be out there fighting with them, not here, making love to my beautiful wife. She was a beautiful woman. King David went into the house and then into his wife, this brother went to sleep on her front porch, TALKING ABOUT LOYALTY!

King David realized that the trick that he and Bathsheba tried to set for her own husband Uriah, BACKFIRED! Now King David had to come up with another plan and that was to send Uriah back to fight the war, but he gave his generals specific orders to make sure that BROTHER URIAH, was put on the front line. Back in those days, everyone would run straight into each other when the main word "CHARGE" was yelled. That's what brother Uriah did, he went back with this man to continue fighting the battle for King David and the Israelite military and he was killed. WHY? He was being a loyal soldier, but he was not respected nor treated as a loyal man by his own loyal wife and also BY HIS OWN LOYAL KING! King David repented and that story is found in Psalms 51, when he asked God for forgiveness for what he had done to Bathsheba and Uriah the Hittite.

I don't want to deviate from what I was saying about my brother wanting to find out who did this to me and having someone negative speaking in his ear about getting revenge but also about me taking full responsibility and accountability for my actions, my choices and learning how to deal with the consequences. I had to ask my wife and kids, my parents, siblings, nephews and nieces and the rest of my family members for their forgiveness. There are so many other people that are involved in your life, that can affect them by the choices that we make. Even the mention of suicide, which is a very selfish act, because you are just thinking about yourself and not how it may affect or will affect so many others. If you took your life, THE COWARD ROUTE out, I can say this because I've been tempted multiple times to do just that, but thank you Lord for always being there with me even when I've been tested and tempted by the opposer.

I THANK ALL OF MY FAMILY MEMBERS FOR THEIR PRAYERS, LOVE, VISITS AND EVERYTHING ELSE GIVEN TO ME OVER THE YEARS! ALSO, THE SAME GOES TO MY SPIRITUAL FAMILY MEMBERS FROM THE CONGREGATION AND THE FRIENDS THAT I'VE BEEN BLESSED TO MEET THUS FAR ON MY PILGRIMAGE OR ALONG THE ROAD!

* * *

SPIRITUALLY IN CHECK

Since I've become paralyzed, I've been praying for healing of my whole entire body, because I believe that Jesus is a healer and He will restore everything that the devil has stolen from me and my family. Though the devil is responsible for every bad thing that happens to you and I, I realized that we have an option to make Godly decisions, versus following tempting demonic forces.

Since I've been injured, there have been a lot of different denominations of churches visiting me; The Catholic followers, The Lion Of Judah, Baptist Churches, non-denominational churches, Seven Day Adventist, and the Jehovah's Witness. Everybody wanted me to convert to their particular faith and doctrine. The members from the Catholic Church asked me have I ever thought about joining their church. I told them that I was trying to learn as much as I could before making a decision.

Every Thursday members from the Catholic church came to visit me, and occasionally we had pizza parties. We became good friends and I tried to give the best advice to her as possible. I was introduced to a lot of their Catholic friends and they would visit me every Sunday at 12 noon after they were finished giving the Rosary. John introduced me to Christina and on Sunday about 12 noon, another young lady from the Catholic church would visit me, and she would help me with opening up mail, or setting up my file cabinet. Sometimes she would visit to just talk about life in general. We are about the same age and that helped a lot to communicate with your peers. John, Christina and I used to talk about me writing a novel and using an alias name.

The Lion of Judah members used to come every Sunday, but now they come on Tuesday. They also have become friends of mine, sometimes they sing songs, and we have prayed together for spiritual healing and blessings. Lynn, a leader among the Lion of Judah, is one of the first members that I met from the congregation. In 1999 Lynn and her husband Tim moved to Israel. Margaret was another friend of mine from the same congregation, who moved to China in the same year. Becky used to also visit me, but I don't see her much now. They have some new members from the Lion of Judah church that come around on Sunday. After they stopped coming to visit with me Sister Bunny and Rose started coming every Sunday. Sister Bunny and her husband have been very helpful to me over the years, especially during the Christmas holiday.

The Jehovah Witness members are working all throughout the facility here at Cameron Glenn. One of the nursing assistants named Jackie introduced me to her husband. We started a study session every Saturday or whatever days he has available. This session went on for about a year or two. I learned some different things from him, but there were several questions that were unanswered.

I also met a Seventh Day Adventist named Darnel, who had a brother who was a comatose resident in the facility. His brother's room was right down the hall from me. Darnel is a young lady who would do anything to help anybody. She has been a true inspiration to me. I met her mother, her brother's daughter Jamie, and they were like family to me. Even after her brother died, they all still came to visit with me. I have learned some things from her congregation, and I have somewhat of an understanding of their beliefs.

This is my personal feeling about the different religions that we have in our society today. I believe that there's one God, Jehovah, His son Jesus Christ, and the Holy Spirit. We have so many different religions throughout the world, it confuses the people. I wish that with the power from the Lord, all humanity would become one in Christ Jesus. This would eliminate wars, competition, politics, and all unnecessary drama. Although it is not in my power to discriminate against any church, I asked God to direct me to the right church. Before I was injured I was attending a Baptist church. I also attended a Holiness church, and now that I'm not able to take my children to church every Sunday, it bothers me knowing that Paula's not taking them to the house of worship.

∗ ∗ ∗

EASTER SUNDAY

I met this young lady that was working at the daycare center here at the facility. We started talking, and later became good friends. She introduced me to a lot of her family members and friends. We called her Boo. They would visit me almost every day. Her sister would always come on a Thursday, because we both liked looking at this television show called "New York Undercover." She was really crazy about one of the male actors. Every Sunday they would come, and we would have a little worship service. One of her friends would sometimes come and visit with me. They invited my family and I to come to their Easter Church Service that was located in Ashburn, Virginia, somewhere near Redskins Park. Both of my parents, Marcia, a couple of my nephews, nieces, and Marcia's boyfriend all came to the service. I asked Paula several weeks before I was supposed to attend the Easter service to see if she would bring our children to my parents' house, so they would be in attendance with all of us on Easter Sunday. Sadly, to say, she did not bring the children or give me a legitimate excuse as to why she wasn't bringing them to my parents' house. I had one of the members from that church to make my son a white vest and pants that would match my white suit that I had someone to purchase for me. I had a special outfit made for my son to attend church with us, because my wife insisted that he didn't have anything to wear.

Prior to that Easter, my first two years here at Cameron Glen, Paula brought the children up here to visit with me on Easter Sunday. There used to be a certified nursing assistant (CNA) that was close to my children and I. Those first two years that she brought my children here on Easter Sunday, God had blessed me with the money to purchase their Easter outfits, along with outfits for the following Monday. After several years of attending Easter Sunday service at their church, their visits faded away. I truly enjoyed all of their visits.

∗ ∗ ∗

CHRISTIAN LOVE

I used to attend two different Baptist churches. One was my neighborhood church Matthews Memorial Baptist church, called MMBC, and after I married Paula, I attended Shiloh Baptist Church. The reason why I decided to join another church was because I wanted a change of atmosphere, so that I could grow spiritually with my new family. Paula was baptized at Shiloh when she was about seven months pregnant with our son. I would still go to Matthews Memorial Baptist Church when we were running late and could not make it to Shiloh on time.

We were still getting spiritually fed from both of the congregations, and depending on which church I attended that

Sunday, was where I paid my tithes to God. During the beginning of the days that I was injured, the members from Shiloh were very supportive to Paula, the kids and I. But after a couple of years, my wife stopped attending Shiloh Baptist Church. We were in a group called Sacrifice Circle at Shiloh. When I heard the name of our circle was Sacrifice, I knew that I was in the right group.

Shiloh has many different circle groups, it just depends on when you join their church, and what circle group is open that particular Sunday. Matthews Memorial Baptist Church didn't have circle groups, but they have the 12 Tribes of Israel. After I was transferred from Delaware to Reston, Virginia nursing facility, the Sacrifice Circle members would come out to Cameron Glen to worship the Lord and visit me. They always would come around May, which was also the month that my birthday is in. It would be between 8 and 14 members from my circle for about five of the first years that I was here. Most of the times we would form a circle outside in the courtyard of Cameron Glen, and the other two years we gathered together inside of the facility.

I had ordered some finger sandwiches, chips and soda for them to eat because I knew that they were probably hungry because of their early arrival. I was blessed to be able to have these treats for them two years in a row. They stopped coming out here for a few years but nevertheless in June of 2002, about six of the members from the Sacrifice Circle came to visit with me. I was saddened to hear that one of the lady members from our group had died. I still tried to stay in touch with some of the members, like Deacon Lynch's wife who is our new Sacrifice leader now.

***

COGER CHORALIERS

(The Oldest Choir that they had in Matthew
Memorial Baptist Church)

On March 13, 2000, I was visited by the Coger Choraliers of MMBC. Twelve or fifteen ladies came in to meet me with several different kinds of food. They had just started visiting the sick and shut-in members of Matthews Memorial Baptist Church. One of the ladies suggested that they would start by visiting me first. I wasn't supposed to know that they were coming on that Saturday. It was supposed to be a surprise visit. However, my mother knows my situation here at Cameron Glen Care Center. She knew that I would want to have my morning care done before any visitors came to see me. So she called me in advance to let the staff members know that I had several visitors coming to see me about 12 noon. I cannot remember who my CNA was that morning, but they had my morning care done before the members from MMBC came. They came in three at a time, and every one of them had an assortment of sweets, gourmet cakes, cookies, and delicious foods. During a whole day I have never seen many staff members come into my room until they were offered some of the food that the Coger Choraliers brought in for me that day. I only recognized probably one or two of the ladies that visited me that day. Two of the Choraliers were named Minnie, just like my mother's name. Later I learned that one of the ladies named Minnie actually knew my entire family, with the exception of me. Her family used to live in the Barry Farms area where I grew up. I knew her husband and two of her sons, but I never met her before. The only way we both found out who we both were, was after I mailed her a letter trying to get some information from one of her sons who had a vendor stand. I was trying to find out where to purchase some of the designer perfumes that most of the Muslims used to sell. I was hoping that her son could tell me, and I was going to sell the oils to make some money to get my children some Christmas gifts.

In return Mrs. Lloyd, along with some of the Coger Choraliers, raised over $100 dollars as a gift to my children and I. There were many others and after their initial visit they started coming more frequently to visit. Back to the day when the Coger Choraliers came to visit with me. I had a really special and blessed visit from those 12 or 15 beautiful elderly ladies, it was more than just 15 ladies in the choir, but for the first time they came to visit me. It was probably about 12 or 15 ladies. It almost seemed like they were in competition to feed and get closer to me. I felt special and thank God all of these wonderful ladies came to encourage me. They in return said that instead of them encouraging me, that I was a big encouragement to them. They could not wait to get back to the church and give a report about their visit with me over the weekend.

I felt like I had all of these adopted new mothers and I tried to talk with each one of them while they were here. The following Christmas they took up another Christmas donation to help me get some gifts for my children, again without me asking for anything. Anytime that I contacted Matthews Memorial Baptist Church, I always told the secretary, or whomever, to tell all of the Choraliers hello for me. I tried to send them Mother's Day cards, Christmas cards, and birthday cards every year. Knowing that they visited other sick members from our church, I made several 'Get-Well' cards for them to give to the sick members from the Choraliers.

Unfortunately, Mrs. Wood died in March of 2002, a couple of weeks before her birthday. She was suffering from cancer and any time that I would think about her, I would try to send her an inspirational card or letter. As long as I live these 12 ladies will always hold a special place in my heart. I truly thank God when visitors come to encourage me by praying and lifting my spirits up. So in return, God allows me to encourage, and lift up my visitors spiritually.

* * *

THE COGER CHORALIERS AT MATTHEWS MEMORIAL BAPTIST CHURCH (MMBC)

I was so honored and thankful to God that they would drive all the way out to Reston Virginia, but also make me the first visitor on the sick and shut in list over the years. They decided to make this annual event. They started coming to visit me every year, sometimes, my birthday, and then every second week of December, before the Christmas holiday, they would come out and bring a feast of home-cooked food. Each one of them made something different, just to name a couple of things; barbecue ribs, macaroni and cheese, potato salad, collard greens, string beans, ham, fried chicken. One year, one of the ladies made a whole turkey. A whole turkey, with all the trimmings and all kind of desserts, sweet potato pies, homemade baked cakes, candy yams, cupcakes, I mean they made all kinds of things and it seemed like every year, a different Coger Choraliers would come with them. I had to learn how to remember all their names because I tried my best to individually talk to each one of them during the time that they were there.

I was really blessed by God to meet all of these beautiful ladies over the years. Did I mention that they were the oldest choir at Matthews Memorial Baptist Church. So not only was I blessed with all kinds of home-cooked food, but when they started singing, they had Angelic voices from heaven. Not only could these ladies cook they all could really sing, I mean really. Those old-time gospel hymns that makes you want to cry because they touch your heart and your soul when you hear all of their voices singing together, just beautiful. They have been doing this for at least 18 years, it seems. Not only did I look forward to seeing them every year, but the staff looked forward to seeing them as well, because they were bringing so much food, that it was enough to feed all the staff in my unit, and enough to feed any of the other residents, that could eat from the different units. They were welcome to join us!

When they fed the staff on my unit, it was a way to say to them, "THANK ALL OF YOU FOR TAKING CARE OF OUR BROTHER/SON, JEFFERY D CHAPMAN SENIOR" and the staff would get as much food as they wanted to because they made a lot of food. I mean a lot of food! They would make sure I had several plates of food to eat for a few days. They did this for at least 10 years straight or 15 years straight. Sometimes the other staff members would hear about the food we had on our unit, and they came like a bunch of wild, greedy buffaloes. No one invited them, and at some point I had to put a stop to it because they were getting out of hand and being disrespectful and greedy. I was ashamed to see how some of the staff would get more than one plate, not being considerate of other people that might have wanted some food. They were just greedy and disrespectful.

So the following year, I got a dressy screen and put it by the door. It said: PLEASE DO NOT DISTURB, PRIVATE PARTY! Being in a nursing home, there is a possibility that the majority of them that came to get some food did not wash their dirty hands. Some of them didn't even ask, they just helped themselves in our area. Even though it was a lot of food at the time for everybody, it was the way the other staff intruded on our private party without asking if it was okay to join us. Like I said I had to stop it, now that I had the sign on the door and the screen to block everybody off, I had no problems with the staff coming from the different units. Right before I put the sign up, one of the ladies from another unit already had two or three plates of food in her hand. I told her not to tell anyone else that we had food on the unit. Of course, that was like telling everybody that we had more food, because that's exactly what she did, she told everybody. The next time I saw her I let her know that I didn't appreciate her announcing that I was having a Christmas party. Sometimes our people can spoil everything for everybody else!

The following years, the ladies stopped cooking as much food as they did the first 7 or 8 years. That last time when the uninvited staff members came over to get some food, I asked the ladies from the church to pass out the food and don't let the staff serve themselves, because they did it all the time and the most embarrassing thing was that these were women, neither of them were men. So they messed it up for everybody but the ladies still came faithfully every year to make sure I had this Christmas party. They brought home-cooked food, a lot of home-cooked food! And what we started doing was one of the ladies would feed me my food first. Then, the ladies would take time out to feed themselves. Then it was time for them to put aside several plates of food for me. Afterwards was when they asked the staff members down the hall of my unit to come and get something to eat. I know the staff was waiting for someone to tell them to come on down, because the food was smelling so good, just smelling all of the food would make anybody hungry.

At Cameron Glen, they would make sure that we had a designated area, as a matter of fact I would make sure that I always informed the material maintenance staff that I needed a certain amount of chairs and tables a couple of days ahead of time. I truly appreciate them accommodating us throughout the years. When I moved to the Hyattsville nursing facility I started accumulating a lot of bedsores and I wasn't able to get up in my electric wheelchair like I used to, as a result, the bedsores started getting worse and worse. That enabled me to get up in my wheelchair like I used. When the bedsores would finally heal, my batteries on the wheelchair was not working, so I have been really stuck between the bed and the wheelchair, between a rock and a hard place. To be truly honest about my situation, can you believe that after living in the facility for more than 20 years, I only had four bedsores and sadly to say that since I've been here, I've had more than 50 and counting, which is not allowing me to get up in my wheelchair for years now. They had a designated area that we could've used right here in the facility but the people here at this facility was not as friendly and accommodating as they were a Cameron Glen. But the ladies still continued to come on the Christmas holiday to be with me. They had to cut down on cooking as much food as they used to at Cameron Glen. But they still had enough for all of us to enjoy together. Since I've been here, they still come on my birthday and again on Christmas.

They would go back to the church on fire because FATHER GOD would give me the right words to say to all of them. That was very encouraging and when I got back to the church they would always share all of their experiences with other church members, including the pastor.

I have lost a lot of my adopted spiritual mother's from Matthews Memorial Baptist Church. We have lost several of them over the years, and I thank God that we all were able to enjoy each other's time together whenever they visited. Several of them have passed on to be with the Lord. GONE, BUT NEVER FORGOTTEN!

And if I'm not mistaking, the Pastor of MMBC, decided to dismember **THE OLDEST GOSPEL CHOIR, AND THE CHURCH, THE COGER CHORALIERS.** They will always be the Coger Choraliers to me. I don't know what church that has been around for so long would get rid of their SENIOR GOSPEL CHOIR. They were the pioneers of the gospel choirs in the church, and also the voices that the young generation used to be blessed to hear. Now they have broken the senior choir up to make a larger choir, that doesn't make any sense to me.

I have an idea why this might've happened, that made them decide to break up the choir, but will keep it between God and I. But I'm so thankful and blessed to have so many members from the church to come and visit me. I know that the staff might've fell like; WOW, look at all them, they came to see Mr. Jeffery D. Chapman, Sr. I would try to remain humble, knowing that the Lord had blessed me in so many ways over the years. Each and every one of these beautiful and lovely ladies, The Coger Choraliers hold a special place in my heart, and they always will. May God bless each and every one of them and their family members *AND THE CONGREGATION! Shortly after I got injured, Rev. Russell, who was The Senior Pastor, or should I say The Senior, Rev., passed away, maybe a year or so after I got injured. They had to find another pastor because of the loss. When he was living, I really enjoyed our conversation that we had and most of them were very short conversations, but, I appreciate him taking the time to talk to me every now and then.*

"REST IN PEACE PASTOR RUSSELL"

* * *

HE WILL NEVER LEAVE YOU NOR FORSAKE YOU

God is Good Isn't He? On March 17, 2002, God's goodness manifested when I received an award from Matthews Memorial Baptist church. The members at Matthews Memorial Baptist Church presented my family with a plaque for being the "Man of the Year." My mother, niece sister, and both of my children were there to receive the award. My other sister and my father was also in attendance, but they did not go up with the rest of my family to receive the award. I truly believe that it was a lack of communication with each other. I had no idea that they were giving me an award, but it was a sign, and a confirmation from the Lord.

I had been laying here in my bed for a few days praying that I was doing the Will of God, and God showed me by pouring out his blessings in my life. I was very happy that my children were there to witness how others felt about their earthly father, that was almost more important than just receiving the award. I pray constantly that Paula will one day find a spiritually filled church with God's Holy Spirit flowing throughout the church. I know sometimes that we want people to change the way that we want them to change according to what we want, but I have learned to first ask God to change people according to His will first.

CHAPTER 13

NRH

My stay at the hospital was now over! After only staying in the hospital for six weeks, the doctors told me that I was one of the fastest patients in my physical condition to leave the hospital as fast as I did. I took this as a positive note, hoping that my physical condition would get better because of the progress that I made in the hospital. My next journey would be to the National Rehab Hospital in Washington, DC.

That year when I was shot, Paula came to my room on New Year's night wearing a very fancy and pretty green dress. We had a New Year's drink together and I appreciate her coming there and watching the ball drop on television in New York. It was after she left NRH to go party somewhere with someone. I believe that my children was over my parents' house, and that might have been the only reason why she came to the rehab center that night, because she told my parents that she was going to stop by first. I'm not trying to color Paula bad, I just know how she is. Now after she left, all I thought about is where she was going, and who she was going with, Jealousy yes! Curious yes! But most importantly, I was stuck in the rehab center worrying about my wife having fun with someone else instead of me.

I befriended a few nursing assistants that would come over to the rehab center sometimes to visit with me, and I really appreciated their visits, more than they would ever knew. My voice finally recovered, and I began using a speaking vial called Passey-Muir that really helped my speech. I was now able to communicate with my family and others. While I was in the hospital, I couldn't talk to my wife or children when they would visit me. Even when they got home and called me on the telephone, tears would roll down my face because I was unable to respond and I didn't know if I ever would be able to talk again. We take so much for granted, and something as small as a scratch, or an itch on my face is a challenge because I have to wait for someone to help me. Nurses would take a long time to answer my call light, and by the time they arrived, the itching would be gone. I requested medication because I had a very bad scalp condition called Psoriasis. According to the doctors, my skin condition comes from stress, and yes my heart was heavy. When thinking about my wife and thinking about what she might have been doing with someone else or what somebody else was doing with her, I'M ONLY HUMAN! But I never actually thought that I was stressed, my body was stressed because of the trauma of getting shot multiple times, and I had no control of that. It is something that the body does naturally when subjected to this type of trauma. However, for me to be stressed or even depressed, I refused to accept either one of these titles. My doctor and other staff members might have noticed some of the activities that some of the other patients would display when they are depressed, but not me, and I'm not in denial at all, it is just how I felt.

In the morning I would get bathed, and then get dressed. Afterwards it was time to eat breakfast, and after breakfast I went to occupational or physical therapy. I received a full hour of physical therapy, and 30 minutes of occupational therapy after breakfast. Then it would be reversed, one hour of occupational therapy and 30 minutes of occupational therapy. NRH really had their program together! NRH provided me with two great female therapists. I believe I had the two best therapists in the entire departments, not taking anything from the other therapist, but I believe that I had one of the best physical and occupational services within the entire rehab department. While I was there, I learned a lot about my physical condition. Paula would come for certain training, like how to transfer me from my bed to the wheelchair.

* * *

SOCIALIZATION

Paula had learned how to take care of me. She learned how to use the suction. This was a process that the respiratory therapist and nurses would normally do because of my inability to cough up the secretions. They would have to use a sterile, plastic narrow tube to stick inside of my track, that was located in my throat, to suction out all of the secretion that I could not cough up, because my diaphragm was paralyzed. Because she had this training she would be able to take me outside of the facility if she wanted to and transfer me from the bed to the wheelchair. She learned how to give me a bowel program, and I really believe that was a turning point in our relationship because it involved some very nasty stuff. In all fairness to Paula, after learning about how to do a bowel program, without going into every detail about it, it would've taken a strong person that was more medically inclined to do this and again I believe that it was a turning point. She learned to do these programs for me and I truly appreciate all of her sacrifice that she made to learn the other skills. Also, I thank her employer for being understanding and allowing her to come over because her job was just a few blocks away from the hospital. She had just started this job, that was a no COINCIDENT, THAT WAS GOD!

During those days at NRH, Paula would come every day for lunch and spend some time feeding me while looking at her stories, I appreciated that. She would also bring the children almost everyday, again I appreciate her bringing the children to visit with me while I was in the rehab center. This part of my life was too hard for her to endure. It wasn't something that she was willing to do, now I understand more.

* * *

REAL SPIRITUAL FRIENDS
DEACON HOUGH

When I was in the rehab hospital in Washington, DC, sometimes I would get a surprise visit from Deacon Hough, or Michelle. Deacon Hough was one of the first members at Shiloh Baptist Church that I met. He reminded me of a couple of my relatives in South Carolina. He was always a friendly person, and I always looked for him when I went to church. Downstairs was the overflow room, which had a movie screen in it that showed the upstairs service. I really wasn't that interested in going upstairs to listen to the service, especially with a very active two-year old daughter. I just developed a comfort zone downstairs. I introduced Deacon Hough to my mother one day after church service and she said the same thing, that he reminded us of a couple of our relatives in South Carolina. He said that he admired a young man bringing his family to church. I really appreciated hearing him tell me that, because it motivated me even more to be at church.

Deacon Hough has sent me a check for different amounts of money since I've been living at Cameron Glen. I am truly thankful and blessed to have his support and prayers throughout the years, especially dealing with my situation. I felt that I owed him the right to know everything, that I remember about the night that I was shot. He didn't change his attitude towards me. I really appreciate his understanding and constant prayers and support for my family and myself. The last two holidays I was able to give him and his wife a small gift. It was only some cologne and some perfume. The year of 1999 Christmas holiday, I duplicated the gifts. I sent a different fragrant this time, and both of them were thankful. I believe that he was a little upset with me because I brought them a Tupperware set for their wedding anniversary. I was very hesitant about calling him to wish them a happy anniversary. He told me that I should be saving that money for my family or for my own use, and that I should have not purchased them anything. I'm sorry, but when someone has been so helpful to me I have to show my appreciation any way that I can. I truly didn't want to offend him or disrespect him in any way at all.

In 2000, Deacon Hough was still helping me in a lot of ways. I have adopted him as my grandfather. I truly have nothing but love for that gentleman, for being a real friend. He has come out to visit with me a few times since I've been living here at Cameron Glen. Michelle was a member of our Sacrifice Circle, and she has always been helpful to our family. She reminded me a lot of one of my cousins, she was my mother's niece from her other brother. Michelle did a lot of smiling and she was very understanding. After my accident, she stayed in touch with Paula and the children to be supportive if she needed it. Paula told me that one day Michelle and another member from our Sacrifice Circle had invited her, the children and my mother to one of our members house for a special gathering.

When I was in the rehab hospital, sometimes I would be asleep and awake and see either Michelle or Deacon Hough sitting right beside my bed praying and patiently waiting for me to awake. I really appreciated their prayers and support. When I was in Delaware, Michelle along with another member from our Sacrifice Circle came to visit with me. I don't know if they followed my family there, or if it was all God's arrangement.

Sometimes the members from the Sacrifice Circle would come to visit with me around the same time as my birthday. We all would have prayer, and I would tell them how thankful and blessed I was from God and also to have all of them to make the sacrifice to come all the way up here to visit with me. I was able to supply them all with some finger sandwiches, potato chips and some soda when they arrived, because I know that they would get up early in the morning to get out here. Most of them didn't have time to make anything to eat before they would leave their houses. I was blessed to be able to have something for them during their visit. The last visit that I received from my circle was in the year 1998. I truly was hoping that they did not come in 1999 because I wasn't getting out of bed that much. God heard my prayers, and I didn't get a telephone call or a visit from any of the newer members from The Sacrifice Circle. When they visited me the last time, some of them seemed very distant from me, and she wasn't the same person anymore. Maybe she heard about what had happened to me that night, that I was injured, but I wasn't asking anyone for a hand out, just prayer.

Passing away of My Good Friend Deacon Hough, in the year of 2016

I always called Deacon Hough, he would talk about **God** all the time which is a blessing and every now and then I would get a chance to talk to Mrs. Dorothy Hough, his lovely wife. When I talked to her, it was as if I was talking to a female version of Deacon Hough, they had the same kind of mannerism, and even when they would talk they sounded like one another.

One day I called Deacon Hough, because it had been a while since we spoke to one another on the phone. We talked about the church about how God had blessed all of us and as usual he would always complement me about how I was a blessing to him, and how God allowed me to be a blessing to others.

I know that he met Paula once or twice before over the years and I can't remember if he actually met my kids in person, over the years, but I made sure that he had photographs of them. As we were talking about my family he always asked how they were doing and I would give him the best update that I could concerning them. Again, always trying to remain positive while giving the report and updates to him. On this particular day, as usual I always asked them how is Mrs. Hough was doing, this particular time, he paused for a moment and said, "Oh No Jeff, Oh No, you don't know!" And I said to him; "I don't know what Deacon Hough?" He said, "Jeff, I lost my Dorothy a couple of months ago." I was very, very sad to hear that his wife had passed away, but also a little angry at myself that I didn't call him earlier or sooner, to maybe be supportive or even to send him a condolence card. Because I always sent them a personalized greeting card on holidays and birthdays, and sometimes just because, to let them know that I'm checking in on them, and thinking about the both of them, but also praying for them. I knew that he didn't have a lot of family, as far as I know, especially in Washington, DC area, and I don't think his wife had that many family members in this area either. I think that they both had outlived the majority of their family members. After finding out that his wife had passed away, I tried to call him a little more frequent or often, knowing that he was alone most of the time. I also learned that he did have a cousin that lived in Baltimore that would come around and help out with certain business, concerning him, and other personal things that she was helping him with over the years. Again, especially since his wife had passed away.

And there were a lot of brothers and other Deacons, from Shiloh Baptist Church, that would check on him every now and then. One in particular was a new friend of mine that I met, one after the Rev Felton, Deacon Kearney and then they brought in Deacon Hill, that I met for the first time. So Deacon Hill and I had developed a very special friendship the last two or three years. He would go by to see Deacon Hough at least once a week or twice a week to make sure that he had a full refrigerator. I would get an update through him about how Deacon Hough was doing. During the latter days Deacon Hough was not able to attend church like he used to because he was getting older and also having some medical problems.

One day Deacon Hill came to bring in a few cases of water, this was the year of 2016, and he said that he had to tell me something. Honestly, I had a feeling that he had to tell me something concerning Deacon Hough. Ever since the day we met he made sure I had several cases of water every week. He was truly a blessing to me in so many ways. So while he was stacking the cases of the water in my closet, he nonchalantly said, "Deacon Hough passed away the other day." Just like that! And he said it so quickly, that I had to ask him again; did you say that Deacon Hough passed away? And he said yes, he passed away, the other day. Then he started explaining to me what exactly happened. Deacon Hough had started to get a very bad sore on his ankle, or somewhere on his foot, and at first he was allowing the nurse to come in the house and medicate the bad sore that he was developing. Then I guess he got tired and stopped allowing the nurse to even come into the house. I guess he was tired of living after the loss of his Dorothy and he was ready to meet up with her. Deacon Hill told me that once Deacon Hough had fallen in the bathroom, there's a possibility that he may have hit his head on something, and they found him dead in the bathroom. It was possible that he could have been dead for couple of days, and I forgot who found him. But I think they also contacted Deacon Hill, that was there shortly after his body was discovered.

Deacon Hough was about 96 or 98 years of age when he died. When I received the news from Deacon Hill, in my spirit, I truly felt something was wrong with Deacon Hough, and after Deacon Hill left the room, I started to think back over the years, how blessed I was to know Deacon Hough, that he prayed for my family and I over the years and he truly was a good friend to me.

Knowing the struggles that I was dealing with financially, trying to be a supportive father he would send me some finances every month and I would try to buy certain products that would help me to multiply the finances. Especially during the time that I had to give my checks to Cameron Glen nursing facility. I never told him anything about that. Deacon Hough was just trying to help me be a father to my kids and to be able to purchase things for them. After the facility started taking my disability check every month, they would give me $70, again with my different businesses, that was being very lucrative for little while. I told him that I truly appreciated all the help they provided for me and that, please understand, I mean no disrespect, but you don't have to send me the finances anymore. God provided me a way to be able to make a few dollars here and there, and I thanked him so much for all the finances, prayers and friendship over the years, I told him. So he stopped sending me the checks because I didn't want to seem greedy at times when he was sending me the checks. I was very needy, God knew it, and the Lord blessed me in so many different ways, but I truly appreciated everything he did for me. Even when I tried to do some things for him and his wife as I mentioned earlier, he really didn't want to receive anything from me, like a gift or something. It was just a special friendship God had allowed us to share for many years. I can't remember exactly, but I think it was either a holiday or a birthday when I sent them the last card and I pray to God that he was able to read it before he passed away. He would truly be missed by so many, and he shared with so many people over the years his kindness and love, ESPECIALLY ME, MAY HE REST IN PEACE ETERNALLY NOW WITH HIS WIFE!

Deacon Hough, JOB WELL DONE!

∗ ∗ ∗

WEEKEND STAFF AT NRH

It seems that the weekend staff had a nonchalant attitude towards most of the patients there because they were lazy and did not show that they cared as much as the regular weekly staff. There was a lady that would come from Baltimore twice a week to see her husband Mr. Brooks. I believe that she came as often as she did because she was fully aware of the attitude of the weekend staff. I believe that was one of her main reasons for coming on the weekends, and also just to be a supportive wife. I remember her giving Mr. Brooks a shave and a bed bath. I really respected her for taking care of her husband that way. I wished that I could have received some of that TLC from Paula, but everybody is different. In some ways I believe that Mrs. Brooks had an impact on Paula, as far as visiting with me. She had an attractive daughter and she was probably a few years younger than I. I really liked her a lot and if I would have met her under different conditions, I wouldn't mind dating her. Mrs. Brooks would give her husband a sponge bath and make sure he was comfortable. Mr. Brooks could not talk, but before he left, he took out his trachea, this is a small, stainless steel device, that is inserted inside of a person that is having complications with breathing. If their airway is blocked, they can bypass it by putting this two or three inch

217

device inside of the throat. In my situation this is how they connected the life support machine to my body. Mr. Brooks no longer needed the life support machine, and that is why they took his trachea out because he had made a lot of progress, and he started breathing on his own. He was able to say some words to his family. He was later moved to a facility to Baltimore and we used to say that it was a long way from DC. to Baltimore, but Delaware was even further. Paula and I called Mrs. Brooks shortly after I left NRH, and unfortunately Mrs. Brooks told us that her husband passed away. He was one of my first friends to pass away at NRH.

While I was living at the hospital prior to NRH, I had another friend named Rob, he lived three doors down from me. We would drink alcohol, and watch movies together. We were blessed to have the ability to swallow, so we could eat regular food, and drink everything we wanted to. Our doctors and nurses probably didn't know that we were intoxicated when we were, and if they did, they never said anything or reported us. Rob was also a quadriplegic and suffered this condition because he was also shot. It truly is a small world, because Rob's mother used to get her hair done by my sister. Our families knew each other.

I had another friend named Darnell who I met at NRH. I never actually met Darnell in person, they told me that his uncle would come by and cut his hair for him, so I asked them to ask his uncle if he would cut my hair for me. Darnell helped me a lot, even though we never met, and his uncle never did cut my hair. I always would hear the staff talking about how he had cursed another staff member out. One of the respiratory therapist told me that he wanted to die and he did not want anybody to reposition him. By Darnell laying on one side of his body all of the time, he developed several bad bed sores up and down one side of his entire body. (Sometimes people can help you indirectly that have no knowledge of it), and this is how he helped me, because I would always tell the staff that I was ready to get repositioned. Most of the time they would have an attitude, but I refused to get any bed sores because I didn't want to get repositioned. I wanted to talk with Darnell about giving up, because I learned that he had a daughter, and I was very early in my paralysis situation. Darnell was injured a lot longer than I was, but I still thought that if I had the opportunity to talk with him, that I could help him. I finally had the chance to talk with him and that was when he was transferred to Delaware in the same nursing home that I was in.

When he arrived in Delaware Harbor Health Care Rehab Center, I was in my wheelchair in the front lobby of the nursing home. The respiratory therapist told me who he was and that he was also from Washington, DC. It did not register at first, that this was the same Darnell that was at NRH. I noticed a bandage on one of his ears, and I started thinking that he must have a bed sore on his ear and then it clicked, that's the same guy. I finally had the opportunity to talk with him about three days later outside while we were in our wheelchairs. I told him that despite him being paralyzed, he was still someone's father, and to not give up on her. He was also a victim of violence in SE DC, where he was shot multiple times. There were a lot of gunshot victims in the center.

I used to cut hair in the same general area in which I lived, and I'm pretty sure that we have crossed paths before we got shot, it's a very small world. To let me elaborate a little bit more on this, one of my cousins came up to visit me in Delaware and I told him that I had a friend down the hall named Darnell, I asked my cousin to introduce himself to him. When my cousin came back he had a big smile on his face, he said that they went to school together. Darnell and I became real good friends during that time, up until 1992 if I'm not mistaken.

* * *

3T's

A few weeks before Christmas I caught the flu, and you know how that makes you feel! It was even worse for me because I was unable to move. I had it so bad I thought I was gonna die. They wanted to admit me to the hospital up the street from them called B.B., but I heard that the hospital had a bad reputation, so I didn't allow them to pursue it. I recovered from the flu, thanks to God. Now I take a flu shot every year. Before I caught the flu, one of the CNA's asked me did I ever take the flu shot. I wasn't thinking clearly, because I was telling her that I'm not out there in the public, so why should I take the flu shot. Not thinking that one of the staff members or a visitor could easily bring the virus into my room, and that is exactly what happened. I couldn't eat regular food, but I was blessed that my sister Marcia sent me about one dozen of Florida oranges. That was the only food that I could eat during those three difficult days. I had HBO so I could watch movies if I wanted to, and I always had my tapes to listen to.

Listening to my gospel tapes helped me when I was down in the dumps. I could relate to a lot of the songs that I listened to, like the Reverend James Cleveland, who sang songs about life. Cleveland wanted everyone to remember him when he was living. We all want people to remember us before we die, but it's about what you do while you are on earth. There was a song that he had about someone giving him flowers while he was living. Some people never tell you how they feel until it is too late. I always have been a person to express my appreciation or feelings towards my loved ones. One record by Cleveland that sticks in my mind is, "Lord Help Me To Hold On Until My Change Comes." This record reminded me to really hold on until my own change comes.

The Jackson Southernaires also had a record called, "I'll Be Alright," this record reminded myself that everybody who seems to turn their backs on you should not change your faith in THE LORD because "I'll Be Alright." This helped when my wife turned her back on me (well, that's how I felt during that time). This kind of inspirational Godly music allowed me to pick my spirit up off the ground. I did not listen to the radio much, mainly because the radio music focused on sin. So I tried to stay away from modern music. It was very hard for me to sleep in the midnight hours. I would ask the staff members to come into my room to rewind my cassette player repeatedly throughout the nights. Another reason why I could not sleep at night in the nursing home in Delaware was because I lost my first roommate and friend, David one night about 12 midnight. I knew that they were running to his room, I just had a gut feeling. They were hollering down the hallway to bag him, bag him! We have a manual ambulance bag which you can use, that gets air into our lungs faster than a ventilator, and for some reason I don't think that they were bagging David. He was complaining earlier that day for someone to take his breathing aerosol off of him because it was making him feel uncomfortable. He only had one lung but the nurse just took his precious time getting down to his room that night.

CHANGES

Before I left NRH to go to Delaware, since I've been injured, I've tried my best to manage and control the decisions I've made for myself and not to let others make the decisions for me. But, most of the decisions that were made for me were truly out of my control and they still are. It is sad when doctors, other medical staff and even family members make decisions that you have the deal with you. At times, it sometimes caused me to feel as if I've been thrown under the bus, but that was just from my perspective. Although they may have been correct in their decision, in all reality I guess it had a lot to do with not being able to do for myself.

Paula and the social worker were talking about transferring me to Delaware. I felt like the social worker and Paula were conspiring against me. The time finally came when I had to go and there were nurses that worked with me at NRH, who were familiar with the area where I would be living at. The next morning I was prepared for the journey to Delaware. I told all of my friends and nurses, thanks for everything and good-bye to all. They gave me a sweat-shirt with the NRH rehab logo on it. I really had some good people taking me to Delaware, including a male nurse named Paul. It was a round trip of five hours from DC to Delaware.

* * *

PLANS

I really wanted to stay at NRH until I was able to get proper housing, but Paula had other plans for her life, and mine. Did I mention that while I was at the rehab center, she had a passion mark on her neck? I know that I wasn't imagining that I saw a couple of passion marks on her neck, that was during the New Year's night visit. I said something to her about it and she tried to ignore me. Then she said that I was seeing things. It was very painful to see them on her neck, especially so soon after I was injured. Thanks to God I was able to shake it off temporarily, because there were so many other things going on in my mind. After about four or five months at NRH, my stay there was over, and I was transported to Delaware to a nursing facility. My last night at NRH, Paula, a couple of her friends, and one of her cousins, helped pack up my personal belongings. She seemed so happy that night, laughing, and talking with her friends. All I was feeling was that she was happy to get rid of me. I felt like I was being abandoned and I had made up my mind that I would not come back to Washington, DC alive. I had planned to die there in Delaware since nobody cared (meaning my wife). I know that I was being selfish but I figured if my wife did not care about me, then why should I care about living. That was one of the biggest lies from the devil!

(To anyone that may be reading this, PLEASE don't let people dictate to you whether you live or die, or make you feel like taking your own life, just because they don't show you the love that you think that you deserve from them. Trust God and move on! I'm talking from experience). Especially a lot of young people, that just started living. You will meet somebody else, even better than someone that has mistreated you, so again PLEASE enjoy your life to the fullest, live on to do great things and to meet great people. Do not limit the opportunities that God has Waiting for you.

If God didn't love me, He would not have given His only begotten Son, Jesus Christ for all those that receive. I wasn't on that spiritual path during that particular time because I was looking for love and affection from my wife. I realized that God gave me several reasons to live: one because He loves me, and two because of my two beautiful children. He would not allow me to take the coward way out by trying to end my own life, let me rephrase that, by trying to end the life that God has given me!

CHAPTER 14

DELAWARE

When we arrived at the nursing facility, my family did not stay very long because of the long ride home. My mother saw the expression on my face and she felt bad that she had to leave me there. My father expressed the same feeling about leaving me there, but by me being married, and no longer a teenager, my parents had to go along with the program. I never blamed them for anything. Again, I was a grown, married man and unfortunately my wife was running the show.

I was one of the youngest patients at Harbor Healthcare rehab center, along with a new friend that I had made named David. David and I were the only patients that they'd ever seen that was on a ventilator, that were young, and could talk. News spread around the facility about us and I felt like I was a celebrity. It was God and Jeff, Sr. Delaware was a new place, new faces, with an exception of my friend David, who was also a resident from DC. One day before I came to Delaware and before I met David, he got shot trying to protect his little sister by someone in the neighborhood, somewhere near 10th Street Northeast and as a result he was shot multiple times.

Every time my family came during the beginning stages that I was living in Delaware, we would have a cookout in the courtyard. David would look out the window and see us in the courtyard. If he ever requesting anything, I always offered for the staff to put him in my backup manual wheelchair because his electric wheelchair wasn't working. David wanted me to send him some food inside but I told them to put David inside of my extra manual wheelchair and get him out of that room. After he was up in the wheelchair, he felt better, and we even drank a beer together. I believe one reason why they treated David that way was because none of his family members ever came to visit with him while he was living in Delaware. We were good roommates, but eventually I had to leave out of the room with David, because I was getting too much attention from a lot of the female employees and again I'm not bragging, this is true. I also befriended one of the owners of the facility and several of the female CNA's. As I Mentioned, I'm not bragging, but I had a lot of different female CNA's coming to introduce themselves to me on every shift. Then I noticed that I wasn't helping David by me getting so much attention from the administrators. I asked them for a transfer to another room because David was getting more and more depressed. He used to have the window curtain closed in our room, beside his bed and that was the only window in our room. That was also a sign of depression, from my own personal observation.

* * *

I WAS AN UNCLE 4 TIMES BEFORE
I BECAME A BIOLOGICAL FATHER

I had a friend that was a few years older than I was when I was growing up and his siblings were older than my siblings were, with the exception of two of his siblings. But they were old enough to have children. At the time I would go to his house to visit him, I also had a little niece. I would say to myself; I can't wait for my brothers and sisters to have children so that I can become an uncle. I can't wait!

One year I had a false alarm where I thought that I was gonna become an uncle earlier, but something changed, and I had to wait a long time, but then, God answered my prayers and my brother and his girlfriend had my first nephew and the first grandchild. I was so happy to become an uncle and so was the rest of the family. My parents became grandparents and my two sisters, including myself, became aunts and uncles, and most importantly, my brother became a father. I mean everybody was happy. Nobody was happier than me though. I can remember when my brother's girlfriend at the time and the mother of my nephew came home from the hospital and this was in 1980. I can remember setting up my tripod so that I can be in the photograph with my family. We took a photograph in the front yard of my parents' house and afterwards, my sister and I took turns holding our first nephew.

And just like a parent when they had their first child, you take so many photographs of them, and being that I was a photographer, I took photographs of my nephew, a lot of photographs. I think about two or three months later, if not longer, we had to go to South Carolina because my fathers'-father, our grandfather, grandpa had passed away. We drove down for the funeral service. It was such a sad occasion, something that we had to deal with in life that is unavoidable. During the funeral service, the happy grandparents was showing all the family their newest grandson and the rest of the family members in South Carolina. After the service we all went back to our house in South Carolina and continued taking pictures of my father holding his grandson and my mom changing her grandson's dirty diaper. Nothing but love, happiness, enjoying each other!

And then just a year later I was blessed again to become an uncle to my oldest niece, the second grandchild and the oldest female grandchild. Again, we were so blessed. My niece was the first daughter from my sister Valencia. She was a trip, a real character in so many ways, but loved by everyone. This was during the time that we had our family business and everybody wanted to be the babysitter. Since my nephew and his parents lived in Maryland we did spend a lot of time with them and we hung around as much as possible. Sometimes I would drive to Maryland where my brother and his girlfriend was living at the time, just so I can spend some time with my nephew. I can remember one night staying until the next morning, even though he was not awake all night, I was still able to spend time with him before he went to sleep. I felt good that I was able to spend time with my nephew.

It is a lot different when a man has a child with his girlfriend because most of the time the mother and the baby is around her family members which is understandable. However, when your sister has a child, and she's around our side of the family, meaning her parents and siblings, this allowed us to spend more quality time. Because they lived with us I was able to spend more time with my niece than I was with my nephew. But he still was around and that's all that mattered. Being able to be that uncle, that happy and blessed uncle brought me joy. My friend also had a little niece, he had one niece, I had a nephew and niece. I had both, not bragging, but I waited my time for them to arrive. We had the store and when my niece started walking everybody had to watch her. She was all over the place and even outside. During the summer months it wasn't that hot outside so we would open the door to the establishment to make it easier for the customers to come in and out, but also every now and then just to get fresh air.

My niece was very observant and very quick with her hands so everybody had to be on deck, all hands on deck in all reality. Everybody had to keep their eyes open for her because she would go outside. Sometimes she wouldn't go too far, just right next door to the doorway of some apartments that were above our establishment. One apartment had many different tenants, it was like a revolving door, but the other two were occupied by Ms. B and her husband Harry. Ms. B was a manager to the laundromat upstairs and her husband Harry was a softball pitcher. For years, he played with my brother's softball team located in Barry Farms, called the Satellites. (I forgot to mention that Mr. Harry was an older white guy and very nice and he did not ever have to worry about anybody messing with them, because first of all they would have to deal with all of his teammates, all the guys that lived in Barry Farms for the most part were African-American, but also my brother and family members added a little protection) The other occupants of the other apartment were Bill and his mother Ms. Hill (who also were Caucasians and they didn't have the wherewithal of anybody bothering them. Bill was very nosey. But again thank God they were okay, they were protected and everybody knew that). Ms. Hill, was a regular customer of ours and for some reason she used to like to drink her beer in the back of the store behind the boxes so that she wouldn't bother anybody. She would go outside and sit in the doorway where the apartments were upstairs. She bothered no one and THANK GOD NO one really ever bothered her. She was very old and I can imagine she would drink her beer, one at a time, keeping a six pack of beer with her. I guess in between the time she drank the beer she enjoyed a buzz. She was a very interesting lady. She liked to put salt and pepper in it. I think that she told us one time that it made the beer stronger and it gave her a better buzz or she would get higher because the salt and pepper enhanced the taste and the strength of the beer. But we would allow her to drink her beers and as soon as she would finish drinking her beers completely, she would slowly go outside and sit in the doorway of the apartments. (She would walk slow and sometimes you can tell that she was drunk because she began to walk with a slight slant). I mentioned earlier that my niece would just walk outside as if she was a grown woman, ESPECIALLY if we took our eyes off her, only for a moment, most of the time she would sneak outside and sit down beside Ms. Hill and God only knows what they would talk about, but that was what she did all the time, both of them!

Thank God that society is not as crazy and scary like it is now back then!

Then came my second nephew and the third grandchild. He is my sister Marcia's first child. He is about two or three years younger than my niece, and by his mother being my sister and living at home, again I was able to spend a lot of time with him. That's the advantage of having sisters who have children. Again, even though my friend had that one niece during that time. I'm blessed to have two nephews and one niece. During the time that my second nephew was born, the family still had our family business, so I was able to watch them closely grow up. While I was in school for commercial photography, both of them were my models, I took a lot of photographs of both of them as they grew up and every time my nephew that I didn't see often came over, I would make sure I took photographs of him, because now I didn't see him as much as before.

A few years later, another nephew was born, but now I was anticipating being a father and having my first child, my daughter. I finally got a chance to feel what it was like to be a father and a parent. So I was an uncle four times with three nephews and one niece before I became a biological father. Later on that year, I was blessed to have another nephew. So in a year of 1996, my parents was blessed to have so many grandchildren. The count for nephews and nieces was going up for the family and I.

My second niece was born the following year on May 30, 1987, the family is growing and to top it off, another nephew was born, January 21, 1989. I made a prediction that they would be born on that day, oh I forgot to mention God was about to bless me with my second child. My son was born four days later on January 25, 1989. So I was only four days off of my prediction of the above being born the same day. To round off the 10 grandchildren, my youngest niece and the baby girl of the 10 grandchildren was born on January 30, 1991. She was born several months after I got injured, but she is the youngest grandchild. God willing, I'm praying that my nephew has a child but not before he gets married first.

I know that I have an old spirit but I truly believe that if you're a brother and your sister's baby daddies don't do their job it is your responsibility to step in as an uncle. Yes, I said it! It is your responsibility as a brother and uncle to do the best you can and try to be that father figure/strong male figure to your nephews and nieces. I truly believe this, and where there is a need that your sister is unable to provide for her children, as a man, and their uncle, you should step up to the plate and handle whatever situation it is. It is very hard sometimes for females to try to raise a male or young man. As an uncle, that's when you step in and be that strong role model for your nephews and also your nieces, because a lot of times the little girls and young ladies, really need to have that strong father figure to look up to in their lives. Even if you are married and you have young ones which I did, before I got injured, I tried my best, God knows I tried my best, to take time out and talk to my nephews and nieces. As long as GOD SPARES my life, I will be here for them, no matter what they are going through. "I love you and I'm here for you. Don't think you have to go through life by yourself."

There were several times that one of my nephews and nieces had a birthday and I tried my best to step up to give them a birthday cake, just because it was the right thing to do. That night I made a decision to try to make some quick money, it was the day before my niece 9th birthday, if I'm not mistaken, and my intentions were to use some of the money to take the kids to Chucky Cheese to celebrate her birthday with her cousins. But unfortunately, I was unable to because of the decision that I made and I learned how these things affect everybody in life. We make right or wrong decisions, this is a perfect example of what I mean. As I mentioned, if their father is not in their life on a regular basis, for whatever reason, then uncle Jeff is going to be here for you, all of you! When a young lady does not ever have a father figure in her life everyday they will forever and always be searching in society to find a strong male figure. But instead they run into POOKEY, RAY-RAY AND PEANUT, AND THEN THEY MISLEAD THEM AND LIE TO THEM. SADLY, TO SAY, BECAUSE THEY NEVER HAD THAT STRONG MALE FIGURE THAT GO ALONG WITH THAT OKEY-DOKE AND ALL KINDS OF LIES!

We already have more great-grandchildren, then we had grandchildren and I pray that my parents could have seen all of them.

* * *

MY CHILDREN

I would encourage anybody that has a family member in a nursing home to make sure the facility is close to a family member so that the patient is not lonely and is not neglected. If that particular family member who is in a nursing home doesn't have any family members coming regularly and asking questions, chances are that the family member in the nursing home might get looked over.

When my children would arrive, I wanted them to enjoy themselves. I bought bicycles for both of them when I was living in Delaware, the 1st nursing home, so they could have fun. I looked forward to seeing them and they loved coming to see their father. As soon as they would arrive, they would ask for their bikes, and I always made sure that the nurses and CNA's had their bikes ready. I just wanted my kids to be able to enjoy themselves and visit me at the same time. It also was a form of distraction, to let my kids be kids and not have to really deal with the harsh surrounding environment of so many hurting and sick people. I tried to keep them out of the facility as much possible. Again, that's why I purchased the bicycles, and even if they did not look forward to seeing their father, they did look forward to riding their bicycles, whatever worked during that time when they were visiting.

* * *

DEEP THOUGHTS

Being a long way from home, I had to make a new set of family and friends. Many of the nurses comforted me and I recall this one nurse who had a lovely body, but not a cute face. She was a white woman and I had never been involved in any intimate dealings with a white woman. Many of the female CNA's would come to my room, listen to my stories, and I would just talk to whoever God sent my way in my room. Even though a lot of the young ladies were attractive, I still tried to honor my wedding vows.

229

And by having so many different young ladies coming to talk to me and visiting with me, along with befriending me, it mended a lot of my emotional pain. I remember when I couldn't talk for six weeks while at the MedSTAR Washington, Hospital Center. When I was unable to talk, I now truly thank God when the Lord gave me my voice back with the help of the speaking vial. Every sense I was able to talk again," I haven't shut up since, I talk in my sleep intentionally, trying to make up for the six weeks when I wasn't able to talk."

Despite not being able to move my arms and other parts of my anatomy, I thank God for all my other senses. I can watch my kids grow older even when I am not with them every day. I used to remind people that came to talk with me of the blessings of life. I believe that people should be happy to be able to do the lil' things. I always used this one; being able to scratch an itch or whatever part of your body that is itching, that may be small to someone else but not for me since I'm paralyzed from the neck down. Or like having the ability to give a hug or kiss to someone you love and give them their flowers while they're still living. Flowers are just a metaphor. We must give accolades, the love, the appreciation that they deserve while they can hear and receive them, those are the flowers that will never die!

∗ ∗ ∗

DELAWARE FRIENDS

Doel was about 14 years old when he was injured. He was from the upper part of Delaware. One day he was riding his skateboard, and he accidentally ran into a bus, which caused his paralysis. He had a very high spinal cord injury, about the same level as Christopher Reeves. Doel could not move his neck at all, he actually drove his electric wheelchair with his tongue. He had a little round ball to drive his wheelchair with. He was a Spanish kid, but he could talk English. His mother and other siblings could not talk English as well as Doel could. They didn't visit him as much when he first came to Harbor Health Care. The nursing staff adopted him as their son, and they spoiled him, and he really needed all of that attention. He died about five years after I had left the facility.

Charles was also a good friend of mine from Washington, DC. He came from Greater Southeast Hospital because of his weight problems. He weighed over 1000 pounds before, but I think he was weighing about 800 pounds when he came to Delaware. I would ride by his room sometimes to see him and say hello. Later we became good friends. Charles started losing a lot of weight. Sometimes we would go outside of the facility and sit in front of the facility to talk and watch the people come in and out of the nursing home. Before I left, I believe that Charles lost about 300 more pounds. After living at the nursing home for about two years Charles moved out of the facility into a place somewhere locally in Delaware and he was able to get a job and an apartment. I talked with him a couple of times since I moved down here, and he was still making progress. He showed me a picture of two of his nephews standing in a pair of his very large pants, just to let me know how far he came.

Darnell and I were very good friends. He also was a quadriplegic, gunshot victim from Washington, DC I mentioned him earlier when he was a resident at the rehab center. Sometimes during the night he would fill up a large styrofoam cup with ice and then add brandy and coke inside and Park our wheelchairs in front of the nurses station, and just enjoy talking about the staff or whatever. After a couple of sips of that drink that we had, we started getting intoxicated, but there was no harm done to anyone else. We had to do something that made us happy and pass the time. This seemed to drag out each and every day.

∗ ∗ ∗

ADMINISTRATION

I was starting to feel like the administrative staff did not care for me. There was a time when the administration would only let some of the staff work on me or my friend Doel, only because we didn't have respiratory infections, called M.R.S.A. I realized that after they moved Doel and the babies down the hallway from me, the one administrator kept me where I was at because she was prejudice towards me. I used to get occupational and physical therapy my first six weeks at Delaware. The administrator didn't want them to use the standup device on me and it did not belong to her, or the facility. One of the patients' parents purchased that apparatus to use on her son. I don't think that she would have had a problem with me using it, but you never know.

Jim, along with the other nursing assistants would help position me inside of a frame. The frame belonged to one of the residents. One day I was going to physical therapy class and the nurse who was in charge told me that Jim could not assist the nurses in putting me into the device! I explained to them that he was a great help and that I needed him, because he made me feel comfortable, but her attitude, and her tone of voice was provoking me. Although they held a high position in the center, I realized that you have to let things go in life.

* * *

4TH OF JULY

It was the 4th of July, and the facility paid for my family to stay in a condominium that was located on the beach. They stayed for one week and during that time, I received a check for the amount of $1,600 from the social security benefits department. That was one of the most beautiful days. It wasn't the first time that I had $1600, but it was the first time I had that amount of money at one time after I got injured. By no way did I keep all that money for myself. If I'm not mistaken, I gave Paula the majority of the money. I can't even remember if I gave my mom any of the money. I know that Paula told me that the car needed a lot of work, whether it was true or not, I didn't argue. That's why I said that I didn't keep a lot of money for myself. During the time that they were visiting me for that week, God only knows how many outlets Paula and my mom went to shopping. I'm pretty sure with some of that money they purchased my mom some things to smooth everything over. Knowing that they were there for the entire week, most of the time that they visited was somewhat later in the evening time, which I felt was a sign of disrespect. Not only to me but to the other residents because we had three kids there, one of my nieces, and both of my kids. Why would anyone bring the children to a nursing facility around 8:00 p.m. or 9:00 p.m. knowing that a lot of the people there were very sick and dying! And I truly believe that Paula enjoyed the trip more that anybody else, but it was what it was!

I'm definitely not trying to turn back the hands
of time, it's too painful!

* * *

(PARTY / COOKOUT FOR RESIDENTS AND STAFF) AT THE NURSING HOME IN DELAWARE

After the state had finished their inspection, I thought that it would be a good idea to show the employees my appreciation for a job well done. I asked one of the co-owners of the facility, could I have a cook-out with some of the residents and staff members. He told me that it would be okay with him. I didn't bother to ask the other administrator, because I knew that they would be against my having a barbecue. They never knew about the gathering until the next day. I had brought two cases of beer and asked the other employees to bring any other kinds of food or drinks that they could afford. I also asked one of the owners that I befriended, could I get some chicken from the kitchen. He told me that I could have anything out of the kitchen that I needed.

That weekend one of my friend's family was there visiting and they really enjoyed themselves. I made sure that it wasn't on the weekend that my family came because I'd rather enjoy my family's company in a more private setting. We had a few of the employees show up for the cook-out. In the beginning the staff in the kitchen was reluctant about giving their help to us, but Ray was working that day, and he went in the kitchen and straightened everything out, everything was okay from then on. One of the nurses' assistant helped me cook the food on the barbecue grill. We had enough food for everybody that came, and we had a nice time.

I still remember my friend's little daughter trying to feed him a piece of barbecue ribs. He had barbecue sauce all over his face, but he enjoyed every bit of it, and so did his mother and sister. The next day the other administrators found out about what we did over the weekend. Ray denied having anything to do with the barbecue. A couple of the nursing assistants also denied being there. What really made them mad was that they had a dog that lived in the courtyard, name Harbor. He had scattered all of the leftover trash all over the

233

yard. Then they tried to say that we didn't clean up after it was over. I was responsible for the party and I made sure that the trash and cleanup was taken care of before I went in. They probably would not have known that we had the cookout if we didn't leave the trash bags outside for the dog to get into. Other than that, they would never have known anything, but again I didn't care, I just wanted all of us to have some fun. The real reason that they were mad was because I didn't tell them or invite them at all. They eventually got over it and I really didn't worry about them because we all enjoyed ourselves that day. My friend and I had a few beers and we had a nice buzz. I don't want to get ahead of myself, but I lost about four or five of the friends that I met at Harbor Healthcare, and I often think about those guys, and a lot of the staff and other visitors that I met while I was living there.

CHAPTER 15

CAMERON GLEN

I was transferred to Cameron Glen Care Center Nursing Home in Reston, VA, May 5, 1992, which was my daughter's sixth birthday. I realized that Paula was not interested in finding a house for all of us, so I decided to find a house for my children, where I could have 24-hour care. A few years after living here in the nursing home, I tried signing up for the Section-8 Housing Program in the Fairfax County Department. It took about three to four years for my name to reach the top of the housing list. This time they only had a few CNA's. This was a serious issue and concern for me because the chances of me finding anyone to work with me was very difficult. My case worker did connect me with the Department of Rehab Services, "D.R.S." for short. My counselor was Mrs. Kidwel, she was not involved in the housing situation at all, but she was the number one player in helping me get my computer system. Her department had to get the money to approve the purchase of all of my adaptable equipment. She came to interview me and to sign me up for assistance. She said that I had to at least try. The next Sunday she brought some other church members to meet me. One of the ladies got me involved with the Independents of Northern Virginia. My challenge then was to get my computer equipment from the Department of Rehab Services. I've been accepted into this program for about three years now, and it's time to get some production going. The department of rehab services stopped providing me service about one year after I received my computer. Mrs. Kidwel stopped working with them and they gave me a very prejudice case worker and all he was thinking about was saving the rehab center money. He wasn't concerned about the people who really needed the resources. If I was still affiliated with the Department of rehab services, they would have been responsible for helping me get the nursing and CNA's that I needed because they had a register with the list of nurses and CNA's that they used.

The housing department should have helped me get the proper housing list of accessible apartments and houses, but they didn't give me the adequate care that I needed. They need people to recruit people with disabilities, that need assistance with vocational goals. I was experiencing different challenges in getting proper housing and nursing assistance 24-hours a day. The state of Virginia is the only state that I know of that would give people in my condition a ventilator waiver. The waiver will pay a nurse, or CNA up to 16 hours a day. I would have to find a reliable person to cover the other eight hours of the rest of the days, which was very difficult to find during those years. If and when there is a ventilator waiver available for people in the same situation like I am, it would be able to help others. Right now I'm trying to obtain a skill through this program so that I can become self-employed.

Then the nurses started complaining about me calling them about helping me with entertainment. They complained to administration that I was calling them every 10 minutes to change my tape. If anybody has any common sense, they would know that a cassette takes at least 30 to 90 minutes to play on each side before it stops. When other residents needed help, there was no problem for the staff to help them out as I watched them repeatedly with my own two eyes help the other residents. Why did I have to get treated so badly, different from someone else? I was trying to survive, and not give up, but I believe that they wished that I was a comatose patient instead. I've had a nurse and CNA say this to me, but I shook it off!

EVERY TIME I needed something, it was always an excuse, or negative attitude towards me when it came to helping me with anything. They showed a lot of favoritism towards the other three roommates that I had, depending on who they were, that makes a difference!

* * *

HABITS

Since I've been physically disabled I've developed a lot of habits, for instance having a towel or pillow case laying on top of my face covering my entire face. I think it started because I felt uncomfortable from getting a bed bath from so many different people. The majority of the women were very curious concerning certain body parts. Most of them would not pull the privacy curtain, or even cover my private area up while bathing me. Most of you guys might love to have a female give you a bed bath, but it's no thrill when you can't fill anything. Another reason why I kept a towel on my face was because it enabled me to block certain things like light from my face while I was sleeping. During the morning, I am able to block the light with a towel on my face. There's also a lot of dust flying around this room, and my face is so sensitive, that when the dust falls on it, I'm not physically able to scratch the dust particles, or eyelashes off, but having a towel on my face keeps the dust from bothering me.

Many times my ears would get cold at times, and the towel was a way of keeping my ears warm. Nevertheless, by having a towel on my face, blocks everything, and everybody out, so that I could disappear for a while laying here, especially during my down, sad days. I eventually had to stop wearing a towel over my face, because as the years went on I started selling female cosmetics and when I had the towel over my face, some of the woman would come into my room and take whatever they wanted.

∗ ∗ ∗

STAFFING SHORTAGES

When I first came to Cameron Glen, my unit was called the Annex, and then INOVA health care corporation took over about three years later. Now it is called INOVA Interim Transitional Care (ITC). Within the couple of years at Cameron Glen, the staff has either quit or transferred to a INOVA hospital where they were paid more. The staff here works extremely hard, yet they are underpaid. Sometimes I wonder what people really have on their minds. Because of my condition, I'm in the position where I have to depend on people to help me, many who have, are very good, and have positive attitudes when I ask for help. The first thing many nurses say when you ask them for help is that they have something to do, they have a patient, or they can't stay long. Some nurses say mean things about patients because they are in a comatose state.

I believe that some nurses don't care about the residents, they just want a pay check! One thing about these nursing homes is that they are not ready for younger residents. We become minorities because of our age, race, and in my case, it was both reasons.

One summer, I only got up four times because of the way I felt that I was treated. Several years ago, I fell out of a lift when an agency nurse refused to listen to me and I wasn't properly secured in the lift pad. As a result of his actions, I fell and hit the back of my head on the ground. I don't believe I can survive another fall. I'm picky about who I allow to put me in a lift pad since I had that fall. An inexperienced CNA or nurse need specific training, because to them a small mistake means life or death to a patient. When I continue telling the nurse that I was not safely secured in the lift pad, he didn't listen, just like most staff members. We know ourselves much better anyway!

But I felt a number of things that happened. One instance, my head was just a few inches from the wheelchair petals. If I would have hit one of those petals with my head, I really would have had a large gash or even a fracture from falling the distance and all the solid weight. Thanks Again Lord for watching over me!

∗ ∗ ∗

PICTURE PERFECT

As soon as I come into my room at the nursing home, there are pictures of Paula and my children looking directly at me. Instantly my thoughts are directed towards them. The pictures brought back memories of my studio at home. I have a picture of Paula and I in Puerto Rico on our honeymoon, hanging up in the hallway of our apartment, and that was one of the happiest times in my life. I believe that I will always have feelings for her, despite what she feels about me, because she is the mother of my children. There is a picture of us that was taken on Easter Sunday at my parents' house in 1990. In the background behind the headboard of my bed is a picture of my two children on Easter Sunday, 1994, when my son was into his power wheel, blue big foot truck that I purchased them that previous Christmas. His sister was standing behind him with a couple of friends. This photo was taken outside in the courtyard at Cameron Glen. Then I have a copy of a newspaper article with the first black woman to become Miss America in 1984 Miss Vanessa Williams. Finally I have a picture with my brother and I, we were standing by a tree waiting for our ride to a wedding, that's a special photo because it's the only picture I have of my brother and I together.

SUICIDAL THOUGHTS THAT HAUNTED ME
ALONG WITH THE TEMPTATION

As I reflect back over the years being in this paralyzed state, dealing with all of the challenges, not only physical, but spiritual and emotional, I had suicidal thoughts and considered ending everything! I can remember at least three times that I was tempted to take my life and I knew just how to do it, and I was faced again like I mentioned three times with doing it, but I truly thank God for reminding me of my children and other loved ones. He also reminded me of how selfish it would be if I took the precious gift of life that He gave me.

The second facility that I was at located in Reston Virginia for almost 20 years during the early days, and this nursing facility, I have been living in for more than a decade. When the thought of suicide first entered my mind, I had to remember that I would no longer be able to be with my children, especially when they were younger and the rest of my family members.

All the residents and staff at the facility at Cameron Glen, located in Reston Virginia, were blessed to be able to every now and then get a chance to get away from the facility. Well, especially my respiratory unit. I believe that I mentioned earlier how I was instrumental in doing different activities for the residents that were also on official life support. We would go to the movies every now and then at the Reston town center. We went to restaurants during happy hour or just to get out and away for a while, to almost feel normal again, even though we all were in wheelchairs. We were still able to have some quality of life despite all the different medical conditions.

On this particular outing, honestly, I can't remember where we were going but I know that it was at the town center, they had been doing some CONSTRUCTION on our pathway from the facility to the town center. Most of the time we would drive our wheelchairs on the sidewalk, this day was no different from all the rest. While riding on the sidewalk, there was a deep hole in the ground where they were doing construction and just for a quick moment, the thought came to my mind that I could end everything. I thought if I just speed up I could veer off into the deep hole and put an end to my life. But, as quick as the thought came, God said; "It's not about you son, think about your children and your loved ones." After the thought, I quickly drove my wheelchair away from the sidewalk and started driving on the street where I felt safe. I would always drive my wheelchair for the most part towards the traffic so that I could see the cars and the drivers of the cars would see me as they came towards me.

No one had a clue that I was thinking about committing suicide as we continued towards the town center. However, I remained quiet for a while and started thinking about my children, my parents and other loved ones that would have been affected by what I was thinking about doing, being a coward and taking my own life! No, it's not easy living on a ventilator, being a dependent quadriplegic (from the age of 25 until now, God has blessed me to see 27 years).

After we enjoyed ourselves at the town center and on the way back, I made sure to avoid that side of the sidewalk and again I drove my wheelchair on the busy streets, but always facing the traffic that was coming towards me, because I knew that it wasn't safe having the traffic coming from behind. It was more dangerous because they could drive right up to me and accidentally run me over. So yes, I wanted to live, even conquering this mountain of paralysis that one day it shall be removed from my body and God will allow me to be able to spiritually and physically walk. I have to believe that God is a healer! I have to believe even after all this time.

I'm still trusting in God and what He says in the Bible is true. "But without faith it is IMPOSSIBLE TO PLEASE GOD: but he that cometh to God must believe that He is, and that He is a rewarder of THEM that diligently seek him," Hebrews 11:6. So as I trust and believe in God for healing, even after all these years, I still must believe that he's able to do all things but fail ME! It made me think about when Jesus was fasting for 40 days and 40 nights and the devil came to tempt Him. When he tempted him for the last time he took Jesus to a high place and showed him everything that he would give. He tempted him to jump off the mountain. My situation was similar, but there was no guarantee that I would have died. I could have survived and there was a possibility that I would have been left in a worse situation than I was already in. But I truly thank God for just the small voice that I heard before doing it concerning my kids and other family members. The second time that I tempted to try to end my life, I was also unsuccessful and glad I didn't because I would've WENT STRAIGHT TO HELL and I don't want to go there at all!

But I was at another place of height and again that thought of suicide came into my mind that all I had to do was just ride very fast on this high ledge and it would all be over. But being reminded spiritually where I was at, during a family event, it was a very crazy thought, and brothers and sisters GOD IS REAL! I thank God that I didn't carry this out while I was on this very high platform. I asked the staff if they could please take my chair out a gear so that I would accidentally drive my chair off this platform. I also asked them to please back me up just a little bit because I didn't want to be that close to the edge anymore.

Believe it or not, there was a third time that I was also tempted again to commit suicide after being placed again on another high platform and the same thoughts ran through my mind. I'm fighting temptation each and every day in this SPIRITUAL BATTLE and it is always within! We are constantly fighting against spirit and the flesh, each and every one of us, each and every day that we live. Another way of saying it, "THE ENEMY IS INNER ME" despite everything we have to deal with on the job and other things that we deal with every day. We first must deal with the enemy, fighting against the evil spirit within our bodies CONSTANTLY!

I thank God for the reminder of His word and how He protected me from myself, but mainly from the enemy. Everyday I'm challenged with dealing with the doctors and with the staff, mainly the ones that have negative attitudes. I have enough on my plate living like this, but also waiting for God, but while waiting, I deal with the pain each and every day. Sometimes I think to myself, maybe I deserve to have the many different types of pain for making that decision many years ago that got me in this condition in the beginning.

I struggle with telling this part of my story, concerning the suicidal thoughts, and how close I came to committing suicide and how easy it would've been to take that route out of being physically paralyzed. But then I thought to myself, how would I help somebody else and how dare I even have the thought to take a precious gift that God has given us, despite the challenges, whatever they may be. One of my biggest challenges is dealing with spiritual and physical paralysis. When I think about forgiveness, I have asked my ex-wife, my kids, both of my parents, my siblings and even my nephews and nieces for forgiveness because in a lot of ways I felt like I failed everybody because of my choice to sell a kilo of cocaine drugs that day. So, after asking for FORGIVENESS from everybody else, it was hardest to forgive myself. All I had to do was look down at myself and see my condition physically and then the thoughts would start all over again about making that mistake that cost me a lot, FOR NOW!

I was given too much medication, it really was an overdose!

I can remember one of the nurses gave me a very high dose of Diazepam. She was new working on the respiratory unit. That was no reason to give me that much medication. I was only supposed to get 2.5mg of Diazepam, but instead she gave me 25mg of the medication. This lasted for at least two weeks. I remember trying to talk to my daughter one evening when she wasn't feeling well. She went to the amusement park and like everybody else, she decided to have a slice of pizza that really didn't agree with her stomach. So she called me because she was scared and didn't know what to do. Meanwhile I'm trying to figure out why lately I have been very tired during the evening time more than I was ever before. While I was talking to her I was fighting the drowsiness that the medication caused me because I could not let my baby girl down, and I was trying my best to tell her to relax, but in the back of my mind I'm thinking, where the hell is her mother. I asked my son where was his mom and why was my daughter like this? She was approximately 13 or 14 years old when this happened. I was frustrated that no one was home. I asked my daughter was it possible for her to call her mother's aunt and see if they were together. Now, I'm saying to myself, I have to get Paula a cell phone, not for me to know where she's at or what she is doing, that was none of my business, but my concern was that my kids would be able to get in touch with her.

Thank God, after almost two hours of her throwing up, she was able to relax. I told her to go to her room and turn the lights out

242

and get a cold washcloth and put it on her forehead. She did what I instructed and again thank God. Her mother finally came home, my daughter got up and started to explain to her mother that she was sick on the stomach and that she ate some pizza and she had been throwing up or vomiting for quite some time now. I can't believe what I heard her mother say to her while my daughter had the telephone to her ear. Her mother said to her," WHY DID YOU EAT THE PIZZA?" What kind of response is that when your daughter is upset and trying to explain to you everything that happened and you say something silly out of your mouth like that. I heard it and I'm pretty sure that it hurt my daughter because they were not words of comfort at all. I told my daughter to go back into her room and lay down and relax and GOD WILLING, she would be fine. I can't remember if I told her to make sure that she drank plenty of fluids. Sometimes over-excessive vomiting can cause dehydration.

After this almost near-death overdose episode happened, I did two things, first of all, I addressed the Director of Nursing and informed her that I was given too much drugs, an overdose for 14 days or more. The nurse that made the mistake was transferred to another unit and not reprimanded. The Director of Nursing asked me who told me that I was given too much Diazepam? I let her know that I knew that I was given too much medicine. That was definitely a potential lawsuit to give anybody that much of a dosage of medication. Anyone given that much Diazepam at one time, could have killed them, and I'm not exaggerating, THIS IS TRUTH, GOD SPARED MY LIFE ONCE AGAIN! I was informed by another nurse that was on duty that she had been overmedicating me for more than two weeks. I know that God had a lot to do with me being informed. Someone in particular discovered that she gave me .25mg of Diazepam and not 2.5 which was a pill cut in half. The entire pill would be 5mg and she gave me .25mg. I thank God someone else checked my medication and they discovered the problem because I was on a ventilator and it could have affected my breathing. The second time this happened came from a nurse that was in training on our unit. I was a little leery about this particular nurse. I'm trying to find the right words to describe her. I'd say that she had an air head kind of way about her. I did not feel comfortable around her in the very beginning. I'm not being judgmental but after being in this situation, God has made a way for me to be able to see some characteristics in people, to know whether or not they were right for the job. This comes with experience! It didn't matter if it was a nurse, LPN, RN or respiratory therapist and even a CNA, I could really tell by watching their work ethics and attitude when they provided any kind of medical care for me. I would always say that the acronym "RN" doesn't stand for registered nurse, because I've had a lot of REGISTERED NUTS or REAL NUTS as nurses that did not have a clue. This comes with experience and not being judgmental, but having a good observation concerning the staff.

In the medical field, you really have to have a real hard work ethic in this profession and unfortunately a lot of people knew that when they came from another country that the medical field provided a lot of jobs. For some reason, I don't know why the American people, especially the men and women in this country, do not want to work in the medical field.

One of my good friends who is about 74 years old, who was also born and raised in DC, from Shiloh Baptist Church, Deacon Hill told me that years ago a lot of black Americans worked in the medical field because the jobs were assessable and wide-open for them to get a job, whereas some of the jobs were not available or they would not give a black American man or female a job working in different professions, but the medical field has always been open for everybody. Talking with him, he informed me that jobs in America for black people were mainly labor intense jobs. That could possibly play a big part in why a lot of black Americans don't work in the medical field these days. But as he's telling me this, I'm thinking to myself, that was many years ago, this is a new generation of men and women. I just don't understand it. There is an abundance of jobs working in the medical field and some of the jobs require that they go to school to get their license as a nurse, just to name one profession. I think that he named several other jobs like a bus driver and even the mailman or a woman was occupied by white Americans. At one time or another they would not give a black American these types of jobs. However, these jobs are available today for anybody of any race or color.

Every time I had to go to the hospital for various reasons I never saw a lot of people of color as nurses. I did see other nationalities or races of people. It made me wonder why they didn't take advantage of the medical field. I'm talking about African-American people. But enough of that, let's move on to the next subject, racial issues. God willing, I pray that my story will bless millions and millions of different people all over the world and that it will be colorblind to some extent. Some things have to be addressed and mentioned concerning the racial issues in this beautiful country.

As I was talking about the RN, before administering medicine to anyone she should have been trained by an experienced RN that may have worked here for many years. It just had to be me, being a recipient of her incompetence on this particular Saturday morning. How is it possible to confuse medication when the name of the patient is clearly written on the medication chart? The names are alphabetized, so how could you confuse the letter A with the letter D? I'm still baffled at the thought that I was given someone else medication. She always looked as if she was confused anyway. There were four of us in this particular room and they didn't go by numbers, they would identify each resident by alphabets, ABCD, and our names. I was a resident bed D, and some kind of way she gave me the patient lying in bed A's medication.

The nurse with more experience also worked on the respiratory unit and she would work with me on weekends. I was proud of her climbing up the medical ladder, but for some reason I think she started out as a CNA, then she became an LPN. She went a little further and became a nurse practitioner. Honestly, I was so happy for her making progress like that. She definitely accelerated and took her medical knowledge and career to the next level. If I'm not mistaking before I left the facility, Cameron Glen, she was going to school to become a medical doctor. God bless you, Sister Janet! I'm praying by now that she has the will to becoming a real doctor. By now, in all these years, I know that she is a medical doctor working somewhere. But on this particular Saturday, I believe someone dropped the ball by letting this incompetent RN pass medication to the residents.

At one time I was able to just swallow a couple of pills, capsules, and all. But then, for some reason when I would take medication that was in a capsule, it would feel like they were getting stuck in my esophagus or my throat. Since then I would have to get my medication crushed up and mixed in yogurt. This still goes on even today. Most of the medication that I receive have a very bitter taste. So, on that particular Saturday morning, she brought the medication to me and mixed it up for me. I swallowed it very fast, like I normally did, but this time I felt a large capsule and I asked her what did she give me. Now get this, she responded with "I don't Know." I said to her, what do you mean you don't know? What kind of medication did you just give me? It took the staff approximately 45 minutes before they came back into my room to tell me what medication she gave me. After they quickly called my doctor to inform them of the medication, the nurse was told to monitor me and make sure that I wasn't having any kind of medical effects from the medicine. I know for a fact that she gave me medicine for seizures. It took approximately 45 minutes for them to come back into the room to tell me that I was given 4 different medications. I was told that I was given my roommates medicine instead. I THANK GOD that He protects me from these kinds of mistakes and keeps me from all kinds of harm and danger, seen and unseen. Thank God that my loving father and a spiritual brother, Jesus Christ watches over us and even protects us from ourselves. YES, we need protection from ourselves, from the battle within, the constant battle, spiritually and physically. Not to mention everything else going on in our everyday lives.

The third time I was given the wrong medication was because the nurse did not pay attention. He just gave me the medication without first checking and listening to my vital signs. I cannot remember the name of the medicine, it eludes my memory right now. However, I do know that before the nurses administered me this particular medication, they should first check my blood pressure to see if my blood pressure was high or low, again before giving me this particular medication. The only way I knew that he gave me the wrong medication before checking my vital signs was because I was watching television and I went blind for a few moments. I mean, everything went black and of course, I started praying to my Lord and Savior Jesus Christ and MY HEAVENLY FATHER, ABBA

FATHER or JEHOVAH GOD, to please help me with this situation of being temporary blind. I mean, I couldn't see out of neither one of my eyes, but thank God it was only temporary.

As soon as I was able to get myself together, I was able to call them in to let them have it by using my call light. I called that very lazy nurse into my room, so I could let him know how I felt. Unfortunately, there were a lot of lazy nurses working in the medical arena. They are really there for the money, not because they care. They don't have a heart for the people. I guess he thought he was going to have to call "code blue." Unfortunately, patients are recipients of their laziness and incompetence. I see this every day. I thank God for all the medical staff members that are working in this profession for the right reasons. Some of them do care and have a heart and especially those that I've been blessed over the years to have the majority of my care provided for that really had a heart and cared about the well-being of the residents. Unfortunately, I've seen those people that do care are usually the ones that are stepped over and over looked and overworked. The lazy staff members get away with MURDER, I'm serious when I say get away with MURDER. They've killed several people because they don't care or respond fast enough to help the residents in times of need, because they may be sitting down at the desk talking on the telephone, using a computer or just relaxing. They don't move fast enough when there is a crisis with the patients. GOD BLESSES ALL!

I told the nurse exactly how I felt about what he did to me. I told him that if he was going to continue working as a professional nurse, he should never let this happen again. "Don't you ever, ever give me that medication again without checking my blood pressure," I said. I mean I was livid, very angry and a little scared at the same time but this was a sign of my nurse being very lazy. After that situation, I told the staff, the director of nursing, the administrator and whoever else in charge that day that I did not ever want to take that particular medication. I asked them to please remove it from my medical chart and I explained to them what happened. God knows I cannot take that chance again. I guarantee you that the nurse knew exactly how I felt. My prayer is that he never gives another patient the wrong medication. As a matter of fact, I asked them to remove him from our unit assignment, which they did. They were wrong and they knew it, but since I didn't die, thank God, they just transferred that particular nurse to the unit next door, as if nothing ever happened.

* * *

HOW THEY JUST DISMISSED ME FROM THE NEW OWNERS AT CAMERON GLEN AFTER 20 YEARS

My last two years at Cameron Glen, a new company took over that was headquartered in Roanoke, Virginia, and they had a hidden agenda. The Inova Company told the residents that they were getting out of the nursing home business and someone was going to buy or purchase two of their nursing homes. One of the other nursing homes was located in Fairfax Virginia and the one that I have been living in for 18 years before the new owners took over the facility. There was a conversation about the new medical owners taking over our home at Cameron Glen. During the beginning, the administrator was a really nice guy and he made sure that the residents were provided as much as possible and he insisted that staff make it feel like this was our home. That was very honorable of him to have this kind of mentality, knowing that this was a business as well, but it worked for a while.

As I mentioned before, we would go to the town center along with some of the residents and staff. Some of the employees, believe it or not would come back or come on their days off to the facility so that they could take part in the outside activities. Going to the town center just to get away for a while, and maybe have a decent meal at one of the restaurants was something I liked doing. The administrator would also allow the employees to stay on the clock and the ones that would come in while they were off would punch in the clock, and they all were paid for taking the residents out. He had an idea that the staff was doing this on their own time without pay, and that the employees were coming in on their days off, so out of respect and appreciation for what they were doing for the residents, he decided that they should all clock in, at least the ones that were voluntarily working overtime. They were paid for doing a wonderful job with making the residents feel good about having an outing, even if it is was just up the street from where the town center was located. But there were many things to do there for the residents and the staff together.

I got a little caught up in a moment as I was supposed to be talking about my last two years at Cameron Glen under new management. After I went through my second year, they decided to close down the respiratory department after telling us the year-earlier that they were glad to have a respiratory department within the facility because it was the first time they had one. Unfortunately, they did not know how to run it or to recruit other respiratory patients, so they told the family members that they were building three new facilities to replace the two facilities. They were taking over the Fairfax County area of Northern Virginia. I will have to find another place and so would all the rest of residents that have become my adoptive family members. Upstairs in the facility they had an Assisted Living unit where a lot of the residents would come downstairs and interact with the rest of us while we were doing activities. Sadly to report, that was one of the first places that they got rid of along with all our friends and family members that we had built relationships with and got to know along the way.

They attacked the employees by raising the healthcare insurance payments. A lot of the employees have family members and they were paying insurance to take care of them under the INOVA health care program. They could afford to put their family members on their policy, but this company came in and cut everything. A lot of the employees could not afford to pay the high prices for insurance, so they had to leave the facility. NOW, not only did we lose a lot of our family members from the assistance unit, we have started losing a lot of good employees. Nobody wanted to ask the question, WHAT'S NEXT? What came next was closing down the respiratory department.

When it came time to talk to me about relocating to another facility before Thanksgiving 2011, I told them that I had been here for almost 20 years. I asked if it would be possible to remain throughout the holiday. First, I give God all the credit and honor because I really don't think they did this just for me, but I wasn't thinking about myself. I'm now thinking about my respiratory family because if they were to start moving respiratory patients, which they did to other facilities, I didn't want them to be unemployed during the Thanksgiving holiday, Christmas holiday, and even the NEW YEAR.

So, the respiratory unit stayed open throughout the holiday. A lot of family members that I've known over the years at this facility started moving out. I lost quite a few of them before the transfer. I don't know if it was because they knew they might have to leave and they couldn't accept it or not, but I know a few of them passed away, MAY THEY ALL REST IN PEACE!

I was supposed to go to another facility in northern Virginia and I have been talking to several of the recruiting staff, and I knew of some of the respiratory therapist and other staff members that worked in the facility. They gave me the inside scoop about what to expect and that it wasn't that good of a place to live, even though they worked there. I had already heard about the place many years ago, because at one time it was a possibility that I might have moved there. I was so comfortable with being at Cameron Glen, and knowing the staffing, residents and family members, it was hard to think about leaving way before they sold the facility. When that new company came to purchase Cameron Glen, they really didn't purchase the facility structure itself, they purchased the residents and the beds. That must've been what slavery felt like, being put on the auction block and you had no say so. We were sold to this new company for an unknown amount of money. Just the thought of knowing that you could be sold off really suck!

Prior to me being transferred to my third facility, my social worker continued to lie to me about everything. I mean everything! She would try to avoid talking to me. This was the mindset of the new ownership and everybody's job was in a bubble, they were walking on eggshells. They were slashing and cutting everything including the unit secretary. We had a supply closet that was organized with everything, they gave the supply management assistant an ultimatum, either quit or transfer to the activities department, he did that later. He became a very good addition to the activities department in many ways, that really worked out as well as the rest because he was very talented and also a musician. Well, they terminated his boss, just like that! Everyone was scared, including my social worker that would do or say anything that they wanted her to say so she could keep her job. She had to make a choice, her job was on the line!

They had started preparing to put me into a hospital, just to get me out of the facility until I contacted the Northern Virginia Ombudsman that helped me out in the past. The previous Ombudsmen and I was thankful for the new official that was working within the facility because she was very instrumental in not allowing them to stick me in a hospital. God knows how long it would be until they find a place for me to go. She even went a step further to contact someone from the Washington Post, a reporter that I remember talking to about an issue that I had, but he never followed-up. However, this time he did his job and announced that the facility was trying to personally put me into a hospital just to get me out of the facility so that they can close down the respiratory department for good. I forgot to mention that I was the last ventilator dependent respiratory patient at the facility. After the reporter came to interview me about the situation the representatives for the new company of course lied and denied ever attempting to put me in a hospital. I'm saying to myself, where in the world would I get this concept from if they did not threaten me with placing me in a hospital. So as far as that plan it didn't work because of the public attention that they got from the Washington Post and maybe other friends and family members that contacted them that I had no knowledge of. But pressure was put on them for even thinking about doing this to me.

I was glad that God allowed the respiratory employees and including myself to stay throughout the holidays. On the other hand, I was already preparing to move. I was getting my daughter and her husband to take some of my personal belongings that I had accumulated after 20 years to their place. I wanted to store them because GOD had already warned me and told me in so many ways to start getting ready to leave this place and again listening to that small voice, even though GOD IS A HUGE GOD, I still took heave to what I was hearing spiritually. I had almost got all of my personal possessions out of the facility with the exception of my closet, refrigerator, stereo, television, and a few other things that I was utilizing until I finally knew exactly where I was going to move to. As I mentioned before my social worker was lying to me all the time. She had me thinking that I was going to this Catholic Junior high school that was located in Southeast Washington, DC. I can remember as a kid in Junior high school when I used to catch the

Metro bus home from school, the students from the St. Thomas Moore Catholic Junior high school were real loud, way more than my fellow classmates and other students from the public schools were. You would not believe that they were from a Catholic school because according to everybody else, Catholic students were held to a higher standard than any kid in public school, SO THEY SAY!

Having said that, I was thinking since I've been injured for so many years that they had converted the Catholic school into a long-term facility. My social worker had me thinking that this was where I was going, but never telling me that St. Thomas Moore was located in Hyattsville, Maryland, and she continued setting me up to believe that I was going to a Washington, DC facility. Right up until the day that she came in my room on that Monday morning, January 30, 2012, at 11am, to inform me that they were coming to pick me up. I asked her who was coming to pick me up and that's when I was informed that I was being transferred to St. Thomas Moore, just like that, no notice! It was a one hour notice that I was going to be moved to another facility. It was not enough time to notify my kids or other family members that were far away. Thank God that I was blessed with a lot of friends that I met along the way and I sent out a 911 email form, and everybody that was there was informed that they were going to take me out of this place to replace me somewhere else within an hour. Again, thank God! I had really good friends nearby that I met several years prior that came right away to help me pack some of my belongings, and to inform me to not worry about anything, they would take care of it. I was so thankful for Brother Herb and his wife, Sister Stacey and true to their word, they made sure that I got my computer system, and a few other things that I left there. Since I was rushing, I forgot to get my refrigerator that I was able to have in my room to keep my own personal food and drinks which was truly a blessing.

When my family would bring me food, home-cooked food that would last me a couple of days, I was able to put it in my refrigerator instead of the unit community refrigerator where people used to look in your food, and sometimes they would take it. I was given this refrigerator because my first year at Cameron Glen I gave an in-service about 32 respiratory students and it was free game to ask me any questions that they wanted. Normally it is very hard to find a respiratory patient like myself, that was able to communicate verbally. Providing in-service was very rare and the students took full advantage of it. I also had someone to record it. They were so thankful to be able to ask me any questions. They were really interested in my circumstances and how I was able to deal with the situation about my family members. One respiratory question I can remember was "how does it feel to get suctioned?" And I explained. So they purchased me a refrigerator out of gratitude and appreciation because they wanted to give me something. God allowed me to give them so much more because of the session that we had. Believe it or not, a couple of those same students came to work at the facility for a little while and they remembered me given the in-service and they told me personally, that they appreciated how much it helped them along the way as they became official respiratory therapists.

On that dreadful day when they kicked me out of Cameron Glen, I can't really explain my feelings to the fullest. After receiving the short notice and then not even having time to tell many staff members that I had befriended over the years and the residents goodbye was hard. I guess the word got around the facility that I was leaving and there were a few staff members that shed a tear because of it. As they were taking me out on the stretcher I was able to tell a few of them including my little brother Mike; GOD BLESS AND SO LONG!

When I came to the third nursing facility, I noticed that we were not in Washington, DC. I asked the guy what was the name of this facility and where is it located? Again, he replied; This is St. Thomas Moore and you're in Hyattsville, Maryland. And here I am now, AWAITING FOR GOD TO DO SOME BIG THINGS IN MY LIFE! WAITING ON THE LORD TO ANSWER MY PRAYERS! PRAYERS FOR MANY YEARS NOW TO COME THE PASS, AS I HAVE BEEN FAITHFULLY WAITING!

CHAPTER 16
SPIRITUALLY FIT FATHER

I asked a friend of mine to go to Best Buy and get a cell phone for me that I was trying to get for Paula so that in the event my kids ever needed to get in contact with their mother, for whatever reason, she would have a cell phone. During this time cell phones were really popular and I paid $100 for this particular cell phone and my friend said that the store would activate it for me. I told him thank you very much but I want to make sure that I give it to the person that I bought it for. I was hoping that it would be acceptable. Well, it was not acceptable by Paula, she wanted some kind of flip phone and I told her to take this telephone and trade it off the street and go to Best Buy and choose whatever kind of phone she wanted. I'm pretty sure one hundred dollars was enough to cover the cost of the cell phone she preferred. I just did not want my kids to not be able to get in touch with their mother, for whatever reason, and at any time.

I had a situation with my daughter crying, and I was unable to be there to put both of my arms around her to give her comfort, which really, really took a lot out of me emotionally. After I finally finished talking to her, I really felt drained, spiritually, emotionally and even physically. I said that I had to do something about that, which I did, I purchased the cell phone. What I did was a blessing to Paula as well as my kids. Hopefully, after she finally got the cell phone that she wanted, I prayed that whenever my kids needed to get in touch with her, she was available and there would be no excuses on their mother's behalf. I was praying that whenever they did call her, she did not have a smart or silly remark or response. I was looking out for my two kids' safety and their best interest by investing in a cell phone for their mother. This was also for Paula's safety as well in a lot of ways, just in case she had a problem with her car or anything else. NOW that she had the portable cellphone, anywhere she went she could now contact anybody by her having the cell phone that she wanted. I can't read minds! I'm not a mind reader! But I'm pretty sure she might have some kind of negative thoughts towards me. That was normal behavior that she showed throughout the years. I know that things might've been tougher with me making the stupid decision that I made. I also know that my prayer was that God would make a way for her and the kids. She probably had the negative thought that I was trying to track her in some ways now that she had a cell phone. When she finally did get the cell phone that she wanted, I didn't get her cell phone number right away. It took several weeks or maybe even longer before I was able to get her telephone number. But the most important thing was that she finally had a portable cell phone to take with her at anytime and anywhere that she went. I'm not trying to again make her sound like she's a bad person, because she's not, but she took me through a lot of things after I got injured and this probably was a way to express herself from any hurt it caused her for the mistake I made on that early morning of Thursday, September 20, 1990. I was hurting on the inside and trying to deal with the pain I was experiencing for myself. I always tried to choose the right words to say to her before I said something negative or painful out of my mouth, "Once we say something of our mouth, it cannot be retrieved and in a lot of ways, the damage has been done."

I remember when she finally did get a cell phone, I thank God that I was still able to help her out with the funding, knowing that I did not have a regular job, making a regular income every week or every two weeks, but I did know that, "GOD WOULD PROVIDE MY EVERY NEED, AND SOMETIMES WHENEVER I WANTED." It also took a while before I could get her job telephone number along with her cell phone number and it was important that she and I was able to communicate with each other since we have two kids together. It was a REAL NECESSITY! And thank God that I was able to get both our telephone numbers because the Lord knew I had to call her several times concerning our son and his attendance in school. After he received the automobile that I was able to get for him became a big distraction and he really needed to be monitored by both of us. That was a very hard task because Paula really did not want to open the lines of communication between the both of us for whatever reason. Only Paula and God knew why it was a problem talking to me over the years!

My son's last year in high school, caring teachers and getting his first automobile and job.

I remember one of my son's wonderful teachers, Mrs. Green, just to name one of the many wonderful teachers that my son was

255

blessed to have during his last year at Douglas Senior High School. During his last year in high school, it was very challenging for me. I was trying my best to teach my son a lot of valuable lessons that he had to learn the hard way, because he would not listen to me. He was really blessed to have several caring and wonderful teachers that cared about his education and well-being. Mrs. Green was a very special and nice lady. Both of children had her as their teacher while attending high school. We knew how caring Mrs. Green was towards all of her students. So that's why I mentioned her name. I am not EXAGGERATING at all about how she was towards all of the students that she had while she was working at Douglas Senior High.

I made sure that every year at the beginning of the school years all of the my kids teachers knew my situation. I let them know that I cared about both of my kids and their education and I let them know if anyone had any problems with any class or teacher, that they should contact me. I did not ever want to be labeled as a "DEADBEAT DAD" and that they can contact me at any time. Day or night, it didn't matter! I just wanted to make sure I was aware of what was going on with their lives in education, BY ANY MEANS NECESSARY! If either one of my children was not in school or if they were slacking in their school work, I needed to know all the details in whatever subject matter they were taking at that particular time. I really had to stay on top of my son because of him slacking off doing his schoolwork. (I also tried to find out the information about the classes my kids were taking and both of their teachers names. This went on every year while they were attending school). Both of their teachers and the Principal could either call me or email me. Thank God for modern technology and that I was able to get a computer. Before I had a computer, I would have to get one of the staff members to write down the information that I wanted to provide for their teachers, just so they would know my condition and situation. Mrs. Green for some reason felt a little guilty at times because she always contacted me concerning our son instead of contacting their mother. I had to reassure Mrs. Green that it was okay to contact me, because everything that she would tell me, I would relay this information to their mother either using her job phone or cell phone, which truly was a blessing to have.

MY SON'S FIRST CAR AND THE CHALLENGES

God blessed me with the finances to purchase a used car for my son. I think it was a red color, Mazda. (Thank You Lord for the Money) because I didn't have a job. But God did provide, just as he said he would in the Bible. While stepping out on Faith, God made it possible for my son to get his very first car. I was telling Paula that he needs to get a vehicle if she wanted him to get a job, especially in Maryland and the surrounding area in which they lived, because it was no real public transportation in that particular part of the state of Maryland. He was able to choose exactly what color and style he wanted.

Paula and I went back and forth with the subject of getting him an automobile. It was a possibility that she thought that she would have to come out of her pocket to purchase this car that was faithfully awaiting my son, our family to get. God made a way! GOD MADE A WAY! We really received a great blessing and a wonderful bargain when we finally was able to purchase that particular car that the Lord had provided for my son. It was just a matter of time for him to get it. (I would always try to remind my children that God would make a way. Sometimes it seemed to us that it might not be possible to have the money to get our son a car). The majority of the time whenever we were faced with a crisis or situation during those years, I would remind my kids about several scriptures in the Bible. This particular Scripture was about HAVING FAITH. I remember telling my son that God intends for us to have things, WE MUST HAVE FAITH! The perfect Scripture that I shared with my kids, especially my son when it came to dealing with purchasing his car was Hebrews 11:1 *"Now faith is the substance of things hoped for, the evidence of things not seen."*

* * *

FAITH WE UNDERSTAND

As I mentioned, the car was waiting for my son. All he had to do was believe in the word and exercise his faith. This particular car was a Mazda. As I explained to both of my children over the years, if you exercise and have faith in God and believe that He is exactly who He says that He is without doubting, God will manifest whatever that thought was. In this case, it was a car for my son. Several other very important BIBLE LESSONS that I was able to show my kids about how God made things appear when we thought that it was no way possible for them to happen, but we believed. We were rewarded for that faith and BELIEVING IN OUR HEAVENLY FATHER, THROUGH HIS SON JESUS CHRIST. I have to remind myself every now and then TO JUST LET GO AND LET GOD DO WHAT HE IS GOING TO DO AND GOD DOESN'T NEED OUR HELP! HE JUST NEED US TO BELIEVE IN HIM! SOMETIMES, IT IS VERY HARD FOR PEOPLE TO HAVE THAT MUCH FAITH AND TRUST IN GOD THAT HE WILL DELIVER IF WE JUST FAITHFULLY BELIEVE! THAT'S ALL! JUST LET GO AND LET GOD! EVEN AS I LAY HERE PARALYZED ON OFFICIAL LIFE SUPPORT, BUT I STILL BELIEVE IN MY HEAVENLY FATHER. MY SPIRITUAL BIG BROTHER DIED ON THE CROSS FOR ME, THIS IS PERSONAL! I THANK MY LORD AND SAVIOR JESUS CHRIST FOR MAKING THAT AWESOME AND ULTIMATE SACRIFICE! IT CAUSES US TO BELIEVE IN HIM, AND HE DIED TEMPORARILY! I'VE HAD A LOT OF PRACTICE OVER THE YEARS TO JUST TRUST, BELIEVE AND HAVE MORE FAITH THAN A MUSTARD SEED OR EVEN A GRAIN OF A MUSTARD SEED. I WOULD JUST FAITHFULLY RELAX AND THANK GOD FOR THE LOVE THAT HE HAS FOR ME AND EVERYBODY ELSE THAT BELIEVE IN THE LORD! IF I WAS ABLE TO I WOULD JUST PUT BOTH MY HANDS, PHYSICALLY BEHIND MY HEAD, CROSS BOTH MY LEGS AND JUST WATCH GOD DO HIS THING IN MY LIFE, I STILL BELIEVE!

And the LORD provided just like I knew HE would get the automobile for him, but I didn't want my son crossing the busy highways near where they lived at, during the morning and especially at night without a lot of lit up crosswalks for anybody. It was dangerous. One of my daughters' friends that she took a few classes with decided to sell the car because his father was buying him a brand-new car, what a blessing to him. They quoted me one price. I think it was about $2500 and I told him that it was too much money, especially knowing that the car did not pass the state of Maryland inspection and there were some problems. One of my family members was able to let my son come to his garage and they looked under the car and saw that there was a lot of problems with the suspension. I talked to my daughter's friend's father and explained to him (He Was a Man of God. A Pastor I Believe) about the car not being able to pass inspection and that it would make us have to come out of our pocket for more money to fix the car. Thank God for favor! THANK GOD FOR HIS FAVOR! Her friend's father told me to give him a certain amount of money, which was a lot cheaper than what they quoted before. I kept telling my son that if God wanted him to have this car, then you will get it! And that's what happened, the Lord blessed me with the right amount of money that I had saved for such a time as this and I told him how much I truly appreciated him working with me and my son concerning the sale of the car. Their friend had all kinds of things done to the car, even had a television hooked up on the sun visor, and it had a very nice exhaust system. Anyway, it was a good car for my son to start driving, knowing that he was a new driver.

I've always had favor because when both of my kids started learning how to drive in the state of Maryland, they were required to go to driving school before they got their driver's license. There was No Driver's Ed or classes in high school like we were blessed to have. The driver's school in the DC public school system is totally different from the state of Maryland. Everybody had to go to driving school and it wasn't very cheap. I tried to do my best on my part with my kids father first by providing them with spiritual knowledge of God through His Son Jesus Christ. As a father, it is very important that we teach our children about the Lord and life. This is a spiritual responsibility GIVEN TO US BY GOD HIMSELF, as a man. The Lord wants us to be spiritually minded as we lead our family, my wife and kids, and other family members. I hold each man accountable for doing a pretty good job.

This started in the very beginning with Adam and Eve. In a lot of ways, brother Adam dropped the ball when it came to stepping up against the serpent when the serpent was talking blasphemy and disrespecting God's law and wife Eve. I want everyone to realize that brother Adam was right there beside his wife during that conversation that the serpent had with her. At any time brother Adam could have intervened, and told his wife Eve to step aside and let him handle this.

He could have stuck his arm out and slowly pulled his wife away from the serpent and grabbed this serpent by the neck and squeeze the life out of him because of the deception that he came to Eve with. At any time, Adam could have stopped all this craziness. Knowing that he had named all of the animals and everything that lived in the garden, no animal talked back to him. NO ANIMAL had the ability to speak like the serpent in that particular day. They obeyed Adam whenever any animal might have gotten in the way while he and his wife was walking in the Garden of Eden.

All he had to say was: "I got this baby, step back and let me handle my Father's business." All we should have seen was brother Adam choking the life out of this serpent that was disobeying God, disrespecting Adam and his wife. If the father would've witnessed this happening, even though God knows all, he might have asked Adam, "What are you doing" and brother Adam could've said to our father, father God, the serpent has been talking blasphemy to my wife and disrespecting YOU, as well as ME. So, I had to handle this business. I'm pretty sure that our father would have encouraged him and said, "Carry on my child, continue on, with a big smile on my heavenly father's face, knowing that his child was being obedient and taking care of business like he should have done."

As men, we can live from the story just like I did. I tried to share with you that a lot of times a man needs to step up and be a man and be a spiritual man of God that God created us to be, and also protect his wife and his kids. Brother Adam didn't do that, he allowed this serpent to disrespect Father God, his wife Eve and even himself. He allowed him to test them to see if they would say anything or do anything. Knowing that the circle was wrong, brother Adam stood right there and watched and listened to every word that the serpent had said on that particular day and because of that we have to go through what we're going through every day now. It's still not too late for men to be men and step up and provide for his family and continue to carry the spirit of God within them, and the word of God as well so that he could share the word of God with his wife and children, and anybody else that will listen.

I THANK GOD THAT even though I have been in this temporary physical and SPIRITUAL condition, I pray that I have not disappointed the Lord and that I have been a stand-up father, husband, brother, MAN OF GOD, THROUGH IT ALL!

When I was talking about my children going to driving school in the state of Maryland, God provided me with the finances to pay for both of my kids driving school lessons. My daughter received her driver's license first, and she said that it cost $300, that was with a coupon that she found. A few years later it was time for my son to attend driving school so that he could also get his driver's license. I thank God that I was able to provide finances for both of my children. I had to take care of my responsibilities without excuse or complaint. If anybody had an excuse for not being able to help to take care of their children's financial needs and other needs, it was me, but as I mentioned God always provided A RAM IN THE BUSH! I truly felt good being able to provide finances for both of my kids whenever they needed it and I truly thank God for the friends that were there for me that sometimes would provide me with the financial gifts. They always knew that I was trying my best to take care of my children.

I'm not bragging, but I knew that God would always provide. HE will make a way if you would just trust and believe that God is God and whatever he said in the Bible that he would do for us, he will do it, but it's in HIS own precious time. A lot times WE DON'T BELIEVE and because we don't believe WE DON'T RECEIVE or, we don't ask because WE DON'T BELIEVE IN HIS POWERFUL ABILITIES TO DO ALL THINGS!

I do that every year during the winter months, buy my kids clothing and school supplies, along with things for their birthdays. During the summer months, I know that both of my children needed summer clothing and through my many different businesses that I had I was able to provide for them. The many businesses were; selling cosmetics, design oils, different fragrances of incense, candy, fundraisers, along with the Greeting Card Business, where I provided personalized greeting cards for any occasion. I have some friends that understood the value of getting a personalized card made through the years. I was only charging $3 a card to my customers, especially the residents. I knew that they didn't have that much money, so that price stayed at $3 per card for many years. But as I mentioned, I was blessed by several friends that knew the true value to having their cards personalized and I truly appreciate the support throughout the years, but I thank God for all these different businesses that He allowed me to come up with. I also thank the facility, the administrators and other people that didn't bother me or try to keep me from doing what I was doing, trying to provide for my children. No one had to tell me that I needed to buy this or that for my kids, as a father you're supposed to know these things. Even when their mother would have a birthday, Mother's Day and even Christmas, I would always ask my kids, "What would you like to buy for your mother for any one of these special occasions?" I knew that they didn't have money, well, my daughter probably had some money because she started at a young age working with my sister Marcia at the salon as the shampoo girl and she learned many other things as far as doing hair over the years. But even if she did have money, I would always extend that invitation to find out what they wanted to buy for their mother. I was always blessed to have many friends. A lot of female friends would visit me and I could get them to purchase whatever feminine gifts that my kids wanted to buy for their mother. One example, if there was something in Victoria's Secret department store, I would always ask one of my female friends, if she could please get whatever I needed for my kids as gifts for their mother.

I always tried to stay in the background so that their mother wouldn't know that I was the one that purchased the gifts that they gave her, even Valentine's Day, I tried my best to make sure that every female in my immediate family, starting with my mother received a gift. She liked chocolate and cherries, that was somewhat of a special order. Then I made sure that my daughter and her mother along with my sisters and nieces also got a box of chocolates on Valentine's Day. I didn't want them to feel left out whether they had a boyfriend or not, and you know sometimes guys can really be jerks about these types of things, so instead of being disappointed and not getting the chocolate Valentine's heart from their boyfriends or whoever, it was my responsibility to make sure that they received some chocolate, specially delivered from Jeff.

One year Paula told me that she was trying to cut back on chocolate and this was an indirect way of telling me that she did not want to receive any Valentines chocolate candy from me anymore. It didn't take much to read between the lines, so unfortunately, I had to stop getting her chocolate candy on Valentine but my other female relatives did receive a box of Valentines chocolate from me. Maybe Paula's boyfriend felt some kind of way about receiving a box of chocolate from her ex-husband. I'm a human being and a man first of all. Before I had the title of being her ex-husband, who knows maybe a year, he forgot to buy her chocolate candy. I don't know for sure, I'm just saying I did this from my heart, with no strings attached for many years, almost two decades, for all my ladies. Sometimes I was able to send my adopted sister a box of chocolate candy all the way to the state of New York along with a Valentine's Day card that I made. I just didn't want the females, my loved ones to feel left out, again no strings attached, just trying to be a standup guy for all the ladies in my family. I Love her, YES, again, I always have love for my kids' mother. I just never would cut her off like that, but I've been cut off many times over the years and two wrongs never made a right, if they did, you would constantly be running in circles, if that makes any sense to anyone.

∗ ∗ ∗

DOMONIQUE & SCHOOL

I knew her teacher from when we had our store on Martin Luther King, Junior Avenue in Southeast. On my off days, I would stop by my daughter's school and just check on her during her lunch break. Sometimes I would buy all of her classmates a popsicle. I would then drop by my parents' house for a couple of hours and help them sell some of their stuff to the many different customers that was very supportive over the years. My mother would have different barbecue foods on the grill outside. She would sale hot-dogs, chicken and other foods to the construction workers up the street working on the Metro subway system, green line. I told myself that when they successfully finished working on the Metro Subway, Green Line, I was going to try to be one of the first passengers to ride the subway from that particular subway station. I was very serious about this and just waiting for them to finish the construction of the green line subway station. This station was named after Alabama Avenue or Congress Heights subway station, either way I was waiting for them to finish so that I could get my first ride on the green line subway, which was right down the street from my parents' house.

The construction workers were very important to my parents' business. I guess being down in the whole for so many hours a day, they welcomed and honored buying some of the food and the snowballs. I was very happy that everything was working out for my parents. I gave them a table that I used to have in my studio that was very long, just the right size, and it fit right on the grass in the front yard of my parents' house. Even the firemen would stop by every now and then to get them a nice cold, refreshing snowball or some nice barbecue that my mother had freshly prepared on the grill each and every day. To the other people passing by in the neighborhood on a hot summer day, they would come by for just a nice cold and refreshing snow ball, then they would continue walking down the avenue. Every day after picking Paula up from work we always stopped by my parents' house. We would always get something from my parents' family small business and as I mentioned on my days off, I would come around to help my parents with their many customers. Now, things were starting to pick up, thank you Lord! My parents started to make income that was much-needed because being business owners for many years and my father working with a construction company and my mother working at the airport until she got a hernia and had to stop working that hard job. So that's all we did was the different family businesses. Again, the ice cream truck, before that bootlegging then the family beer and wine store. Even for myself, that was the main job that I had for decades when I was not working in the family business and not ever building any kind of Social Security hours, days and months that you look for when you are applying for disability.

Paula enjoyed those snowballs as well, as I mentioned picking her up from work, and getting both kids. My daughter started attending school near Ms. Jones' house who was our babysitter. She never did anything wrong to me, but, it was just something about her that I didn't feel comfortable with, however, she was someone that Paula had known for years. I don't know why but I think that maybe one of her sons might've dated Paula once upon a time. I never met her son, but I just felt this strange feeling that someone that was related to Ms. Jones used to date Paula. My daughter used to be at her house when she was younger until she able to get her in preschool or daycare at the church. Shortly afterwards I was able to get my daughter into the Congress Heights school, where I mentioned that I knew her teacher very well because she lived down the street from our family business. Her family had a house right on the right hand corner of the other side of the street. She was always nice to me and I'm pretty sure that my daughter had some kind of extra attention from her, knowing that she was my daughter. Not that she slighted any of the other the kids, but because she knew what kind of person I was, and she knew my family, parents and other family members. Sometimes that gives you an extra edge or a special connection with other people while going through life.

Even when I would purchase the other children who were my daughter's classmates' popsicles, they were really thankful. I'm not comparing myself to other parents, but I had a flexible schedule that would allow me that special time to not only buy the kids ice cream but also to be there with my daughter for a little while before they had to go back into their classrooms. My children enjoyed the popsicles also, all this was before my father started with the snowball business. I also made sure that I purchased all of my nephews and nieces that was in my parents' house popsicles as well. My daughter wanted a dreamsicle and I had to make sure that she ate her dreamsicle before we got to her grandparents' house. I did not want my other nephews and nieces to see that my daughter had something different from their ice cream and I would purchase another popsicle for my daughter when we got there. It kind of reminded me of when I was a little kid and my father would take the other kids in the neighborhood to McDonald's and buy them a cheeseburger or hamburger meal, but I would get the fish sandwich. Even when other parents would take my siblings and I to McDonald's, I always wanted to get the fish sandwich. I'm pretty sure my siblings wanted fish sandwich or something like that also. My father would get them whatever they wanted, not just me. I'm pretty sure they had a certain request for food that they wanted from McDonalds as well.

My wife, children and I would always try to patronize my parents' little small family business. I couldn't support my family financially like I wanted to because of my own family needs and expenses that I had. Opening up my photography business put me in a financial bind, but at least I tried to fulfill my goal as far as having a photography studio. GOD KNOWS I TRIED! I believe that my father was motivated to do this snowball business again after he went to Baltimore with me one day, and spotted this little snowball stand, and he purchased one of the snowballs. That was the eye opener for him, this was in 1989. When we returned home, he mentioned something about starting to sale snowballs, and it didn't take him long to put it together. When we had our ice cream trucks in the 70's, we also sold snowballs back then, and it was very successful.

* * *

HOLIDAY TALKS WITH MY SON

I started giving the facility $500 a month and I would keep the rest of the money to do the things that I needed to do for my kids. During the school months, I would not give the facility money at all because my kids needed it more. Finally, I had to give them all that was required to them, or they were threatening to put me out. By law I was required to give them my disability check as rent. I had to trust in God to help find the money to help support my children and responsibilities. God provided as usual and Deacon Hough, a special friend of mine from Shiloh Baptist Church would send me money faithfully for several years since I have been here. God knows that I appreciate all of Deacon Hough's help over the years. He is like a grandfather figure to me and I thank God for a real friend.

I started selling personalized greeting cards to staff members to make money, especially around the holidays. Later, I started selling Spanish cosmetics from a company called Jafra to staff members and friends that would visit me throughout the last three years. I did very well for a couple of years and I would used the money to purchase the things that my children needed throughout the years, just like I had been doing in the past. I never stopped providing for my children. God blessed me to still make enough money to sell many different products. During those years of selling Jafra cosmetics, I had about $300-$400 worth of cosmetics stolen from me by staff members at Cameron Glen. That's not all that they had stolen from me. They stole a camera, clothing, dresses, money, and shoes from me. In the year of 1999, I started selling little bottles of designer fragrances and incense to the staff members, and friends. I would purchase the larger bottles of designer oils and get my children or visiting friends to help me label and pour the oil into the bottles. Between my oldest sister and I, business was good for about two years, but now I'm blessed if I can sale two bottles a week. If I only sell one bottle, I am thankful, God knows what I need!

* * *

JEFFERY JR.'S GRADUATION
FROM ELEMENTARY SCHOOL
MONDAY, JUNE 9, 2001

I was successful in making it to my son's graduation. The agency nurse went with me, free of charge. We left the nursing facility about 6:20 a.m. I was up and ready in my wheelchair at 5:30 a.m. There were several CNAs that were on the night shift that helped me to prep for the next day's graduation. I had a lot of help and God knows I was thankful for it. I wasn't able to sleep much the night before, anticipating the help and being ready at the right time for the morning pickup from Metro Access. I wasn't able to wear my new shoes because they were too tight. I wore my old black slippers that I had to wear the year prior because someone stole my other black dress shoes.

Before I left the facility, several other CNAs arrived to assist me with getting dressed. They forgot to put my wheelchair seatbelt back on. While we were about three minutes away from the High School where the graduation was being held, I started sliding out of my wheelchair and they had to stop the bus and pull me back up into my chair. After they put me back into my chair, we continued on to our destination. We arrived almost two hours before the graduation ceremony started. So the bus driver put us off in front of the school. We learned later that we had to go around the side of the building again after riding my wheelchair in the wrong direction. We had to turn around and ride back towards the front of the school to get on the right sidewalk and then go around to the side of the school. We passed three students dressed in black with bandannas covering their faces while we were on the side of the school building. As we passed by them, I really was tempted to stop and talk with them about life. But

I didn't and now I wish that I would have stopped. Another missed opportunity to share with some youth about real life. I wanted to tell them exactly what happened to me as a victim of gun violence and maybe some other chapter about real life. I pray that the next time I have an opportunity to talk with the youth I will take total advantage of the movement.

Normally, when any children come into this facility and come into my room I'm in their ears telling them about God and how to respect their parents. This has been bothering me ever since I left Friendly High School. What's up with that? I Just couldn't shake it! After finally finding the wheelchair ramp and the auditorium, we still had to wait for almost one hour until they opened the auditorium door. While we were waiting, I started talking with a couple of mental retarded students that attended Friendly High School.

Finally, they opened the auditorium doors, about 30 minutes later my wife and daughter arrived and joined us right on the front row. It was supposed to be a surprise that I was there but his big sister was so excited she told him that I was coming. I quickly told him to fix his long white dress shirt that was just hanging all off of him. He really looked roughed up. So he put his dress shirt into his pants and then adjusted them. Then I noticed that his sleeves were too long, so I instructed him to fold them back one time and then button them again, his sister helped him with that. He also had a necktie and I always thought before I even had a son that I would love to teach him how to tie a necktie and a whole lot of other things about life. But it has been over 11 years since I've even thought about trying to tie a necktie, but I gave it my best try from memory. My daughter looked very nice and I told her that I'm not familiar with seeing her in dress clothing, only blue jeans. She was trying to work the video camera and she finally figured it out. My CNA assistant was also videotaping the ceremony. My wife was really looking nice and I was praying that I could really become physical with her after everyone went out to eat afterwards.

God you know how much I would have loved to have been with my entire family and not in this wheelchair. I started watching my sister's boyfriend videotaping everybody and noticed his angles of the video camera. He has been at most of the family events that I should have been attending. I was glad to see that my parents, sister Marcia, nephews and my niece were all there to represent the Chapman family. While we were waiting, my daughter made the statement that they never come to any of our activities. That hurt a lot, but thank God for answering my prayers.

Paula's side of the family was also represented. After the graduation ceremony was over we all stood outside and took some videos and still photographs of everybody. The entire family on both sides took pictures afterwards. Then it was time for me to leave. God, please give me a perfect ending to my life! I started thinking about being with Paula all night and most of the morning. God I'm really tired of living in this condition and in this facility away from my wife, children and family members!

I really enjoyed seeing our son walk across the stage and receive his graduation certificate. He was headed to middle school. I was also praying to watch my daughter graduate from High School and college. I prayed that I would also live to see my son graduate from middle school, High School and college. I'm putting my total trust in you, Lord Jesus Christ to make this all come into reality for my children and I!

* * *

PROTECTOR

I remember when I was home, I always tried to protect my kids from danger. When we would go shopping and come back with bags, I always made sure that my kids got in safely first because of the neighborhood that we lived in. Then I would come back outside and bring the bags inside the house. I didn't witness it myself, but one day some guys did a drive-by shooting in front of our building. Then, one day a drug dealer was sitting in his car at the traffic light in front of our apartment building and he was shot dead in the middle of the street. Paula, my daughter and I had just walked into our apartment 10 minutes before it happened. One other close call was one night after I finished taking pictures at a party, I came back outside two hours later to go to work, and I noticed that my car windows had been shot out. I was very angry, but I was thankful that my children or anyone else was not in the car when it happened. The bullet went through the left cargo back window of my station wagon and continued through the right back window on the passenger side. That just added more pressure on me to try to get my family out of that neighborhood as soon as possible. I learned later who the person was that actually shot out my car windows. As I lay here in my bed, I constantly think about my children and how much I miss them. When it is a nice sunny day, I'm always wondering what they are doing.

* * *

MISTREATMENT

My most challenging and difficult times came from dealing with Paula and the way I believe she mistreated our kids. When I moved to Cameron Glen, I learned about another one of her boyfriends and how he was mistreating my son. They moved to Maryland into a townhouse and I wished that I could have been a part of that, but that wasn't in the plan. I would hate to call the house because I didn't want to hear her boyfriend answer the phone. I refused to let him stop me from calling my children. I had to swallow my pride and deal with the situation every day. A lot of people would say that she was entitled to live her life, which is true, but don't mistreat your children, and don't let anyone else mistreat them. I called the child protective service twice on her and her boyfriend. The second time he hit my son he put a bruise on the upper part of his leg. My daughter told me what happened, and I felt helpless. I really felt paralyzed physically and mentally. It was a difficult task for me because I couldn't physically do anything. How could she allow this to happen to her son? Prior to the protective service agents arriving, Paula told our son that if he showed the Child Protective Agents his bruised leg she would beat him. After seconds, minutes, hours, days, and months of a lot of prayers, God removed her boyfriend out my children's life. Well, out of their house, but not out of their lives. My mother and I contacted a friend who was like family to us, who was a Metropolitan, DC police officer. He knew how much this situation was bothering me and my mother. God Bless his soul because the boyfriend is no longer living in their house! The children seemed a lot happier. I was seriously considering finding someone in my old neighborhood to go over to their house and break both of her boyfriend's legs and arms. I was willing to take whatever punishment or consequences that I would have to get from God for getting someone to do this for me. I suffered a lot of sleepless nights, thinking about how to help my children resolve this problem. I prayed to God for help, but it seemed like at the time they weren't being answered fast enough, so I was going to try and take care of this situation myself by any means necessary. People, it is truly hard to sit back and watch someone hurt your children and you don't try to do anything to help them. If they can't come to their own parents in times of need, then who do they run to when they are so young and don't have the full knowledge of God? I thank God that He did take care of that situation, really faster than I thought. All we need to do is truly wait and trust in God whenever we are having any problems and I thank God for that lesson. Our friend who helped us died several months later after having some problems in the hospital with his heart.

Please don't let anyone come between you and your children. If your kids can't turn to you for help, who can they turn to? I don't know how any parent can put anyone before their kids, but several times throughout the years, she did this to my children, putting someone else before them. Every time I found out it really bothered me a lot. No sleep at night, ONLY SLEEPLESS NIGHTS, wondering how I can make this situation right concerning my kids' safety and well-being!

* * *

FATHER OF THE YEAR

One morning my daughter called me astonished to let me know that they entered my story into the Tom Joyner's father of the year contest. It was quite early and at first, I was startled until I heard the beautiful news. Tom Joyner is a popular radio air personality, who has a radio show that is syndicated throughout the nation. I thought to myself; Wow! Now if I would have won the contest, they would have given Paula four passes to Walt Disney World and though that would have been nice, I know that the 4th person would've been her boyfriend, so I am thankful that my name was submitted during a time that Joyner was awarding money.

My daughter finally got out the words, "Daddy you won!" I was elated and I thanked Paula for entering my name. Shortly after talking to my daughter, my sister called with tears of joy in her eyes. I could hear her feelings over the phone. She said she caught the tail end of the show, but she knew it was me. A few relatives in South Carolina also heard the interview. The morning show is a funny show and Paula mentioned that I sold boot-leg tapes. The comedians made a real big deal out of that on air. They said, "This man is in a nursing home selling boot-leg tapes." I knew it was all for fun, but I was embarrassed that she gave them that information. I called the radio station and requested a copy of the winning announcement. They sent me a copy of the tape, and I really felt bad listening to them cut on me. Overall it was a blessing to be chosen for that reward!

* * *

LETTER THAT WAS SUBMITTED TO TOM JOYNER MORNING SHOW REAL FATHER, REAL MEN

I would like to include JC as one of your "Real Father/Real Men" because he is the ultimate example of a real father and a real man. I am using the name JC because I don't want his benefits to be cut due to what I'm going to expose about him. He is the father of our two children (boy 9 yrs. and girl 12 yrs.) and continues to do more for us than the average man should do for his family. However, he is not your average man. Over seven years ago, JC was involved in an accident which left him a quadriplegic and dependent on a ventilator. He is in the same condition as Christopher Reeves for those who don't know what a quadriplegic is. He lives away from us in a nearby nursing home outside the Washington, DC area.

Tom, let me tell you about this man. Given his condition, he continues to provide for us. He receives social security, all but sixty dollars goes to the nursing home, but this does not stop him from providing for us. He has a business in creating greeting cards, business cards, flyers, etc. This is done by a voice activated computer system that was donated to him. JC also sells newly released movie videos with the help of an outside source and continues to seek and find other ways to provide for us. All the money he makes he spends

272

on us and sometimes others. He never misses a birthday, Christmas, Mother's Day or any day that has a celebration connected to it. He is one of the most giving person that I know. He always put others before him and looks out for their best interest.

He truly loves his kids and there's nothing in the world he would not do to see them happy. JC calls the kids every day after school and goes over their homework since I'm not able to be there when they get home. He follows their daily and ongoing activities and keeps in touch with their teachers about their schooling. He also provides the teachers with banners and other display items for their classrooms. The kids call him the "best dad in the world."

Tom, I could go on and on about this man, but I must keep this letter to a minimum. Since his accident, he has never spent a day home with us. Therefore, if JC is selected as the "Tuesday Morning Dad," I will use the money to have him brought home for his birthday, which is the latter of this month, and have the biggest celebration imagined. Because he treats each day as his last I would like to make this a day he will remember. (The kids wanted me to add this sentence) Knowing dad, he would want to use the money on us to help pay for our dream vacation to Disney World. Tom, I keep telling them that it takes much more money to go to Disney World!

Thank you,

Signed wife of JC

LETTER I WROTE TO THANK TOM JOYNER

Hello Mr. Tom Joyner

My name is Jeffery D. Chapman, Sr. (JC) was the name my wife used to protect me from losing my health benefits. I was the winner of the real man of the week on Tuesday, September 29, 1998. I'm writing to personally thank you and your staff for selecting me as a winner. The happiest moment about winning this title came from the early morning telephone call from my 12-year-old daughter. Just hearing her excitement on the telephone was music to my ears.

Mr. Joyner I will do anything to make my children happy, it's because of them that I'm able to continue living under these conditions. I refuse to give up on life, because if I did that means I will give up on them. I've never been a quitter, and despite living on life support I'm not quitting now. Mr. Joyner, I wasn't able to tape the announcement, and I would really appreciate it if you could mail me an audio copy of the announcement.

I am so thankful and blessed to have two beautiful and wonderful children. I have said several times that if it wasn't for my trust in God and His Son, Jesus Christ, my two children and my family members, they could have disconnected my ventilator/life support years ago. I cannot thank God and Paula enough for giving me two beautiful children. I know that life isn't fair, but I can't understand how a man, a real man would not want to have anything to do with his children. I made a promise to God and myself that if I was to get anyone pregnant, I would be a responsible man and father. I would make sure that I went through with my promise. Every time I look at my children, I thank God that I wasn't a selfish person. Remember, I was only with Paula three months before she was pregnant with our daughter. Abortion was not even an option, and I believe that I surprised her when I showed how happy I was when she told me that she was pregnant. I know that I will never get the years back that I lost when my children were younger. I always imagined having my son trying to do whatever he saw me doing.

There was a television show out in the late sixties called "The Courtship of Eddie's Father." I always remember the little boy trying to help his father wash their car and the little boy was using a water pistol while his father was using a water hose. I could have only been about four or five years old when this television show was on. Talking about planning for the future! God is my Witness, I want to walk out of this facility with them and enjoy whatever life God has for me. I would love to visit both of my children during their lunch break and have lunch with them and their friends while they are in school. I have so many things that I pray God will allow me to do with my children before my life is over here on this earth. I always tell both of my children about life. I don't try to cover up anything. I keep my conversations real with them.

In today's times, you can't beat around the bush with your children because life is short and real. For years I have been telling my children to call their grandparents and just say hello. One year I said that to my daughter, she responded, "Grandma never calls us!" She was talking about my mother, which is true, but when I was telling her this, I was referring to her grandmother on her mother's side of the family. I know that my parents didn't call them like they should and I don't have any excuse for them. But when I tell my children that they can call me sometimes, they have no excuse. I call my children every day.

CHAPTER 17

MY WIFE/EX-WIFE

"I still consider her my wife because when I made my wedding vows, I first made them to God, and then to her. I will not be free from my wedding vows until death do us part!"

Paula decided that she wanted to move on with her life, and she told me this during my first months here at Cameron Glen. In 1995, I received a document from the Washington, DC. District Court Building. I opened it up and it was some divorce papers that she filed. I was really surprised and hurt at the same time. It was October 3, 1995, which would have been our 8th wedding anniversary. I was scheduled to talk with a divorce mediator before the divorce was finalized. I asked the respiratory therapist to go with me to the court building. He used to be a metropolitan police officer before he became a respiratory therapist. When we arrived at the court building, Paula spotted us and waited until the mediators called us into this small room. She had filed grounds of divorce because I was not living with her for over one year. That reason was because I was paralyzed, living in a nursing home. I know the main reason she divorced me was because I was paralyzed and no longer of any use concerning her personal needs.

I did not contest her divorce request, it really was a very difficult day for me, but Paula handled it like a champ. While we were talking with the mediators, she acted like everything was just roses. I told them that I knew that I was subject to alimony, but I waived my spousal payments, so that they could go towards my children's child support payment. The mediators set our final appointment on January 28, 1995. I remember that day very vividly. It was raining earlier in the morning. My transportation didn't arrive on time and when he did arrive, the wheelchair van wasn't large enough to accommodate my wheelchair. When the proper transportation came, we were one hour late. After we arrived at the Washington, DC., District Court building, it was all over. Paula spotted us going down the elevator and when she finally caught up with us she said that everything was finalized. I did not get a chance to represent myself, and she came out smiling. We caught the elevator back upstairs and I felt the hurt all over again. I told her that I bet she had a bottle of champagne waiting for her to get home.

She said it's chilling in the refrigerator, in a very impassive way. Her boyfriend was living with them at that time. All I could think of was them drinking the champagne and having sex while celebrating her divorce from me. I told her good luck, and she went on her merry way, smiling as she walked away. I had some sunshades that covered my eyes, and they were like small mirrors on the outer part of the lenses. We had to wait for almost an hour before our transportation was scheduled to pick us up from the court building. I remained silent for a little while, thinking about what had just transpired concerning Paula and I. When our transportation finally arrived, I was ready to get back to Cameron Glen. That was another long day for me, but I granted her freedom. I still consider her my wife, because when I made my wedding vows, I first made them to God, and then to her. I will not be free from my wedding vows until death do us part!

* * *

L-O-V-E

Paula has always been impassive and somewhat unaffectionate. Sometimes we all need a hug, or a little kiss, just because we love each other. I would always try to hug or give her a kiss because I was trying to do that romantic thing, but she always pushed me away. Unfortunately, my two children are being pushed away because she has a bad way of showing her love to them. My daughter told me one day that she noticed how my sister Marcia would hug and embrace her children. My niece also did not like her mother hugging on her, but my daughter wished that her mother would hug her sometimes. She said, "Dad I feel jealous sometimes when I see aunt Marcia hugging her children because I wish that mommy would hug us like that."

The next day I emailed Paula and told her exactly how our daughter felt about not getting any hugs, or hearing her say that she loves them, but I did not receive an email back concerning the message that I sent her. One day my son was watching a movie with his mother and sister called "A Beautiful Mind." After he watched the final minutes of the movie, the main actor stated; "if it wasn't for her love for him during those difficult years, he would not have been able to make it without her!" My son told me that he stood up and looked at his mother and said; "Mommy, you were a bad wife a couple of times." I was told that she didn't say anything after that statement.

Recently, I had a discussion with my daughter about their mother sharing and showing them how much she loves the both of them. My daughter said; "Daddy, every time Jr. sees on television, or in a movie, a parent showing their children some love and affection, he says; 'Mommy you never show us love like that or tell us you love us like Daddy do, he talks to us.'" I told my daughter that's when she should speak up about what her little brother is telling her mother, because it affects both of them. It was difficult for me to deal with Paula not showing me affection, but I really feel bad for my children. All children really need to be shown that they are loved especially from their mother. If you can get no love from your parents, God knows there are a lot of negative people out there, just waiting to give them that artificial love and false advice.

∗ ∗ ∗

DIGGING DEEPER

Paula can draw and sing. She is very creative artistically and she can decorate very well. When the children show me some of the pictures from their previous houses and the new house that they live in now, I look at how warm and nice the house is decorated and how much I am not a part of it all. I know that a lot of you may not think that this is a big deal, but after living with Paula and our children for a few years, and enjoying our nice apartments, I can't help but feel left out.

Several years ago, I had to live with the knowledge that someone else was enjoying the life that I should have been enjoying, instead of living in a nursing home, paralyzed on life support, after all that I have been through, dealing with the emotional roller coaster with Paula. If I was able to have another child, I would've wanted to have it by Paula, because I would not want to have any outside children from another woman. I know that this may sound crazy to a lot of my people, but after being blessed to walk out of this nursing home, I would consider giving her another chance, knowing now about the power of forgiveness!

* * *

HER STRENGTH

I have no regrets that I married Paula! We have two beautiful children, and thanks to God, for the last 12 years, Paula had to take care of our children 24 hours a day, seven days a week, and 365 days a year. She had to pay rent, car payments, insurance for the car, and their house note. She had to pay for their everyday meals and any other financial responsibility for the last 12 years. She had to take off of work if the kids had any health issues, or problems at school for the last 12 years.

During the summer months, Paula had to find the money to take our children on a summer vacation somewhere every year. For the last 12 years, twice a month, she would bring the children to come and visit with me, whether or not she stayed, she still brought them to see me. When it was time to purchase the new furniture for their new house, Paula had to find the money to get all of those new items. When her car had problems, she would have to pay for getting her car fixed. She has been a very strong woman, despite her inconsiderate ways, and how she may have treated me.

Maybe it is because of the situation that I put her in for the last 12 years, that she has had no choice but to be strong, and that helped her to endure. After thinking about all of the things that Paula had to deal with all of these years, I really feel for her. I always will love her, until death do us apart.

I know that she gets a disability check for both of our children every month, and hopefully that helps her and the children out. But as God is my witness, it really hurts me to know that I am responsible for putting them in the situation that they are in today. I take full responsibility of my wrongdoing. I cannot even blame the devil for what happened to me. All I had to do was "say no!" I should have waited patiently on God. I have asked Paula and the children several times to forgive me for putting them in the situation that they are in today. I've asked God first for forgiveness for all of the things that I've done in my life and for being disobedient.

* * *

TODAY

Paula is a very strong woman, just like a lot of other women out there today. There are many women in the world who are at home raising our children and taking care of business because of the absentee of a man in the household. I must say that today they are doing a wonderful job by themselves. Every time I think about being home with my wife and kids, it hurts because of a mistake that was made. I can't replace those 12 years that she had to take care of our children while paying all of those bills by herself. I do know when, and if, it is God's will for me to walk out of this facility, but if I ever get the finances, I will make sure that they are financially secure.

I'm praying that God will answer all of my prayers very soon! I know that she has treated me bad and she has said some things that really ripped my heart right out of my body. But I thank God for teaching me how to forgive, and the more I learn how to forgive, the easier it gets!

Thank you, Jesus Christ, for dying for me, and taking care of Paula, my children, and the rest of my family for me over the years. I don't believe that you brought me this far to leave me now. My only comfort is knowing that God knows my situation, and He is working it out for all of Us!

We must all remember to put our trust and our faith in the Lord, no matter what situations may be. Not to look down on anyone, but there's always someone worse off than you are, count your blessings and count them one by one, giving God all the honor and praise. I thank Him for all that He has already done and even those things He's going to do for us, but we must believe! FAITH

WITHOUT WORKS IS DEAD, AND IT IS IMPOSSIBLE TO PLEASE GOD WITHOUT FAITH!

CHAPTER 18
FAMILY MEMBERS AND FRIENDSHIPS

"A man who has friends must himself be friendly. But there is a friend who sticks closer than a brother." Proverbs 18:24

FAMILY MEMBERS

My sister Marcia has made so many sacrifices for me over the years. Since I moved to the Cameron Glen nursing facility, she has been here. She has sacrificed every Monday to come up here with my mother and sometimes my father would come with them during my first year here. During the summer months and sometimes holidays throughout the school years, she would also bring my nephews and nieces with her.

When I lived in Delaware, I only saw her once, and that was on my 26th birthday. I didn't see much of my other family members with the exception of my parents, wife and our two children every other two weeks while I was living in the nursing facility in Delaware. It was hard for me to get a good hair cut so I wore a lot of hats, and I would not let anyone cut my hair for me during that year in Delaware. Thank God for my sister, for many, many, many, things! Marcia would bring me home cooked food, cut my hair, and she has been my power of attorney, and overall, she has just been there for me. She has shown and given me a lot of love, and I can't thank God enough for blessing me with my sister. I'm not taking anything from the rest of my family members, or other siblings, I love them just the same, and I'm equally blessed to have each and every one of them in my life as well.

Still to this day, Marcia continues to give up her Mondays for me. She gave my daughter a job working in the hair salon as a shampoo girl. That helps us out, knowing that she is in a safe environment, but mainly that she is still around family. I pray that one day I can return all of the things that Marcia has done for me over the years. I would love to take care of my entire family, first being the spiritual leader, and hopefully being able to take care of all of their financial needs. My sister is a very hard working, single mother of two children. She works long hours and I know that it gets difficult for her at times. During the weekends, sometimes she may have three of my nephews, including my son, and a couple of my nieces over her house, sharing her love with them. When I was at home, a lot of responsibilities came my way especially from my parents. Now that I'm not home, those responsibilities have fallen in my sister's hands. She made sure that our parents get to their doctor's appointments and that they got their medications. She really needs some help and a break. I'm just waiting for God to heal my body and soul, so I can get back out there on the battle field. Though I realize that I may not have many visitors coming to see me, God will never leave me or forsake me. Thank you, Jesus for caring, and giving me such a loving family. My father stopped coming out to the nursing home shortly after he started his ice cream truck business. During the summertime is when a person with an ice cream truck makes most of their money. I understood his situation, because it reminded me of when I would be outside taking pictures, it was seasonal. That didn't stop my mother, sister and my nephews and nieces.

$$* * *$$

COUSIN CHAMP

We called my closest cousin Champ. We both grew up together because he was the only male cousin that lived in Washington, DC. and we were only two years apart. He was the oldest. As a child it would be a special treat when I got the opportunity to spend the night over his house. Like I mentioned earlier, we both grew up together even up until we were adults. In 1983 he went into the Army National Guards and for several months and I was without my big cousin. I am thankful that he has been successful throughout the 20 years that he was in the Army Reserves, April 2003.

Prior to him going into the reserves we had some very wild experiences with the girls, starting at a very young age and again after we got older. I will not go into details because it was very rated X, but boy was it a lot of fun during those days. In the year 1985-86 we were blessed to work together at St. Elizabeth's Mental Hospital.

Champ got the job first as a psychiatric assistant. We were both supposed to go to the same job that day, but he stood me up and went without me, that was okay. He was so excited about getting the job and how much he was paid that he started showing off, again that was okay. Hey, this is my cousin we're talking about, I was happy for him. I thank God that I never was jealous of anybody's success, especially my family members.

Two months later, his brother and I were getting high across the street from the hospital (smoking love boat). I tried to tell my cousin not to go to work like that, but he would not listen to me. I could have driven him to work, but I thought by him walking that distance, it would help his high come down, but several months later I learned different.

With the help of God, my cousin and another gentlemen that lived down the street from our store, was very instrumental in me getting the job at St. Elizabeth. My cousin helped me fill out this very long application. The gentlemen who lived down the street from our store, used to take care of elderly people in his house and he let me use him as a reference. Well, you know God is God and I don't have to say any more about Him!

My first day of orientation I was working on the unit where my was also working at as a psychiatric assistant. Champ had lost his job that same day when he went to work high. After I started working there some of the employees told me what happened to my cousin that day. I felt bad for my cousin because he wasn't himself after they fired him from the job. I remember one day after I started working there, I went to pick him up and we were going to hang out for a little while that day, but the way he was acting I had to turn the car around and take him back home.

While I was taking him back home I asked him to do me a favor, "He asked what". I asked him to apply for a job in the same building, but with the security department. He told me that they would not hire him. I told him that the security department was separate from the psychiatric department. Thank God he listened to me that time. By him already being in the Army Reserves, that along with the help from God, he was able to start working in the security department as a guard. That really worked out for both of us because I knew his boss and his boss was a good friend of mine. We both worked on the 11:00 p.m. to 7:00 a.m. shift. I used to pick him up from home and take him to work. When we arrived at the hospital, I would always ask my friend, Champ's supervisor/boss would he put my cousin on the same unit with me. This way if either one of us was tired the other one could watch out while I took a quick nap or vice versa.

Anytime I needed help with anything, I could always depend on my big cousin and I pray that I was there whenever he needed me. He would wait until after I got injured to get married and have a baby girl. He also started driving his own car after I got hurt. I would have enjoyed being a passenger in his car and to be around his little daughter. I did get to see her for about one year and that was when my mother was her babysitter. They would bring her up here on Mondays when they would come and visit with me in the nursing home located in Reston, Virginia. We really had some wonderful times together in the past.

∗ ∗ ∗

NIECY, DONALD, D.J., DASEAN AND JESSICA

I had other cousins who started visiting me in 1997, and it was a joy to my heart because I hadn't seen them in 10 years. I remember when her mother and father came out to Olan Mills portrait studio where I used to work. They came to see me and I took a couple of pictures of them. That was the last time that I saw my cousin, and she looked a lot different when she came to visit me here at Cameron Glen in the year of 1997. She was married and had two little boys.

I really enjoyed their first visit, and they stayed for a few hours. Maybe three months later, they would come by again and stay for three to four more hours. I always enjoyed their visits, and it worked out well because her husband was stationed in Virginia Beach, at a Virginia Navy facility, but they lived off base. One day my cousin cooked me some home cooked food and brought it up here from Virginia Beach. I ate almost two plates of food. Sometimes I would ask them to stop by this fast food chicken restaurant called

285

Bojangles. There were two of these chicken restaurants in Southeast Washington, DC, but they closed them down. So I would ask them to bring me some of their spicy Cajun chicken up here when they were on their way up to visit me.

That same year my cousin and her husband took my children to Ohio for our Chapman, Mufford family reunion. I really thought that was a very special thing to do for me, because I wasn't physically able to take my children there, and my parents sure weren't going to Ohio for a family reunion. After they left Ohio, they took my children to South Carolina with them, and they were able to meet their great grandmother, which is my father's mother. I was truly grateful and thankful for all that they did for my children and me. They were used to driving anywhere they wanted to go, and they had no problem getting in the car and going.

Several months later they were stationed in Mississippi. I would call sometimes, and they came to see me once when they were living in Mississippi. Several months later they were stationed in San Diego. I was praying that the Lord would heal me and I would be able to bring my children out to San Diego to visit with them, but that didn't work out. After they lived in San Diego for about one year, they finally received the papers that they wanted. Her husband was talking to one of his fellow colleagues that was stationed in Puerto Rico. His friend wanted to finish out his remaining years in the states. Well, he wanted to be transferred back to Puerto Rico, where both of his children were born. God worked it out, and they were transferred back to Puerto Rico in February 13, 2000. Before they went to Puerto Rico, they drove up and down the East coast. They came to see me one day, after they had been in South Carolina. My grandmother sent me some food from home, and I really enjoyed eating it. After they left me, they drove back to Virginia Beach, then from there they went back to South Carolina, and I believe after that they drove to Arkansas, where his parents live. They finally went to Florida to visit my cousins' parents and to take the children to Disney World.

I haven't heard anything from them yet, but I know they should be okay. I called my cousin's mother last month and she said that they are doing well. She and her husband really compliment one another, and I hope that God keeps blessings them. I'm praying for them throughout their lives now! I'm hoping that the Lord Jesus Christ will bless me spiritually, physically, emotionally, mentally, financially and every other way, so that I can take my children to visit with them and her family in Puerto Rico, one day soon.

I told my cousin that she was going to have another baby, and it would be a little girl. She said that she was finished with having babies, and if she did have another baby, that it would be a miracle. Guess what? She had a healthy baby girl in May 2002. I talked with her a couple of weeks before she had her baby and she really sounded weak. She told me that her pregnancy was taking a lot out of her, because she was a diabetic. But thanks to God, both of them are safe and healthy!

* * *

MY FAMILY FROM PHILADELPHIA

My father's oldest brother used to visit me a lot in the '90s. He was very excited and supportive to me when I told him that I was going to write a book, an autobiography. He showed me a book that he had written and had published years ago, however, I wasn't able to read his book because I didn't have the proper book holder.

Anytime I would write an article about myself or about some of my life experiences, I would mail him a copy. He used to try and inspire me to finish writing the book so he could help me get it published. I guess I wasn't moving fast enough for him, but he still remained faithful to me.

At the family reunion that was held in Ohio, he gave a little speech to our family on my behalf, trying to get some family support, but it wasn't that successful. My Uncle lives in Philadelphia and years ago, if I am not mistaking, during the early '70s, he and one of his partners were featured on the front page of Life Magazine as being the first African Americans in Philadelphia with their home Insurance Business. I always admired him for that accomplishment and his spiritual advice throughout the years.

I haven't talked with him in a long time. The last time I saw him was on videotape at the reunion. He sent me a letter along with the rest of our family members informing us that him and my Aunt were moving into a smaller place. They sold their large house and moved into an apartment. I received that letter in 2002, but I still haven't talked to him in a while. Our last conversation, he told me that he had another Christian Bookstore in Philadelphia. The first bookstore was a learning experience for him, now he is better prepared to run this new store. If I'm not mistaking, I believe that he said that he had published another one of his books, but I don't know the title of it, hopefully I will hear from him so I can give him a telephone call one day soon.

* * *

MY FRIENDS

Ms. Shirmaine was an agency nurse that I have known for several years now. I consider her as my sister and a good friend. During the night when she is working on my unit, we always had a long conversation, sometimes I really feel guilty because I kept her in here talking for quite a while. I believe some of the other staff members started complaining about how much time she spends in my room talking to me. My first time going out of the facility with her was a trip to Shiloh Baptist Church. This was one of the two churches that I used to attend in Washington, DC. Mr. and Mrs. Wiggins were very instrumental in getting me to church that year. They were a couple that Deacon Haugh introduced me to.

Paula, my children and her favorite aunt were already at the church when we arrived. It was good to have all of us in the house of God together. My son came back there where I was sitting and that was another blessing to have my son in church sitting right beside me. Before the church service was over they asked me to say a few words to the congregation, I just said whatever God put in my mouth. I was a little nervous but I felt that this is my opportunity to share some of the Godly wisdom through my temporary physical condition. After talking with Mr. & Mrs. Wiggins and Deacon Hough weeks later, they told me that the congregation was really inspired by the words that God gave me to say that Sunday. The sad part about that day was that they did not record the words that I was telling the congregation and I felt a little disparaged because of that, but then I had to remind myself that it really wasn't about me, but about God.

Before Shirmaine and I left Cameron Glen, she told me that her husband and children were going to church with us. But she said that he probably would not be there. I told her that I guarantee that he would show up. No man or woman want to hear their wife or husband talking about the opposite sex to them. I believe that her husband really wanted to know why she was going to church. Before we could finish talking he walked up with her two beautiful children. He was very friendly and helpful to me, especially when they were transferring me in and out of the wheelchair van.

After church service, all of us went next door which is still a part of church and had a really wonderful lunch. Lord knows how much I wished I could have brought my family every Sunday and enjoyed worship service and afterwards having a nice lunch together.

Shirmaine went out with me a couple other times. The second time was at the Rotary Club meeting where I was somewhat the guests of honor. Mr. Troy sponsored that trip for me and he is one of my friends that I'll talk about later, a very nice guy. The third time she and I left out of the facility was to attend my son's 6th grade graduation ceremony. She didn't charge me for taking me out and that really meant a lot to me to be in attendance at my son's graduation.

Shirmaine has a really, really, really big heart and if I could ever do anything to help her there would be no hesitation. I pray that God will continue to bless her and her entire family.

During this time while I was in the center, I wanted some help with my English and grammar skills, so I contacted my representative from the Department of Rehab Services. They sent out a very nice, older lady named Lydia. I met a lady named Tina a year before from the Catholic church. We had become friends, and she would come by on Sunday's sometimes and read to me about angels. It was one particular angel story, discussing this man named Mr. T. That was a very interesting story, and she would read parts of it every Sunday that she visited with me. Tina was another one of the first friends of mine from the Catholic church, and I forget to mention her with the other friends of mine. She had a son, John, and he was only about 17 years old when I met him. He was about 6 feet, 4 inches tall, and I tried to encourage him to play basketball. One Christmas, they brought me a colored angel that looked like the singer "Little Richard". They hung it above my bed, and I enjoyed their company as well. That was the last time I saw either one of them for a while. When Ms. Lydia started coming to work with my grammatical skills, she started encouraging me to try to write some stories.

I had a few articles published in a few newspapers, prior to her making this request. She would bring me different publishing companies that were interested in short stories, about different subjects. A magazine newspaper was having a writing contest on the subject "Learning from a disability." This subject was right down my alley, because I've learned a lot about being physically disabled. So we started working on the project together for about two weeks. We finished everything and made the deadline.

She was very instrumental in helping me with my grammar on this article. We waited for a few weeks and received the news that our article won first place. I received a small award and a fifty-dollar check. This was the first time I've ever won anything as far as a writing contest was concerned. I never even considered writing anything involving a contest, but Ms. Hertz encouraged me a lot to do this article. I was truly thankful for all of her help. After we had made this accomplishment, she told me that I knew her sisters. I asked; who are your sisters? She said that her name was Tina. I never connected the two names. I was happy to know this because I always wanted to know what happened to Tina. I really missed her visits, she really had a good since of humor. They were totally different. When I first met Ms. Lydia, she was a very strange person, and her sense of humor was very different.

Tina finally came to visit me, and we started talking about her sisters and how different they were. She told me that Lydia never got married but was engaged a long time ago. I used to look forward to seeing Ms. Hertz coming in to my room every Wednesday. We would work for about an hour on different stories that I was writing. Ms. Hertz came to visit with me a few days before the Easter holiday season. She brought me a beautiful white chocolate cross, that I still have in the box on my shelf. A few days later Tina came to visit me, and it truly was a surprise visit. She had told me that Ms. Lydia was killed in a car accident a couple of days prior. I was shocked to hear that, because she was just here. I had just received another fifty dollars for a story that was published. I sent twenty-five dollars to Ms. Hertz as a token of my appreciation. But she never lived to receive it. Her mother came to visit me a couple of weeks later, and Lydia looked just like her mother. She gave me the twenty-five dollars back, with the business cards that I had made for her, all as a surprise. Lydia's mother came to visit with me a few times. She told me that Lydia talked about me to her a lot, and that she was very proud of my accomplishments. Ms. Lydia was my inspiration to write, and after her death, I lost a lot of motivation to write again. I really miss seeing her, this little old lady, she wasn't a senior citizen, but she was getting close to it.

* * *

KIRK, ANGIE, & FAMILY

I met this young lady that was taking CNA classes downstairs in the basement of this facility. She came to my room one day along with one of her other friends. Her name was Angie and the other young lady was pregnant with one of the CNA's step-son's baby. The lady's name was Jackie, and the young lady that was trying to get a job here as a CNA, both her and Angie were expecting. I believe that the reason why they didn't hire Angie was because she would always come by and visit with me when she got a chance. They didn't like that, and they held that against her. We still remained friends even though she wasn't hired here. I later met her boyfriend and he and I became friends as well. They had a younger daughter. She was only about two or three years old when I met her. They brought me a box of food to give my family for one Thanksgiving Day. They had put my name in this charitable organization that helped families during this time of the holiday season. Angie's family fixed me a delicious Thanksgiving Day dinner. The food reminded me of the way that my mother cooked. During the Christmas holiday season, they went to the store and purchased a couple of items that I needed for my children. I really appreciated their help because I didn't know who I would have gotten to go and purchase these toys for me at the time.

Sometimes during the winter months, they would bring some of their other family members to meet me, and we would have a drink or two. I always had some drinks around, just in case I had some visitors. They were married that year, four months before their baby was born. I wish I could have attended the wedding ceremony. A few years later they had a little boy named. He was born on September 11, 1995, the same day as my parents anniversary. They made me the godfather, I don't know why, but I felt honored. As the years past, they would occasionally drop by with the children and stay for a while. Sometimes we would order out for dinner. He was a Dallas Cowboy football fan, and I'm a Washington Redskins fan, so we only disagreed during the football season. He would be in heaven when the cowboys would beat the Redskins.

I always tried to get both of the children something for Christmas, with the exception of the year 1999. Angie said that she wanted to get her son this educational computer toy that cost about fifty dollars. I had sold some cosmetics that year, and I gave her the money to purchase his computer game. Prior to that, they promised me that I would see them on Thanksgiving Day, and that they would bring me a plate of food. I did not hear anything from them that entire day, and it wasn't until I called a couple of weeks later that I talked to them about that promised that they did not keep. That was when she was telling me about the computer game. I told her to come by and I would have the money for the game. She and her sister came that night to get the money from me. I truly believe that the money went towards something else instead of the computer game. Again, she promised me that they would bring me a plate of food for Christmas dinner this time, I said okay! My parents and my sister went to South Carolina for the Christmas holiday, and in a way, I truly was hoping that they would come through this time. But again, they didn't keep their word, and her son never called to tell me thanks for the Christmas gift. That almost confirmed that they purchased something else with the money that I gave them that night.

Paula and the children surprised me with some food that she had cooked for Christmas dinner. I really was thankful for that. I finally received a telephone call from Angie in late February 2000. She said that she hasn't heard from me in a while, and she was just checking up on me. This message was left on my answering machine, even though I was listening. I received a telephone call from Angie in July of 2002, and she told me that she was two months pregnant again. They said that after the movie that day, they were going to stop by for a visit, but they never called or visited me at all.

I befriended a lot of residents that had the AIDS virus! On many occasions, when I was outside enjoying myself, I would invite them over for something to eat, and I believe that made them feel excepted. I had two friends with the virus, that was really annoying. Mr. A was one resident that had AIDS, and one day while my family was outside passing out food, we offered him a plate of food, and that started everything. He would always come to my room when they were giving my bed bath, and that made me feel uncomfortable. We would close the curtain with some safety pins, and we would put up a "Do not disturb" sign outside of the curtains, hoping that he would get the message. He never opened the curtains, but he would come to my room like clockwork. One day he wanted to show me some pictures, I said okay! When I noticed that it was of another man, naked with his penis showing, I asked him why are you showing me these pictures, because I don't go that way? He really didn't say much after that. Every night he would come to my room for a few minutes with his robe, again he never said anything obscene, with the exception of those x-rayed pictures.

Mr. A always wanted to repay me for the food that my family gave him that day outside in the courtyard. I told him that he didn't have to worry about bringing me anything to eat, but he wanted to give back. While he was here, he purchased a nice car that he would drive back and forward to his home town somewhere down south. After he was here for a few months, he was discharged and he went back home. The next year on my birthday he brought me a plate of food. I really appreciated it, and it really looked good, but excuse my ignorance, I just couldn't eat it. A few years later, Mr. A came back here for only a couple of days. They transferred him to the hospital and he died shortly afterwards.

Ms. R was another resident that had the HIV virus. She wanted something to eat while we were outside doing our thing. I told her to come and get a plate of food. She sat right at our table and really enjoyed the food. Anytime we had an outside gathering, she would come right over and get her something to eat. She would say some really nasty things out of her mouth, when the two of us were sitting in the courtyard. A lot of it would be indirectly towards me, but I asked her a couple of times to not speak to me in that tone. She would sometimes come to my room while I was asleep and look into my personal items' drawers. I had to report her to the nurses, because she could do anything while I was asleep. The disease was really starting to affect her, so they transferred her to another unit right beside our old unit. A few months later she died, the disease had taken yet another one of my friends away.

My last friend that had the virus name was Mr. E. He lasted for a long time and he also enjoyed our fried chicken wings. Sometimes we would sit outside and talk about life. He used to be an architect before the symptoms started getting worst. Eduardo liked to go out to the restaurant and eat there, because the food here really sucked. His stepfather was the main person that helped him, and visited with him daily. They both would go out to the restaurant. Eduardo started losing his balance, and they gave him an electric wheelchair that used to belong to Ms. E. When he first started driving the wheelchair he was okay, but later his driving was terrible, we both would get a laugh out of that. He survived for a few years but later developed pneumonia. From pneumonia, the virus had triggered, and he died shortly.

Since I've been living in this physical condition, and in two different nursing facilities, I have lost several good friends from many different illnesses. If any of you have a friend or family member in the hospital, or nursing facility, please don't wait until they're dying to bring them some flowers and gifts because when they die, the flowers and other things won't make a difference then. They can only enjoy the love from their family and friends when they are living. Even if you don't have a family or friend in the hospital, or nursing facility, take a visit sometimes to see the condition of people, so that you can appreciate your own life.

Another friend of mine, Mr. C was one of the first respiratory therapists that I met here at Cameron Glen. We used to talk about everything, he was cool with me. A lot of the nurses and other staff members didn't get along with him that much, because he wasn't taking any of their bull. He was in the Navy, and he was married without any children. They had two little dogs, and I guess in a way the dogs were like their kids. He lived in California and in Hawaii when he was younger. He used to tell me a lot of stories about when he lived in Hawaii, and they were pretty interesting. He could come directly from one job and come here for eight hours. He really knew about computers. When I received my first older model computer that was donated by one of the nurses' friends, I couldn't use it because I needed some special adaptable equipment.

He tried to show me different functions on how to use certain programs with this machine. After waiting several months, God had finally answered my prayers. The Department of Rehab Services finally purchased me the computer. It was a Gateway 2000, one of the top of the line computers in the early nineties. He knew all about this system, and he started to educate me about it every night he worked here. Some of the lazy staff members would complain about him being in my room on the computer all of the time. He was just showing me how to work certain programs on my computer. Every time he had a few minutes, he would come into my room and show me something different. The department of Rehab Services didn't send me anybody to educate me on how to work this computer, so Mr. C was truly a blessing. He worked here for about three years and was then transferred to Japan. Since he moved to Japan, I received a couple of Christmas cards, but I thought that we would be corresponding over email eventually. I have received a few Christmas cards from them during 1999-2002. I learned that they finally had a little girl, and I was very happy for them.

Another friend of mine, a respiratory aide, Mr. D and I went out of the facility on many occasions. When I needed someone to go with me, I would always request that they called him to go with me. He reminded me of my father, facially. He was really a nice guy, and he had raised both of his children, an older daughter, and son. Sometimes he would talk about his children, and one of his granddaughters.

He painted and renovated houses and apartments as a side job. I was hoping that one day after I moved out of this facility, I would have him help me paint and renovate whatever area that I needed renovated. Mr. D worked the night shift as a respiratory therapist, we would talk late at night about whatever subjects that came up: women, sports, children, places that he had renovated, and what was the next project that he had to work on. He had just purchased this beautiful older model BMW automobile. I never had the chance to see it, but he purchased it from one of the people that he had a contract with to do certain renovation jobs.

One night, Mr. D had come to work and was moving very slow. I asked him what was wrong, and he said that he wasn't sure. From looking at him that night, it looked like he had lost a lot of weight. The next night he was walking even slower. He thought that maybe he was coming down with the flu or something similar. He told me that night that he was going to see a doctor the next morning. Later that morning, someone called to Cameron Glen and said that Mr. D was in the hospital, in a coma. Just that fast, he had slipped into a sugar coma. A few days later I was making a get-well card for him. He was a big Dallas Cowboy fan, and I'm a Washington Redskins fan. I found the upcoming football schedule for the Cowboys and I printed it on the back of his get-well card. I tried real hard to make this card for him the night before, but my computer kept acting up. Before I could finish the card, one of the CNA's that used to work here, came into my room crying, because she was a good friend of both of ours as well. She said that he died. Within three days his life was over. Another one of my friends have left this earth and went on home to live with God.

I'm reminded of another respiratory therapist named Ms. K, she was a young lady that worked here at the Glen. When she started working here, she had a leg brace on one of her legs, that didn't stop her at all. She was walking around this unit like nothing was wrong with her at all. She was a very hard-working young lady, she did her job very well. She worked mostly night shifts, and she was able to help me out a lot. I had a lot of thoughts running around in my mind, but I had no way to write them down. She would sometimes set beside my bed after she did her rounds and I would dictate whatever thoughts I had to say to her. She would write them down for me, and later rewrite them while making some corrections.

Most of the time we would do our writing sessions between 2:00a.m. and 3:00a.m., or during the late-night early morning. This was the only down time that she could do the writing for me. She truly was a blessing to me in many ways, but especially being there to help me write down my thoughts. She also helped me compose a letter that I sent to several different newspaper companies. As a result of me sending these letters out, one of the local newspapers in Reston, sent out a photographer, and later a reporter to interview me concerning my story. Ms. K eventually left Cameron Glen to go work at a rehab center, it was the same rehab center (NRH) that I lived at in Washington, DC.

I always stayed in touch with Mr. J, who is the person in charge of the respiratory department, and he called me one day to get a reference concerning Ms. K's work ethics. I told him about when she first started working here, and about the leg brace. I told him that despite her having that brace on her leg, she out-worked everybody on this unit, and that she really is good at what she does. I felt good to be able to help Ms. K get the job. I guess in one way it was my way of helping her after all of the help she gave me over the years. After she worked at NRH for several months, the respiratory department closed, so she started working here again at Cameron Glen. I was glad to have her back here again, but I didn't need her to help me write anymore. God had blessed me with this voice activation computer system. Ms. K worked here for about another year, during that time she got married. She was really a very attractive young lady. I always used to ask her was anything in the oven, meaning was she pregnant yet? She stopped doing the respiratory therapy job and went to school to become a Registered Nurse (RN). Her and her husband moved to Chicago because her husband got out of the military and was offered a wonderful job in Chicago.

A couple of years later, she emailed me and told me that she was pregnant. They had a little boy, the year after they moved. I received another email message; she was pregnant again. I was very happy to hear that something was finally in the oven. She surprised me in June of 2002, with a visit. She now has two children, a little girl, and a little boy. I was glad to see her and her daughter, her husband was outside in their car with their son who was sleeping during her short visit with me that day.

* * *

MS. E. and MR. DELGADO

Ms. E had multiple sclerosis, which is a rare muscular disease among the Black race. She was like a mother to me, and to a lot of employees. She also was a Dallas Cowboy football fan, and you know we didn't have that in common. That was the only subject that we didn't agree with because I'm a Washington Redskins fan. If anyone knows their history Cowboys and Indians, they never got along. This was our highlight of the football season. Ms. E had her room decorated with Dallas banners. She also had earrings, socks, t-shirts, cups, and finally a bed cover. Ms. E was a sweet, and understanding lady, she was diagnosed with this disease since she was a teenager.

When I left her, she was in her late forties, or in her early fifties. Our CNA at the time would relay messages back and forth to the both of us. Every Friday our unit would go to happy hour upstairs, and we had our own section because we were the youngest residents in the facility. Sometimes I would visit Ms. E in her room, and in return she would visit my roommate Wayne and I. She would visit everybody else, just to chat, and to bring encouragement to us all. Our unit used to go to the local shopping area, and also to the movies. The area was called the Town Center which is located in Reston, and was only a 10 minute walk, and in our case, a 10 minute ride in our wheelchair. During the summertime about seven or eight of the residents, and about five employees, would ride to the Town Center just to break up the monopoly, or to get away from this everyday environment at Cameron Glen. We would stop at a bar and get a couple of drinks before coming back. I liked the cold beer, or frozen drinks, mainly because it would cool me off. We also would sit by the water fountain and enjoy a lunch with actually real food. That was another highlight to eat real food. On our way back, we were never ready to come back after enjoying ourselves. But like they say, "Every good time must come to an end."

Ms. E and I were invited to go to an outdoor blues concert at Wolftrap. Two respiratory techs took us to the Wolftrap where they held outdoor concerts. Anyway, we had a really nice time together. This was a couple of weeks after Ms. E received her electric wheelchair, and I was very happy for her, because she could go around the facility whenever she wanted to without waiting for somebody to push her around. Ms. E got a new roommate and when you saw one, you saw the other. They became real close friends, and it was healthy for the both of them, because they were able to communicate and also relate to each other. Both were on ventilators, but Ms. E only needed hers at night. During the mornings or daytime, she was able to breathe without it, that was a blessing to have that much freedom from the machine.

Another friend Mrs. P was married, and her husband would come to stay with her every day. He became a part of our family. He was from Louisiana. He was in the second World War and had a lot of stories to tell about those old days. He told us funny stories about the war, and about the Louisiana life style. He would tell us about his wife's partying days during the Marti Gras in the Streets of New Orleans. He would do anything for you if you asked him. They had a lot of children that would visit both of them especially during the weekend. He also came faithfully everyday about 9-O-clock every morning just like clockwork. He also would hang out with us on our special gatherings.

Another special friend of mind was Mr. D. He was an older gentleman living with AIDS. When I first arrived, there were a few other residents that had AIDS. Several of my friends passed away due to this disease. He passed away during my first year here, but before he died we used to talk about certain things, and he even had a friend that would spend a lot of time with him before he died.

I knew a little bit about the AIDS epidemic, but since I lived around people that had AIDS, I actually had an opportunity to see how this disease affects a person. Mr. G was doing okay until one day all of a sudden he started to have major problems, and within a day or so after it was all over, just like that he died. Mr. B was an older gentleman, and he was starting to lose his awareness. His sister used to come almost every day to visit with him, she was a very sweet lady. We used to talk all of the time when she was here. They later transferred him to another unit. He might have lasted a little longer if they didn't put him in a different environment. But I think he started getting depressed, and that triggered the disease to work faster on him. Anything can speed the process of that disease up, and trigger the symptoms of AIDS, because the person's immune system is already weak.

Mr. D was one of my closer friends out of that group. They used to drug him up because they didn't want to watch him for their entire shift, and they also would put restraints on him. I think he used to be an alcoholic because one day he escaped from the facility. When they found him, he told them that he wanted a cold beer, and that he caught a bus to the 7-Eleven store. They found Mr. D at Reston hospital down the street from this nursing facility. He apparently got lost on his way back. Sometimes he would watch football games with me in my room. Mr. D loved taco bell, so I would treat him to a taco or any Mexican food that he wanted. I wanted to offer him a cold beer, but I didn't want to cause any problems for him.

Then I asked the nurses why he couldn't have a beer if he wanted one. They told me that he was an alcoholic before, that confirmed my earlier theory. They said that it wouldn't agree with the medication that he was taking. We started getting him some nonalcoholic beer, and he seemed to enjoy the flavor. Mr. D and I used to sit outside and talk about getting out of here. When they would drug him up, he thought that he was in jail. Mr. D used to say;

"why won't they let me the hell out of here!" Then his doctor must have told them not to sedate him with those drugs. After that Mr. D. started acting as if nothing was wrong with him. They even started letting him walk wherever he wanted to inside of the facility. When I was outside, I wasn't able to get back inside of the building without someone opening the door. Mr. D would help anybody with getting in and out of the door. I remember him coming outside with a large cup of ice and sitting in the courtyard enjoying the sun. He used to call me big man or sometimes call me Jeff. Mr. D. was a very short man. The administrators and social workers would make him mad anytime that he talked to them, because they would take his social security check every month, and he wanted to have his own money. I understood how he felt about his money because most facilities will take your disability or social security checks, even though your insurance paid your bills. I feel that it is wrong to take advantage of your personal checks because if your insurance is paying your medical bills, why should they take your benefit check?

Later on in the years, I felt victim of them taking my disability check, and only giving me $60 dollars a month. The administrators would take five to six hundred dollars. I really understood how Mr. D. felt. Anyway, this really made him angry, so eventually he left the facility. It was fall and I tried to tell him to wait until the weather was a lot warmer, but he was frustrated with everybody and he wanted to go. He was married but his wife wasn't interested in him. I guess Mr. D. and I had something in common concerning our marriage situation. Sometimes when you treat a person bad, you never know what might happen to you. Before Mr. D. left, his sister-in-law was also admitted here, and she also had the AIDS virus. His mother-in-law, and his brother-in-law would come and visit. Finally, I had a chance to meet Mrs. D. I later learned that she had died from AIDS several years later. I think that he felt the same way about her, as I did about Paula. Like I was saying before, Mr. D. was doing real good, he was putting on some weight, and it seemed as if his condition went into a remission state. He also used to tell me that I might have made a hell of a linebacker, if I would have played football. He finally left the nursing home and they put him in a shelter that was located across the street from here. That didn't last long, because he started getting sick, and they had to admit him to the hospital. After a couple of days, he left and tried to find his way back to the nursing facility. One of the employees spotted him and brought Mr. D here.

He made it to my room and we found him something to eat. It was the coldest day of that year and he had no place to stay for that night. We had a fat and inconsiderate unit manager who wanted to put him out of the facility. I told her that he is visiting me and if you call the police on him my visitor will make sure that I contact a lawyer and see where we go from there. Then she called the police to take him out. I told her that he was my guest and that she couldn't put him out, so she ran and told the police that everything was okay.

Mr. D thought that he could live with his brother-in-law, but when we called him, he said that Mr. D couldn't stay with him. After everybody started to complain about his being put out into the cold weather, the administrators decided to let him live on another unit. He was put on the Jamestown unit, and they put Mr. D in a room far in the back of the unit. His sister-in-law died a couple of weeks after he moved in and on February 22, 1994, Mr. D finally died from the AIDS disease. One month later Ms. E also died March 23, 1994, from MS.

When Ms. E went to the hospital, I had no idea that she was as sick as she was. I remembered a few days before she went to the hospital, she said to me how much we were going to miss Mr. D. The staff here never told me how bad Miss. E's condition really was, until the night before she died. One of the nursing assistants told me that she had to go to the hospital to see her because they didn't give her long to live. She died that same morning, and it hasn't been the same since. She had a niece named who reminded me of Paula when I first met her. I couldn't take my eyes off of her. There were so many similarities, except she was a lot more compassionate than Paula was. They came to see me after they came from the hospital, but I wasn't able to talk to them because of my emotional status. After losing two of my friends, I had to let them go, and not be selfish. I had to say to myself that they didn't have to suffer anymore. Happy hour wasn't the same after Ms. E passed away. Shortly after Ms. E died, Mrs. P had moved to another facility. After living there for about one year, her husband CD had died. It wasn't much longer before Mrs. P died too.

Howard was another one of my good friends. When he arrived at this facility, he was unresponsive, and had a trachea. He was slowly coming out of a coma, and his girlfriend was very supportive throughout his stay here. We became good friends after about three months. Everyday Howard was making progress, and that was music to my ears. Anytime that I see or hear about another resident making progress especially getting off of the ventilator, it does my heart good. I'm waiting for the Lord Jesus Christ to free me from my ventilator and allow me to breathe on my own again. Howard had progressed so fast, that they removed the trachea, and they started taking him to therapy. As I would pass him in the hallway, I would always say hello, and tell him to keep up the good work. Four months later, we would be outside holding a regular conversation. God had truly blessed him. It was a blessing to me to be able to witness his progress. However, he wasn't able to fully use one side of his body because it was very weak. It reminded me of when I was paralyzed at the age of 12, when I wasn't able to walk or use my right side of my body. One other problem that Howard had was because of all of the physical damage that was done to his brain, that caused his accident, he had an eating disorder. The side of the brain that was damaged always made him feel like he had to eat or that he was hungry. The nurses used to tell me that every morning when they would go into his room, he would have a lot of junk paper under the bed from potato chips, candy bar wrappers, and cookies.

I remember one year I was selling some Girl Scout cookies for my niece. Howard was not supposed to be eating a lot of junk food because he had started picking up a lot of weight. Every other day he would come to my room, try to swindle me for cookies. I told him that I'm not helping him by selling him these cookies, even though I was selling them for a worthy cause. If I had some when he would come, I would limit him to only two boxes. I was so glad when I sold all of her cookies, because I know that Howard couldn't help himself. But I also knew that I wasn't helping him either. Sometimes during the summer evening, I would drink a beer, and fall asleep outside in my wheelchair. It was so relaxing outside, getting that fresh air, that

God had provided. I didn't drink a lot of alcohol, not as much as I could have. I didn't want to use it as a crutch, only for socialization amongst my friends within the facility. After Howard and a couple other residents and I would have a beer outside in the courtyard, that started Howard wanting to drink a beer every day. He would say; "all come on man, it's nothing else to do around here." Sometimes it worked on me and sometimes it wouldn't, because I know that the beer was making him even larger.

They transferred Howard to another unit next door to my unit, where he used to live. I noticed when they started walking Howard with the assistance of one of the CNA's and Howard's walker, that Howard gained a lot of weight within several months. Eventually his mother had him transferred to another unit located in Kansas City, Kansas. This is Howard's original home place. Several years passed by and I asked one of the nursing assistants about Howard, because he had a daughter by her sister. She said that they had to put Howard back into another nursing home because he had gotten even larger than he was before he left this facility in 1999.

I met two sisters her 1994, they had just brought their father here to live. They were very nice looking middle aged ladies, and we all became good friends. Every time they came to visit with their father, they would make sure they came to visit with my roommate and I. I later met a lot of their children, brothers, and some of their other family members. If I ever needed anything from the store, I would just call one of them, and they would pick it up for me, and bring it on the weekends when one of them visited with their father. One sister would assist with me with putting my check in the bank because she worked at the bank. They were very helpful to me throughout the years. I would try to make sure that I gave them something for Christmas as a token of my appreciation. Ms. V had a few of the Washington Redskins players come to visit with us. Bryant Mitchell number 30, a running back, and punt, and return for the Redskins was the first player to come and visit me. He stayed about two hours, and we sat outside and talked about football and life. I really enjoyed his visit, and three other Redskins players came to visit me: Andrew Collins, Tim Johnson and Wilbur Marshall.

I was truly thankful for Ms. V for bringing them to meet my roommate and I. Even to this very day, these sisters come to visit with me every weekend, after they come from seeing their father upstairs. They have never refused helping me with anything that I needed and again I'm truly blessed to have friends like them. Ms. B stops by every Tuesday, and occasionally her daughters and granddaughter also come by. She would go and get different items for me from different stores. Mrs. V still helps me cash my checks and money orders. She has been married now for over one year. I met her husband before they married. Occasionally their brother and grandson would come to visit. All of them have been a real blessing to me over the years.

* * *

JOHN

John was one of the first members from the Catholic church that I met and he introduced me to several other members from his church. He introduced me to several of the women from the Catholic church, and they introduced me to some of their families and friends. John has really helped me out a lot throughout the years, especially during the Christmas holidays. He would go out and pick up some of the gifts that I needed for either my family or other friends and I really appreciate his friendship. I was able to meet his parents by way of email and we occasionally email each other sometimes.

During the holidays, his family would send me some homemade goodies, cookies, candy and chocolates. Both of his parents are a lot older than my parents are, but it is really good to communicate with them, if only to say hello.

* * *

MR. FRED

I met Mr. Fred about nine years ago when he used to visit a couple of the residents that lived across the hall from me. After they passed away, Mr. Fred started visiting me more. He is really a very nice man and very intelligent. He is a real rocket scientists, and that's no joke.

He has helped me a lot through the years, especially with my computer. I have had several problems over the years with my old computer. One year, my hard drive crashed on me, and if it wasn't for God and Mr. Fred, I would not have gotten my computer fixed.

Sometimes when he comes and visits, we have some serious religious discussions. He is also from the Catholic church, and we never debated or compared our religion in a negative way. I don't see much of Mr. Fred anymore, because the year 2002 he was getting sick. Prior to that he was very active with all of his grandkids with soccer practice and any other athletic sports. I forget to mention that Mr. Fred is about 70 years younger.

* * *

ANNE

I met Anne through Mr. John because he knew that we both were interested in graphics. She is a real graphic designer and she was able to give me some professional advice when we met. Anne told me that she had nine sisters and two brothers. My reaction was; "Wow, that's a really big family." Later on as our friendship grew, she introduced me to her father, one of her brother's and two of her sisters.

In the year 2000, Anne moved to California to pursue becoming a nun. That's right, she packed up all of her stuff that she could carry and moved to California. I didn't talk with her much after she moved, except maybe a couple of email messages, but never a telephone conversation.

The last time I talked with her sister, she told me that her sister was considering leaving California and coming back home. This conversation took place on February 23, 2003, so we will see!

* * *

MARIA

One of Annie's nine sisters, I met Maria about six or seven months after I met Annie. She brought Maria and one other sister to the facility, who were both attractive in their own way. But Maria was more attractive and stood out more than her two sisters did for a couple of reasons. She was very attractive, she had a very nice body, and a lot of sex appeal. I never dated or considered dating any other women outside of my race until I was injured. Maria along with about three other white women that I have been exposed to since I've been injured, I found attractive, and I would have considered even dating them, if I was physically able. Maria is a very attractive young lady to me, and I don't know why she hasn't gotten married yet. I'm very puzzled about why the guys out there haven't picked her up. She and I are the same age, and I really enjoyed her company. She works out at the gym and takes good care of herself. Anytime she comes to visit me, the other male employees ask questions about her, and always comment about her appearance, and how good she looks. All I can really do for Maria is give her the best spiritual advice that I can, while remaining true, and controlling my lustful thoughts about her. I try to give her some real advice from a real male friend, about other men that may be playing games with her mentally. She has been very helpful to me in many ways, just like her sister Annie was before she left to become a Nun.

Maria would go Christmas shopping and help pick up gifts for my children and other family members. Also, during the beginning of school, she would go and pick up the necessary school supplies for me. During the week, we would have dinner together most of the time, usually on Wednesdays. I would suggest something from a restaurant, and she would pick it up. I tried to pay for our meals, but most of the time she would not accept the money, and she would always tell me that I could get the next one. Our conversation is a lot different from her sister Annie and I, maybe it was because of our age compatibility. As much as I wished that my physical situation was different during the time that I spent with her. I have to thank God for helping me with any lustful thoughts that I had for her, and the other females that I met during my testing at Cameron Glen Care Center. I have met several ladies since I've been paralyzed, and I wished that I could have helped them with several different things, (not sexual), I'm talking about maybe helping them do some painting around their homes.

I enjoy watching the home improvement television shows. I love to do that kind of work, even though I only did renovation work once when I was a teenager. I helped do some renovation work at one of the churches located in Washington, DC. I wasn't a "Bob Vila," but I liked to learn from the many different programs. I prayed to God that He would allow me to build my temporary house here on earth, using my arms, legs, and being free from paralysis, and life support. I would also like to help the ladies with any automobile, mechanical work, and I'm not even a mechanic. I would just like to help the single lady friends that I have, especially the single parents, with financing, friendship, and spiritual guidance. This is with no strings attached.

∗ ∗ ∗

JOE & JOAN

Joan was a resident here and she was the roommate of Ms. Linda, another good friend of mine. Joe was Joan's husband, and he would almost be here every day for a couple of hours with his wife. They would come to my room just to say hello. Joan was a very sweet lady, and she also suffered from the MS disease. She had a brain tumor, and needed surgery, and that was before she became a resident here on the Williamsburg unit. She loved to sing and one of her favorite songs was "You are my sunshine." Her voice was slurred, and you really had to listen very close to hear what she was trying to say. She had a beautiful smile and she did a lot of that around here. We needed someone that was cheerful. We went on a shopping trip to the local shopping mall, and she talked to me all the way to the mall. I really couldn't understand most of her words but I gave her my undivided attention.

Joe had a lot of friends in the neighborhood, and occasionally they would come to visit with Joan. She would bring them to my room and introduce them to me. I met several new friends and one friend's wife lived in Hawaii, all whom were nice people. Joe told them that I made and sold personalized greeting cards for all occasions. One year all of them ordered some Christmas cards from me and with the money that I made, I was able to get the toys and clothes that my children wanted. Joe and Joan ordered one hundred Christmas cards from me two years in a row. That really helped me with my Christmas shopping. One year we were celebrating the Father's Day holiday outside in the courtyard, and they were grilling hot-dogs and hamburgers, so I said that they should be cooking some steaks for us on Father's Day. Joe agreed and said I'll be back, within 30 minutes he went to the gourmet store and purchased us some really big steaks. He only brought three, one for Eduardo, himself and I. I really was the only father amongst the three of us. I really enjoyed that steak, but most of all, I appreciated Joe for taking the time to make it happen.

I really appreciated their business as well as their support. Unfortunately, Joan died in 1997, and Joe asked me to make one hundred obituary cards for him. I must say that I did a really good job on them. I even put a small picture of Joan on the back of the card with her million-dollar smile. I saw Joe one time months after his wife died. He was in the neighborhood and he said that he just wanted to drop by and say hello.

∗ ∗ ∗

TROY

Joe's friend is an airline pilot for one of the largest airline companies. Troy really helped me out during the Christmas of 1999. I made some birthday cards for his club called the Rotary Club. Later he told me that he was the president of the club. I asked him to see if his club would be willing to donate some money towards getting my children a computer for Christmas. Within a few days I had an answer; "Yes!" And shortly after that, I received a computer for my children. They had purchased a refurbished computer system for my children and I was truly thankful for their help. Several friends put up the majority of the money for the computer, and a couple of the Rotary Club members put up the rest. I made sure that I gave each one of them a personal thanks by making them a card especially for them.

That wasn't all that Troy did for me, he and his wife ordered almost $200 dollars worth of personalized Christmas cards. Jim also ordered about $40 dollars worth of cards with the addition of $60 dollars, as an extra Christmas bonus for my children. God truly blessed me spiritually and financially over the years.

* * *

MRS. PEGGY

Mrs. Peggy is a very special friend of mine. I met her years ago from my roommate Wayne. She used to work with one of Wayne's sisters. She would bring Wayne, Mrs. Stewart, and I lunch sometimes and believe me it was always on time and appreciated by me. During the holiday seasons, she would always bake Wayne a cake, and she would make me a delicious homemade sweet potato pie. Mrs. Peggy reminded me of my mother, and she was always going, and doing things that she should not be doing instead of staying home and resting. Her mother was living with her husband, but Mrs. Peggy had to finally put her mother into a retirement home, and I know that it really bothered her to do that, but she really had no choice. She also had to look after her two brothers that needed some special attention. Occasionally, she needed me to make birthday cards for her family members. She is very active in her church and sometimes she needs some labels or something else for the church. I really appreciate her visits, friendship, prayers and the business that she gives me. We also correspond with each other over the computer by way of email messages. May God continue blessing her and keeping her in good health, and spirits!

* * *

MRS. MILDRED

During the holiday season she would always purchase a large order of Christmas cards, or calendars for her and her church members. Mrs. Mildred also reminds me of my mother, always going above, and beyond. For years she would get all kinds of baked goods from one of the larger stores in the area and give them to the staff members here at Cameron Glen. They really were for anybody that wanted them. The products were still good and sometimes she would bring me a variety pack of cookies for my children, and my other family members that wanted them. Occasionally, she may need me to make birthday cards for her family members. She is very active in her church, and she always needs labels, or something else for the church, just like Mrs. Peggy. I don't want to charge them a lot of money for the work that I do for them most of the time. Mrs. Mildred lost her only son to AIDS years ago, so that is another reason why I call her Mom, I always end our email messages like this, "Love your son, in Christ Jesus." I really appreciate her visits, friendship, prayers and the business that she gives me. We also correspond with each other, over the computer by way of email messages. May God continue blessing her and keeping her in good health and spirits.

∗ ∗ ∗

MY EX-WIFE'S MOTHER

I have stayed in contact with my mother-in-law within at least eight of the years that I've lived at Cameron Glen. Either she would call me and say that she was just calling to check up on me or she would call to tell me that she was proud of me. Before she would hang up the telephone, she would say, "I love you my son-in-law and God bless you." I call her mom, and I would in return call her just to let her know that I was thinking about her, and to listen to whatever she had to say.

When I was home with Paula and the kids, occasionally she would stay with us because I really didn't know if she had a stable place to live. She was very helpful when she stayed with us especially helping us with the children. Every morning I had to take Paula to work and if her mother wasn't there, we would have to wake our daughter up and take her with us in that cold weather. This was when I was working at a portrait studio, and I had to be there at 12 noon. A few years later our son was born, and I was working at the airport. On my days off, again Paula's mother came back to stay with us from time to time. Which again was great because I didn't have to bring our son outside during those cold winter mornings because mom was there. Sometimes she would cook dinner for all of us and help us clean up our apartment, which her daughter should have been doing.

311

Believe me I had no problems cleaning up our apartment, but I wasn't going to be no slave or Mr. Mom, and let Paula get away without cleaning up, I wasn't raised that way.

Occasionally, Paula's mother would come knocking at our door at 2:00 a.m., 3:00 a.m. or whatever time she wanted to, under the influence of alcohol. I would get up out of our bed, and 9 times out of 10, I knew who it was at the door. I would go back into the room and tell Paula that her mother was at the door. This way I would not express my anger and say something disrespectful to her for coming that late and intoxicated. So, I let Paula handle that situation every time she did that. I understood that she had a drinking problem, and I still respected her more than Paula did. After I was shot, my son heard his grandmother say that I was just a drug dealer, and that really bothered him. He told me this several years ago about how his grandmother spoke bad about me. I never mentioned to Paula's mother about what she had said about me. It really hurt me after my son told me what his grandma said about me. I still give her all of my respect, and I try to share my love with her, because I know how she has been treated by her family over the years.

I truly thank God for a spirit of forgiveness! Mother Barbara got married a couple of years ago. I asked my sister Marcia to fix her hair for her, and I was going to pay my sister for doing it as a wedding gift from me. Paula got angry at my sister for not doing her mother's hair. Marcia told Paula's mother to be at the salon at a special time. It must have been an opening during the time that my mother-in-law was supposed to be there. However, she called Marcia several hours later and was not able to get there at that scheduled time. She told her that she would have to try to catch the bus to the salon. Marcia had some paying customers scheduled during the time that Paula's mother would get there so she had to cancel her appointment, so Paula called Marcia with an attitude asking her why she did not do her mother's hair and hung up the telephone on her. All of this could have been avoided if Paula or her sister would have driven their mother to the hair salon in the beginning. My sister called me to apologize for not doing Paula's mother's hair, and then she explained what transpired. I told my sister that she didn't owe an apology.

Friends come and go, but what will we do without a friend? Through the good times, and the bad times, a good friend is hard to come by, but what a friend we have in Jesus. The bible says in Proverbs 18:24, "A man who has friends must himself be friendly." I bless the Lord my God for putting so many encouraging friends in my life for seasons, yet He is the only one who lasts a lifetime!

CHAPTER 19

NEAR DEATH EXPERIENCES

I have had several bad, life-threatening experiences since my injury. My first experience was when I was in the ICU unit at the Washington Hospital Center and I could not talk. It was about 10:50p.m., during the change of shifts, and I could not talk, but I was trying to get the attention of one of the staff members by kissing. All I remember is that she replied, "All shit, another one of them." I was kissing because I did not want to die because my ventilator had been disconnected. I recall the ladies just standing in the doorway staring at me with negative attitudes. I told the nurse who was working my 3:00pm -11:00p.m. shift that I did not want that lady to work with me during the night. I requested someone else because I suspected that the nurse disconnected my circuit. That was a very frightening experience because I knew that if I did not have this machine providing air to my lungs and diaphragm, I would die. After that life-threatening situation, I would panic every time my ventilator was accidentally disconnected.

I had another scary situation at the Washington Hospital Center, when one of the nurses were working with me and I did not feel comfortable with her because I questioned her knowledge in taking care of me. The incident took place while I was being transferred from my bed into a reclining chair, and I noticed her transferring skills were not accurate like the other CNA's. As soon as she put me into the chair, my circuit was disconnected from the ventilator, and I was really nervous and scared. I felt like I was suffocating. When I was transferred to NRH, the staff was better prepared with ventilator-quadriplegics. There was an alarm on the outside of my room that would sound off if I was disconnected for any reason, which was effective. Although I had another bad experience with my ventilator being disconnected, I turned on my call light, and the outside alarm sounded off, but no one came to my room right away. One minute seemed like five minutes, and two minutes seemed like 10 minutes when you can't breathe. Finally, a CNA came into my room, and connected the circuit back into my ventilator. It was hard to stay calm, and I don't believe any of the staff members could truly understand how frightening it was for me to be in that predicament. I truly thank God for being there for me during those times, days, weeks, months, and years to come!

It was my second day at NRH, that a respiratory therapist named Ray asked if he could try a new device on me that would help me talk again, I told him yes. The device was plastic, and round, and it was called a speaking vial. After a couple of minutes of using it, I was able to talk, and say a few words. That was a blessing for me. Prior to being introduced to this device, I didn't know if I was gonna ever talk again. I realized that having a voice is a blessing from God, and now I am able to talk to the world. I don't know what my first words were, but they should have been, "Thank you Jesus!"

When I moved to Delaware, I always liked sitting outside in front of the building. The building did not have electric doors, so when I would go outside by myself, I would have to wait until someone either came out or in. One day I was sitting outside of the facility by myself, but spiritually I was in tune to God. All of a sudden my circuit to my ventilator came apart due to the strenuous heat. Thanks to God some visitors came within seconds and I got one of their attention. I was able to direct him to my circuit, and he was able to reconnect my circuit. I know that they were sent by God because I had no way back into the facility. Once again, I have to thank God!

I felt secure by going outside the facility with staff members and friends after that episode. One of the reasons why I enjoyed being outside the facility was to meet different people, listen to music, or sometimes wait for Paula, my kids, or my parents to arrive. When I was at Cameron Glen, I noticed that my ventilator was disconnected mainly because of an inexperienced staff member, someone repositioning me, or the thermometer popping out of the circuit, inputting a new circuit. Five minutes had past, she walked out of my room, and the fire alarm went off. My circuit came off, and the alarm was louder than my ventilator alarm. I turned on my call light outside of my door, but they were taking their time to see what I was calling for. I needed someone to reconnect my circuit, and I was beginning to see shadows outside of my door. While I was waiting I started praying to God, not knowing if it was his will for me to die that night. Immediately I started asking for forgiveness for all of my wrong doings. The nurse came in with a nonchalant attitude and reconnected my circuit. I had to thank the Lord, and I then thanked the nurse. Something did come out of my near-death experiences! The respiratory department had a panel board installed at the nursing station, and it was connected to all of the ventilators in every room. Now when the fire alarm goes off, the respiratory therapist that is on duty will be able to watch the panel and see if any of the ventilators are low pressuring, or if something is wrong with the patients. Every now and then, when the fire alarm goes off, I feel uncomfortable, but I have to put my trust in God! "God does not give us the spirit of fear, but of power, love, and a sound mind," I Timothy 1:7. Probably the worst experience was when the electricity went off at Cameron Glen, and we were on the back-up generator system. We almost lost all of the internal power from our ventilators which had a lil' back-up battery inside of the vent, but the generator was being drained from all of the other units.

At that particular time, my other three roommates were on life support machines, and I wasn't scared or worried because I had an external battery on the back of my wheelchair, and that was my last line of defense. I wasn't being selfish, and therefore I told the staff members that if we ran completely out of power, they could bring my wheelchair closer to my bed, then this would give them the freedom to help my other roommates. Thank God we were able to get our electric back on before the generator was completely drained. After that happened, the facility bought some extra external batteries that they put on the bottom of the ventilator cart. These batteries would always be charged up just in case we had another shortage. God is Good!

CHAPTER 20

WHAT HAPPENED TO MY FAMILY AFTER I GOT SHOT ON THAT DREADFUL NIGHT

As I mentioned earlier, I learned that my oldest niece called my wife and told her that I was dead. I can imagine her first reaction was a total shock to hear that I was dead. She called her aunt and she brought her to my parents' house and learned later that I was shot and hurt pretty bad. In the beginning I'm sure that she was hurt about what happened to me.

I really can't tell you how she really felt inside, only Paula can truly answer that question. I do know that while I was in the hospital and rehab center, she brought the children during the day time. I would see her at lunch time, and I really appreciated all of her visits and support during those very difficult days. I always enjoyed her visits, but even now when her and that kids leave, I still wish that I could walk out with them.

After several weeks and months of being in the hospital and in rehab center, I felt our marriage slowly slipping away. I started noticing that Paula was changing towards the latter days when I was about to get transferred to Delaware. Prior to that time, I could not ask her for any more than what she was doing every day. I know that she had a lot of responsibilities dropped right on her overnight. I have to give her a lot of credit for handling the situation the best way that she knew how. I know that it was not easy for her to handle two young children, however my parents were very supportive in the beginning years.

After living in Delaware for one year, our marriage was over. I know that all of us are human and we have needs, again I guess she handled her business the best way that she knew how. My main concern was my children and how they would be treated, because I knew that she would have lots of freedom. There was no telling where my children would be staying any given weekend. Now, I'm not going to lie about how it affected me knowing that Paula had another

317

man laying with her and sleeping in my bed. YES, my bed because I can remember paying several hundred dollars for that bed, and now another man is enjoying my wife in the bed.

God has blessed her and the children to have several houses. They moved from our old apartment to Virginia after they lived there for two years. He blessed them to find another house in Upper Marlboro, Maryland. It was a townhouse where they lived for several years. During the time when they were living there, her boyfriend was living there with them.

I had a very difficult time dealing with him living there with my children. Yes, I will be honest, it did bother me that she had another man sleeping in my bed. I was also very disappointed and angry because she allowed her boyfriend to beat my son and bruise his leg.

When I first learned that her boyfriend put a bruise on my baby boy's leg, that's when I made the telephone call to the child protective service. I had to call child protection twice on her and her boyfriend twice, because of the way that they were treating my children. I don't think my daughter experienced quite as much of the abuse as my son did. (Unfortunately, sometimes women will be angry at the children, especially boys if they look like their fathers, not the kids fault, and he should not be punished for that, which I truly believe had a factor in it, that every time she looked at my son, she would see me).

I had many sleepless nights thinking about how I was going to handle this situation. I had contemplated getting someone from my old neighborhood to go over to Paula's house and break both of his arms and legs. I also had a family member that was used to doing things like this and I was trying to contact him as well. This situation was getting the best of me. Every day and especially at night, and I was ready to do whatever I needed to do to protect my child.

I was ready to accept whatever consequences that I had to face from God. It was very stressful for me not to be physically able to protect my children from Paula and her boyfriend. As a parent, it was my God given responsibility to be there to protect my children and do whatever I had to do in order to help my children, by any means necessary.

I thank God that I didn't have to go in that direction, because shortly afterwards God took him out of their house. But the people that I had on standby wanted to know when to make the move and I explained to them the whole situation. They even asked me, what about Paula? They wanted to know what to do about her because they knew that she was wrong for allowing this. I told them that I needed them to go over to her house and take care of her boyfriend, not to kill him, but to make sure both of his arms and legs were broken really good.

After he was gone for a few weeks, I could tell the difference in the way my children acted, especially my son, he was only about eight or nine years old during that time when these things happened, and my daughter acted like she was oblivious, and had no knowledge that her little brother was being mistreated. I guess as long as she wasn't being mistreated, that's all that mattered in a way to her. When I told her about that years ago about how all these things happened, again, she said she had no knowledge of it. I know that my son can tell a whopper every now and then, but I believed him, and why would a man put handcuffs on a child? They had to call the police to use their handcuff key to take the handcuffs off of my son's arm. That was the truth. It wasn't no pretend or make-believe, this really happened to my son. I think a lot of times my son would tell his mother's boyfriend that he wasn't his father. He feels the same way now that his mother made a choice, her son or her boyfriend. I remember telling my son years later to just let it go son, just let it go! As he got older he never forgot.

When Paula was dating this guy, she wanted to drop my children off at the front of the nursing facility. I had to tell her that she would have to bring the kids to my room and when she comes back to get them, she would have to pick them up from my room also. I wasn't going to send my kids through the hallways of the nursing home, anything could happen to them within a short distance.

After dropping both of my kids off, she stopped coming to see me, her and her boyfriend would go somewhere else together. While my kids were with me, just knowing that at one time he was right outside the door of the nursing facility before they finally broke up, bothered me. He would be outside in the car waiting for her return. All these things weighed very heavy on my heart, knowing that there was nothing physical that I could do about it. I didn't even have my own place that would allow my kids to stay overnight with me some days over the weekend or during the summertime.

I really felt alienated from her. I told Paula that when it was time for her to come and pick up the children from my room, she had to personally come in to get them. She wanted to call my room from the front of the facility pay phone and tell them to come out. She didn't want to come into my room for whatever reasons, maybe because of her boyfriend. This lasted for a few years until after he moved out of their house.

Later they were blessed with a brand new home, and I really wished that I was a part of that new home. However, Paula started coming into my room with the children more often than before. I used to order some seafood because I knew that she would come inside to enjoy eating the seafood. Sometimes it would cost me $60 or $70, but I could not put a price on having the four of us together, only if it was for couple of hours.

Things got a lot better as the years past, we would communicate over the computer by way of email. I tried to send Paula some inspirational email's every day, until one day I sent her an email message on a rainy day, to hopefully bring a smile to her. I was going to email that same card to one of my old female friends but first I said let me send it to Paula. I had always suspected that Paula was not reading the past email messages that I was sending her. Well, this email was confirmation of what I had suspected.

When you send anyone an electronic greeting card, it will send you a confirmation note informing you when that particular person opened and read the greeting card. I never received that confirmation email letter from the greeting card company. After that, I stopped sending Paula any more email messages unless it concerned the children, and I would make sure that I titled the email message kids or children, then I knew that she would open and read that message. My friend that I sent the same inspirational card was thankful and appreciative. She thanked me three times that day for sending her the inspirational card.

Now, the only way Paula and I communicate is by way of email during the Christmas holiday. I asked her to get a list from both of our children and send it to me. I also asked her to put something on the list for herself. We have been doing this since 1999 and it seems to work out very well for both of us. I always ask the kids, do they know what their mother want for Christmas? The year 2002 Christmas holiday was very successful, Paula was able to purchase everything that our children wanted for Christmas and all I had to do was reimburse her several hundred dollars. Our daughter was able to purchase a few gifts for her mother from me and I reimbursed her for getting them.

Despite all of the negative and painful things that Paula did and said to me over the years, I thank God for the power of forgiveness. Every year during those special holidays, Valentine's Day, Mother's Day, her birthday and Christmas! I try to make sure that I give her a gift or some money to show her that I still care, and I appreciate her taking care of our children over the years.

I also have to be a spiritual example for God and my children, truly two wrongs don't make a right. Our conversations are about our children and I always ask her how she is doing. I'm always trying to give the best spiritual advice to Paula, our children and everybody else that I talk to every day.

I REALLY DON'T KNOW IF PAULA HAS EVER FORGIVEN ME FOR MAKING THE CHOICE THAT I DID ON SEPTEMBER 20, 1990

MY CHILDREN

I know that they were affected especially when they wanted their father to be home with their mother. That is a natural reaction or feeling to have both of their parents together. They had to grow up very fast, especially my daughter, because she had to take care of her little brother when mom was out somewhere. As I write this paragraph I feel so sorry for my children, Paula and other family members that I put them through this situation. Because I am totally responsible for my actions that night and the decisions that I made. I wish I would have waited and thought about the consequences before I committed myself to what happened that night. (I read this story in the Bible one day about King David and Bathsheba. He decided to have sex with this married woman and because of his decision he had to deal with the consequences for his actions, even though God forgave him). II Samuel

People, please think about whatever you're going to do before you do it, because I guarantee you that if it is something wrong, you will have to deal with the consequences. I have been dealing with my consequences for more than 12 years now. "God said, do not be anxious about anything." I would like to add to this statement, "Anything worth having it's truly worth waiting for!"

Both of my children are teenagers now and they had to grow up fast and without my physical presence with them every day. I pray to God every day and ask Him to restore my health and reunite me with my children and other family members. I have to wait and faithfully trust in God.

* * *

MY EARTHLY FATHER, JOE

He found me laying outside on the front porch dying. I know that it bothered him for a long time, thinking that I had died right there in front of him while he was talking to me. Again, it bothers me to think that both of my parents had to come outside and see their son dying. God is truly a merciful and forgiving God! I don't know how my father felt inside, but he continued to be supportive throughout the years. Now his health is not as good as it used to be because he is now 68 years older. I pray that I could be home now taking care of my parents, my children and the rest of my family like I was before I got shot. He worked on his ice cream truck to make some extra money so that they could pay these overwhelming bills. I pray that this will be my father's last year working on the ice cream truck and hopefully he will be very successful. Maybe one of my nephews could work on the truck and give my father a break. I asked God would He give me the money so I could take care of my entire family's bills including paying for Paula's and my parents' house off. I am still trusting in the Lord.

* * *

MY MOTHER, REE REE

That's what Paula and the grandchildren called her, she's Mom to me! As a mother you can imagine how she felt when she saw me laying on the ground in a pool of blood, her baby son. Just 12 years old, she had to rush me to the hospital when I suffered my first experience with paralysis, and I promised her that I would not take her through anything like that again, but I didn't expect to hurt her again.

A few years later my mother started studying with the Jehovah's Witness congregation. I believe that she was searching for some answers from anywhere and they started coming around. She started studying with one lady, then she started studying with Jose's mother. Yes, the same Jose that partially paralyzed me when I was 12 years old. My mother never mentioned about what her son did to me years prior. Jose's mother wanted to tell my mother something, but she never could get up the nerve to tell her that her son was the one who injured me when I was younger. My mother even saw Jose at some of the Kingdom Hall service sometimes, but again nobody ever said anything about the past.

My mother remembered Jose's mother acting very nasty when we were going to court about what he had did to me. The judge dropped all of the charges that was brought up against Jose despite the injuries that I suffered. They studied together for about two years until my mother decided that she did not want to continue studying. She said that they were pressuring her to join their congregation. I told her that God gives her a free will and why should she feel forced to join anything or group.

My mother wasn't feeling that well during the years when she was studying with Jose's mother, but she still kept trying to force my mother to come to their Kingdom Hall service anyway. His mother finally was able to relate to how my mother felt after she had surgery herself. One day she admitted to my mother she understood how she felt during the times she didn't feel well because she too was in so much pain.

As the years passed by and I was getting stronger in my religion and closer to God, I started telling my mother that we both are God's children and He will take care of all of us if we would just Trust in Him. I remember telling my mother one day not to let the devil use my situation to destroy her. Sometimes the deceiver can use a certain situation to destroy us if we yield to his deception.

In May 2002, mom had to have surgery on her knee. She had one knee replaced and that surgery took a lot out of her. She stayed in the hospital for a couple weeks and then she had to be transferred to a nursing home for rehab. I was hoping that I would have the time and funds to take care of both of my parents so that they would never have to go into a nursing home. She really had some rough times and experiences while she was in the nursing home. In the beginning she was drugged up because of all of the pain that she was in. A few of the staff members there did not treat my mother right and that really angered me, because I know how I have been treated these last 12 years living in this nursing home.

I thank God for taking care of my mother when she was so very sick. I was so thankful when she was able to go home. She now can really understand what I may be going through sometimes here at Cameron Glen.

During those months that my mother was a sick, I wished I could have been there right by her side, every day. I'm still praying every day that God will answer all of my prayers one day. She is doing a lot better now, her and my father, thanks to God!

* * *

MY BROTHER

He really had a hard time handling what happened to me that night. He asked me later, why didn't I let him know what I was about to do? I truly believe that if I would have told him what I was about to do, both of us would be dead. Even to this day my brother is trying to find out who did this to me. I told him that I do not know who shot me, nor who was involved in it that night.

I really believe that he is being pressured by some of the knuckleheads out there that might be telling him, "Man you haven't straightened out what happened to your little brother." He never knew that the person saying these things to him may know or could be the same person that shot me themselves.

My brother is nine years older than I am and he took care of me when I was a baby. I know that it must be hard for him to see me like this. I probably would have the same revengeful attitude, God only knows. I'm constantly reminding him that vengeance is the Lord's and He will take care of everything in time. This reminded me of when I was 12 years old and my father wanted to hurt Jose for what he had done to me. I remember telling my father, "If you do something to Jose for what he did to me, then you must answer to God for what you did to Jose." It's called accountability!

* * *

MY OLDEST SISTER

When I was living in the nursing home in Delaware, I had a lot of hats because I didn't have anyone there to cut my hair for me. Since I was suffering with a very bad scalp condition called psoriasis and my head would be itching all the time, I would ask certain staff members to please cut my hair for me. I didn't care what it looked like, I just wanted some relief.

After I was transferred to the nursing facility in Reston, Virginia, my sister was at my parents' house the night that everything happened. I remember pushing her back into the house and closing the door to protect her from getting hurt. After I was shot she came out of the house chasing one of the gunmen. I thank God that she did not get hurt. It was very traumatic for her for several months and also she was pregnant. On January 30, 1991, she gave birth to my youngest niece. My mother actually helped deliver my niece right in our living room. By the time the paramedics arrived, my mother had my niece in her hands. The paramedics took my sister and my niece to the hospital. Both of them were healthy and released from the hospital in a couple of days.

I was in the rehab center when I learned that my mother delivered her last grandchild. I was telling all of the staff members at (NRH) National Rehab Hospital that my mother delivered my sister's baby. This was the only one of my nephews and niece that I was not around when she was a baby. Two years later (1992) my sister and her two youngest children moved to South Carolina to live. I was very happy that she decided to move away from Washington, DC.

When she first moved to South Carolina she had a very difficult time adjusting for various reasons. She was living in an older model trailer that needed lots of repairs. My uncle was helping her with some of the repairs. After living in the trailer for several years, God blessed her with a brand new home, God is Good! Since she and her two younger children moved to South Carolina, she has been back to Washington, DC several times during the holidays and after my mother had surgery. I called almost three or four times a month. For a couple of years we had a designer perfume business and we did very well. I was able to help her make some money for her children and anything else she needed money for, but in 2002 the business was slow for both of us. It was good while it lasted, and I'm truly thankful to God for everything.

MY YOUNGEST SISTER

After I was shot, I would see some of my family members when I was in the rehab center every weekend. My sister's old boyfriend's father came one time to cut my hair and my sister came every week to cut my hair. I still suffered from the psoriasis (which they said was caused from stress) and believe me, my body was really stressed out. However, after getting shot multiple times, my body was traumatized and that's with the stress but not mentally stressed or maybe I was in denial. I finally went to a dermatologist and she prescribed me some medication to treat my psoriasis problem. God helped me with all of the stress that I was going through after I surrendered all of it to Him.

It truly has been a blessing to see my mother, sister and my nephews and niece during some of the summer days in the past. We used to have some fish and chicken fries outside in the courtyard during the summer days.

I have been able to get rid of all of my hats that I used to have, now that I'm getting a real hair cut every week, thanks to God and my little baby sister. She is a single parent and I really pray that I could give her a break and show her how much I appreciate everything that she has done for me and my kids over the years.

Every time I got a chance I would let my sister know how much I appreciate her for everything, especially teaching my daughter different business techniques that allowed her to get her own income. Whenever she would bring my son to visit me, she always made sure he got his hair cut. I want her to know every chance I get that I APPRECIATE EVERYTHING SHE HAS DONE FOR ME OVER THE YEARS.

If it weren't for God, my sisters and my parents, my children probably would be stuck every weekend in that house alone or dropped off at someone else's house, while their mother did whatever she wanted to do. After I got injured, it was like Paula was set free. She wanted to hang out with her girlfriends in the club. She would just hang out there like that. While I was home, I just wasn't having it. I don't think people realize when you get married you make a covenant to God and a commitment to your spouse. It is necessary to change the old ways of what you were accustomed to doing, old friends, old environments, maybe I'm just old school, OR MAYBE I'M JUST A FOOL! But this is what I believe once you get married and you're no longer single, you should conduct yourself in such a way that reflects God and your marriage along with respecting your wife or husband, and mainly have a respect for yourself.

* * *

WHY ARE PEOPLE SO AGAINST AND JEALOUS OF MY FAMILY?

As long as I can remember from a child, up until I became an adult, people have been against my family because we have tried to better ourselves over the years. When I was a little boy my parents had an ice cream truck and the rental office management gave us so many problems because we had the ice cream truck business.

Then years later God blessed my family with a mom-and-pop/beer and wine store, and we had problems with people coming in trying to steal our merchandise and cause us problems throughout the 10 years that we had our business.

Several years later I had my own photography business and I encountered a lot of jealousy throughout the years that I had it up and running. I was very successful with my Polaroid photography business and the word was getting around that if you needed a photographer for your party, contact Jeffery D. Chapman Sr.

Even now that I am paralyzed and on life support, the people in this facility still have something against me and all I am trying to do is to do my time and whatever God has for me to do while I'm in this temporary physical condition.

Jealousy and envy have always been one of my worst enemies because the Devil doesn't want me to be prosperous.

FAMILY REUNIONS THAT I MISSED OVER THE YEARS

I have missed several family reunions since I have been paralyzed. The next year after I was shot, (1991) I was supposed to help my cousin with our first Chapman & Mumford family reunion in Washington, DC and I was very excited about being a part of the committee. I have always been serious about my family and keeping everybody together. In the past years, before I was hospitalized, I was able to help organize about three of our family reunions on my mother's side of the family with my older cousin who also lived in Washington, DC and a lot of help came from my cousins who lived to South Carolina.

* * *

ACKNOWLEDGING OUR SENIOR FAMILY MEMBERS

Family reunions are very important to all of us, but especially our senior family members. Some of them have lived through wars, depression years, and also the civil rights movement. It is very important that we recognize our senior family members to let them know that we appreciate everything they did for us over the years. Dealing with segregation, I can't imagine myself living during those difficult times. Our senior family members not only had to deal with getting equal rights, but just the right to be treated like a human being. Can you imagine today, not being able to use the public bathrooms or set in the front seat at McDonald's? That would blow your mind!

The family reunions are equally important to the younger generations. You don't have to go to your local library if you have an elderly family member living today and is very alert, sometimes their short-term memory may not always be there, but I guarantee you that their long-term memory is very vivid and sharp. So, let us recognize the older family members as well as the younger family members because they are our future, Amen!

Our reunions were held in several different states; Washington, DC., Ohio (where my cousin and her husband took both of our children), South Carolina, Myrtle Beach, and the last reunion was held in Jacksonville, Florida.

I have been blessed first by God and secondly by my aunt Doris and her husband Uncle Earl. They have videotaped most of the family reunions for me over the years and I am very thankful for them doing that for me. *"**Truly, the Family That Prays Together Stays Together!"***

One of my father's sister's, Aunt Madge and her husband Uncle Jimmy sponsored that reunion on July 12th-14th 2002. They were willing to pay for me to be in attendance with them at the reunion. However, my doctor was against me traveling that far under my temporary physical condition. I was very thankful that they were willing to put out all of that money for me to come to Florida.

I stayed in contact with my aunt by way of the mail messaging. She is really a fascinating lady and I'm thankful that she is a part of my life and my family. The next family reunion will be held in Greensboro, North Carolina and I'm praying that my immediate family, including myself will be in full attendance and I will be free from paralysis, God Willing!

CHAPTER 21

MEMORIES OF (MEMORIAL)

BOTH OF MY MOTHER'S BROTHERS
DIED THE SAME YEAR-2001

I lost two of my uncles last year, both of my mother's brothers, my uncle Sam was disabled, and he lived like that for years. He was in his early seventies when he died. One of my mother's sisters took care of him for years. Out of all of the family members, she dedicated her life to take care of him and one of my older aunts but died several years ago. My uncle Ike was the only uncle that I grew up around, I believe that I talked about this in the letter below.

This is a letter that I wrote to my Aunt B in hopes that someone would read the letter at my Uncle Ike Memorial Service. I normally send the mail to my sister's house and I could almost guess how long it would take to reach South Carolina.

Unfortunately, after staying up all night crying while I was trying to get the words out and thinking about my Uncle Ike, the letter never made it to her house. I really was hurt about losing my uncle and also that the letter never reached its destination.

WEDNESDAY, AUGUST 15, 2001

This Message to my mother, brother, wife and kids and family

I know that you may have remembered hearing this same card being read to all of you just a couple of months ago at our Uncle Sam's funeral service, but two months later I had to make another card for yet another Uncle.

I'd prayed to God Almighty that I would not have to make another condolence card again this year. (Especially after hearing that my Uncle Ike was very sick. I prayed every day, evening and night, I even fasted for two days).

331

Then knowing that this situation was not in my control, I prayed to my Heavenly Father to let His will be done. Sometimes we get a little selfish, but that's the human part of us.

As I type this letter on my computer at 1:35 a.m., laying here in this nursing home bed, paralyzed from the neck down and on life support, I realize that one day I will meet my maker/creator.

We all will one day, but until that time, please thank God for His son Jesus Christ, and the many blessings that He has given us over the years, including My Uncle Ike. (I don't mean to sound selfish, because he was all of our uncle) but I'm paying a personal thanks to him today.

Since my injury on September 20, 1990, I've seen my uncle several times. I thank God that I was able to thank him for everything that he had done for me over my entire life.

As a child and as an adult, my Uncle Ike was the only uncle that I actually grew up around. I'm not taking anything from the rest of my uncles, I love them as well. But Uncle Ike only lived about 20 minutes away from my parents' house, and later on in the eighties, he lived about six blocks down the street from my parents.

I thanked him for coming around and visiting us, taking me to his house in Washington, DC. where I would spend the night with my cousins, especially my youngest cousin because we were close in age. I thanked him for taking me to South Carolina several times. I just overall enjoyed being around him.

When I used to remind him of everything that he did for me, he would say that he couldn't remember, but even now, the memories are still fresh in my mind.

I also prayed that if it was God's will to spiritually and physically heal me from this demon of paralysis, I would one day have an opportunity to use his barbecue pit outside of his house. It would be my turn to barbecue him some food this time, because he has sent me several plates of his famous barbecue foods and I wanted to return the favor.

Again, this was not God's will for me to return the many gifts that my uncle had given me over the years.

I apologize for taking so long with this letter, but my uncle and other family members and friends need to know how much I loved my uncle and how special he was to me. I know a lot of other people like my uncle because that was the type of person he was, sharing and caring.

Again, I'm glad that I was able to share this information and appreciation with my uncle while he was still living. I would encourage all of you today to let that special someone know how much you love them, whether it's a husband, wife, sister, brother, aunt, uncle, cousin or just a friend. Please don't wait until it's too late, and don't let your selflessness or foolish pride get in your way.

Brother, Rev. James Cleveland made a record several years before he died, and the title of the song was "Give me my flowers." It said, "Give me my flowers now, So I can see the beauty that they bring while I'm Alive".

So, family members, and friends, please if someone has done something good for you today, yesterday or years ago, it's not too late to tell them thanks today!

I used to call my Uncle Ike "Big Wheel." It was a little inside saying that we had amongst his children and I, and his response would always be **"Roll-on"**.

So now in my closing statement to my much-loved Uncle Ike, **"I'll say to his Soul" Uncle Ike, roll-on into God's Kingdom!**

To my Aunt B, all of my kids and all of his grandchildren. From The Entire Chapman Family I would like to offer our condolences to you and your family during these difficult times. All of you are in my prayers every day. I wish I could have been there physically!

We will truly miss him and anybody that knew our Uncle Ike Wilkins can also echo the same condolences. May your soul now rest in peace, you are now free from all of the earthly pain and suffering. Free at last, free at last, Thank God almighty through your Jesus Christ, my uncle is free from this earthly, sinned filled world!

Please tell Uncle Buddy, Aunts, Mag, Flouretha, Irene, Cousins and In-laws, that I love them also and they are in my daily prayers.

* * *

UNCLE FARRIE

The year 2000, one of my father's younger brothers died. Uncle Farrie died after he was working on his car and a part of his automobile dropped on him, if I'm not mistaking, on his chest. He did not go to the hospital right away, because he did not get any external injury. Later he started feeling bad because the injuries were internal which caused his death.

Uncle Farrie had a very good sense of humor. He would have everybody laughing all day long. I remember one year when my parents and I went to South Carolina for a few days' vacation, Uncle Farrie came over to our house in South Carolina and stayed overnight. He had my friend and I laughing all night long, I was in tears because of all of the jokes that he was telling us.

In the Chapman family, we always have an uncle Farrie in each of the different families within the Chapman family. My brother is the comedian in our family, some of my other cousins in the Chapman family have a comedian in their family as well, but I haven't been around most of my other cousins to positively identify them like I have my other two cousins.

Uncle Farrie was in the Vietnam war, and he told me that he was exposed to a lot of bad things in Vietnam. He said that his job was to stack up the body bags and body parts and how it had an emotional and mental effect on his life every day afterwards.

Sometimes he would relive some of the things that he saw during his time in the Vietnam war. Readers, I'm sure that you may have some family members that were mentally and physically damaged from that senseless war, even today.

Uncle Farrie was another one of my uncles that I grew up around more than my other uncles. Years ago, he and his family lived in Washington, DC, but I believe he got involved in something dangerous up here during the time when he was living in DC. So, he took his wife and one of his sons and moved to South Carolina. I believe he only came back to DC one time for a very short visit during the late seventies.

When he was living, I could catch him over my oldest sister's house. He would stop by and visit with my sister and another one of my cousins, that was my mother's nephew and they would hang out together. I always enjoyed talking with him because he always made me laugh. He looked like that comedian that's on BET Comedy View, Renardo Ray on the host of the Comedy View show. Uncle Farrie even talked like Renardo Ray.

I will miss all of my uncles. Since I've been living in these two nursing homes, I've witnessed a lot of people dying and I have learned that after we lived our last day here on earth that all we become is a memory, whether they are good memories or bad memories, that's what we leave here with our loved ones.

I TRULY THANK GOD FOR THE MEMORIES THAT ALL MY LOVED ONES THAT HAVE PASSED ON HAVE LEFT WITH ME. EVERY TIME I THINK ABOUT ONE OF THEM, THERE IS ANOTHER MEMORY THAT FOLLOWS. THEY ALL MAY BE GONE, BUT NEVER FORGOTTEN! TO ALL OF YOU, REST IN PEACE - ETERNALLY!

WITH THE FATHER AND THE SON, JESUS CHRIST, AND GOD WILLING WITH EACH OTHER!

CHAPTER 22

WRITTEN EXPRESSIONS

Within my last 12 years, I have dedicated a lot of time towards giving my own testimony so that others may be comforted, even in their trials and tribulations. Many publications have published articles about my injury, and I truly feel blessed by that. I have also contributed columns for other publication. I have written several letters and short stories on life. It feels good to know that by God's grace, and through Jesus' blood that I am healed and that I am here. Since I have been injured, I have not let my circumstances hinder me from inspiring others, as I have been inspired. I would like the Washington Times, Reston Times, The Connection, Fairfax Journal, Mobility Outlook, church newsletters, and a couple of other magazines that I am grateful for. I thank the Lord for them giving me another chance.

All of these publications or magazines that I spoke about above God has allowed me to either write a letter that was published or they wrote a story about me and my kids, especially Reston Times newspaper even though they no longer exist. I was featured several times in their newspaper. I have copies of all these articles, but unfortunately, I cannot put my hands on them, literally, because I moved so many times, no telling where these publications are. However, through all the publications that I mentioned above, they allowed me to touch a lot of people. I sometimes hear people say that if I can just reach one person that they would feel like it is all worth it, but I have a different mindset. I would like to bring millions of people to Christ and witness to them. I can't just settle for just one person.

* * *

AWARENESS

My second year here, I wanted to share my experiences with other people, so I started talking with the head of the respiratory department, Mrs. D. On March 29, 1993, she called the Northern

Virginia College to set-up a seminar with the respiratory students. It was my first time ever talking with a group about living on life support. The class had about 35 students and 4 instructors. Before they came I dictated some information to her since she was in charge of the respiratory department here at Cameron Glen. I gave her some general information about what happened to me. After I entered the room, I was getting nervous, but I tried not to show it. I had someone videotape my session for my personal records, it lasted about 90 minutes, but it seemed longer. I told them about how scared I was living on life support, and how many times I thought it was over because of my ventilator incidences. They asked me questions about my family situation, and I didn't hesitate to tell them my marital status. After it was over they rewarded me a $50 check because they were so thankful for me helping them out. They brought me a small refrigerator as a token of their appreciation. Three of the students got a job working at Cameron Glen as a respiratory therapist a couple of years later. I didn't recognize them, but they remembered me, and they told me how much my conversation helped them. The seminar encouraged me to do more.

Kathy, my respiratory therapist would sometimes write down my thoughts when I couldn't sleep at night. She was very instrumental in helping me communicate my feelings to the masses. I would try to make my letters to the people universal, to avoid re-writing letters. I sent letters to the Washington Post, the Washington Times, and finally the Reston Times newspaper. I received one response, and that was from the Reston Times newspaper. Their office was located up the street from Cameron Glen. I didn't want the staff at the facility to know my business, so I told the photographer who came from the paper to act like we were friends. Because they knew that I was a former photographer, they didn't question the visit. The newspaper sent a female journalist to interview me, and the story took about five to seven months to be printed. Clarence went with me out of the facility a couple of times to get an evaluation from the National Rehab Center in DC. I also went for an environmental control unit (ECU) evaluation to test the latest devices. He photographed the session with Paula, who came to be nosey. This was the first time I had been to DC. since I was injured. The second time I went to DC., the driver stopped in front of my parents' house where I was shot, and I got chills. Clarence photographed the scene and the front of the house and the surrounding area, but I never got out the van.

When we returned to Cameron Glen, he photographed me being transferred from my wheelchair into the bed, and those were the final pictures that he took. When the story came out, it made the front page of the newspaper, with an additional part on the inside pages. I was pleased with the story, although there were a few misprints, and quotes by the reporter. When the administrators read the article, they were upset because of the comments that I made. I wasn't trying to bad mouth anyone, I was just trying to get my story to the public. I had several other articles published in the Washington Times paper, and the Connection (Fairfax, VA) newspaper. The story in the Connection was about the importance of celebrating the life and great accomplishments of Dr. Martin Luther King, Jr., this was more of an informative piece. The second article that I wrote was published in the Washington Times February 13, 1994, and that piece introduced all the African American leaders who fought for freedom and contributed to inventions that we use today. I also connected my own testimony into the story, letting the readers know the importance of life.

* * *

MY BROTHERS KEEPER

I have befriended a lot of Africans from Sierra Leone, Ghana, Cameroon, Niger and several other countries in Africa since I have been a resident at Cameron Glen Nursing Facility. I've met a lot of African employees, and I really enjoy talking with them about Africa. Africa is the largest continent in the world, the land of milk and honey. Africa is also one the riches continents in the world as well, full of diamonds, gold, silver and some of the most precious minerals known to mankind. When I started living at Cameron Glen, I noticed that it was about 85 percent of Africans working here, mainly as CNA's. The majority of the Africans working here in 1992 when I arrived were from a country called Sierra Leone, in Africa. They don't call them countries, they call them providences. I haven't met anyone from South Africa yet, but I know that it is the richest country in Africa. Nigeria and many other countries in Africa are very rich in minerals, diamonds, gold, silver and all kinds of natural resources, all located within the continent of Africa. If I'm not mistaking, Sierra Leone is very rich with diamonds and gold, located in West Africa. Years ago, the Europeans came to Africa and raided all of the countries in Africa, beginning with Britain, Portugal, France, etc. They all came and invaded large parts of Africa, taking their diamonds, gold and anything else that they wanted from the African nations. They are still doing that today, taking whatever they want from Africa, and leaving large populations of Africans starving and living in poverty, while they reap the benefits from all of the wealth that they have stolen. Several of the African CNA's that work here at Cameron Glen have advanced themselves into a better way of living.

One married couple from Sierra Leone opened up their own little grocery store located in Woodbridge, Virginia. I remember one day the owner of this grocery store (when he was working here as a CNA), wanted me to call the shipping company that was holding his merchandise because they were giving him a hard time. He asked me to call the shipping company and tell them that I wanted my merchandise that they were holding. He wanted them to hear an American voice so they would not keep giving him the run around, because he was an African. I made the telephone call for my friend, and told them that if I did not get my merchandise within a couple of days, I would be calling my lawyer to take care of this situation. My friend told me that he was able to get his merchandise the next day. I was truly thankful that I was able to help them out in their time of need. Just hearing my voice spoke volume and maybe some fear in their heart. He informed me the next day that he didn't know why they were withholding his merchandise, knowing that everything had been paid for by him, and there was no need to try to hustle him out of his money.

What is wrong with people? I know God has given me the wisdom and knowledge on how to make money for my children, so I can help them and their mother the best way I know how. I might not make a lot of money, but God provides the necessary money so that I can provide for my children. I'm writing you this letter while lying in my bed, paralyzed from the neck down and living with a ventilator (life support machine). What my children needed throughout the years were school clothes, supplies, winter clothing, summer clothing, but most importantly love. God has given me His wisdom and knowledge on how to be a spiritually guided father. I pass that wisdom and knowledge to both of my children every day that God has given me to wake up and see.

Thank you, Lord, Jesus Christ for everything! I pray that one day I will be able to travel and see several countries in Africa with my children and wife, helping the last fortunate people of the mother land. I often wonder, what did the Black people from all over the world do to get in the situation that we have been in for hundreds of years? Did our ancestors do something to anger God? Remember we are our brothers and sisters' keepers! But we don't help each other out. First of all, some family members can't get along, whether it's the parents, brother against brother, sisters against sisters, and what is really sad is when the children can't get along with their birth parents.

I thank God for both of my parents and the opportunity that He has given me all of these years to let both of them know exactly how much I love them. As long as I can remember, I have been trying to find a way to take care of my parents, sometimes by any means possible. Even while I'm lying in this bed temporarily paralyzed, I'm still trying to help them first spiritually, and financially. Sometimes I would just call them on the telephone to tell them some jokes or anything that will make them laugh because they both are getting older and they still are under pressure financially and physically. I really get disappointed when I hear that the government isn't helping our senior citizens, especially when it comes to purchasing that expensive medication.

Listen, all of our senior citizens have helped the United States of America in many, many, many different ways and they have given their blood, sweat and tears for years. Now they can't pay for this expensive medication and some of them have to make the decision whether they are going to buy food, pay a bill or purchase that much needed expensive medication, something is definitely wrong with this picture. I would like to just say something a little different; I believe that after a while, the children should start taking care of their parents once they get older. All of our parents have made sacrifices for all of us to better ourselves. Now it is our time to show them our love and appreciation for everything that they have done for us. Yes, we Owe Them!

∗ ∗ ∗

FORGIVENESS AND COUNTING
YOUR BLESSINGS

What a Powerful blessing it is from God to be able to forgive. Why is it that we can't forgive one another? When we do something wrong, we always ask God for his forgiveness, and being the merciful God that He is, He forgives us! But when someone does something to you, you find it hard to forgive, why? It doesn't work that way, if we truly want God's forgiveness, we should be able to forgive others when they do something wrong to us. Remember this part of the Lord's prayer, "Forgive our trespasses, as we forgive those who trespass against us?" We are so quick to hold a grudge against someone as soon as they do something to us. Sometimes people hold grudges against family members and friends for years. It could have happened 10, 20 or even 30 years ago, and we won't forgive that person. Many times we don't even remember why we were mad at the person but yet we're so unforgiving. Brothers and sisters, life is too short to hold on to your unforgiving ways. Life is truly too short to be holding on to whatever may have happened years ago or yesterday. *"Yesterday is history, tomorrow is a mystery, and today is a present."* Today is a gift that God has given you, take advantage of it and let go of your unforgiving ways of living.

Sometimes we can hinder our blessings when we don't forgive and we often wonder why the blessings take so long. God will forgive us if we ask for His forgiveness. The laws of physics says, "For every action there's a reaction." We have to show accountability for whatever we do to others. "Remember love thy neighbor as you love yourself!" We have brothers against brothers, sisters against sisters, children against their own parents because they will not forgive them for whatever occurred in their lives. Some family members and friends haven't spoken to one another in several years because of something that happened years ago, that's not right! The topic is forgiveness and counting your blessings!

I was injured on September 20, 1990, I put myself in harm's way. I should have been home with my wife and children, but I wasn't. I was robbed, setup and shot several times, which left me on a ventilator, dependent (on life support). At 25, I was a quadriplegic, paralyzed from the neck down. Our children were very young, my daughter was only four years old, and my son was only 20 months old when I was injured. My wife and I were about to celebrate our third year of marriage, which was on October 3rd. A lot was taken from me and I lost my physical independence. Believe me, you cannot put a price on having your physical independence. I'm not able to feed myself, dress myself or do anything physical for myself. I've missed so much since I was injured, but mostly I miss watching my children grow up every day, watching them go to sleep at night, and having them running into our bedroom early in the morning. I used to get so much joy out of holding my children and receiving hugs with their little arms around my neck and sometimes around my legs. When I would pick my daughter up from school, she would run towards me, that gave me so much happiness. I felt a tremendous amount of pride when I would hear her call me daddy. She would be so glad to see me, and I was equally as glad to receive that acknowledgment from her. My son was very young, but I was looking forward to having him mimicking some of the things that little boys would do after watching their father.

Even before he was born, I was looking forward to watching him mimic me, but that wasn't to be. I will never be able to get those years back. Any father that doesn't get joy from their children, there is something seriously wrong. Yes, I said it! I always carried both of my children, especially when taking them to and from our car and into our apartment. It was a dangerous area where we lived in Southeast Washington, DC. My wife and I used to stay up late at night on Christmas morning, wrapping their gifts up, and putting their toys together. The highlight of waking up early Christmas morning and watching the excitement on their little faces was priceless. My wife was very creative and could really decorate a Christmas tree. I remember our first tree, it was before our daughter was born, I had come in from work that night, and the Christmas tree was the first thing that I noticed when I came into our apartment. It was the most beautiful tree that I've ever seen. Maybe because it was ours, but I remember that is was a beautiful tree.

Since my injury, I've missed 12 Christmas mornings watching my children wake up early to give thanks to God for another opportunity to celebrate His son Jesus Christ's birthday. I miss watching them open their gifts. Now, we had two separate Christmas celebrations. The first one is celebrated with their mother and then she brings them to the nursing home to get their gifts from me, and the four of us celebrate it together for a few hours. I'm praying that I will be able to spend this Christmas morning with my children and their mother. On Tuesday, June 6, 2000, our daughter received seven different achievement awards from each one of her classes including a trophy for her outstanding science project. I truly wish that I could have been there to take her pictures or videotape her receiving these awards. Because of the bureaucracy that I face every day here at this nursing facility, it wasn't possible for me to attend that special event. This part that I'm about to tell you, I thought that I'd never miss. I used to hate going shopping with my wife. She would go into the stores and pick up something, then walk around the entire store and then purchase that first item that she picked up earlier, while I dealt with two rambunctious kids. But brothers, I never thought that I would say this; if I were able to go shopping with her again, I wouldn't complain. I would just enjoy standing and playing with my children, only if the Lord would allow me to walk out of this facility.

Now! Really a serious statement, because if you ever go shopping with some women, they are never in a hurry to leave. I miss putting my arms around my wife. I was a very emotional guy, and I'm not ashamed to say so. This injury has cost me a lot, including my marriage. But I'm thankful that my wife/ex-wife still brings my children to visit with me. The hardest part to deal with is when they come to visit me and then I have to watch them walk out of my room. I never know if this will be my last visit with them, so I cherish every second, minute, hour that they are here with me. I'm constantly praying for them, every morning, noon, night, and every day. I've been living in a nursing home for over nine years. I'm not asking anyone for sympathy, I'm still thankful that God has allowed me to live this long under these circumstances. God blesses me for an eternity.

We always complain about the things that we don't have, but we never thank God for what He has already given us. I'm not trying to contradict myself, I said all of these things to make a point. The two gunmen that shot me made a statement while they were shooting me. They said, "Make sure he is dead." This statement was later confirmed by my parents' next-door neighbors, because he heard everything that was said during my attack. They left me laying on the front of my parents' front porch dying. This was where it all happened to me, on my parents' front porch that late night. Now! After telling all of you all of that information, I thank God that He has given me a forgiving heart. I have forgiven the two guys that tried to kill me, and take me away from my family. I forgave these gunmen several years ago. Jesus says, "Vengeance belongs to me," and he has already made my enemies my footstool. Because of the trauma that I suffered, I couldn't identify the people that shot me, but I truly believe that there are two kinds of judgment, "Man's and God's." I have put them both into God's hands. I just hope that they are not out there hurting anymore people. I hope that they have accepted Jesus Christ as their Lord and Savior. Forgiveness is good for the Soul!!!

This portion is for the fathers that are out there who don't take care of their children because of their selfishness: How could you not want to be a part of your child's life? Just because you and the mother don't get along, please don't let your child, or children, suffer the absence of their father. Put aside your foolish pride and be a real man! Brothers and sisters, it is very important to learn how to forgive one another!!!

* * *

THE LESSON OF FORGIVENESS

I've learned a very viable lesson over the years about the Spirit of Forgiveness. It doesn't come overnight, it takes time to forgive someone who have wronged you, and in my case, several times trying to take my life.

When I was only 12 years of age, I learned a viable lesson about forgiving others. My instance with forgiveness came when an older teenager, probably 16 or 17 years old almost killed me, I was only trying to protect my younger sister. I know that I mentioned parts of my story earlier, but I wanted to get the point across that it is so important to be able to truly and honestly forgive people when they have done something to you. The human side of us instinctively tells us that we should get revenge on people as soon as they do something to you. But, we must give it up and truly forgive. The Old Testament says, "AN EYE FOR AN EYE," and that's what they did back then, and it was considered righteousness. But the New Testament tells us that VENGEANCE is the Lord and He will repay. HONESTLY, it is really hard to forgive someone that tried to cause bodily or emotionally harm. The flesh tells you that you should get that person back for what they did to you, stating that the Old Testament was justifiable.

However, the New Testament tells us differently, and as Jesus Christ was being crucified on the cross, He said to his father, "FATHER FORGIVE THEM, FOR THEY KNOW NOT WHAT THEY'VE DONE." Even though the Romans knew exactly what they were doing for the most part. But, as my Lord and Savior JESUS CHRIST is dying on the cross for your sins and mine, He had enough strength in his body to say these words to our HEAVENLY FATHER before He gave up the HOLY GHOST.

Again, I truly thank God that I learned a viable lesson about forgiveness at the age of 12. My father wanted to shoot and kill the guy that hit me in the head with a bottle that caused me partial paralysis. As a 12-year-old kid, and even to this day, I ask myself "what kind of a threat could I have been to these almost grown men and their friends?" I have been under attack by the enemy for a very long time, but I know that the battle is not mine, it's the Lord. After I recovered I had to tell my father to let it go and let God take care of the situation and the guy that hit me. At the age of 12, these words had to have come from God that would relieve my father from getting

345

into trouble with the law, but also with God. As I explained to my father, again I said; "Pop, if you do something to that guy for what he did to me, you will have answer to God one day for what you've done to him, so just let it go." As I lay here thinking about all these things, this was really deep stuff coming out of the mouth of a 12-year-old kid, but I truly thank God for being able to tell my father these words.

At this point, it was time to practice forgiveness. It takes work and it is truly the spirit of God that helps you to learn to forgive spiritually and mentally. Believe me, I had a lot of experience on learning how to forgive others. It really hurts sometimes, but I have to be true to God. I am truly a believer in the Lord! I've had several attacks against me over my life and they have not stopped at all to this day. But every time I have to deal with my tongue and not saying a word. I am always being tested. One day, I had to get a urine specimen done by the nurse, and it was time to get repositioned but I noticed that there was some urine in the tubing on my catheter, I asked the young lady and the young man could they wait a couple of minutes and call the nurse so that she could get this urine specimen before they turned me. I was trying to help her and make her job easier. As I was trying to explain myself to her, she said out of her mouth in a negative tone, "Can you let me do my job." That was unnecessary because again I was trying to help make her job easier. There are a lot of wicked people that I had to deal with over the years, including her, hating on a person for no apparent reason. I would never falsely accuse anyone, but one night I was trying to sell uniforms, she would tell the people not to come into my room anymore. I wasn't bothering anyone and for the most part, I'm able to sleep at night anyway, but this was just an evil and wicked spirit that she has shown over the years.

I had a refrigerator in my room on the right side of my bed. There is enough light so there was no need to turn on the bright lights in my room. She would intentionally come into my room and tell the staff that she was going to turn on the bright lights. There was absolutely no need to turn those lights on, but she was wicked. I've had to deal with this type of wickedness for five years.

Not to sound redundant but as I mentioned, she does is to be spiteful. Sometimes I try my best not to even get pain medication at night to prevent her from turning on the very bright light. Sometimes the medicine would also give me headaches and I don't need any more pain that I'm already dealing with. Even though I know that she has a wicked spirit, I have to forgive her. It is hard and sometimes she has said things to me out of her mouth that was very disrespectful. Sometimes I address the issue, most times, I don't. I know that was her simple, wicked ways, and I have to pray for her. Again, it is hard when I know that she does things intentionally.

✳ ✳ ✳

INSPIRATION

This poem was written by my friend and it is truly dear to me!

The poem is entitled:

YOU ARE THE CLOSEST TO JESUS THAT I HAVE EVER COME
Written for JEFFERY CHAPMAN SR.

*YOU ARE THE CLOSEST TO JESUS THAT I HAVE EVER COME,
IN YOUR COMPASSIONATE EYES I CAN SEE HOPE
THROUGH GOD'S SON.*

*THOUGH YOU LAY THERE PARALYZED AND UNABLE TO MOVE, YOUR
SPIRIT IS TREMENDOUS AND WITH YOUR WORDS I FEEL SOOTHED.*

*YOU ARE THE CLOSEST TO JESUS THAT I HAVE EVER COME, I SENSE
HIS PRESENCE LIVING WITH YOU, THOUGH YOUR BODY MAY BE
NUMB.*

*I FEEL INSPIRED BY YOUR STRENGTH AND YOUR WILL
TO EMBRACE LIFE,*

*YOU RISE ABOVE YOUR CIRCUMSTANCES, HOLDING FAST TO YOUR
FAITH, AND OVERCOMING STRUGGLES AND STRIFE.*

*ALTHOUGH I VISIT HOPING TO CHEER YOU, AND GIVE YOU MY TIME,
I LEAVE FEELING MOVED,*

ENCOURAGED AND GRATEFUL THAT YOU ARE A FRIEND OF MINE,

I REALIZE THAT THE LORD HAS CAREFULLY PLACED YOU IN MY COURSE,

SO THAT I CAN BE CLOSER TO HIM THROUGH YOU,

AS
HIS
SOURCE

~M.M.

CHAPTER 23

VICTORY IS MINE

James 1: 1-4 "My brethren count it all joy when you fall into various trials, knowing that the testing of your faith produces patience. But let patience have its perfect work, that you may be perfect and complete, lacking nothing."

THE VICTORY! THE HEALING! THE POWER!

After years of heartache, pain, sorrow, love lost, and heartbreaks, I've learned how to "Count it all Joy!" You never know how God can use a bad situation in your life and turn it into a prolific testimony.

THE SECOND-GENERATION OF THE CHAPMAN FAMILY

When I got injured, my father was able to get a trailer that he converted into an ice cream truck. This was one of the reasons why I was trying to sell a kilo of cocaine, hoping that things would work out for them. I was trying to also buy equipment, new photography equipment so that I could get off the streets. I had a goal to start taking more family pictures inside of the homes of different people that had money. I understood the value of someone coming into your home to take family portraits.

But as I think about the new generation, my children, nephews, nieces and family business, it was necessary to pass down the business mindset of how my father was able to convert a trailer into an ice cream truck and was successful for many years. He was able to purchase the ice cream truck and park it in the yard next to the house. Again, this was a safe haven for the children because the stores weren't close by. They had to walk a distance and having the truck in the community was a blessing to everyone except for one lady, God bless her. Ms. P would always call the police on my family. Now 20 years later, my family, through my nieces and nephews are experiencing this same crazy emptiness and jealousy from one particular woman and I know there are several others who complained but weren't as vocal as she was. They would conduct community meetings and she'd always complain about the ice cream truck. It wasn't bothering anyone. It is sad how history repeats itself in a negative way. Now my nieces and nephews and their kids can see just how much people hated our family, just because we wanted better and more for our family. What's wrong with that?

And just like my siblings and I, my oldest niece started working on the ice cream truck, went to school and did her homework. History repeats itself, she worked on the truck for a few years. We had parents taught us to have the mentality to work and help out the family. This started when he was a kid in South Carolina, working to help the family out. I understood early the dynamics of working and supporting one another. I don't know if my siblings fully understood. However, she hung there for quite a while until she got tired and wanted to get another job. I couldn't blame her and I respected her for having the mindset to work. In most cases, our family business was our job.

After she stopped working on the truck, my nephew stepped in. He reminded me so much of myself when I tried my best to run the family business. My father would work in the morning on the ice cream truck and sometimes my mother would do as much as she could, and just like when we had the family business during the morning time my father would have his buddies come in and they would all talk and laugh about everything. I would open the store with my father and cook breakfast for us before I went to Junior high school, we did this almost every day. It was no different when it came to the ice cream truck with the exception of them not being able to come inside the truck, they would stand around and talk with my father. Unfortunately, a lot of the young ladies that were on crack, turned Alabama Avenue into a prostitution area. They walked the streets at night and sold their bodies to make money in order to support their drug addiction and I'm pretty sure some of them had kids. But it was really serious that these ladies of the night would be on the street that we lived on. If they were up during the mornings when the guys would be hanging around ice cream truck, they would flirt with the young ladies and the young ladies would flirt back with them, and, possibly some of the guys might have had sexual relationships with them.

My nephew would make sure that the money was counted out right, again my father showed my niece and nephew when they worked on ice cream truck how to organize and count money, just like we did when we were younger, again history repeats itself. My nephew would also help keep my father straight because sometimes my father would have too many beers and start acting up. Sometimes I had to be the referee between my mother and father. I had to remind them that WE have been through too much for them to be acting the way they were acting. My nephew had to do the same thing but mainly with my father and dealing with the money, just like when we had the store. I would bring the money to my father and my nephew and niece had to do the same thing, he was in charge of all the money and he did what he wanted to with it, which wasn't right at all. That was the downfall to us eventually losing the store, mostly because my father mishandled the money.

While my nephew is working on the ice cream truck one day, something kicked off about this family coming over to beat us up, again my niece was fighting somebody, and another person tried to jump in and my mom grabbed this person and threw her somewhere. The young girl was surprised and I couldn't understand why they came from where they came from and tried to intimidate us. These things are happening all over again and now the next generation is able to see these things. Again, I don't like using these words, but it is what it is when I say that the jealousy and envy continued to plague my family. When all we were trying to do was make it and make ends meet back then. I know the struggles that we had to go through, losing the store, filing bankruptcy, and getting another store in the Anacostia Southeast area, and trying to start over and having them to protest against our license. They did have an organization come against us in that area. In the beginning I was very angry at all of them including the pastor that I ended up helping renovate the church, was the biggest person that was against us.

I know that I jumped from subject to subject at different times that things occurred within the family, but I was just trying to show the resemblance of how we were treated and what's still happening today, some 20 years later. My mother was accused of sticking a knife in her tires. That's ridiculous, really ridiculous, but the accuser had some kind of mean and evil spirit against us even to this day. She and all the others felt the same way as if my family did something to them. We had to endure these things for decades and even to this day. It must be some kind of generational thing, it must be! But my nephew hung in there for a long time. Even when my son would come to visit over the weekends he would get on the truck and try to help out and my other nephews would come on the truck and chill out with each other, and keep him company, but also learning as they watched. They did the same things that we did, especially eating up the profits like, potato chips, sodas and candy. My father would say to us, "How could I make a profit if you're eating everything up?" It was true. But God made a way! Even in my present condition, IF IT WAS NOT FOR GOD'S MERCY AND GRACE, I WOULD NOT BE HERE NOW! After a while my father got tired of working on the truck. What bothered me the most was when he saw money laying around the house, he would claim it as his own, even if it was change, he would pocket it and you would be out a luck.

All four of us were able to help our parents financially in different periods of time. I mean, I was thankful to be able to help them because of what they had done for me over the years and my siblings, so if they ever needed something and I had it, there would be no problem giving it to them, NO PROBLEM AT ALL!

When my father was working on the ice cream truck he really lost a lot of patience, especially with certain people that would ask some stupid questions. He would really get frustrated. One example, if somebody asked for a bag of potato chips, he would ask what kind and then they would ask him what kind do you have? He would really get frustrated! All they had to do was ask for the particular type of potato chips or soda that they wanted. I'd also find myself getting frustrated with some of the questions at times. All they had to do was ask and we could tell them if we had it or not. I didn't have time to deal with all those questions. Believe it or not, my father's popularity was well spread throughout Southeast DC. I know for sure and I was surprised that one day my daughter told me something that I didn't know. She told me that when her mother moved them to Maryland schools she had a conversation with a classmate and she mentioned that her grandfather owned an ice cream truck on Alabama Avenue in Southeast DC. She told the classmate that she was raised in Southeast DC. Just that quick the guy said, "You mean Mr. Joe is your grandfather?" I was surprised to know that this kid knew my father well. He told my daughter that her grandfather was off the hook. The young man was blown away. It was a surprise to me as well. It's a small world AFTER ALL!

And after working on ice cream truck for several years, my nephew started acting the same way as his grandfather, getting frustrated. I can say that for any public servant to deal with the public it can really be challenging and difficult, and it takes a lot to continue. So, hats off to all the public servants working out there. I have much respect for you because I know what you go through sometimes.

It was very lucrative, and I was truly thankful to God that my parents were able to bring in some finances to pay their bills. For so many years we had been working for ourselves with the exception of when my father was a construction worker and my mother worked at the airport, other than that we were blessed by God to have our family businesses. Even myself, when I went to school for commercial photography and I mentioned this earlier in the story when my photographer instructor wanted to get me a couple of good jobs as a photographer, and I truly appreciate it, but I told her that I had to help my parents out. I was responsible for a lot of things within the business. These words she said to me haunted me as we lost our first store, she said to me, "What about the day that your family can no longer have the store, then what are you going to do?" And when we finally did lose our first business, I could hear her voice, and those words that she told me that day. God blessed me with opportunities for those couple of photography jobs that I could've had and no disrespect to my other classmates but I really got an early start learning about photography and the age of 11. So I was a little more advanced than some, but always called upon to represent my commercial photography class which was an honor and a privilege. But the jobs she had lined up for me, I know that I must have been a disappointment to her, and I'm sorry that I couldn't take those jobs. I was even offered a job working on computers. My first year in high school, they only gave out two or three positions and I was blessed to receive one, but I didn't follow through because of the family business. Another missed opportunity, but I wouldn't change it for anything in a world to work with my family, and I tried my best to make my parents proud, because of the love, honor, respect, appreciation and all that they did for my family, I COULDN'T TELL THEM NO!

***

HOSPITAL VISITS OVER THE YEARS

I have had many hospital visits, several times I remained for several years. Yes, I was concerned about whatever surgery or procedure I was scheduled for. I know for sure that two of the procedures were life-threatening, but that's when your trust in God kicks in, AUTOMATICALLY! Over the years of being hospitalized, I thought that overtime I had to go in for whatever type of procedure that it was a sign from God that I was supposed to minister to someone there. Although I never knew who the person would be, it took the focus off of my situation. This would not be hard to do, especially since I've always communicated with everyone. Most of the time they would come into contact with me, mainly the staff or someone passing through by way of ambulance and on a stretcher. Whenever I had to enter through the emergency room entrance and pushed through the hallways there would be people lined up against the wall or some even waiting for help. While passing by them, I would try to say encouraging words to them, if it was just to say hello, hang in there, have a blessed day, keep the faith, or any of these little words. Although I'm temporarily paralyzed and on official life support, over the years I've learned that it is not about me, but it has been about God, family and trying to be my brothers and sister's keeper.

I believe that every opportunity that I have to encourage someone else, it keeps me believing and trusting in God. I ask God to keep me humble! Over the years, I have had numerous visitors that I would encourage, some were members from the church or other residents. Sometimes when the church members would come to visit the sick and shut it, I would even find myself encouraging them. I thank God that I have heard this numerous times over the years by many church members. They have told me "they came to encourage me, but I thank God that he allowed me to be the one that was encouraging them." I always remained humble because I know that it's not about me but again I'm so thankful that I was able to be an encouragement to so many others, known and unknown over the years.

I learned something just recently from one of my nieces. We were talking on the telephone about life and she told me that she just recently received a promotion. I congratulated her about that and she told me something that was very enlightening and really surprising. She told me that when they were really young, whenever they were faced with a challenge and thought that they couldn't accomplish it or get through it, my nephew would always tell them to "THINK ABOUT UNCLE JEFF." When they thought of me and my temporary physical situation, it always helped them to accomplish whatever they were struggling with. She let me know that they all used this method. I THANK GOD that they were able to accomplish a task because they thought about Uncle Jeff. That was very touching and very emotional to hear my niece tell me that story. I'm truly honored that I was still able to be there with them even though I wasn't physically there with them. GOD IS AWESOME! I'm grateful that I was able to motivate them and in turn they were able to gather strength from my situation and get through whatever challenges they were up against.

CHAPTER 24

Dealing with the Death of Both of My Parents just eight Days Apart from Each Other

Throughout these last 26 years, I had to deal with all kinds of life challenges, just being paralyzed from the neck down and on official life support. It is a challenge in itself, every second, every minute, every hour, every day, every week, every month, every year and every decade, God has brought me through thus far.

Losing both of my parents just eight days apart from one another is really hard to explain. This story has to be told about how God brought me through it. They will never be forgotten, and I will never forget what happened on Saturday, August 11, 2007. I remember this day so clearly, emotionally and very vividly, starting from that Saturday morning. Two days prior to that my mother had to go to the hospital because she wasn't feeling well, and for a couple of days I was able to communicate with her and my father like I normally do every day. It was my job to call my parents three times a day, very early in the morning, the evening and before 9:00 p.m. until it was time to turn off the computer for the next day.

Well, this day felt very sad, even before death that Saturday was different from any of the Saturdays and the weekends always were long and drawn out living in a nursing home. The weekends seem to last forever, on the other hand, the weekdays would go by fast. But this Saturday morning, like I normally would do, I called my parents to check in on them to make sure everything was okay. The day before my mother passed away, Mrs. Minnie R. Wilkins Chapman, I had to call my own sister and my oldest niece to go and check on my mother to see if she needed anything, like breakfast, lunch or even dinner. I remember calling several family members, siblings, nephew and nieces several times to ask them to check in. I have to say that I was a little disappointed with my sister and my niece because they were close by but I had to call on the nursing home in Virginia to check on my parents. The frustrating thing about it was that all they had to do was drive by the house.

On the morning of Saturday, August 11, 2007, I called my parents and my father answered the telephone, so I asked him if I could talk to mom. I knew that she had been hospitalized and I was unable to talk to her. So, my dad said that she didn't feel that well and she was throwing up or vomiting, but he did not tell me that she was vomiting blood, because at that time I would have insisted that someone take my mother to the hospital, but again he didn't tell me. I can remember very clearly saying to my father, "Okay, Dad, GOD WILLING, I would try to call back later on during the evening to see if I could talk to mom." He said, okay and as usual I always told my parents how much I loved them.

I can remember, after talking to my father, I started listening to my gospel music that helps me get through each and every day, first with the help of God. I listened to a gospel artist by the name of Reverend James Cleveland, one of the gospel pioneers in the music industry. This particular record, if I'm not mistaking the title was "ON THE BANKS OF THE JORDAN" and occasionally I would listen to the entire album, but when I got this one particular record, I skipped over it, I just didn't feel right that entire day, like something was very wrong, seriously wrong with my mom. As I listened to the CD and when he would get to that particular record, I would skip over it because the lyrics of the song was very painful. The late Rev. James Cleveland was singing about how God took his parents. He started singing about how the Lord had taken his father first and then later on he came back to take his mother. In my case, it was just the opposite. The Lord took my mother first and then later as I mentioned, eight days later, the Lord came to take my father.

I truly believe that my mother passed away of a massive heart attack before they could get her out of the house. When my father and other family members went to the hospital, my mother was pronounced dead. Around 11:00 p.m. while I was laying in my bed just thinking about everything that was going on my telephone rang and I don't get telephone calls after 9:00 p.m. On the other side of the line it was my sister telling me that mom had passed away. Normally a person that hears news like that would start hollering and screaming, however, in my case I could do neither. I could not holler because of the life support machine. I did have air in my lungs and diaphragm to push out a scream or holler. I couldn't even grab my head in my hands to try to hold on to keep myself together, NO, I just had to lay there and cry with the tears running off my eyes. I couldn't holler out for the staff because again, I did not have enough thrust and air in my lungs. I wasn't even able to jump up and down, or just run, no not me. I had to lay there and exalt all the pain, but then shortly afterwards, maybe five minutes of talking to my sister, my son called to confirm whether or not it was true. I said, Yes, son, she has passed away. I was trying my best to hold back the tears and to be strong for my son and the rest of the family. A few minutes later, my daughter called from Miami, she was down there on summer break with some of her college girlfriends. She asked me the same question, still fighting back the tears, I answered with a yes. I asked my daughter to put one of her girlfriends on the phone, I asked her to comfort her for me because her grandmother just died, and I was unable to console her. She said, Okay Mr. Chapman, I will be there for her. I thanked the young lady multiple times for helping my daughter out during this tragic time. They were down there in Miami, Florida for summer break, enjoying themselves, only to receive this very sad and painful news that her grandmother had passed away.

I don't know, maybe after talking to my sister, my son and my daughter for just a few moments, I was able to muster up and cry out for help, and one of the nurses came in to see what was wrong with me. I told her that my mother just died, and she said a few comforting words, which I appreciated, but the tears continued to roll down my face. I did not receive any more phone calls that night, I couldn't take it. As I laid in my room crying, I had three other roommates, but they are mostly comatose, so I would not disturb any of them, in any way that night. I just could not go back to sleep, and ever since then, anytime that phone rings after 9:00 p.m., I'm afraid to answer it, because I was traumatized receiving the call and receiving the news that I lost my mom, my best friend. It is very painful to lose a loved one, but even more painful because I couldn't be there to console and help my family members and comfort them with maybe a few words, maybe just to talk to them. NO, I just had to lay there that night thinking about everything. The following morning, the record that I didn't want to play by the late Rev. James Cleveland, was the first record that I played that morning and I played several times throughout the day. It was like I knew that there was a possibility that I was going to lose my mother that Saturday. This was the song that I wanted to avoid playing but found myself playing the song over and over again, all through the day.

One of my friends in a nursing home, Linda or Sister Edna, may she rest in peace now, must've told her Pastor, Pastor G., to come over and pray with me because I just lost my mother. God knows I was appreciative of them coming to check on me because I really needed it. Pastor Patten came and introduced himself and prayed with me and my family and I truly appreciated that as well. Pastor G. and I became good friends after that day and as a matter of fact, he was the one that performed both wedding ceremonies for both of my children, which was a blessing. A little later on that Sunday, another good friend of mine came by to visit, Brother Ken Baker. The both of them would stop by on some Sundays. God has blessed me over the years with so many good friends and to this day I'm thankful for both of them and all the other friends that have come to the nursing home to visit. Sometimes they would stop by before their service actually started and then return afterwards to check on me. A lot of times when someone loses a loved one and you want to help them out, the best thing you can do is to just be there for the person. That means so much to me, just to have somebody sitting there with you so you would not be alone while you're mourning the loss of a loved one.

I reminded brother Baker, every now and then, as days and months went by, how much I appreciate him coming back and sitting in the chair and just listening to me talk about whatever, not just the loss of my mother but so many things that popped up in my mind. Again, I was in a room with three other residents and most of them couldn't communicate, so I was physically alone, but God was always with me. I was used to calling both my parents three times a day to make sure they were doing okay. Sometimes I enjoyed making them laugh. But it was mainly to check in on them to make sure they didn't need anything. With the help of God, I would find a way to get them what they needed, mostly through my siblings.

About three weeks before my parents passed away, they took the trip to South Carolina to visit with some of our family members and I truly believe that they both knew that it might be the last time they would be able to visit family. My father was scheduled to have surgery to have a pacemaker inserted because he had a weak heart and he didn't really want to go through with it. So, having said that, I was calling my father EVERY DAY, VERY early in the morning, just like I used to before my mom passed away to see how he was doing and I tried my best to ENCOURAGE MY FATHER TO CONTINUE TO TRUST IN GOD! MY MOTHER AND FATHER HAVE BEEN MARRIED FOR 52 YEARS OF THEIR LIVES TOGETHER AND HIS PARTNER FOR LIFE HAS PASSED ON! When I called my father, we talked about some of the relatives that were coming from out of town for the funeral service of my mother, he also told me about all the visitors that he was getting. I can hear in his voice the hurt, the pain and the emptiness of losing his wife.

After the funeral arrangements were made, my father did not want to go into the funeral home to see his wife of 50 plus years laying in the coffin, so we stayed in the car. One of my sisters went inside to do the paperwork. Although he sat in the car and was physically alone, he was not alone spiritually. There was something that he needed to sign, some kind of document, so he had to get out of the car to give his signature. That same day, my sister said something to upset my father. I cannot remember all the details, but I know that I called my sister and told her what she did wasn't right. I told her that whatever it was she said to my dad really upset him and I didn't appreciate it. Nevertheless, everybody was going to be an emotional roller coaster, trying to put all these things together. Neither one of our parents' health was great, especially my father, dealing with a weak heart. But, we thought that if we were going to lose a parent, it would be my father first because of his heart condition. God saw it differently.

After we left the funeral home, I called my father to see how he was doing and after the little episode concerning my sister. He said that he was okay. As the days went by everybody was just hurting. I was talking to my niece one day and she started explaining some of things that I really didn't know concerning how they found

360

my father dead. They found him laid across his bed stretched out. My niece said that she had just finished talking to her grandfather, just a few minutes before and he told her something very important, but I can't remember what she said it was. Her brother, my second oldest nephew is the one that found his grandfather. My Father, Lee Curtis Chapman, nicknamed Joe, died of a heart attack, although I believe it was mainly from heartbreak caused by the loss of his wife. This affected my nephew very much because my sister and both of her kids were living with my parents for a while. During this time, my father's relationship with my nephew grew stronger. This closer relationship ensued during the time that my nephew and niece decided to start an ice cream truck business. Ironically, 20 years later, they would mimic the same entrepreneurial goals as my siblings and I had. Although I started in the family business at the age of 13, it allowed my relationship with my father to grow. (Just like the old saying goes, "History has a way of repeating itself in more than one way" is true. Just like my siblings and I when we were younger, we had people in the community that was jealous and envious of my family. Trying to be productive, 20 years later, my nephews and nieces and my kids have expressed the same thing).

When I talked to my sister shortly after our mother passed away, she asked my advice about when we should have the service, the HOMECOMING SERVICE for our dearly departed mother. I can remember saying to her, "Sis, I think we should wait until Monday because we have a lot of family members coming from out of town. It would be fair to give them enough time to make it here." She agreed. I truly believe that was God instructing me to tell her that because, if we would have had the service earlier than Monday, August 20, 2007, there would be no telling how things would've turned out with our father passing away before Monday.

I have been calling my father early every morning because he normally get up early. So, on Sunday, August 19, 2007, I decided to just give them a little time to relax and maybe call them around 12:00 noon, which I did. Like I said, I had been calling my father very early in the morning to check in on him and talk to him. When I called around 12:00 noon, I can't remember who answered the telephone, but I asked the question, "HEY, WHAT'S GOING ON AROUND THERE?" Their reply was, we lost DAD! Again, I could not let out a scream. I cannot grab my head. I could not walk away. I couldn't do a lot of things that people only do when they receive bad news like this. I had to just lay in this bed, paralyzed from the neck down and on official life support. I had nowhere to run, no one to talk to at the time, I just laid there and took the bad news. I tried to control my emotions as I'm grieving for my mother. NOW, it has shifted to GRIEVING for both of my parents. Again, I must've mustered up enough air in my lungs to holler just LOUD ENOUGH for another staff member to hear me crying. They asked what was wrong. I told whoever it was that morning that my dad just passed away. So now everyone is aware that my mother had passed away. NOW, MY FATHER!

On that Sunday, Pastor P came to visit me to see how I was doing, and I told him that he wasn't going to believe that my father just died. I thank God for him being there to pray with me and for my family. But lightning striking twice, just eight days apart from one another is very hard, very hard on everyone. When you have your health and you receive news like this, you can react differently by walking, running, crying or whatever. Instead, I'm stuck, paralyzed in the bed, dealing with this grieving process while hurting on the inside. My sister and a few of the family members came to the nursing home late on that Sunday and gave me a haircut so that I would be ready for the funeral service. The following day, Monday, August 20, 2007, as family members were traveling up for the homecoming service for my mother, we had to call them and tell them that our father just passed away. These were three out of the four of my father's sisters, and they had to pull on the side of the highway after receiving such shocking news. But thank God that my aunt had knowledge of the Jewish culture that when someone dies in Jewish families they have to bury them within 24 hours. My sister didn't have the knowledge, but one of our aunts who was a pastor did and thank God for that because we had enough time to prepare my father's body within 24 hours, so that they could be laid to rest together.

I arrived in the church relatively early and had no idea that the time had been set a little later because my father had to be prepared for the homecoming service as well. I really was trying to sit away from everyone that I hadn't seen for 17 years or longer, after I got injured. I had distanced myself away from a lot of people, but I found myself sitting right there where everybody had to walk pass before they got to see my parents' body for the last time.

I couldn't sleep the night before the service, so I made some small obituary cards, photo obituary cards that had four different answers on each one with the Scripture below. I think I made about 60 or 80 of them to pass out to the family members and friends. They came to pay their respects to my family. The original obituary, for some reason was not ready, so the little photo cards that I made that night were just in time. I was able to get one of the staff members to cut the cards for me, so I could pass them out. I was thankful that my ex-wife Paula was sitting right beside me. I TRULY HATE USING THE WORD EX-WIFE, but it is what it is. Again, I was thankful for it. She remained by my side throughout the ceremony. I'm pretty sure about 99% of the people that came to pay their respects with the loss of my mother had no idea that my father passed away as well. Even while getting there to my childhood church, Matthews Memorial Baptist Church, one of my cousins in South Carolina tried taking in everything. They brought my mother and father's coffins in and positioned them in front of the congregation. My cousin Richard asked me, "Why are there two coffins?" I said to him, "You don't know that my father passed away?" Did I mention how one would react to such news? You let out a holler and a scream. That's what he did. My father passed away a couple of days after my uncle and aunt came to visit. I remember my dad telling me that they came to visit him. EVERYBODY was VERY SHOCKED to find out that my father had passed away. The possibility that the HOMECOMING SERVICE would've been even larger, BUT THAT'S THE WAY GOD SET IT UP. As I lay in my room, the majority of the time physically alone, BUT NOT SPIRITUALLY ALONE, I WAS ABLE TO UNDERSTAND THAT GOD KNEW EXACTLY WHAT HE WAS DOING. THE WAY BOTH MY PARENTS PASSED AWAY WAS A PART OF GOD'S PLAN!

I believe that my father could not handle seeing my mother in the casket. He only saw her in the hospital. There was a possibility that things would have been a lot worse. You may be wondering how something like this could be any worse. But, I think that if my father would have walked in the church and saw his wife of 50 plus years in that casket, he would have died right there in the church. That would've been very, very, very traumatic for everyone to witness! SO, THANK YOU FATHER GOD, AND THE NAME OF JESUS CHRIST, that you know exactly what you're doing and that we had time to prepare my father's body so that he and my mother could be laid to rest eternally together. If I had to write a script to the situation, this would fit perfectly, "When you get married, you take these vowels and you say for better for worse, sickness and health and finally UNTIL DEATH DO US PART." They only stayed apart for eight days. Numbers are significant in the Bible. One example, Jesus Christ really started his ministry at the age of 33, he also was crucified at the age 33, 12 disciples, the Trinity (THE FATHER, SON AND HOLY SPIRIT, THE NUMBER 3) and these two numbers are related to my parents passing away. The number seven means finalization or finished, the number eight means NEW BEGINNINGS. So my parents had a new beginning as they laid to rest together Eternally with the Lord. So, I pay a lot of attention to numbers because they have a significant meaning and a lot of them are related spiritually.

The night before the service, THE HOMECOMING SERVICE, I wanted to say something to everyone that came to show their respect for the loss of our parents. I wanted to say something, all the while trying to remain strong, but hurting so much on the inside. I tried to be strong for God, my parents and my family members. I did not prepare any kind of speech, but I know I had to say something to those that were in attendance. The closer he got to the ending of the homecoming service, I started getting nervous, but I had already informed the pastor that I wanted to say something to everyone before the service is over. I THANK GOD that Matthews Memorial Baptist Church Congregation/Family allowed us have my father eulogized in the church because he was not a member. However, my mother and brother and I were and had been a member of the Matthews for many years because it was my CHILDHOOD CHURCH. It also was the neighborhood church. But again, I thank them for allowing us to have the service there and also all the church volunteers, the ushers, the cooks. We had the repast service downstairs in the church and most of the church members volunteered their services. I'm truly thankful for them for volunteering their time to help my family lay to rest both of our parents, Mr. Lee Curtis, "Joe" Chapman and mother, Mrs. Minnie Ree Wilkins-Chapman. MAY THEY REST IN PEACE ETERNALLY TOGETHER!

And if I may say so; "MOM AND DAD, JOB WELL DONE!"
From Your Baby Boy,
Jeffery D Chapman Sr.
THANK YOU JESUS!

* * *

BOTH OF MY KIDS ARE NOW MARRIED AND HAVE CHILDREN OF THEIR OWN AND I'M ALSO THANKFUL TO GOD THAT HE HAS ALLOWED ME TO SEE MY CHILDREN GROW UP AND BECOME A GRANDFATHER

The year before I left the nursing facility located in Reston Virginia, I was blessed to be able to attend my daughter and her husband's wedding service. The facility paid for the respiratory therapist and for the transportation which was a blessing. However, this place that I'm currently at now will not even provide me with a respiratory therapist to go anywhere, which feels like a form of incarceration or imprisonment.

But we all had a very nice time at the wedding, and even though I wasn't physically able to walk my daughter down the aisle, my son did that part for me. But when it came to giving my daughter away to my son-in-law, I was able to roll beside her as she walked up to her future husband, when the question was asked, "Who gives this bride away" that was my cue to say, "I do" and then I backed the wheelchair back to where I was and the ceremony proceeded.

They were running very late, trying to get everything and everybody in order and I was supposed to help to direct the photographer and show him what photographs to take, but for some reason I started feeling sick. Out of all times I was feeling awfully bad at my daughter's wedding, but I was able to hold everything back until the end. At the reception, I tried to get Paula to sit beside me to show some kind of unity, even though we were no longer married, but this was our daughter and I wanted to show some type of solidarity, but for some reason she wasn't having any parts of that. She continued to ignore me while I was trying to get her attention. After making several attempts, I asked the guy that drove the wheelchair van to sit between her and I.

I really could not eat food because I wasn't feeling great. While we were waiting for the ceremony, my son's stepfather's brother Mr. V was able to give me a drink. There were a lot of family and friends at the reception, including my sister from New York and my old friends. They used to help us when we had our family business. They started out as young employees until they graduated high school. It was good to have both of them there along with everyone else.

I truly thank GOD that I could be in attendance to be able to witness my daughter get married. This was very huge to me. The following year she graduated from George Washington University with her master's degree. Again, another problem moment because I wanted to be in attendance, but I was glad to see that she had accomplished some of her goals. A few years later, my children had two of my grandchildren, again another blessing.

Unfortunately, when my son got married, I was unable to attend the wedding ceremony because this facility would not provide me with the respiratory service transportation or anything else. The day that my son and his wife got married was a very significant date for the Chapman family. Early that morning, one of my nephews and his wife had a little girl who turned two years old on August 20, 2017. On that same day, my son and his future wife got married. It was a beautiful wedding from all of photographs that I saw, but I really wanted to be there for him. I felt like I let him down again, I can't take too much more disappointment! The reason the date of August 20, 2007, has such a significant meaning within the Chapman family is because it is the anniversary of the day that we laid both of our parents TO REST IN PEACE INTERNALLY!

Now, not only do we have memories of the service for my parents, but now there are two other beautiful things to think about, the birth of my grand-niece and my son's wedding anniversary. As this date comes around, all these memories will come to mind, just like they had been for the last 10 years when we think about the loss of our parents. I don't think we will ever forget these days or this date within the family, happy and sad, with mixed emotions throughout the month.

I thank God that both of my kids were able to find their partners for life. My daughter found her husband, he found her and my son found his wife and she found him. The main thing is that they found each other, and that's what started the next generation of the Chapman family with the great grandchildren. Blessings all around and as a father you want to make sure that your children make the right choices. I don't care how old they are they will always be your children, but I'm happy for all of them.

* * *

LOTS OF DAYS I STRUGGLE CALLING
FAMILY MEMBERS AND FRIENDS.
THEN I FEEL LIKE I DON'T WANT TO BOTHER NO ONE.
I DON'T WANT TO BE A BURDEN TO ANYONE OR TO
MAKE ANYONE FEEL LIKE THEY'RE
OBLIGATED TO TALK TO ME

During the earlier years when I first got injured, I was able to use a telephone that I got at the National Rehab Hospital, in Washington, DC. It was truly a blessing to be able to call founding members. My family members are really the only ones that I communicated with, especially my kids, my mother and my parents. Just to have the ability to use a telephone with the special device that they provided me with (ECU Environmental Control Unit Device) gave me the ability to do various things.

Even when I moved to Delaware and lived in a nursing home for the first time, as a promise they would also provide me with an ECU system to use. Again, that was truly a blessing and I definitely used the telephone even more than when I was in the rehab center, because now I'm miles away from all my family members. It was somewhat of a necessity to be able to use a telephone on a regular basis, and I utilized it all the time while I was up there in Delaware. However, when I moved to the nursing facility in Reston Virginia, even though they promised to give me this device, it didn't happen right away until I was able to communicate with DRS, The Department of Rehab Services and The Independence Center Northern, Virginia.

They were very helpful and very instrumental in helping me to get my adaptable equipment. They were very resourceful. I also wanted to make sure that others that were in my condition would be provided with the necessary equipment. My circle of communication, especially on the telephone extended to my parents, my kids and their mother, and my siblings and nephews and nieces and a few friends that I met over the years since my injury. They were the fair amount of people that I would call regularly. However, now that I've been in this facility my circle of friends and family members that I communicated with diminished tremendously. I guess it started with the lost of my parents, knowing that I would call them at least three times a day to check in on them and to make sure they didn't need anything. I made telephone calls to my siblings and other family members to make sure they were provided with whatever they needed.

I was lost when my parents passed away, seriously, I was lost because I was used to calling them every day. Again, three times a day. That's a lot of phone calls, but I was checking up on both of them, while trying to reassure them that I was okay and not to worry. That was a great loss and they can never, ever be replaced. So now my circle of communication with my family members is starting to get smaller.

When I first arrived in this facility they tried to charge some outrageous prices for their telephone services. It was ridiculous and besides that I hardly talked anyway for the first 14 days when I was here because of the loss of moisture in my lungs. If someone from the other facility was trying to call me, I could hardly talk to them which is very challenging and painful in more than one way physically and emotionally. Finally, I was able to get my telephone situation working by producing a magic Jack system that only charges me one fee a year, but the computer had to be working because it is used by the web. I'm glad that I am able to communicate again. I'm telling you, you never know how much you miss the use of your body and good health. It is also extremely hard to deal with the loss of a loved one, your parents and when you love somebody that doesn't love you back or they get tired of you and your drama. It's hard to get them back, if in fact you ever get them back. I always say that one of the saddest things in life is to lose somebody. You don't realize how special they are, like a job. You might complain every day about how much you hate your job and for whatever reason you lose the job and get fired or you decide to quit the job for whatever reason. After a few days reality sets in and you realize how much you miss the job and what a big mistake you made, but now it's too late. It's a hard lesson to learn in life and I've been down that road, unfortunately before, but I've learned.

It is really bad that we have to go through these things before we realize how good we really had it, SUCH AS LIFE! In the last three and a half years, I've found myself not wanting to call or bother anybody and my circle has gotten very small! I used to call my daughter almost every day when she was in college, now she's graduated and moved to the state of Florida. I try my best to communicate with my son, both my kids. Since the clock in life is moving very fast, I would try my best to keep the lines of communication open with my kids and siblings and other family members as much as possible. Honestly, sometimes I really feel like I don't want to call anybody and bother them or be a burden to anyone. The weekends are very long and most of the time that's when you might want to call somebody. This generation doesn't really believe in talking on the telephone, it's usually a text message, a very quick conversation, no long conversations. I guess a lot of times when I do get the opportunity to talk to my children I'm constantly trying to make up for lost time or to see how they are doing. I imagine them with the phone away from their ears. I lay here a lot of times contemplating should I call this person or that person. Again, because I don't want to be a burden to anyone. I want to call my children on a regular basis and my siblings and nephews, nieces and other members from the church. This is just one of those things that I struggle with every day.

* * *

FINAL WORDS, JUST FOR NOW

ALWAYS TRUST IN THE UNIVERSAL GOD, JEHOVAH GOD, ABBA FATHER, THROUGH HIS SON JESUS CHRIST! LEAN NOT UNTO YOUR OWN UNDERSTANDING, SEEK THE WISDOM OF GOD FIRST! This lesson I had to learn the hard way and up close and personal. BE ANXIOUS about nothing, but in all things, IN PRAYER AND SUPPLICATION make your requests known unto God.

On the night that I got hurt, all I had to do was wait, but the flesh took over. Even though I pray, believe it or not, before these things happened to me, I know it is only God that has allowed me to share these words of wisdom with all of you.

Seek first the Kingdom of God and everything else will be added to you. These are not just clichés, this is God's truth. There are so many lessons that I've learned throughout this journey that we call life, or pilgrimage either one. We live, we learn, we don't have time to waste or to go back. We must keep moving forward in search of the Kingdom of God here on earth and in Heaven.

I know that there is a system that is against us, especially the black man in this country, this is the truth, and I just want to be honest with myself and everyone else about my experiences. There's no doubt about it, concerning the system that is against people of color, but THANK GOD, there is also a spiritual system that God has orchestrated, developed and built by the LORD, MADE BY GOD ALMIGHTY or ALMIGHTY GOD, that no man on this planet can tear down, THIS IS TRUE.

But we must believe that it is so because the Bible tells us so! Yes, there are questions that people have about the King James version of the Bible, and just in case you didn't know there is a Black Heritage King James version of the Bible as well.

But I know for sure that illegal drugs have destroyed millions of us over the years, it has destroyed millions of families over the years, directly and indirectly, and the selling of crack cocaine on a higher level was developed to kill the African-Americans and the powers that be did a very good job because it is still working as of today. I do know that the only guarantee is that when you are selling drugs, you may become your best customer, depending on what title you have, whether you are a mule, the Lieut., runner or kingpin. They're out to get you. Not just the law, but the stick-up boys are your competitors. It is guaranteed that selling drugs will one day catch up with you. It is no escaping it! You really don't realize that you're selling drugs, you're helping to kill our people!

Unfortunately, no matter the amount of drugs you carry, whether it's a nickel bag or not, you're labeled "A DRUG DEALER." I know for certain that if you really tried hard, there is employment out there. Unfortunately, I do realize that a lot of opportunities have been taken away from our communities and neighborhoods and what remains is a lot of labor, which our ancestors were used to. This country was built on the free slave labor. That's another true story!

Living this type of life guarantees one of two things, prison time or getting killed. If you're in prison, you would have to defend yourself or be killed. This is not make believe. In my case, I have to deal with physical disability as a result of being setup, robbed and shot multiple times. Who wants to be a paraplegic or a quadriplegic on official life support? People, these are the guarantees that you will be faced with one day if you choose the life of a drug dealer. I have heard some say that if their family members didn't get it from them they would get it from someone on the street. Which is true, but why would you want to be their source? Again, I know that the system makes it hard for brothers to make it out here in this country, a beautiful country but there is so much ugliness behind closed doors, but they're coming out in the open, they just don't care.

I just pray to God, honestly! Yes, people write books to make money, and some have a passion for writing. I can say that I'm a published writer until this get out. However, I pray to God that whoever purchase my book, they recognize that there is a viable lesson to learn about God, FAITH IN HIM, THROUGH HIS SON JESUS CHRIST about the love of family, and how much we need to get back to where we came from Spiritually and to get unified like we used to be with God and each other. Think about the choices that you make because THERE ARE GREAT CONSEQUENCES that follows every choice and decision that we make. I've been with this condition for quite some time now, more than two and a half decades and I'm reminded of my mistake as I deal with the consequences. Every time I look down at the life support circuit laying on my chest and look at my arms and legs and I'm not yet able to move them, it gets me the most. It especially bothers me that it has been many years since I've been able to hold and embrace my children like I used to in both my arms and carry them. I used to receive SOME OF THE BIGGEST HUGS AROUND MY NECK, and oftentimes I would walk with them on my feet. I received the biggest grabs around my legs, BECAUSE DADDY WAS HOME!

MY CONSEQUENCES for making that choice that night and affecting my family, my kids and their mother (and now my grandkids that are around the same age that my kids were when I got shot). God knows I want to wrap my arms around all of my grandkids, just like I couldn't wrap my arms around my kids because of the CONSEQUENCES. My mother and father, siblings and nephews and nieces and other family members have to come and visit me as I lay in a nursing home bed on official life support for a very long time, but these are my CONSEQUENCES just to name a few. Or every time they have to stick that suction catheter down inside my lungs to help me cough up the mucus or secretions because my diaphragm is paralyzed, and I can't cough it out, then comes the gag reflex, because of the catheter that has gone down my throat and I started to cough and my body started to spasm because of the gag reflex getting suctioned every day throughout the decades. CONSEQUENCES!

I CANNOT BLAME NO ONE BUT MYSELF! Thank You Father God, His Son Jesus Christ, and the HOLY SPIRIT for watching over all my family members and friends, OUR FAMILY BUSINESS, STARTING AS A LITTLE CHILD, AND GROWING UP TOO FAST AND SEEING TOO MUCH AT A YOUNG AGE. I WAS JUST "LIVING JUST ENOUGH FOR THE CITY, AND WITNESSING THE GANGS, RAPES OF A LOT OF THE ST. ELIZABETH FEMALE PATIENTS. I WAS ONLY ABOUT SEVEN OR EIGHT YEARS OLD, JUST TOO FAST, AND JUST SEEING SO MUCH DESPAIR, ABUSE, ALCOHOL AND DRUG ADDICTS. SO MANY THINGS THAT I SHOULD NOT HAVE BEEN EXPOSED TO OR EVER SEEN, BUT IT WAS MY REALITY AND I DIDN'T CHOOSE THIS LIFE, IN A LOT OF WAYS IT CHOSE ME!

WHEN I WAS SURROUNDED AND LOCATED ALL AROUND THE SOUTHEAST PARTS OF WASHINGTON, DC, I COULDN'T GET AWAY FROM IT BECAUSE THAT'S WHERE ALL OF OUR FAMILY BUSINESSES WERE LOCATED AND PLEASE DON'T MISQUOTE ME OR EVEN MISUNDERSTAND WHAT I'M TRYING TO SAY ABOUT SOUTHEAST, WASHINGTON, DC, IT HAS ALWAYS BEEN A BEAUTIFUL AREA. THE SYSTEM IN THAT AREA, THE NEGATIVITY, DRUGS, THE KILLINGS ALL HAPPENED ARE ALLOWED IN THE AREA, SO NOW THEY HAVE A NEW OCCUPANT OF SOUTHEAST WASHINGTON, DC.

THESE ARE THINGS THAT THE SYSTEM ALLOWED TO HAPPEN SO THAT IT WOULD SOUND LIKE IT WAS HELL LIVING IN THIS PART OF WASHINGTON, DC AND NOT JUST THIS, THE SYSTEM IS NOW GOING THROUGH THE COUNTRY AND TAKING THE COMMUNITIES AND NEIGHBORHOODS THAT ONCE WAS OCCUPIED BY PEOPLE OF COLOR, AFRICAN-AMERICANS, AND KEEPING THEM FOR THEMSELVES.

THE ENEMY COMES TO STEAL, KILL AND DESTROY!

EVENTUALLY, EVERYTHING THAT I THOUGHT I GOT AWAY WITH FINALLY CAUGHT UP WITH ME!

www.ingramcontent.com/pod-product-compliance
Lightning Source LLC
Chambersburg PA
CBHW062147080426
42734CB00010B/1591